THE BOOK OF

The
Aran
Islands,
Co. Galway

TírEolas

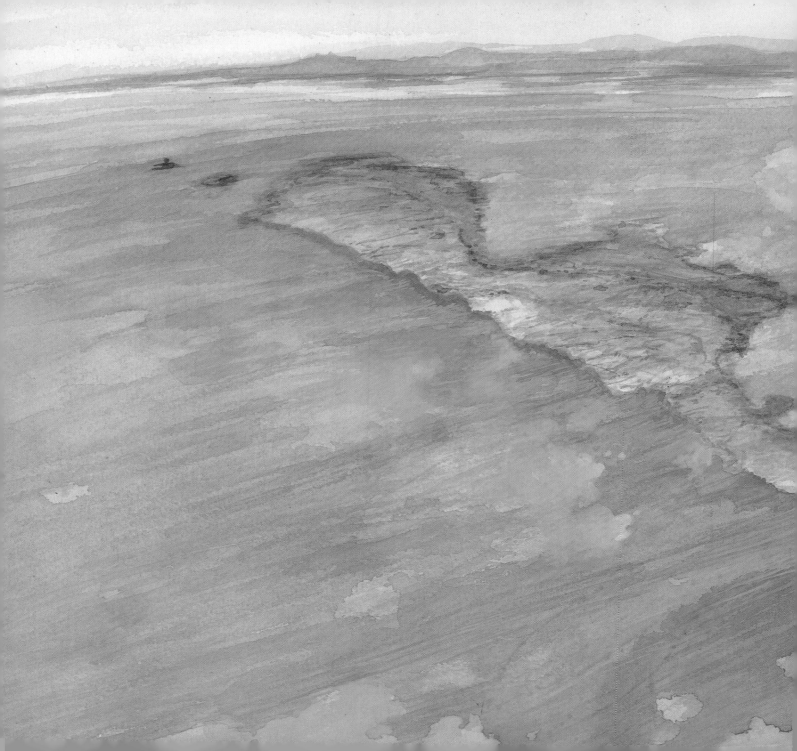

THE BOOK OF ARAN

The Aran Islands, Co. Galway

by

John Feehan
Cilian Roden
Michael O'Connell
Gordon D'Arcy
J.W. O'Connell
John Waddell
Paul Walsh
John de Courcy Ireland
Anne O'Dowd
Dara Ó Conaola
Pádraigín Clancy
Lelia Doolan
James Duran
Anne Korff
Joe McMahon
Patrick F. Sheeran
Pádraig Standún

Editors   John Waddell
J.W. O'Connell
Anne Korff

Published by   Tír Eolas

First published in 1994 by Tír Eolas,
Newtownlynch, Kinvara, Co. Galway.
Copyright © **Tír Eolas**
Illustrations © contributors and listed sources

Production Manager: Anne Korff
Text Editors: John Waddell, J.W. O'Connell
Visual Editor: Anne Korff
Editorial Assistant: Ailsa Ellis

Editorial Policy:
Place-names are normally given in the conventional Irish form as in Tim Robinson's 1980
detailed map of the islands or the more general
1993 Ordnance Survey 1:25000 bilingual map
of Aran. In deference to popular mis-usage the
large island, Árainn, is rendered as Inis Mór
and the islands are collectively called Aran or
the Aran Islands.

1st Reprint 1996   2nd Reprint 1999

ISBN 1 873821 03 4 PAPERBACK
ISBN 1 873821 04 2 HARD COVERS

Cover: Anne Korff
Layout and design: Anne Korff
Typesetting: Johan Hofsteenge
Printed by Colour Books

Contents

*Illus. 1. 'The Irish Field Clubs Landing on Aranmore',
on the 15th of July 1895,
photographed by Robert John Welch.
Photo, Ulster Museum, Belfast.*

*Illus. 2. 'A busy day in
Spring 1952' in Cill Rónáin.
Photo, G.A. Duncan.*

'Any fine day in Summer 1993' in Cill Rónáin. Photo, Joe Geoghegan.

Introduction

'Of the making of books there is no end!' cried the brilliant 17th century essayist, statesman and scientist Francis Bacon, although this did not stop him making several himself. But the important point we may take from Bacon's complaint is that authors or, in the case of this particular book, editors have a responsibility to their readers to explain, either explicitly or implicitly, their motives for imposing yet another book on the world.

This is even more the case when the book in question is one devoted to the Aran Islands, surely one of the most written-about places in Ireland. So, in order to discharge our responsibility, let us ask three related questions:

What is the book about?

Why has the book been written?; in other words, what is the aim of the book?

For whom has the book been written?

The Book of Aran is an exploration as well as an examination of a particular place and culture. The nineteen chapters comprise a detailed and scholarly survey of almost every aspect of this place and culture, drawing upon the knowledge and understanding of a group of authors who have devoted themselves to the study of their own special fields of interest.

The Aran Islands are unique, in the quite particular sense that there is no other place in Ireland where you will find such a wealth of archaeological and cultural material to hand. Ever since the islands were rediscovered in the 19th century by the great antiquarians like Petrie, O'Donovan, Ferguson and Westropp, and taken as the inspiration for works of cultural and artistic transformation by such people as J. M. Synge, Lady Gregory, James Joyce, Patrick Pearse, the film-maker Robert Flaherty, and native islanders like Liam O'Flaherty, Máirtín Ó Direáin, and the late Breandán Ó hEithir, and adopted sons like Tim Robinson, they have exercised a fascination that is as easy to account for as it has been impressive in its results.

To deal with such a diversity as the islands and their culture represent is no easy task. The editors have tackled the problem by literally taking the islands 'from the ground up'. Roughly speaking, the chapters fall into three broad divisions: the natural history of the islands; the archaeological and historical dimension; and the culture that has evolved over the centuries, including everything from folklore traditions to the literary, artistic and even cinematic treatment of the islands and their people.

Of course it goes without saying that it would take several books to adequately describe the islands in all their particularity, which is a tribute to the wealth of resources available to the student of the Aran Islands. The Bibliography at the end of the book suggests the extent and depth of this material. Yet within the compass of these pages, a genuine attempt has been made to do justice to the incredible richness of this very special place. It has not been possible to cover the extraordinary contribution of recent Aran writers such as Liam O'Flaherty, Máirtín Ó Direáin or Breandán Ó hEithir, and others. The literary legacy of modern Aran is worthy of another book.

The Book of Aran has been written both to celebrate and to caution. The first of these intentions is the easiest to explain. All the authors who have contributed chapters write out of a background of real love for the islands, their culture and the people who keep this culture alive today.

The academic approach to a subject runs the risk of becoming very dry and even dismissive. Especially is this a danger when the apparatus of study is applied to something living. It is like the story of the professor who, after completing his study of the lion, opened his office door to be confronted not with his tidy manuscript but an actual roaring lion, its tail swishing back and forth menacingly. The lesson here is that a healthy respect must always be maintained for the dynamic actuality of what is being studied. While it is, of course, up to the reader to determine this, the editors are convinced that each of the authors has succeeded in keeping this firmly in the forefront of their minds.

However, the book is also something of a caution to us all. It has become a commonplace today that we live on a planet that is much more fragile than previous generations could ever have imagined. As long as there were vast, unexplored areas of the world, represented by map-makers as tantalisingly empty spaces just waiting to be filled in, it was possible to hold a laissez-faire attitude to the environment.

This, as we all know, is no longer possible. The delicate balance of man and environment requires care if it is to be maintained for future generations. We have become increasingly conscious of the fact that each generation is more like a caretaker or a custodian than an outright owner with the absolute right to do as it pleases with the heritage it inherits.

This custodial aspect applies as much to the cultural environment as it does to the more obvious natural environment. It is just as easy (if rather more difficult to detect in the short term) to destroy a culture as it is to destroy an eco-system.

Here we encounter the subject of tourism, one of the most important aspects of the present-day economy of the Aran Islands. Tourism, as the poet Robert Graves pointed out many years ago about his own island home of Majorca, is a two-edged sword. While it provides an economic boost to a community, it also, unless consciously controlled, runs the risk of destroying the very things that attract visitors in the first place.

Tim Robinson, one of the most brilliant commentators on the Aran Islands this generation has produced, has raised this question in his introduction to a recent edition of Synge's classic *The Aran Islands*. Since Ireland is what he describes as an intriguing island off the west of Europe, and Aran an island off the west of Ireland, then Aran itself, he argues, is doubly intriguing; it is, he suggests, 'Ireland raised to the power of two', and he asks, 'Whether the grain of wonderful truth in this can survive the trampling of the hundred thousand tourists who now visit the islands each year, remains to be seen'.

This is a question also asked by some of the contributors to this book, one invariably prompted by their particular knowledge of some aspect of the islands and by their affection for Aran as a whole. In fact, some feel, rightly or wrongly, that this island world is at a crucial point in its long history.

Decisions taken now may well shape the future of the islands in a fundamental and irreversible way. The extraordinary rise in the number of visitors is now a very significant factor in island life and has brought many benefits – witness the transport revolution in plane and ferry. However developments like these in particular initiate other pressures. What changes are these pressures likely to bring about? In other words, what impact will all these visitors, and the islanders' response to them, have on the fabric of the islands? Aran and its people have shown how well they have adapted to an ever changing world and how well they can keep pace with developments elsewhere, but can they continue to cope?

Fr Pádraig Standún has observed that 'some people look at the Inis Oírr waterfront and see a mini Manhattan sprawl of unplanned-looking oversized buildings', but he sees instead vibrant young families where children were scarce in the seventies.

He is right, of course, to see the people first. However, the choice is not one between buildings and people. The shabby conglomeration that confronts the visitor must – and does – affront the eyes of Aran people as well. Happily insensitive building is still rare, but it does exist. If it increases, it will, like a creeping fungus, scar and irrevocably damage the image of Aran that has captured the imagination of a great number of ordinary people as well as a host of artists, poets and novelists who have always regarded Aran as a place of special beauty and cultural integrity.

Imagination is not limited to artists, and there is an urgent need for sensitive development in areas such as architecture, road building, wall building, sign posting, and transport policy. On the negative side, Gordon D'Arcy, for example, notes the threat to some vulnerable wildlife habitats such as coastal sand dunes. On the positive side, Fr Standún, dealing with the islanders and their children on a daily basis, is encouraged by an increase in environmental awareness.

Perhaps the most fundamental question to ask is, why do people visit the Aran Islands in the first place? It is obvious to us that they do so because they are attracted by the special qualities of the place, culture and people. They come seeking to touch the past, which is so evident here in the many monuments scattered over the three islands; they come for the peace and solitude of a landscape that has so far escaped the worst ravages of the 20th century spoilation of the environment; they come for qualities almost too intangible to pin down with words – warmth and hospitality, reverence for an old and still vital tradition of song and dance, folklore and craftsmanship.

They come, in other words, because Aran is different from other places. If they want the sun, they can go to the Mediterranean. If they want golf courses, there are plenty on the mainland. If they want karaoke, there are the pubs of Salthill and Galway twenty miles away. Visitors to Aran come because they are seeking something that cannot be found, or at least not easily, elsewhere.

No one would suggest that Aran should become a quaint time-capsule. The islands are, and should remain, living, changing, developing places. However no one would wish to see them become cultural theme parks either.

The great challenge for the people of Aran (and here we speak with the greatest respect and with a deep awareness of the dangers there are in offering advice as outsiders, for that is what most of the contributors are) is to preserve that which is special about the islands and their heritage, and their childrens' heritage. In the end, it is the Aran people themselves who will determine how the islands develop in the future, and how they deal with the problems confronting them in the last decade of the 20th century. Yet, because it is our heritage also, we feel it would be irresponsible if we did not address these problems as we see them as well.

Finally, for whom has this book been written? Quite simply, it has been written for all those who cherish these islands and their people and what they represent, now and in the future. *The Book of Aran* is not an elegy, not a nostalgic picture of something which has ceased to be. It is a testimony to the vibrancy and vitality of a culture that continues to have much to teach the contemporary world, as Synge himself recognised when he came here early in the 20th century.

To take just one example, the tradition of craft work that is still evident on the islands and as it flourished for so many hundreds of years is an enduring legacy to us. The qualities of skill and design that arose to meet the immediate needs of the islanders, whether it be the building of currachs or the knitting of finely-made garments that have influenced modern designers is something we can not only admire but emulate. Modern technology can learn from traditional ways of doing things, adding a humanising dimension that many in the modern world seem to find missing in the mass-produced goods and contrivances that claim our attention so insistently wherever we turn.

The Book of Aran is an offering to readers, a guide-book and a source-book for all those who would explore a place, as we have repeatedly emphasised, like no other. As we make our offering we, as editors, are all too conscious of how we have only scratched the surface of this unique world, and we are comforted by the words with which Tim Robinson concludes his own personal confrontation with Aran: 'But for a book to stand like an island out of the sea of the unwritten it must acknowledge its own bounds, and turn inward for them, and look into the labyrinth'. It is our hope that this book will act as a thread to follow in exploring this labyrinth.

Anne Korff
J.W. O'Connell
John Waddell

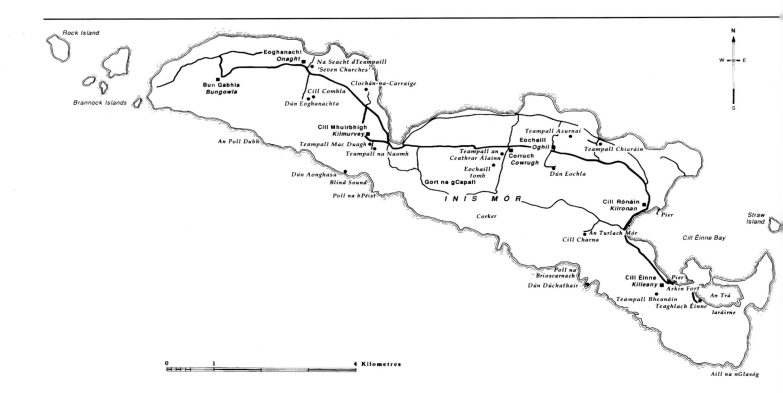

*General map of the Aran
Islands showing the principal
localities mentioned in* The
Book of Aran.
*Considerably greater detail
will be found on Tim
Robinson's map and guide to
the islands (*Oileáin Árann:
The Aran Islands - a map
and guide, *Cill Rónáin,
1980) and on the Ordnance
Survey of Ireland's 1:250000
map (*Oileáin Árann: The
Aran Islands, *Dublin,
1993).*
*This general map is based on
the Ordnance Survey by permission of the Government
(permit no. 5878).*

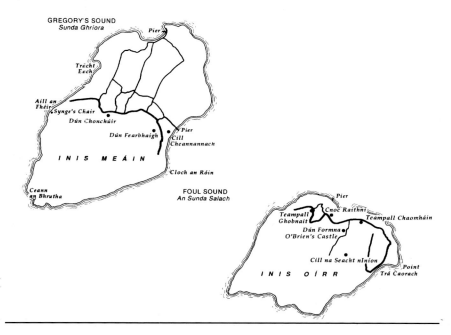

Illus. 1.1. This remarkable photograph was taken by Fr Browne in 1938. It looks from near Teampall Bheanáin towards the Clare coast, and makes it easier to believe that the Aran Islands are but recently detached outliers of the Burren mainland.

CHAPTER 1

The Geology of the Aran Islands

John Feehan

The soile is almost paved over with stones,
soe as in some places nothing is to be seen but large stones with
openings between them, where cattle break their legs.
Scarce any other stone there but limestone, and marble fit for tomb-
stones, chymney mantle trees, and high crosses.
Among these stones is very good pasture, so that beefe, veal, and
mutton are better and earlyer in season here than elsewhere.

Roderic O'Flaherty, *Ogygia* (1685)

Every landscape is built upon a solid framework of rock formed at an earlier time in earth's history. Though it is usually hidden from view by a thin blanket of soil and vegetation, the nature of this hidden rock skeleton profoundly influences everything that happens at the surface. There are few landscapes where this is more clearly demonstrated than the bare limestone lands of the Burren in north Clare and south Galway, where much of the rock skeleton has been stripped of its superficial covering and is now exposed. The Aran Islands are satellites of the Burren, marooned by marine erosion and encroachment of the sea in the not-so-very-distant past. They extend in a north-west to south-east direction across a distance of about 16 miles, from Carraig Éamonn Mhac Dhonncha at the north-western extremi-ty of Oileán Iartharach (Rock Island) the western of the Oileáin Dá Bhranóg (Brannock Islands) to Trá Caorach Point at the south-eastern end of Inis Oírr. And although they cover a much smaller area, they are no less fascinating; of all the landscapes of Ireland, theirs is perhaps the one which is most redolent with the richness of the cultural heritage of the past, and most profoundly shaped by its geological heritage.

This little archipelago consists of three larger islands – Inis Mór, Inis Meáin, and Inis Oírr – together with a number of small ones, the most prominent of which are the four small islands known as the Brannock Islands off the north-western end of Inis Mór, and Straw Island on its east coast at the entrance to Cill Éinne Bay.

Inis Mór is 14km at its longest, from north-west to south-east, and it varies in width from about 0.75km to just over 3.25km. Inis Meáin is 5km long from north-east to south-west and half that across at its widest. Inis Oírr is less elongated; its maximum 'diameter' is about 4km. At times of lower sea level in the past, Inis Meáin and Inis Oírr were possibly joined, because the narrow and dangerous passage between the two – Foul Sound – is only a league (3km) across, and has a ledge of rocks covered by only two metres of water.

The Aran Islands are themselves, in fact, a relatively recent geological phenomenon. The depth of the sea between the Burren mainland and Inis Oírr is less than 30m, and the three islands are separated from each other by submarine valley-like features of about the same depth. This means that for much the greater part of the Pleistocene period Aran must have been just another part of the Burren. A rise of 100m today would have something like the same effect on such inlets as Turlough and Ballyvaughan on the mainland – but of course such a rise would also forever drown the Aran Islands!

The rock of which the islands are composed is the same Lower Carboniferous limestone as the Burren: pale grey to blue-grey rock formed from the muddy sediment, rich in lime, which accumulated in the warm, shallow seas that covered this part of the earth between 325 and 350 million years ago. That sea teemed with life of all sorts: corals, sea-lilies and the different groups of shellfish – brachiopods, gastropods and bivalves especially – whose dead remains were often preserved in the mud and, just like the mud itself, later hardened to stone. The limestone is packed with the fossil remains of these extinct plants and animals, though it is only when the beds have been etched and

sculpted by the careful action of the elements that they become obvious – they are part of the stone, so when you break the rock the fossils break with it. But sometimes the patient, slow, careful processes of weathering wear away the surrounding rock in such a way that the fossils stand out, and on Aran this often happens in particular to the beds of shale which occur at intervals in the limestone sequence and which are particularly rich in good fossils. The sea often etches out the muddy matrix in which the fossils occur, and we can sometimes have the thrill of seeing whole rock surfaces with the fossils all lying there in the very positions they occupied on the floor of the Carboniferous sea 330 million years ago. Sometimes the etching away of the shaly material has been so delicate that we can see every detail of the shell – even the spines on some of the brachiopod shells – sometimes with a golden coating of iron pyrites (fool's gold) precipitated over them from the ancient muddy sediment.

The geological structure of the islands is very simple, and it essentially determines the entire character of the islands. If we were to make a traverse of Inis Mór beginning at the north-east end, we would find ourselves ascending all the time as if climbing a great stairs. From the highest point of the island the land falls away south-westwards to the cliffs that face the Atlantic. The form of the islands is a classic example of a *cuesta*, the dip slope facing the south-west, and the scarp looking north-east to Galway Bay. The dip is very gentle however, so that the beds appear almost horizontal, and in the absence of folding the rock has been sculpted into a magnificent series of gigantic terraces along the bedding planes. The islands lack the variety of karst features for which the Burren is so renowned, but all three display a magnificent variety of pavement types.

Illus. 1.2a. A cross-section across the north-west part of Inis Mór, running NNE-SSW. The successive terraces are numbered I-VII. At the base of each terrace there is usually a thin shale bed. This is easily weathered, and it is the weathering of these shales which is responsible for the alternation of cliff and terrace.

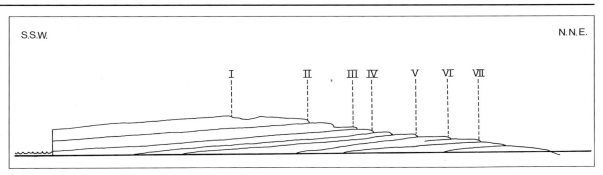

On Inis Mór and Inis Meáin the beds of limestone are everywhere inclined to the south-west at an angle of 3-5°, very occasionally up to 10°. On Inis Oírr they dip gently (1-3°) to the south or south-east. The limestone is replaced occasionally by dolomite. Dolomite is a limestone where some of the calcium is replaced by magnesium, usually through alteration of ordinary limestone by percolating magnesium carbonate solutions.

Geophysical measurements suggest that the Galway granite extends southwards under Galway Bay and north Clare, and westwards under the Aran Islands, so explaining the great stability of north-west Clare as exemplified by the undistorted character of the Carboniferous rocks of Aran and the Burren.

If you look across to Aran from the south coast of Connemara, Inis Mór sometimes has the appearance of being three separate islands. This is because two low valleys traverse it from north-east to south-west. One of these valleys runs west and then south from Cill Éinne; the other is immediately south-west of Cill Mhuirbhigh, and since it is only 15m above the sea it was occasionally mistaken by ships inward-bound for Galway for one of the channels into Galway Bay – a circumstance which

Illus. 1.2b. Most of the terraces are separated from each other by cuestas, each consisting of a gentle dip slope on one side (usually parallel with the bedding), and a steep escarpment on the other.

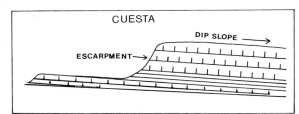

earned it the name of the Blind Sound. In O'Flaherty's famous *Ogygia* there is a fascinating reference to an event which took place around the year 1640 during which 'an extraordinary inundation' took place, causing the sea to sweep right across the island through the Blind Sound. The event has been attributed to an earthquake known to have affected northern Europe about this time. A tidal wave may also have been responsible for another tragic and extraordinary event. On 15th August 1852 a freak wave, coming in from a calm sea, swept away and drowned fifteen Aran people who were fishing off the rock terrace at Aill na nGlasóg.

One of the most obvious structural features of the rock is the way in which it breaks along three regular sets of fissures or joints. These develop along lines of weakness which are due to pressures sustained by the rock since its formation. Weathering concentrates along these lines of weakness, the main set of which runs

Illus. 1.3. above left. A colony of productid brachiopods, splendidly entombed in the limestone.

Illus. 1.4. A colonial coral (Lithostrotion) etched out by elements on a beach cobble. Weather-etched fossils are also often seen in their original position in the rock.

Illus. 1.5. Beach cobbles of varied lithology and prove-nance! Beach cobbles are often of fossil-bearing limestone, and the sea's wearing away of the surface highlights the fossils. Here we have corals, brachiopods and sea lilies (crinoids).

in a direction 10° east of north. The sea-filled sounds between the islands have developed along joints, and good examples inland include the valley north of Poll na Brioscarnach and the Maum or Pass in Inis Meáin. The joints do not however account for the formation of the Blind Sound, nor of the whole of the Cill Éinne Valley, which runs westwards for a time before meeting the glen leading south to Poll na Brioscarnach, which does follow the natural line of break. When these valleys cross the ter-races there is a line of break or fissure, along which the terrace is undercut, and it appears very likely that these valleys and fissures result from marine erosion at a time of higher sea level in the past. The formation of the terraces is due largely to the same agency, which swept from them much of the debris of subaerial decay and morainic material with which they would otherwise be covered.

Illus. 1.6. Where the limestone terraces occur at sea level, they often function as wave-washed platforms.

The terraces

There are nine terraces; five of these are well-defined, and there are four others below them which are more obscure. Some of these run beneath the sea into Galway Bay to the north-east of Inis Mór. On Inis Mór two of the terraces can be followed all the way from the south-east to the north-west of the island. On Illus. 1.2a these are numbered 3 and 4 (counting from the highest terrace); they can be followed all the way from Gregory's Sound to the cliffs near the north-west corner of the island. Cill Rónáin is situated on terrace no. 6. Seven terraces can be identified on Inis Meáin; the three lowest extend almost across the island,

and the four highest not only go all the way across, but also curve around the south-east side to overlook the Foul Sound.

The terracing is due to the occurrence of soft and easily eroded thin beds of shale which interrupt the limestone sequence. These shales occur at the base of the cliffs separating the terraces, and they are largely responsible for the way the sculpturing of the islands has taken place. But these thin beds are profoundly important in another way. Because they are impermeable, they trap water seeping down through the overlying limestone; the water then flows laterally and emerges as springs at the base of the cliffs. Continuous beds of chert are sometimes found to have the same affect, but they are less reliable because they are generally fractured. The beds of shale are usually thin, although some of them are well over a metre thick; individual shale beds vary in thickness from place to place. The vertical distance between shale beds is also very variable, but around 12m is a common interval. The shales are often full of brachiopods, goniatites and other fossils, sometimes beautifully preserved, especially where they are exposed between terraces along the cliffs. The springs usually yield an abundance of clear water, but in dry years they sometimes run dry, and in earlier times water had to be brought from the mainland, or the cattle themselves moved there.

The cliffs

Their appearance, on approaching, is awfully impressive; the dark cliffs opposing to the billows that roll impetuously against them a perpendicular barrier, several hundred feet high, of rugged masses shelving abruptly towards the base, and perforated with various winding cavities worn by the violence of the waves.

Samuel Lewis, *A Topographical Dictionary of Ireland* **(1837)**

The most dramatic aspect of the geology of Aran is the way in which the forces of weathering and erosion – which severed the islands from the mainland in the first place and later from each other – continue their steady work of destruction. The agents of demolition are dominated by the sea, which concentrates its destructive action mainly on the sheer, vertical,

Illus. 1.7. The beds of limestone which make up the islands are interrupted by thin beds of shale. These are very easily weathered, and have much to do with the pattern of erosion shown by the islands. They also control the movement of groundwater inland.

precipitous cliffs which are found especially on the west and south-west coasts. These awe-inspiring cliffs are often more than 50m high, and at their highest exceed 120m. Cliffs are found all down the west coast of Inis Meáin from Trácht Each to Aill an Fhéir, where they attain their maximum height of nearly 60m before beginning to fall gradually again to sea level at the south-west corner of the island.

The pattern of vertical jointing in the rocks is responsible for the sheer nature of the cliffs. Large block falls characterise some of the cliffs. Where the joints are close together the sea in storm is able to detach enormous blocks of rock. This is best seen south of Gort na gCapall in Inis Mór, where the limestone in the cliff is divided up by a set of regularly-spaced east-west master joints about 2 metres apart, and criss-crossed by a second set at right angles to this. Where the cliff has been undercut by the waves, these have collapsed like ranks of gigantic rectangular building blocks, and they now form an effective breakwater helping to shield the cliff – for this brief geological moment at least – from further attack by the sea. When the last great collapse took place here, one vertical stack of these giant bricks managed to avoid toppling into the sea; it steadied itself after it had become detached from the mainland, while all the adjacent columns tumbled into a chaotic heap all along the cliff. It now forms one of the most spectacular features of the south coast. Appropriate though the term is, the column of great blocks is not quite a sea stack in the strict sense, because it has not originated through the collapse of an arch formed by the meeting of two caves eroded into opposite sides of a headland.

Illus. 1.8 and 1.9. The forces of weathering and erosion are slowly eating away the land of Aran. Lowering of the surface takes place at a rate of a fraction of a millimetre a year – but even at this rate – and without the help of any rise of sea level resulting from global warming – the islands will disappear beneath the waves in as little as 7 million years. But apart from this horizontal shrinkage, the sea is steadily dismantling the cliffs along the ready-made joints which divide the limestone into conveniently movable blocks. Here at Gort na gCapall the waves disassemble the limestone into artificial-looking rectangular blocks of great regularity. At some later time, these will be picked up again by the waves, and used as battering rams in some future onslaught on the fragile cliffs.

The formation of the cliffs

The destructive power of the waves is obviously normally concentrated on the few metres at the base of the cliff, acting like a slow and enormously powerful horizontal saw. When the rocks here are softer than those above, these will be deeply undercut, and a deep, continuous wave-cut notch may form at the cliff base, undermining and further weakening rock which is already divided up by such structural features as bedding and jointing into blocks which readily collapse into the sea. Once these have fallen, they provide the surf with new weapons for its battering. If this happens in a bay or inlet, the force of the waves will be most concentrated at the apex of the inlet, and water will be directed into any cavities which have developed along joints or other lines of weakness, trapping the air in the cavities and forcing it between crannies in the rocks with great force. When the wave then retreats the decompressed air expands in the crannies it was forced into and exerts further force on the surrounding rocks. This is repeated over and over again, and gradually the cavity enlarges into a cave which may retreat further and further inland. Eventually, the compressed air at the

end of the cave may find a way out upwards, and once it does, this new opening is quickly enlarged until the weakened rock collapses to form a chimney or puffing-hole opening to the surface. The cliff retreats as erosion proceeds over the centuries, leaving sea arches and stacks as a last reminder of earlier conquest. Seaward from the cliffs, the surf will usually create a wave-cut bench or platform along a rocky shore, often bevelling the tilted layers of bedrock, but on Aran the bedding is so nearly horizontal that the benches are usually bedding planes, covered with sediment or cliff debris in gradual transit from the shore to deeper water.

Illus. 1.13. When the limestone bed is not weakened by joints, it may be undercut by the waves and project as a ledge over the sea.

These benches are under tidal influence, and their surfaces have a pattern of weathering which is distinct from the physical battering of the surf. An understanding of these principles of the physical geology of coastal erosion provides the key to interpretation of the detail of the coastline, and adds enormously to the interest and excitement of a walk along any stretch of Aran's shore.

Perpendicular or terraced cliffs are among the most awesome features of the west and south coasts of the islands particularly. Prominent sea-terraces developed below the high water mark of the spring tide are a distinctive feature of many of the cliffs. On Inis Mór terraced cliffs extend from the north-west corner as far as Gregory's Sound. These sea-terraced cliffs are best developed south-east from Dún Dúchathair, where they are surmounted by the impressive rampart of the block beach. The cliffs are 60m high at Dún Dúchathair, rising north-westward to 78m at Corker. They fall again across the Blind Sound before rising again to 88m at Dún Aonghasa, and reaching their maximum height of 92m about a mile further north-west, just to the south-east of An Poll Dubh.

The northern coast of Inis Meáin is fringed by beaches of sand and shingle, and low cliffs. From Trácht Each to Aill an Fhéir on the south-west the cliffs rise in steps. They are perpendicular and about 20m high at Aill an Fhéir, and from here they fall to about 12m at the south-west end of the island. Sea terraces are well developed from the south part of Aill an Fhéir (where the cliffs reach heights of over 50m) south to Ceann an Bhrutha, and then north-east to Cloch an Róin, surmounted by a block beach for most of the way. On Inis Oírr, terracing is developed mainly on the north and east sides of the island. The coast is nearly all rocky, except for a beach on the north-east side.

The puffing-holes

Several spectacular blow-holes or puffing-holes occur on the Aran coast. Two can be seen to the east and west of Aill na nGlasóg (the Glassan Rock), where two caves run inland, that to the west for 85m and the one to the east for 33m, before opening to the surface through the puffing-holes. The latter is much the more spectacular of the two, because it is a great yawning chasm through which the sea below can be seen and heard advancing and retreating through its tunnel far below. When the sea is calm, the puffing-holes are peaceful enough, but according to Samuel Lewis 'during the prevalence of strong westerly winds, prodigious columns of water are projected to the height of a ship's mast'. The prodigious power of the water is shown by the fact that there is a block beach north-east of the puffing-hole, and there is evidence of earlier ones further back. A number of much smaller puffing-holes occur further to the north-west. There are puffing holes also at the south-west corner of Inis Meáin.

The block beach

Looking at the gentle swell of the waves breaking against the low terraces on a calm day it is difficult to imagine the awesome might of the sea in storm. But the size and extent of the storm beach is tell-tale proof of the force at work here at a time when nobody may approach to observe. A beach is not just sand beside the sea; it may be defined as wave-washed sediment – the particles of which can be anything up to the enormous boulders of

storm beaches – extending throughout the surf zone, and generally in active movement; it often extends seaward below low tide as a wave-built terrace or carpet of sediment.

Undoubtedly one of the most dramatic features of the geology of the Aran Islands is the extraordinary storm beaches which occur atop the cliffs. They consist of prodigious assemblages of enormous flaggy boulders up to 5m high and several times that width, found mainly (in the case of Inis Mór) on the western cliffs

Illus. 1.14. In calm weather the puffing-holes are at rest, only haunting echoes in the caverns below giving an indication of the hidden sea. During storms, however, the force of the sea rushing through these caverns forces great columns of spray up through the puffing-holes.

Illus. 1.15. Storm beaches made of massive blocks of limestone up to several metres each way occur on all three islands. They occur even on top of the cliffs, at heights of over 60m above the sea. These block beaches are formed when the sea in times of heavy storm picks up loose blocks of loose rock at the cliff's edge and hurls them inland to a distance of up to 10m. Such is the power of the sea that it was able, during the night of the great storm known as the Big Wind in 1839, to bury the clochans inside Dún Dúchathair under rocky debris.

between Poll na Brioscarnach and Gleann na nDeor. It also occurs elsewhere on Inis Mór, especially on the cliffs west and south of Gort na gCapall, as well as on both Inis Meáin and Inis Oírr. On Inis Meáin it occurs at an even higher level above the sea than on Inis Mór – at nearly 60m, and in some ways it is more impressive than on the larger island. What happens is that the great storm waves overtopping the cliffs pick up the loose blocks and slabs from the limestone pavement at the edge of the cliffs and hurl them back to a distance of up to ten metres. And when you consider that the cliffs are 100 metres high in places you have some idea of the incredible power of the waves responsible for the work. In 1839, during the 'Night of the Big Wind', the great storm which has etched out an enduring memory in

the folk tradition of the entire country, several clocháns inside Dún Dúchathair, Aran's other great cliff fortress, were smothered under the debris of the storm beach. The block beach is built up and added to only by the most spectacular storms, and in places the retreat of the cliff-line by erosion has caught up with it, and the storm beach now stands at the very edge of the cliff.

On Inis Mór the block beach is confined mainly to the cliffs of the south-west; on Oileán Iartharach, the westernmost of the Brannock Islands, it is perched 11m above sea level. On Inis Meáin it commences at 52m, and continues round the west and south-east sides of the island. The block beach recurs on top of the cliff on Inis Oírr, extending to the south-west point of the island.

Geology and the cultural landscape

When people first arrived on the islands, the limestone pavements were strewn with loose blocks and slabs of broken stone of all sizes and shapes, which provided early farmers with an abundance of material for building. The cultural fabric of the islands was built almost in its entirety from these products of subaerial decay – from the great stone forts, the clochans, churches, crosses, tombs and homes of earlier centuries to the drystone walls which are such a characteristic feature of the cultural landscape of the islands. Some of the blocks used in the building of Dún Aonghasa are over 2m in length, and there is a massive block of limestone measuring nearly 4m which spans the entire width of Cill Cheannannach on Inis Meáin. They also provided the islanders with suitable material for blocking up the grikes so

that seaweed and sand could be spread on the rocky little fields within their protecting encircling walls of stone to produce the soil which in time acquired its own highly distinctive natural vegetation – though many of the enclosures consist largely of bare rock. These walls are up to 2m in height, and only one stone thick as a rule, which makes the fields very difficult for the uninitiated visitor to traverse. In these little fields the islanders grew their crops of potatoes, black oats and rye, and grass which produced the finest calves 'reputed to be the best in Ireland, and much sought after by the Connacht graziers'.

The pattern of the fields is essentially determined by the structure of the rocks, because the steps or risers which separate one terrace

Illus. 1.16. The remarkable little church of St Benan (Teampall Bheanáin) is an outstanding example of the use of Aran's limestone in shaping the cultural landscape of the islands. It is made of cut stone, and some of the blocks are of very large size. A single stone composes nearly half of the west side wall (seen here on left). The very steep gables originally rose to a height of 5m. The church stands on the high ground overlooking the village of Cill Éinne, which is 300m to the NE (seen in the background); beyond the village are the blown sands of the dunes and machair

from the next (and which can be up to 6m high) act as natural field boundaries. Many other field boundaries follow the joints, into which upright slabs of rock have been wedged. The limestone occasionally found other uses. At the time the lighthouse was built on Inis Oírr, a layer of dove-coloured and black marble was being exploited in a quarry at the southwest point of the island near Ceann na Faochanaí, blocks from which were exported to Dublin to be worked.

The Ice Age on Aran

The ice sheets of the Pleistocene scoured the surface of the islands clean before leaving behind a blanket of boulder clay or till when they finally retreated 10,000 or so years ago. However, Aran was robbed of this precious inheritance almost as soon as the glaciers had melted, because it was simply stripped from the surface of the limestone by the Atlantic gales at a time of much higher sea levels. Only the boulders in the till survived this onslaught. They were left behind as erratics on limestone pavements polished smooth by the moving ice. But the forces of wind, rain, frost and sun did not stop their campaign of destruction when they had stripped away the boulder clay; they have continued ever since to eat away both at the surface of the limestone pavement and at the exposed erratics. The joints in the limestone were opened and widened further and further to give the pattern of clints and grikes so familiar on Aran and in the Burren. The pavement lost its polish and its glacial *striae*, the scratch marks made by rocks held in the grip of the moving ice, and its surface began to be slowly eaten away. Only where the large erratics provided a measure of protection, and in the very few areas where the rock did manage to retain

the original covering of boulder clay, has the limestone resisted this downward process of weathering.

The glacial erratics which are so prominent a feature of Aran's landscape are mainly of three kinds: Galway granite, sandstone similar to that which occurs near Oughterard, and limestone which could be of local origin; erratic boulders of other kinds occur occasionally. The erratics have also been subjected to weathering since they were exhumed by the stripping away of the boulder clay, but the weathering is most evident on the limestone erratics, which have been fluted and deeply pitted by weathering – especially the lower half. This is because wind erosion is most effective only up to about half a metre above ground level, this being the maximum height to which the wind can effectively lift sand and other weapons of erosion.

The larger erratics frequently rest on little pedestals of unweathered limestone, and if the difference between the tops of the pedestals and the surrounding exposed pavement is measured we can get some idea of how rapidly the limestone surface is being eroded away. We must be careful in drawing conclusions here however for several reasons. Sometimes the loose surface blocks of the pavement have been removed to build walls, and the difference in height between the limestone surface and the base of the erratics in the vicinity – which can

Illus. 1.17. When the Ice Age retreated it left behind it a blanket of till or boulder clay: rock debris transported by the ice across from Connemara. The winter gales in the immediate post-glacial period stripped away most of this legacy of the ice, leaving behind the large erratic boulders which it could not move. In that short interval of a few thousand years, the surface of the terraces has been further lowered, but the mass of the erratic sometimes preserves the limestone immediately beneath from subaerial erosion, and provides us with a rough-and-ready calendar with which to calculate the decay of the limestone.

sometimes be as much as half a metre – is obviously not entirely due to natural weathering in these cases. Where the surroundings have not been disturbed, the pedestals are usually 75 to 150mm high. Moreover, the rate of erosion may well have varied with time. Keeping this in mind, it appears that since the limestone pavement was first exposed to the elements it has been lowered by something like 75 - 150mm. If we assume that this process of erosion began almost as soon as the Ice Age ended 10,000 years ago, the rate of erosion on Aran has been between .0075 and .015mm a year. If Aran was once partly covered by woodland, and erosion only commenced after this was removed, the figure will be higher. This cautious estimate is still much slower than the figure of .05mm a year estimated for the Burren, but it still means that the Aran Islands will have disappeared under the waves completely in as little as 7 million years, even if the processes of erosion at work on the Atlantic coast (very possibly accentuated by the effects of global warming) have not claimed them long before then.

It is interesting to see how the early Irish geologists of the eighteenth century, who knew nothing about glaciation, accounted for these granite erratics. Richard Kirwan claimed that there was formerly a vast mass of granite on one of the Aran Islands, but that this had been shattered by lightning in 1774. Galway Bay, he claimed, had originally been a great granite mountain subsequently shattered and swallowed in an upheaval of the earth.

Many of these granite erratics still survive; they were often too big and too tough to break, and the expedient of digging a hole into which they could be tipped – resorted to in most other parts of Ireland where large erratics hindered agricultural practice – could not be employed on Aran. Praeger remarked on how 'some of the tiny fields look as if their walls had been built solely for the enclosure of these defiant erratics'.

The abundance of rounded granite erratics is largely due to the proximity of Connemara, just across from Aran on the opposite side of Galway Bay – a gap of great geological width in terms of the ages and kinds of rocks on either side, but geographically very close. And it is a geological contrast and proximity which has had profound consequences for human life on the islands, because the islands have next to no fuel of their own – no timber or turf, whereas much of the impermeable granite across the bay is covered in bog. The absence of bog is partly due to the virtual absence of surface water: it's even hard to store rain water on Aran.

There are several sheltered hollows running north-south across the limestone where the glaciated pavement still survives under a protective skin of boulder clay. The best example is on the cliff edge north-west of Dún Aonghasa, where the polished and striated pavement can be seen at the cliff edge where the surface material has recently weathered away. There may have been local peat deposits in earlier times.

Illus. 1.18. A granite erratic above the sea – eloquent memorial of the last cold stage of the Ice Age.

A whisper from the Tertiary

During the progress of the Geological Survey, G. H. Kinahan recorded 'patches of a bed very ferruginous as well as dolomitic [which] weather into a blood-red ochre clay' on terrace no. 7, due south of Port Chorrúch on Inis Mór. This insignificant deposit is very likely all that remains of Tertiary weathering, a rare relic of the time before the Ice Age when the limestones of Aran carried a covering of red *terra rossa* soil developed under the warm climate which then prevailed. One of the best places to see this special Tertiary clay is in the area of an Turlach Mór, south-west of Cill Rónáin.

Depositional processes

The rocks of which the coast is made are levered out by the waves, before being pounded against their parent cliffs and against each other so that they gradually lose their edges and become ever smaller. The resulting debris is carried away by the currents and deposited somewhere else as sediment. These sediments may accumulate around other coasts and eventually go to form new land. In the longer term they may build up great thicknesses of sand and mud which in the patient fullness of geological time may harden to produce the new rocks of the future.

Erosion by the sea and other processes is the most spectacular contemporary geological activity on the islands, but it is by no means the only one. While the land is being steadily eaten back all along Aran's south-west facing Atlantic coasts, on the opposite side it is being built up and added to by sand brought in from the sea. Around Cill Éinne on Inis Mór for instance deposits of blown sand are accumulating as dunes and machair, as they have for millennia, their constant change measured by the covering and uncovering of such cultural datestones as fields, tombs and churches. When the first people arrived on Aran there was probably little or no sand being deposited on this angle of the island; it had the same rock pavement, broken by patches of flowery grassland, as the rest of Aran: except that there was rather more of it, because at that time the land stood higher in relation to sea level than it does now. The rising sea drowned the fields and dwellings of Aran's coast-dwelling communities. Under the deep cover of the sands which have built up over the millennia around Cill Éinne and Iaráirne there is a hidden network of ancient field walls which divides the land into fields and gardens which run out beneath the sea, and which still awaits full investigation. Having been partly drowned by the rising sea level, this prehistoric field system was buried beneath the sands brought in by the same sea. These subaerial and submarine sands are constantly moving and shifting about, and around 1840 or 1850 the tops of some of the ancient walls, and several clochans associated with them, emerged again when between three and six metres of sand were swept from the dunes round Cill Éinne and the north-east corner of Inis Mór into Gregory's Sound, which in consequence became much shallower.

By the time St Enda's little church was built at Teaghlach Éinne in the early Christian centuries, the coastal fields of these early people of Aran were probably completely buried. And in time, Teaghlach Éinne was itself buried by the relentlessly encroaching sands: and with it his grave, and those of the 120 other nameless saints of Ireland who are buried with him here in this holiest corner of Aran. The same thing

has been happening on the other islands. The little hillock on which Teampall Chaomháin on Inis Oírr is situated was a grassy open plain in the 17th century; by the 19th it too was buried in sand, which was then dug out every year on the saint's feast day. And in O'Flaherty's *Ogygia* (1685) we find mention of several other ancient churches, tombs and fields which were buried beneath the sands in the centuries which followed.

Illus. 1.19. Teaghlach Éinne on Inis Mór.

Acknowledgements for Illustrations

Illus. 1. 1, Fr.Browne S.J. Collection.
Illus. 1.2, *Memoirs of the Geological Survey.*
Illus. 1.3, 1.4, 1.5, 1.6, 1.8, 1.9, 1.11, 1.12, 1.13, 1.15, 1.17, 1.18,
Anne Korff.
Illus. 1.17, T.H. Mason.
Illus. 1.10, O.P.W.
Illus. 1.14, Bord Fáilte.
Illus. 1.16, John Feehan.
Illus. 1.19, John Waddell.
Illus. 1.20, Fr Browne S.J. Collection.

Illus. 1.20. Poll na bPéist, *the Worm Hole, on Inis Mór. The 'péist' in the name is the reptilian monster with which Gaelic imagination often peopled the deep in past ages. In spite of its regularity, the feature is a natural one, dramatic evidence of the power of storm waves to excavate enormous blocks where the limestone is conveniently divided by the regular vertical joints which traverse it. Even on calm days the sea can be heard gurgling ominously in the hidden caverns that connect Poll na bPéist with the ocean.*

CHAPTER 2

The Aran Flora

Cilian Roden

For the inhabitant of the continent, the three islands of Inis Mór, Inis Meáin and Inis Oírr must seem to be amongst the most remote and isolated parts of Europe. They are, after all, six hundred kilometres north and west of France and even further distant from the Low Countries. Two large islands and three seaways lie between, and the vast and empty Atlantic stretches west from their very shores. Indeed, the deep ocean, marked by the 1000m isobath, lies less than 150 kilometres west. Impressed by this very remoteness, it is all too easy to equate geographical distance with diminished human impact and to imagine that the natural history of the archipelago will show natural features, now lost in more developed places.

It is sufficient to stand in the centre of any of the three islands to realise how misleading this idea can be. To reach such a viewing point it will have been necessary to negotiate innumerable stone walls or to walk down any one of the small lanes or paths that traverse the territory. If you are a newcomer, there is every probability that you have a copy of Robinson's meticulous map in your hand.[1] Your first glance will have shown you that the entire surface is gridded by paths, roads and tracks, which lead between endless kilometres of carefully built dry stone field walls. Navigation, especially on the two smaller islands, bears comparison to making your way about the blocks and alleys of an unfamiliar city. With the exception of the seashore and perhaps some of the cliffs, there is no such thing as 'natural vegetation' on these islands. The present day flora is one which exists only in balance with human activities.

That is not to say that the flora appears degraded or impoverished. On the contrary, the islands abound in beautiful and often rare plants. Even along the roadsides pink mallow, *Malva sylvestris*, and white greater burnet saxifrage, *Pimpinella major*, are to be seen. Many of the small fields enclose what seem to be pieces of limestone pavement; in spring and early summer the gentian, *Gentiana verna*, and the Irish saxifrage, *Saxifraga rosacea*, provide a display that rivals that to be seen in the Burren – the grey limestone hills of Clare which lie to the east across the South Sound. By mid summer bloody cranesbill, *Geranium sanguineum*, yellow rattle, *Rhinanthus minor*, and kidney vetch, *Anthyllis vulneraria*, make an unforgettable combination of magenta and egg yolk yellow, while along the shore the sulphur yellow flowers of the wild radish, *Raphanus*

raphanistrum, stand out against the shingle. Many of the springs and wells are decorated by the apple green and purple black fronds of the maiden hair fern, *Adiantum capillus-veneris*, while the pale blue sea holly, *Eryngium maritimum*, and the huge pink and white flowers of sea bind weed, *Calystegia soldanella*, grow amongst the sand dunes. In autumn, the blues, purple and carmine of harebells, *Campanula rotundifolia*, devilsbit, *Succisa pratensis*, and knapweed, *Centaurea nigra*, are everywhere in the fields.

Illus. 2.3 below. Sea stock (Matthiola sinuata). This most attractive plant was once known from several places in Ireland, including Straw Island at the mouth of Cill Éinne Bay and the nearby coast of Clare. During the first half of this century, it disappeared from the last of its known Irish stations. It has not been seen on Straw Island since the nineteenth century. Its history is thus the opposite of wild sage (Illus.2.2). The photograph is of a plant in cultivation.

Illus. 2.1 above. Primroses in the cashel of Dún Fearbhaí on Inis Meáin. Often thought of as a woodland plant, the primrose (Primula vulgaris) frequently grows in more open situations in the west of Ireland. This extension of range reflects the lack of strong sunlight characteristic of the wet oceanic climate of the region. The primrose is frequent on all three islands and can flower as early as February.

Illus. 2.2 right. Wild Sage (Salvia verbenaca) growing on Inis Mór. Ireland is at the northern edge of the distribution of this plant which grows in the south and west of Europe and north Africa. The plant is only known from a few localities in Ireland and it is illegal to disturb it in any manner. Botanists were surprised when a new colony appeared on Inis Mór as recently as the 1980s. This species is not the cultivated sage of herb gardens and is of no culinary value.

An island flora

The flora of the Aran Islands is surprisingly large given their size; four hundred and thirty seven species in a total area of forty three square kilometres.[2] The total flora of Ireland is about a thousand species in an area of eighty three thousand square kilometres. At first glance, the three islands appear to have a proportionately much richer flora than the country as a whole, but it is now well established that island floras do not increase in direct proportion to area. Instead it is suggested that a tenfold increase in area usually leads to a doubling in species number, but even by this yardstick the flora seems very diverse. By comparison, Achill which has an area of 164 square kilometres, has, according to Praeger,[3] only four hundred and twenty species.

Illus. 2.4 above. Maiden Hair Fern (Adiantum capillus-veneris). *This frost-sensitive fern is a southern species, but it occurs in great abundance around many of the island wells and springs.*

Illus. 2.5 far left. Purple milk vetch (Astragalus danicus). *This clover like plant grows both on Inis Mór and Inis Meáin, but not on the Irish mainland. It is found both in the sand dunes near the air strips on both islands and also along the cliffs of Inis Mór. Here it forms a close sward along with Fescue grass and sea pink near the cliff edge.*

Illus. 2.6 left. Irish Saxifrage (Saxifraga rosacea) *is both a striking and common wild flower amongst the rocky island pastures in spring. The characteristic reddish foliage contrasts strongly with the large cream flowers. It is also common on the nearby Burren coast but further afield it is a mountain plant. It occurs occasionally in southern and western Ireland but is now extinct in Britain.*

While islands have always been of interest to naturalists – their natural boundaries and isolation help to avoid all the difficulty of defining 'natural units' – only in the last thirty years has a general theory of island biogeography been established.[4] Two predictions may help explain the size and composition of the Aran flora. According to theory, the flora should increase with island size and this is indeed the case; Inis Oírr contains 289 species with an area of 4.1 square kilometres, Inis Meáin 352 species on 9.1 square kilometres, while 417 species grow on the 30.1 square kilometres of Inis Mór itself. More intriguingly the number of species is assumed to be a balance between extinction and new emigration, rather than an always fixed population. It is expected that smaller islands will suffer greater extinction and emigration rates than larger ones. The idea that an island flora might be in continuous flux is not always an obvious one; that island floras are in flux has been demonstrated by experiments in various parts of the world. So far rigorous investigations have not been performed on Aran.

However, the flora has been repeatedly studied over the last hundred and twenty years and it is striking how species appear and disappear from the flora lists as decades pass. Indeed D.A. Webb in his 'Flora of the Aran Islands' notes that the number of alien (i.e. introduced) species appear to be waxing and waning at a greater rate than for any comparable area of the mainland. Some extinctions can be assigned to known causes; juniper, *Juniperus communis*, for example, became extinct in Inis Oírr possibly because the few trees were used as a source of palm on Palm Sunday. Other species, sea stock, *Matthiola sinuata*, for example, became extinct early in the last century for unknown reasons. It is probably extinct at all its Irish stations by now[5] but no convincing cause has been advanced. We also know that certain species suddenly appear. The seashore plant, frosted orache, *Atriplex laciniata*, was not recorded before 1970, but in the mid seventies it flourished on several beaches, only to decline subsequently. An even more striking example is wild sage, *Salvia verbenaca*. This rare but striking species (it is legally protected) was found for the first time along a well travelled road in 1984 by two separate observers, T. Robinson and T. Curtis.[6] Mr Robinson was a resident on the island and knew the area well; it seems unlikely that it had been overlooked previously. Either the plant was present but concealed as seeds or leaf rosettes or, alternatively, it is a recent immigrant. The matter is made more complicated as the nearest mainland colony is over eighty kilometres distant. While it will never be possible to explain every species change, it would appear that the Aran flora is not constant.

In general however, it is the less established species which come and go (and genuine new arrivals and long established but undiscovered rarities can be difficult to tell apart). There is a large number of unusual and distinctive species which have been part of the Aran flora since recording began over two centuries ago. Many of these are typical of the Burren and they underline the great similarity between these two areas of bare Carboniferous limestone. The gentian, the hoary rock-rose, *Helianthemum canum*, the Salzburg eyebright, *Euphrasia salisburgensis*, the pyramidal bugle, *Ajuga pyramidalis*, the bloody cranesbill, the spring sandwort, *Minuartia verna*, the Irish saxifrage and the maidenhair fern are as much Aran plants as Burren species and indeed some are commoner on the islands. However some Burren species, surprisingly, do not occur; a good example is the mountain avens, *Dryas octopetala*.

Aran is also the home of one species which does not occur on the island of Ireland; the purple milk vetch, *Astragalus danicus*, which occurs both on sand dunes and the grassy cliff tops. It is a most unlikely location for this species. Abroad it is mostly confined to areas of more continental climate, eastern Britain and Europe east of Denmark – although it does occur in Tiree in the Hebrides and the Isle of Man. It is assumed that it is a survivor of the early post glacial period when open grassland covered north-west Europe. In Ireland it is now confined to this last island outpost where, perhaps, tree growth was less developed. Indeed several other species are assumed to have a similar history, including the pyramidal bugle, the gentian and the hoary rock-rose. Unfortunately no record of the former vegetation cover of the islands is available and the deposits of bog or mud which could preserve the necessary pollen from former times are very scarce. By analogy with the similar Burren, some type of forest cover may have existed, possibly of the now extinct pine and almost certainly low hazel scrub. To this day hazel remains on the two largest islands, but forest trees such as oak and elm are not found (A nineteenth century record for oak, *Quercus robur*, is thought to be an error).[2] It must be remembered that the coast line was very different in the period immediately after the ice age, nor is it established when the islands became detached from the mainland.

Flowers and habitats.

While the vegetation of Aran before the arrival of people is conjectural, archaeological remains and historical tradition show that the islands have supported a relatively large human population for at least two thousand years. Most of the ground is now enclosed in fields of varying quality; in places glacial drift allows tillage, in other areas the rock is so bare as to make one suspect some form of soil erosion, as it appears quite pointless to enclose such naked rock. In addition, as is well known the islanders laboriously manufactured a new soil in many fields from sea sand and decaying sea weed. This practice demonstrates how close was the link between community and land on Aran. On an island where this new soil is a necessity, there can be no possibility that large areas of unmodified vegetation or soils will still persist.

So two major habitats can be identified, the currently cultivated fields and managed grassland and, in contrast, the semi-natural grass and herbs that grow on the almost exposed limestone, especially in the centre and southern parts of each island.

The cultivated ground is by no means the least interesting place to find wild flowers. Aran is unsuitable for large scale commercial farming and many agricultural practices, extinct on the mainland, still persist. In certain places rye is still grown in small plots, as much for straw as fodder. The seed is gathered and resown without any of the sorting or screening of large scale tillage, consequently certain weeds are still to be found in the fields. The most interesting examples are darnel, *Lolium temulentum*, and cornflowers, *Centaurea cyanus*. Both species were found by Dr T. Curtis and his colleagues in 1987.[7] As the authors note, these once common weeds have now almost vanished from the rest of the country. The continuation of small scale tillage has preserved these and other weed species, several of which are now so rare that they are legally protected.

Illus. 2.8 left. Geranium molle *growing in sandy soil on Inis Oírr. There are extensive tracts of sand dune and sandy soils on the Aran Islands. These places have a characteristic flora including many annual plants such as G. molle. Annual plants can survive the occasional droughts typical of light soils as seeds.*

Illus. 2.9. The magnificent and exotic tree mallow (Lavatera arborea) *is a native plant of the west coast of Ireland and much of southern Europe. A colony occurs near Dún Aonghasa but it is now much commoner in island gardens than in the wild. A biennial it can grow to two metres or more in height.*

Illus. 2.11 opposite page. Sand dune flowers in June. Magenta pyramidal orchids (Anacamptis pyramidalis), *yellow kidney vetch* (Anthyllis vulneraria) *and white squinancywort* (Asperula cynanchica) *combine in one of the many displays of colour to be seen on the island. The thin reddish stems of the parasitic plant dodder* (Cuscuta epithymum) *can be distinguished in the foreground.*

Illus. 2.10 left. Babington's leek (Allium babingtonii) *is now only found in the wild but some naturalists think that it is descended from an ancient garden variety of leek. It is confined to the west coast of Ireland and south-west England. The flower heads carry not only flowers but small bulbs which can also give rise to new plants.*

Neither pesticides or herbicides are widely used on the islands, nor are cars common except on a few of the surfaced roads on Inis Mór. The effect of the absence of such pollutants is difficult to specify, but several naturalists have commented on the diversity of roadside flowers, insects and the varied weed flora. Only careful research could demonstrate if a direct link existed between this supposed diversity and the absence of chemicals. Be that as it may, the variety of plants amongst fields and lanes is noticeable to a mainland visitor.

The greater part of each island is rocky pasture, enclosed in larger or smaller fields. This vegetation is directly comparable to the vegetation of the Burren crags. Indeed Praeger[3] was of the opinion that the limestone flora of the west of Ireland attained its greatest development on the Aran Islands. Much of what has been written about the Burren flora also applies to Aran. It is a meeting place of northern and southern species and many species are relict from early post glacial times. The most famous southern plant of the Burren flora, the dense flowered orchid, *Neotinea maculata*, now occurs on all three islands. It was first recorded by Prof. J. J. Moore only in 1966, despite previous efforts to find it by nineteenth century botanists. Whether it is a recent colonist or an overlooked species is impossible to say. Certain species are commoner on Aran than in Clare though for no obvious reason. An example is the hairy violet, *Viola hirta*. Although very rare throughout Ireland and hardly present in the Burren, it is occasional on both Inis Meáin and Inis Mór.

The most awe inspiring habitat on the islands are the southern cliffs and storm beaches. There are no houses here and paths are infrequent. The ocean extends west as far as the eye

Illus. 2.12 below. Frog orchid (Coeloglossum viride); this well camouflaged orchid occurs occasionally on the two larger islands, because of its drab colouring it is easily overlooked.

can see, and winter storms have swept the rocks clear of all but the most enduring plants. Not surprisingly, only a few species are to be found including wild samphire, *Crithmum maritimum*, sea pink, *Armeria maritima*, sea spleenwort, *Asplenium marinum*, and sea lavender, *Limonium recurvum* (subsp. *pseudotranswallianum*). An interesting plant is roseroot, *Rhodiola rosea*, which grows on the cliffs and pavement at the west end of Inis Mór. It is more usually a plant of high mountains, but in northern latitudes many of these species also descend close to sea level. The presence of roseroot on the Inis Mór cliffs is a reminder of how far north the islands lie, despite their almost frost free climate.

Perhaps surprisingly, Inis Mór has well developed sand dune systems and a number of plants such as sea rocket, *Cakile maritima*, marram grass, *Ammophila arenaria*, storksbill, *Erodium cicutarium*, and sea holly are abundant amongst the dunes and foreshore. As is so often the case on these islands, unusual plants also occur; the wiry leafless red stems of the parasitic dodder, *Cuscuta epithymum*, can be seen and the magnificent glaucous rosettes of sea kale, *Crambe maritima*, are to be found in a few places.

Plants and people

As I have noted people's influence is everywhere on these islands. There is no comparable terrain to the empty boglands or mountain tops of Connemara which can be seen across the North Sound. Instead every space has a function and a boundary. When you stand in the narrow cleft between Baile an tSéipéil and Baile an Chaisleáin on Inis Oírr and look up towards O'Brien's Castle, you see that even the escarpment is carefully divided into small gardens enclosed in beautifully made dry stone walls set against the vertical limestone. This scene is almost a metaphor for the islands as a whole. They are populated and cared for oases in a surrounding wilderness, but the wilderness of course is the ocean; the land is human territory. It follows that there are many connections between the people and the plants with which they share the territory. Cottage gardens are everywhere and the sight of wall flowers, old fashioned pinks and iris beneath white washed walls is encountered time and again. One species has been recruited into gardens from the wild. This is the two metre high tree mallow, *Lavatera arborea*, which grows along the cliff near Dún Aonghasa. A plant of south and west coasts of Europe, it is a biennial or perennial and grows easily from seed. Whether the plants in island gardens are descended from Aran or imported stock is an open question.

Conversely, the wild leek, *Allium babingtonii*, may have spread from ancient gardens. It is a tall, impressive plant, possibly a relict of cultivation but now no longer sown. Instead, it is to be found in fields and roadsides. It has a very restricted distribution, growing only on the Atlantic coast of Ireland and the coast of south-west Britain. Some botanists think it is an ancient cultivar of the leek *Allium ampeloprasum*.[8] Others regard it as a native plant confined to the coasts of north-west Europe.[9] Both theories create difficulties. If a cultivar, why are there no plants still in cultivation? But on the other hand, a world distribution limited to western Ireland and south-west England is most unusual for native plants. People do more than grow plants. They give them names, describe their uses, and make up

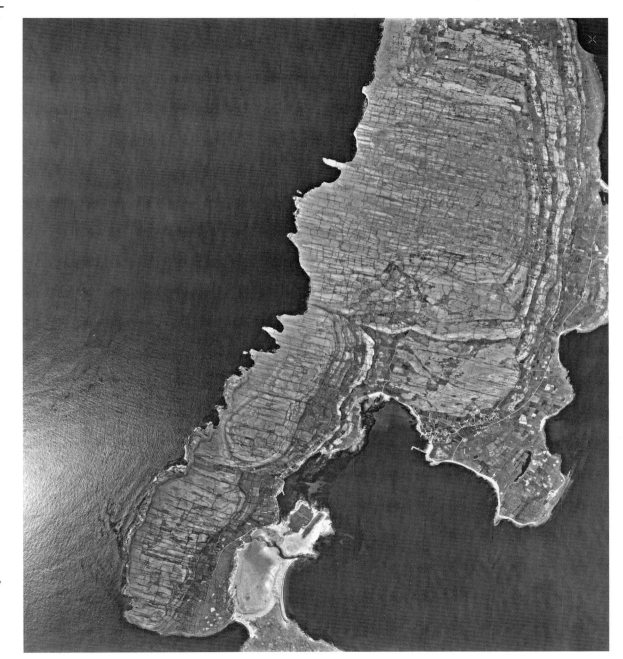

Illus. 2.13.   An aerial photograph of Inis Mór. Note the division of the whole land surface into fields bounded by stone walls, the complete absence of either houses or trees on the southern side and the extent of bare limestone pavement.

Illus. 2.14. Sea spleenwort (Asplenium marinum); *this sea-side fern exploits the shelter of a large gryke to grow a great deal bigger than the eight to twelve centimetres of more exposed plants. It is frost sensitive and only grows on the warmer coasts of Europe.*

stories about many of them. The people of Inis Mór have preserved an exceptionally detailed folk knowledge about plants. While Lelia Doolan explores this topic in chapter 12, I include here one remedy that was told to me on Inis Meáin. Seeing a plant of wild valerian in a collection, a woman remarked that its leaves, soaked in whiskey, were a well known relief for pains and aches. Unfortunately few botanists have been Gaelic scholars and few Gaelic scholars have had a detailed botanical knowledge. One exception was Eoin MacNeill, founder with Douglas Hyde of the Gaelic League.[10] He first encountered spoken Irish when he came to stay on Inis Meáin in 1891 and he returned annually until 1908, returning for a final visit many years later in 1944. As he relates himself, time spent alone was time wasted for one learning Irish, but he did acquire a detailed knowledge of plant names which he subsequently inscribed in his copy of E. Step's *Wayside and Woodland Blossoms*.[11] Many of these names are not to be found in the latest edition of the *Census Catalogue of the Flora of Ireland*[12] and it is possible that some at least were learnt on Inis Meáin. Curiously that most striking flower, the spring gentian, is not annotated, perhaps because it flowers so early in the year. Mr. Michael O'Connell says that it is now known simply as Bláth Mhuire or Our Lady's Flower; the *Census Catalogue* gives

Illus. 2.15. English stonecrop (Sedum anglicum) *growing in the unusual habitat of a limestone solution hollow on Inis Oírr. Normally the plant avoids limestone, it is one of the peculiarities of the island's botany that the species has colonized the rock in a few places.*

Illus. 2.16. Salzburg eyebright (Euphrasia salisburgensis) is a tiny member of the snapdragon (Scrophulariaceae) family and is a distinctive member of the flora of the limestone of western Ireland. It occurs in many places on the island but outside Ireland it is mostly found in the mountains of central and southern Europe.

Ceadharlach Bealtaine. Other less well known names recorded include tae scailpeach (maidenhair fern), pabhsaer Bealtaine and pabhsaer na seangán.

It must be admitted that scholarship has an unfortunate tendency to interpose layers of paper between the object and the observer. A marvellous example is the history of an insignificant plant variously known to botanists as *Sedum anglicum* or English stonecrop. No less a botanist than Robert Praeger[3] started the confusion when he noted that this plant often monopolised ant heaps on the islands and was called an póirín seangán (in English, the ant's nest). This apparently simple statement caused problems for two reasons. The species is rarely found on limestone and Aran is composed exclusively of this rock, nor has it any special link with ants on the mainland. Modern botanists, struck by its absence on all three islands, assumed that it had grown on the acidic debris of turf stacks

Illus. 2.17. An illustration of rock samphire in Eoin MacNeill's copy of Step's Wayside and Woodland Blossoms *published in 1905. MacNeill, one of the founders of Conradh na Gaeilge (the Gaelic League) and a pioneering historian and patriot, first learnt Irish on Inis Meáin in the early 1890s. Note his handwritten list of Gaelic names for the plant. Rock samphire (Crithmum maritimum) is common on the rocky shores of the islands. The leaves and stem were formerly used as a vegetable and have a distinctive but pleasant taste.*

Samphire.
Crithmum maritimum.
UMBELLIFERÆ.

which are now vanished from the island. In 1976 Mr J. White discovered a small colony in the centre of Inis Oírr growing in limestone solution hollows, a most unusual habitat for the species. Two other small colonies have since been found but neither have any connection with ants, so Praeger's statement remains a mystery. Few present day islanders have heard of an póirín seangán but one old man interviewed by Lelia Doolan in 1993 was familiar with the plant. He confirmed that it grew over ants' nests, but when shown a sample of stonecrop said the póirín seangán bore no resemblance to it whatsoever. His description seemed more suited to wild thyme, which does indeed grow on ants' nests.

So, as so often happens, scholarship ends by making itself an object of study and perhaps even an obstacle to approaching the original material. But there is no need to ponder the subtleties of the póirín seangán to appreciate the flora of the islands. All that is required is a willingness to leave the established route and strike out along the cliffs and fields. There, with some of the most interesting limestone pastures in western Europe to one side and the illimitable Atlantic on the other, you will find yourself in a most exceptional place.

Acknowledgements

Illus. 2.1, 2.2, 2.3, 2.4, 2.6, 2.8, 2.9, 2.10, 2.11, 2.12, 2.14, 2.15, 2.16, 2.17, Cilian Roden. 2.5, Dónal Henderson. 2.13, Geological Survey of Ireland.
Special thanks to Micheline Sheehy-Skeffington for reading this chapter.

Illus. 3.1. Storm waves breaking against the cliffs in an Sunda Caoch or Blind Sound west of Gort na gCapall. As these cliffs are thirty metres high, the size of the breakers can be appreciated. Such large waves are caused by wind blowing over the open ocean for thousands of miles, their destructive power is immense and is reflected in eroding and undercut limestone cliffs.

CHAPTER 3

The Natural History of the Sea

Michael O'Connell and Cilian Roden

The marine environment of the Aran Islands is rich in habitats and diverse in flora and fauna. The diversity is partly the result of being at the meeting of north and south temperate waters where species from both water bodies meet and mix in this region.

The bedrock of the shores and inshore waters of these islands is Carboniferous limestone which occurs in horizontal layers. This limestone weathers into a variety of structures – depressions, pits, overhangs, crevices and gullies, which provide a wide range of habitats for living things. Indeed some of these structures have been formed by the animals and plants grinding their way into the limestone.

The marine environment can most easily be sampled on the seashore, particularly at low water of spring tides. This occurs on the west coast of Ireland between ten in the morning and three in the afternoon. There are two spring tide periods, taoilí rabharta, alternating with two neap tide periods, taoilí mallmhuir, each month. The average range between low and high water spring tides in the Aran Islands is nearly five metres. This results in a fairly expansive piece of shore being uncovered. The influence of the tide on the life of a shore results in different species being confined to horizontal bands, usually called zones. The upper limit of a species is mainly determined by its tolerance to drying out and its lower limit by competition for space with more vigorous species.

A further factor affecting a shore is its exposure. This is a consequence of the area of open sea facing the shore, called the fetch, the prevailing winds and the direction of the swell. It is possible to tell how exposed a shore is from its flora and fauna. The Aran Islands are an excellent place to study shore exposure in a limestone environment. They have shores which range from 'extremely exposed' to 'very sheltered'. This covers all the accepted grades of exposure except 'extremely sheltered'.

Inshore seawater temperatures vary from 8 to 18° centigrade and are caused by oceanic water of subtropical origin. Frost is also prevented on the more exposed shores by a steady spray of salt water from the continuous Atlantic swell. The seawater of the islands is primarily oceanic, as demonstrated by the clarity of the water. It is little influenced by freshwater runoff from the mainland which passes out of the North Sound hugging the Connemara coast.

Extremely exposed rocky shores

A good place to start an account of the marine environment of Aran is on the extremely exposed shores, those directly facing the Atlantic Ocean where the fetch is greater than a thousand miles. On calm days they are washed by a continuous heavy swell while in bad weather they are pounded by enormous Atlantic breakers. Here the tidal zone is wider than on more sheltered shores, as the waves and spray move farther inland. The physical outline of these shores is of vertical steps separating horizontal benches or platforms that slope gently towards the sea. Storm beaches delimit the landward side of the shore where the cliffs are low and the shores more accessible. Such shores occur on Inis Oírr, Inis Meáin and at both ends and the middle of Inis Mór.

At the top of these shores is a wide zone regularly wetted by the sea spray. Lichens are the dominant plants growing there. Orange, grey - green and white ones on top are followed by a broad, black tar-like band of the lichen, *Verrucaria maura*. In damp conditions the lichens are grazed by the small periwinkles, *Melaraphe neritoides*, faocha bheag, which occur in large numbers in the cracks and crevices. The fertilised eggs of these tiny snails are released into the sea when it reaches them at high water of spring tides. Thus it is through reproduction that these essentially land snails maintain their link with the sea. The developing young spend a few weeks drifting in the upper layers of the water (in the plankton) before settling on a shore which may be many miles away.

Immediately below the spray zone the bedrock is smooth with many pools. Streams of fresh to brackish water issue from the layers of impervious shale sandwiched between the blocks of limestone. In winter the rock is covered with a thin layer of edible purple seaweed, *Porphyra*, sleabhcán, making it very slippery.

Illus. 3.2. An exposed shore at Carraig Fhada north of Cill Rónáin. The eroded limestone is covered by mussels and other attached animals while breakers erupt along the water line.

The pools and streams are covered by the green seaweed, *Enteromorpha*, líneáil ghorm, which can tolerate very low salinities. In summer it is often bleached white by the sun. A small silver fish, the three spined stickleback, *Gasterosteus aculeatus*, lives in these pools. The male makes a nest among the green seaweed using secretions from his kidneys. After the female has laid her eggs in the nest he chases her away and then guards the nest until the young have hatched. The young remain in their pools until the first storms of autumn tear away their seaweed cover. The fish spend the winter in deeper water and return to the pools the following April. Three spined sticklebacks are also found throughout the year in the brackish water lakes of the islands.

The next zone consists of barnacle, garbhán carraige, covered rock with pools of various depths. The barnacles are southern species of the genus *Chthamalus* which have a range that extends from the Mediterranean to the north of Scotland. They appear to favour the more exposed shores, being absent from the sheltered ones. The cone shape and small size of the barnacles offer little resistance to the waves. The next zone is populated by a black band of small mussels, *Mytilus edulis*, diúilicíní, which are attached by byssus threads glued to the rock. As the mussels grow and get bigger the surface area they expose to the waves increases until they are eventually knocked off by the waves. Young mussels from the plank-

Illus. 3.3. A moderately sheltered shore at Barr an Phointe north-east of Cill Rónáin. Here the rocks are covered in brown sea weeds, mainly Fucus vesiculosus, *and in contrast to 3.2, the sea beyond is calm.*

Illus. 3.4. The cliff shoreline. A vertical rock face confronts the ocean near an Poll Gorm south of Mainistir. Except at low water mark, few animals or plants protrude above the rock surface. Instead encrusting forms such as the yellow lichen (Caloplaca), and further down, red seaweeds colour the rock. The green streaks are algae indicative of nutrient enrichment, probably from freshwater seeping out between the limestone layers.

Illus. 3.5. Not a seaweed, but a patch of the marine lichen (Lichina pygmaea) on an exposed shore surrounded by barnacles. Such clumps contain many small animals. Here grazing periwinkles can be seen.

ton will soon replace them. The mussels and barnacles feed by filtering the water for the tiny microscopic plants and animals in the plankton. In turn they serve as food for animals such as the dogwhelk, *Nucella lapillus*, cuachma. This bores through the shells of mussels and barnacles to eat the flesh. The most obvious feature of the mid-shore zone (the barnacle and mussel zones) is the lack of large seaweeds and the abundance of small animals and low rock hugging plants such as the purple laver, *Porphyra*, sleabhcán, and the small red *Ceramium*. This results from the heavy seas tearing from the rock any large or weakly attached plants and animals.

The sides of the pools in the mid-shore zone are coated with small slow growing seaweeds with a lime skeleton. In depressions in the pools there are purple sea urchins, *Paracentrotus lividus,* cuán mara. These urchins also belong to a southern species and are confined to the west coast. It is likely that each urchin has made its own depression because the entrance to each of these depressions is smaller than the animal within it. As a result each remains in its depression on the exposed shores. It is known that they can absorb food directly through their body from the seawater, which probably accounts for most of their feeding on these exposed shores. On more sheltered shores urchins can be found outside the depressions where they graze the tiny algae growing on the bare patches of rock. Sea urchins bore through the limestone rock by mechanical means using a combination of teeth and spines.

They have a life span of six to nine years, with each individual excavating up to ten millimetres of rock per year. When the large numbers on these shores are considered it becomes obvious that they must be responsible for a considerable amount of erosion. Indeed, bioerosion by boring plants, sea urchins, sponges and molluscs can be a significant factor in the destruction of limestone coasts.

Large seaweeds, which can tolerate the surf but not drying out, are found on the lower shore. They are mainly northern species, also occurring in the Arctic. The uppermost is the thongweed, *Himanthalia elongata*, rúalach, followed by *Alaria esculenta*, sraoilleach. Both of these seaweeds tolerate and indeed indicate extreme exposure. They are pliable and bend to assume the shape of the incoming and departing wave, moving with it rather than offering resistance to it. Below these weeds and extending into the sublittoral is the kelp, *Laminaria*, coirleach. It can form dense forests where it is not heavily grazed by sea urchins.

Other rocky shores

On the shores facing the North, Gregory and Foul Sounds, patches of brown seaweeds become apparent on the mid-shore, indicating that exposure is not as extreme. At the top is the small channel wrack, *Pelvetia canaliculata*, casfheamainn, followed by the spiral wrack, *Fucus spiralis*, caisíneach, and then a bladderless form, cosa dubha, of the bladder wrack, *Fucus vesiculosus*. Below this, particularly where the sea breaks at low water on sublittoral reefs, is the saw wrack, *Fucus serratus*, míoránach, and a lush 'algal turf'. The latter is composed of small red and green seaweeds that keep this area very wet.

In more sheltered inlets on these sounds there is a more extensive cover of brown seaweeds, with the bladder and saw wracks dominating the mid shore. As shelter increases still farther, the egg wrack, *Ascophyllum nodosum*, feamainn bhuí, is found to the exclusion of the bladder wrack. This plant is indicative of shelter and on Inis Mór it is found only on the west side of the inlets of the North Sound, where it is sheltered from the prevailing swell. It has a similar distribution in Cill Éinne Bay.

The west and south shores of Cill Éinne Bay have small localised beds of the only flowering plant growing in these waters, the eel grass, *Zostera marina*, meilsceánach. The largest bed is between the two piers in Cill Rónáin. It is only visible at extreme low water of spring tides.

Several periwinkle, *Littorina*, faocha, topshells and crustacean species feed on the large seaweeds while hydroids, spirorbid worms, sea mats and smaller seaweeds attach themselves to the surface. These large seaweeds and stones

Illus. 3.6. A rock pool full of the purple sea urchin (Paracentrotus lividus). Although this sea urchin is at the extreme northern edge of its range in Ireland, populations of thousands are found in Aran rock pools. Attempts to cultivate the species were recently undertaken on Inis Oírr.

of the sheltered shores cover a wide variety of animal species that patient uncovering will reveal. The fish include the butterfish, *Pholis gunnellus* (péist an dhá shúil déag) and the eel, *Anguilla anguilla*, eascann. The crabs include the shore crab, *Carcinus maenas*, portán glas, and the edible crab, *Cancer pagurus*, portán rua.

Pollack, *Pollachius pollachius*, mongach, mackerel, *Scomber scombrus*, ronnach, ballan wrasse, *Labrus bergyla*, ballach, are the main fish species caught by rod or hand line from the rocks and cliffs. The red sea bream, *Pagellus bogaraveo*, bréam nó deargán, was formerly caught in some numbers on rod and line. It is a southern species that overwinters in deeper waters appearing off the Aran coast in summer. It has become rare of late probably due to overfishing well offshore

Illus. 3.7 above. Brown and red seaweeds of a rock pool. The large brown alga is Bifurcaria bifurcata, *a species near its northern boundary in the Aran Islands. The pink growths are species of red calcareous algae of the Corallina and*

Lithothamnion genera.

Illus. 3.8 below. Near low watermark mussels give way to large brown algae such as Laminaria digitata *seen here as well as characteristic red algae such as* Palmaria palmata.

Illus. 3.9 above. On weed covered sheltered shores a variety of richly coloured algae can be seen if the weed is moved aside. Here a large growth of a calcareous alga, of the Lithothamnion genus can be seen.

Illus. 3.10 below. Periwinkle (Litorina mariae) *crossing a frond of the red alga,* Lomentaria articulata. *Note the presence of the large brown weed (Fucus serratus) which forms a canopy above the smaller red weeds.*

Uses of seaweeds

Several species of seaweed are edible. They include the purple laver, *Porphyra*, sleabhcán, creathnach, *Palmaria palmata*, and *Alaria esculenta* of the exposed shores, and caraigín, *Chondrus crispus*, dilisk, *Palmaria palmata*, sea lettuce, *Ulva*, glasán, and *Laminaria saccharina* of the more sheltered shores. Creathnach is an exposed shore form of dilisk that grows among the small mussels. The stem-like stipes of the kelp are dried and exported for the extraction of alginate. All of the large seaweeds are used as fertiliser, some from driftweed, others are cut.

Sandy shores

Most of the sandy beaches of the islands are very exposed. They consist of a shelly gravel that is constantly shifted to and fro by the breakers. These beaches contain little organic matter and support few animals. Amongst these are the razor shells, *Ensis,* sceanna mara. These are suspension feeders and depend on the food the surf brings in. Others such as sand eels, *Ammodytes* and *Hyperoplus* (Illus. 3.15) scadán gainimh, burrow into the sand for protection. The large non-compacted sand particles have pores large enough between them to allow sufficient space for these fish to breathe. The sand eels remain buried in the sand throughout the winter from November to March and during the hours of darkness for the rest of the year. In the waters of Aran there are five species of sand eels, three small species (20cm or less) and two large species (up to 40cm). The small species eat zooplankton (animal plankton) while the large ones eat bigger zooplankton and small sand eels. Both species often swim and feed together in shoals. Sometimes they can be observed on bright sunny days in summer over a sandy bottom

Illus. 3.11 above top. Sandy shore at Cill Éinne Bay. As sand grains are both small and mobile, there is no point of attachment for attached organisms. While such strands may appear lifeless, a large variety of burrowing forms are present.

Illus. 3.12 above. Cobble shore at Trá na bhFrancach. Shingle shores are hostile to life. The large moving cobbles crush any organisms which attempt to settle. Such strands are perhaps the most inhospitable coastal environment around the islands.

from one of the piers of the islands. The smaller ones, with due cause, are very wary of the larger ones. Four of the five species occur on the sandy shores, with *Ammodytes tobianus* being the most common. This species consists of two breeding populations in these waters, one that breeds in winter to early spring and the other that breeds in autumn. In the north of its geographical range (Iceland) it only breeds in autumn and in the south (Spain) it only breeds in spring. The more compacted sheltered beaches of Cill Éinne Bay contain some cockles and clams, but only in small numbers.

Offshore

The most westerly tip of the islands, the lonely Oileáin Iartharach (Rock Island) Light stands less than ten miles east of the 100m depth contour. This isobath is often taken as the boundary between shallow inshore water and the open seas over the continental shelf. The deep ocean which lies beyond the continental shelf commences one hundred and fifty miles further west. This borderline position near the open sea means that the ecology of the surrounding water is more typical of offshore than

Illus. 3.13 below. Plankton. These extraordinary forms are in fact microscopic marine plants which drift in the upper layers of the sea. They form the base of the marine food chain. The fish which sustained so many of the islanders ultimately depend on these organisms as a source of food.

Illus. 3.14 right. Animal plankton; this variety of creatures includes both the young stages of crabs, fish and sea urchins as well as copepods. These are small shrimp-like creatures which consume the plant plankton and in turn are consumed by larger creatures.

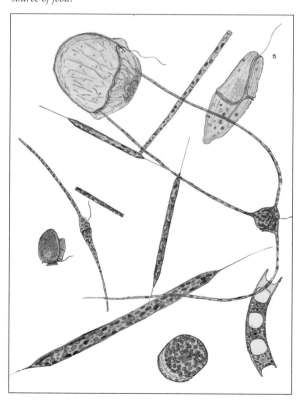

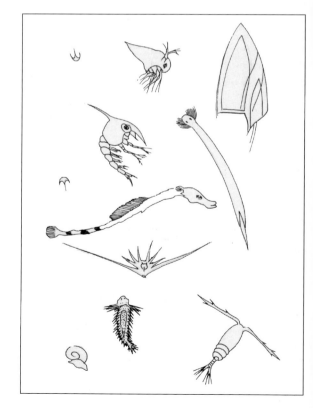

of inshore or estuarine conditions. Indeed salinity, an indicator of oceanic conditions is usually high (34.5 - 35.0 ppt). A more impressive if subjective measure is the clarity and colour of the surrounding water; it is often possible to see objects fifteen metres below the surface of the deep blue or even turquoise water. Another characteristic of the open sea is a small temperature range; off Aran temperatures between 8.0 and 17.0°C have been recorded.

To a traveller crossing from Rossaveal to Cill Rónáin the water may appear empty; this deception reflects the microscopic size of nearly all plankton plants and the only slightly larger size of the associated animals or zooplankton (Illus. 3.14). But the plant or phyto plankton constitutes a huge part of the living matter in the sea and often production of biomass is greater than production on the nearby land. While detailed measurements have not been made off Aran, in comparable coastal waters up to thirty tonnes, dry weight, of plant matter per hectare are produced each year. It is this production, transformed into fish through the food chain that provides so much of the food of the islanders (although only a small fraction of the total ends up as edible seafood).

This invisible plankton is made up of innumerable single celled organisms, while they can only be seen using a microscope, they have a beauty of form and colour that rivals other types of plants (Illus. 3.13). There are several hundred different species in European waters and the annual succession of species in the sea to the north west of Aran has recently been described. In spring increasing day length provides sufficient light for growth to commence even though the temperature of the water is near the annual minimum. A series of large

populations or 'blooms' grow between mid March and early May, only diminishing as the dissolved plant nutrients, nitrogen, phosphate and silicates become exhausted. In summer the surface of the sea warms and by late June two distinct layers are to be found in the deeper waters around the islands. South-west of the Oileáin Iartharach Light, for example, in August 1973, the temperature at the surface was over 17°C, but six degrees colder at a depth of seventy metres. As the colder water does not reach the surface, the plant nutrients it contains are unavailable to the surface living plankton and consequently far smaller populations occur at this time. This lack of plankton in

Illus. 3.15. Sand Eels. These small fish are extremely abundant in coastal water, where they feed on animal plankton. In turn they are devoured by sea birds and many other fish. They play an important ecological role by making the microscopic plankton available to larger marine fish and sea birds. Two genera are shown: the larger Hyperoplus sp. and the smaller Ammodytes. Both species bury themselves in loose sand on the bottom at night and throughout the winter.

Acknowledgements for Illustrations

Illus. 3.1 to 3.12, 3.14, 3.15 and 3.16, Mick O'Connell. 3.13, Cilian Roden.

Illus. 3.16. Luth or Leathery turtle (Dermochelys coriacea). These huge reptiles live offshore and feed on jellyfish and other drifting animals. There has been a notable increase in strandings along the west coast in the last fifteen years and several have been seen around Aran. This specimen was stranded near Renvyle, County Galway, in Autumn 1981.

July and August may give rise to the characteristic deep navy blue colour of the sea at this time, in early spring the greener colour is partly caused by the green chlorophyll of the plant cells. In Autumn large blooms can again occur, characteristically these are formed by organisms called dinoflagellates; in other parts of Ireland these sometimes are so dense that the water turns a red brown colour, this has not been recorded around Aran. In winter, growth ceases as light fails, a most interesting feature of the plankton is that species normally found in sub-tropical water are occasionally found. The winter storms so disturb the water that colour is often due more to re-suspended sands and silts than living plankton.

The sandy grounds offshore support several commercial species of fish such as plaice, *Pleuronectes platessa*, plás, cod, *Gadus morhua*, trosc, and turbot, *Scophthalmus maximus*. At different times of the year herring, *Clupea harengus*, scadán, and sprat, *Sprattus sprattus*, síol, come close to the islands. Prawns occur on the muddy bottoms to the west of the islands with hake, *Merluccius merluccius*, colmóir, and jumbo prawns farther west in the deep waters of the Porcupine Bank.

In late spring and summer giant basking sharks, *Cetorhinus maximus*, liamhán, can be seen feeding in the waters off the islands. These gentle giants, which can be over 11m in length, move slowly through the water with their mouths open sieving water with their gill rakers. In winter they cease feeding, shedding their gill rakers and moving into deeper water. Sadly in recent years basking sharks have become rare probably because this slow-breeding species is vulnerable to overfishing. A large species like it is especially vulnerable to the modern trawlers of the open ocean.

The south westerly winds and currents also bring many southern species of jellyfish, smugairle rón, to these waters. Some such as the metre wide *Rhizostome pulmo* feed on plankton while others like the by-the-wind sailor, *Velella velella* feed on small fish and other small animals. Large numbers of these occur each summer off this coast. The native species of jellyfish *Aurelia aurita* (contains four purple horseshoes), *Chrysaora hysoscella* (brown colour) and *Cyanea lamarckii* (blue colour) are also plankton feeders. The latter can inflict severe stings. Seeking and feeding on the jellyfish come the sunfish, *Mola mola*, liamhán gréine, and the leatherback turtle, *Dermochelys coriacea*. The latter is a giant warm blooded turtle weighing up to 1000kg, which is not unusual in the North Atlantic.

CHAPTER 4

The Wildlife of the Aran Islands

Gordon D'Arcy

Illus. 4.1. Chough (Pyrrhocorax p.) This maritime crow is found on all three of the islands where it makes its nest in caves and crevices on the sea cliffs. On Inis Oírr, however, a pair nests in a most unlikely site, on the rusty upper deck of the 'Plassey', the wrecked ship which lies high-and-dry on limestone pavement along the shore.

Choughs spend much of their time in the close-grazed fields where they use their strong claw-shaped beak to good effect in probing for invertebrates and their larvae which are their staple food. In these circumstances good views are to be had of these normally wary birds whose hallmarks are sleek plumage, red legs and beaks and unmistakable far-carrying call. This call contains for me, evocations of the original bird-shout, the communion of bird with man rather than with other bird — a reminder to us perhaps that we are, by 140 million or so years, comparative newcomers.

A peculiar bee with a rust back is to be seen buzzing around the flowers on the Aran Islands. It otherwise resembles the moss carder bee, *Bombus muscorum*, a well-known ochre-backed species found over most of the Irish mainland. The naturalist is inclined to assume that it is a totally distinct species restricted to Aran, but it is not. This bee is simply a race – *Bombus muscorum smithianus,* one of a group of sub-species – which is found on a string of islands along the western seaboard from Scilly to Shetland. The Aran bee may be well on its way to evolving into a discrete island species – an endemic – but not yet.

Islands all over the world do indeed have endemic species. Those of the Galapagos and Hawaiian archipelagos are so distinct as to have given substance to the notion of evolution in the first place. The key factors in the development of these endemics has been the isolation of their island homes and their long-term occupancy by wildlife castaways. Some of the results of nature's quirks in these situations have been bizarre; the Mauritius dodo which looked more like a sheep than a pigeon – its original predecessor; the Cook Island tuatara, the only living reptilian survivor from the age of the Dinosaurs which still retains a sensitive receptor on its forehead – like a third eye!

Comparatively speaking, exploitative man has come recently (over the past few centuries) to such places. His effect has nevertheless been devastating. Either by direct exploitation, for food for instance, or indirectly, as a result of the introduction of predators, he has put paid to enormous numbers of these most special of species – the dodo, for instance, over three hundred years ago. Indeed, 90% of all the birds which have become extinct in the world in historic times were island dwellers.

In the case of the Aran Islands, proximity to the Irish coastline – within rowing distance of Connemara at one end and the Burren on the other – and their relatively long-term occupancy by humans have been the most significant criteria in their colonisation by wildlife. Both have militated against the possibility of endemicity. Whatever fauna existed prior to the Ice Age was eradicated by the glaciers, and invasion began anew within the past ten millennia. Whether this occurred primarily 'on the dry', before the melting of the ice restored the sea level or by wind and sea drift it is now impossible to say.

Archaeological evidence suggests there has been permanent human settlement on the islands for well over a third of that time. In view of the obvious limitations of the island resources down the ages, human influence on the island wildlife must have been profound. Given that today it is only possible to speculate on this, it is reasonable to assume that more wildlife has been imported (and perhaps subsequently lost) than has survived since before man's arrival; exchange rather than continuity.

The geological location of the islands, wedged between two radically distinct land masses – acid Connemara to the north and alkaline Burren to the east – has also been a significant factor. Such biotypical opposites have ensured that diversity and enrichment have occurred, and continue to occur. In view of the fact that the Aran Islands are geologically speaking no more than a fragmented reef of the Burren extending into the Atlantic, the influence on the fauna from this quarter has been the more significant of the two (though probably less so than in the case of the flora). In comparing Aran's wildlife diversity with that of other similar-sized islands around the Irish coast it is important to take account of the undoubted calcicolous (lime-friendly) bias due to the proximity the species-rich 'mother island' of the Burren.

Despite the relative accessibility of either end of the island chain, its overall alignment, at right angles to the predominant wind and tidal directions must have rendered colonisation more difficult than the map would suggest. Above all, small creatures which rely on drift, both in air and in sea, should have had particular difficulty in reaching the islands in sufficient quantity to form permanent settlements. In fact the diversity and abundance of some of the smallest creatures, terrestrial invertebrates, tend to suggest the opposite. How this has come to be, is something of a puzzle.

Invertebrates

As in the Burren, it is the showy fliers that make their presence felt. The abundance and variety of butterflies and day-flying moths suggest that wind-drift to the west has been a significant factor in populating the islands with insects, for many of those familiar on the limestone mainland are also found on Aran. There are at least 19 resident butterflies and three migrants – 22 compared with 30 in the Burren. Some of the resident butterflies are amazingly common on Inis Mór. Grassland species such as the grayling, *Hipparchia semele*, common blue, *Polyommatus icarus,* and small blue, *Cupido minimus,* and the marsh fritillary, *Euphydryas aurinia,* appear to be as common as in any similar sized area in the Burren. The two Burren specialities, the pearl-bordered fritillary, *Boloria euphrosyne,* and the brown hairstreak, *Thecla betulae,* are, however, absent though this may be as a result of the paucity of their caterpillar food-plants.

Of the moths, the well-known black-and-red day-fliers, the transparent and the six spot burnets, *Zygaenidae,* and the cinnabar, *Tyria jacobaeae,* are common and fairly widespread. One of the most striking of the day-flying moths is the forester, *Adscita statices,* which, with its iridescent turquoise wings, lights up the summer pasture. The status of the nocturnal moths, on the other hand, is as yet cloaked in darkness. It would be most interesting to compare their diversity and distribution with their counterparts on the mainland and to establish whether the isolated population of the rare Burren green, *Calamia tridens,* extends also to the islands.

Representatives of the other groups of insects are also widespread. Bees in general are noticeable. The famous Clare Island survey, which visited Aran in the period 1909 - 1911 identified five different bee species but appears to have missed *smithianus*. The striking red-tailed *Bombus* is certainly common nowadays on all three of the islands. Beetles, bugs and other arthropods abound. *Geotrupes stercorarius* and the orange and black *Aphodius fimetarius* are found in the open and woodlice, centipedes, and yellow and black ants are found abundantly beneath the rocks.

Predatory invertebrates are widespread on all three islands. Dragonflies are seen in freshwater localities; most common are the red sympetrums and the common aeshnas – 'hawker' dragonflies which hunt on the wing. But the 'darter' *Libellula quadrimaculata* is also known from Inis Mór.

Hunting spiders, particularly wolf (Lycosidae) and the tiny jumping spiders (Salticidae) are widespread. The miniscule, but nevertheless obvious red velvet mite, *Eutrombidium,* is noted frequently.

The abundance of land snails on the Aran Islands is intriguing. They appear to be disproportionately common there; more than forty species have been recorded, a high percentage of those found throughout the Burren. Most eye-catching are the beautiful banded snails, *Cepaea*, which in their colourful abundance provide an appropriate compliment to the wildflower meadows. How do we account for this plenitude ? Did it come about as a consequence of inadvertent transportation by man, or as a result of random water drift from the land, at either end of the islands? Could birds or other snail predators have been responsible?

Whatever the vectors have been these gastropods are surely the islands' most successful invertebrates reflecting their capacity to multiply in favourable circumstances and their significance in the ecology of limestone regions generally.

Freshwater snails also occur but they are much less diverse than their terrestrial counterparts. The thin-shelled pond snails are the most abundant. The little amphibious pond snail, *Lymnaea truncatula*, is locally abundant in Leac Chrannail well on Inis Oírr. Jenkin's spire shell, *Potamopyrgus jenkinsi*, another diminutive

Illus. 4.2. Aran Island Bee (Bombus muscorum smithianus). Of all the wildlife of Aran this humble bee has the strongest claim to distinctiveness. Though in fact merely a race of the moss carder, a common mainland species, it differs markedly in appearance in having a russet-coloured, not straw-coloured, back and a blacker base to the abdomen. A.W. Stelfox, who described it first in 1931 stated that the Aran bee foraged for food among thistles, wood sage, thyme, and mallow. Though this would require it to frequent the flowering meadows throughout the islands, along with the other handful of bee species, its home (as far as is known) is to be found in the sandy places – such as the machair – near the shore. Here it burrows beneath the dry turf to construct its nest. Stelfox described the nest as 'a detachable, cushion-shaped wad of moss in which the comb, a shapeless agglomeration of cells is imbedded'.

Illus. 4.3. Butterflies and Day Moths. The Aran Islands have a surprisingly rich Lepidoptera reflecting that of the Burren. The great diversity of limestone plants supports many species allowing each to lay its eggs on specific food-plants on which the caterpillars must feed. Notable among these are the marsh fritillary (Euphydryas aurinia) which favours plantain and devil's bit, and the small blue (Cupido minimus) which utilises kidney vetch. The common blue (Polyommatus icarus), and the greenveined white (Pieris napi) have less specific requirements, utilising a number of meadowland plants among the legumes, (clovers etc.) and crucifers (cresses etc.). The highly coloured day-flying moths are easily distinguished from the butterflies by their more clumsy-looking flight and by tent-like manner in which they fold their wings when at rest. The caterpillars of the common forester (Adscita statices) feed mainly on sorrel.

species, is common in the turloughs and streams on Inis Mór despite being rather local in the Burren.

The invertebrate life of the freshwater bodies of Aran has been investigated and compared with that of the Burren proper.[1] It was found, predictably, to be noticeably impoverished. Less than half of the Burren's pond snails were noted. In addition, many of the water beetles and bugs – the water boatmen, water measurers, water scorpions, so abundant in the swallow holes and wells on the mainland – are either scarce or absent from the islands. It would appear, therefore, that the relatively narrow sea passage which has not proved to be a barrier to a plethora of terrestrial invertebrates, including land snails, has acted as an effective barrier to their freshwater counterparts.

Vertebrates

Among the lower vertebrates the most obvious absentees are the amphibians, the common newt, *Triturus vulgaris,* and the frog, *Rana temporaria.* The absence of the newt is explicable in view of the paucity of other freshwater life: newts are rarely found too far away from water. The frog, on the other hand is so widespread and common in the Burren – even on apparently dry land – that its absence from the islands is both noticeable and noteworthy. Doubtless they could not have reached the islands without manual intervention but given the level of tooing and froing between the islands and the mainland it is strange that Inis Mór, at any rate, is still without the frog. (It is found on Cape Clear, off Cork, and on Tory, off Donegal, which is considerably more offshore than Inis Mór).

Ireland's only native reptile, the viviparous lizard, seems as common on Aran as in the Burren. For instance, twenty have been seen in a day in June on the largest island[2] and several were noted on Inis Oírr in April, 1993. This little creature seems to have had little difficulty in populating most of Ireland's larger islands – Aranmore (Co. Donegal), Sherkin and Cape Clear (Co. Cork). Achill and Clare Island (Co. Mayo). It does not follow, of course, that it colonised them by its own means – before man's arrival – though this in fact may be the case. It seems more likely that lizards have been unknowingly transported to Aran, perhaps in a state of hibernation, within a supply of winter turf from Connemara. They are commonly found thus. A slow worm, *Anguis fragilis* – a legless lizard apparently introduced into the Burren in the early 1970s – was discovered recently, hibernating in a turfstack at Gleninagh in the north-west corner of County Clare. Is it only a matter of time before Aran also accommodates this newcomer?

In seeking to resolve the question concerning the colonisation of islands by common lizards the naturalist R.F. Scharff, writing at the turn of the century, examined specimens not only from Ireland but from different parts of their world range. Strangely, he found that those which he examined from Clare Island were indistinguishable from 150 specimens found elsewhere, including those from the island of Sachalien in the Pacific! It is tempting to deduce from this that *Lacerta vivipara* is a relative newcomer to islands; that it is a recent coloniser from a remarkably homogeneous common lizard population throughout the world.

Birds

There is more information available about the natural history of the birds of Aran than about the remainder of the wildlife. The literary references are nevertheless few and mainly sketchy. A likely repository of additional information exists in the form of bones from kitchen middens in the dunes – birds that were eaten as food by the island's earliest residents. However since excavation of this kind has yet to be undertaken we have to make do with historical references and recent surveys. Roderic O'Flaherty alludes in passing to the birds in his *Chorographical Description of West or H-Iar Connaught* (1684). He mentions 'Cornish choughs with red legs and bills', 'ayries of hawks' and 'birds which never fly but over the sea' (auks and their relatives, undoubtedly). He also comments on the harvesting of these birds as food for the islanders: 'They go down with ropes tyed about them to the caves of cliffs by night and with a candle kill an abundance of them'.

Lewis in his *Topographical Dictionary* (1837) also refers to this dare-devil activity and mentions the quarry as 'puffins'. However as puffins normally nest underground in burrows he probably means the others of the auk family – guillemots and razorbills – which are cliff-nesters. He also mentions (as does Haverty in 1857)[3] that the birds were hunted for their feathers. This seems to differ from the bird-catchers of Shetland, St Kilda and the Faeroes whose primary goal was the birds and eggs as food, though they did make use of their oil and feathers besides. Were the feathers used for crude brooms as elsewhere or perhaps in the millinery trade? These uses would seem to be highly trivial compared with the danger involved. The activity is now a part of island folklore since it gradually died out in the first half of the present century. One or two of the older residents on Inis Mór remember its last practitioners.

Padraic Pearse spent time on the Aran Islands, especially on Inis Meáin, at the turn of the century where he compiled a list of the bird names, in Irish. He compiled more than twenty names and the editor of the *Gaelic Journal* (in which the list was published in 1899) added a further eight which were known to him.[4] This list is interesting, not for its total (it is obviously quite incomplete) but for the allusion to birds which are now no longer found on the islands; the eagle (presumably the sea eagle which still nested on Ireland's western seaboard at the time – iolrach, but normally iolar or fiolar; the corncrake – traonach; and the owl (probably the barn owl) – ulchabhán.

The *Atlas of Breeding Birds of Britain and Ireland* (1976) suggested a breeding population of about 58 species including, at that time, the corncrake, *Crex*. Nowadays the total is probably a few species less though the magpie, *Pica*, and the grey heron, *Ardea cinerea*, which did not nest there then, do so now. The present day breeding tally is of the same order of the other large islands around the Irish coastline such as Clare Island and Rathlin.

The most significant (and vulnerable) of Aran's birds are those which nest on the cliffs and on the sandy machair. For three or four months of the spring and summer Inis Mór's sheer cliffs are converted to a 'seabird-city' – a seething, garrulous avian community. Here, more than a thousand guillemots, *Uria aalge*, and kittiwakes, *Rissa tridactyla*, vie with each other for the best ledges on which to make their meagre homes. Lesser numbers (hundreds) of herring gulls, *Larus argentatus*, fulmars, *Fulmarus glacialis*,

Illus. 4.4. Little Tern (Sterna albifrons). With its white fore-head, yellow bill and legs, the little tern is the most easily identi-fied of the five species which nest in Ireland. It is also one of the scarcest; the Irish breeding population is less than 300 pairs. Of these, a few dozen pairs nest on Aran machair, the Inis Meáin colony holding 5 - 10% of the entire national population. Disturbance by visitors has been shown elsewhere to be intolera-ble to these habitat-specific birds and conservation measures will undoubtedly be necessary to enable them to survive on Aran. The decline in sand eel stocks which appears to be adversely affecting seabirds generally is probably also affecting terns which rely heavily on such food during the summer months.

razorbills, *Alca torda*, and shags, *Phalacrocorax aristotelis,* also breed here, each species occupy-ing a predominant location on the cliff – the fulmars usually near the top; the shags near the sea. Other seabirds such as great black-backed gulls, *Larus marinu*, black guillemots, *Cepphus grille*, and cormorants, *Phalacrocorax carbo*, nest in smaller numbers again. Most of the gulls nest on the rocky Brannock and Rock Islands at Inis Mór's western end. From this detached location they attack the eggs and young of the other seabirds as is the norm in seabird colonies. By late July the surviving young have been raised and the seabirds vacate the cliffs to begin the pelagic phase of their lifestyle.

Concern has been voiced about the steady decline in the numbers of these seabirds which has been noted over recent decades[5] and is reflected in other western seabird colonies. There seems to be a correlation between this decline and that of certain fish stocks such as sand eels, *Ammodytides*. The decline of the puf-fin, *Fratercula arctica*, on island breeding colonies off the Scottish mainland has been attributed to overfishing of sand eels. Surely this is a clear example of nature indicating (once again) to mankind that it is time to cut back on exploitation.

Other birds, rock doves, *Columba livia*, choughs, *Pyrrhocorax p.*, and ravens, *Corvus corax*, occupy the cliffs all year round though the wild doves have inexplicably declined dramatically since the *Atlas* survey of 1976. Kestrels, *Falco tinnun-culus*, and a pair of peregrines, *Falco peregrinus*, usually nest also; the falcons have an abun-dance of prey on which to feed their own young, at least for the critical period of upbringing.

The machair, na muirbhigh on Inis Mór, is flat-tish sandy ground near the sea. Another area

Illus. 4.6 right. Grey Heron (Ardea cinerea). Formerly known only as a visitor from the mainland, the heron now nests in a small colony on one of the islands. Due to the lack of high trees (the heron's normal nest-site) the island's birds have chosen a relatively inaccessible site amid a tangle of ivy and crag. They are nevertheless still highly vulnerable being visible at eye-level. The herons counter their vulnerability by being remarkably silent and secretive at the nest-site: despite their large size and conspicuous plumage, the immobile adults display an amazing capacity to merge into the mottled shadows of their background.

As there are no frogs on the islands (an important food item on the mainland) the young herons are fed on the eels which are available in the lakes and turloughs and on the rock-pool tiddlers such as the ceannruan, or shanny.

Illus. 4.5 left. Goldfinch (Cardulis c.). This beautiful finch most suitably represents the small birds of Aran for it is found commonly on all three of the islands. The abundance of unsprayed headlands and meadowland has provided the circumstances whereby this bird has become established. There is certainly no shortage of its favourite seed-bearing plants, thistles, docks and salt-resistant coastal varieties.

Goldfinches elicit unanimous approval from those who have watched them closely. Everything about them appears to have been designed to please the eye. Not only do they add sparkling colour – red, yellow, buff – to the fading pastel shades of the dying year but their mellifluous twittering has an unerring capacity to ameliorate even the bleakest of winter days.

exists on the northern edge of Inis Meáin. The machair and its associated dunes is a wonderful habitat for a wide range of flora and fauna. It is especially an important breeding habitat, mainly for wading birds – lapwings, *Vanellus v.*, ringed plovers, *Charadrius hiaticula*, and oystercatchers, *Haematopus ostralegus*. One of Irelands scarcest terns, the little tern, *Sterna albifrons*, also nests there.

The machair is also a favourite resort for human visitors in high summer, by which time the birds' offspring are at fledgling stage and thus particularly vulnerable. The overall effect of human disturbance on Aran has yet to be measured but evidence from elsewhere in Ireland suggests that breeding shorebirds are often adversely affected in similar circumstances. In addition machair represents a delicate ecosystem of habitat-specific plants, invertebrates and higher animals which is vulnerable to people pressure, and particularly to that of their vehicles. It would seem that with Aran's burgeoning tourism some conservation measure will be necessary if this most precious of the islands' habitats is to remain as a wildlife haven.

The geographic location of the Aran Islands renders them obvious 'stop-offs' for migrating birds. While manned lighthouses were in operation it was a common occurrence for the birds migrating at night to be attracted to their light and many subsequently perished by flying into the glass surrounding the light. A century ago R.M. Barrington collected records of bird casualties from light stations all around the Irish coast in an effort to better understand the phenomenon of migration. From Inis Mór light he collected specimens of the wryneck, *Jynx torquilla*, and the barred warbler, *Sylvia nisoria*, birds from the European mainland which were otherwise virtually unknown in Ireland. There is no doubt that many other commoner migrants; thrushes, finches, buntings, use the Aran Islands as staging posts on passage to northern and arctic breeding grounds. Long term observation at different times of the year would help to clarify these migration patterns.

A list compiled on Inis Mór over three days in 1957 gives a clue to the status of the winter birds. Fifty two species were recorded. The majority would be regarded as all-year-round residents, but some including the redwing, *Turdus iliacus*, and the snow bunting, *Plectropheax nivalis*, and the flock of 55 whooper swans, *Cygnus c.*, on Loch Phort Chorrúch were visitors from the far north. Notable was the record of seven black-throated divers, *Gavia arctica*, which, considering that Galway Bay is now known to be their premier wintering resort in Ireland, is certainly significant. It indicates perhaps that these arctic birds which are scarce in Ireland have perhaps been coming to the area for longer than recent records indicate.

There is a good case for establishing a semi-permanent bird observatory on Inis Mór. Others such as Copeland (Co.Down), Saltee (Co.Wexford) and Cape Clear (Co.Cork) have added greatly to our ornithological knowledge down the years. This would have a three-pronged beneficial effect. It would help to develop a better understanding of all the islands' birds (and indirectly, the other wildlife); it would act as a 'watchdog' in helping to protect the increasingly threatened habitats on all three islands; and it would act as a valuable educational resource for the islands' schools.

Mammals

The first reference that we have about the mammalian fauna of Aran comes from that enthusiastic reporter of all things Irish, Giraldus Cambrensis, at the end of the twelfth century. He reported at that time that 'while the whole of Ireland is infested with mice there is not a single one here' (on Aran). Can we believe Giraldus' report? Can it be used as an historical bench-mark in our quest to understand the mammalian colonisation of the islands? I don't think so. Most of his information was second-hand and may have been 'coloured' before he received it; he had a propensity to do this himself. The islands today have both the house mouse, *Mus musculus*, and the field mouse, *Apodemus sylvaticus*, which undoubtedly arrived there as stowaways on boats, perhaps centuries ago. The even more unwelcome brown rat, *Rattus norvegicus*, also occurs, though it is probably a more recent coloniser.

The pigmy shrew, *Sorex minutus*, is most probably a long-term inhabitant of Aran. It is thought to be a prehistoric resident in Ireland and it is conceivable that it populated the islands of Ireland before, or without man's influence. It is known from Rathlin, Saltee, Cape Clear and Sherkin, the Blaskets, Achill and Aranmore. It is well known nowadays on Inis Mór. In a trapping programme carried out by F.L. Clark in 1970, two pigmy shrews were caught near the shore.

Those other tiny mammals, bats, have been seen in Cill Rónáin in recent summers. This is not to say that there is a colony on Inis Mór; bats are capable of wandering considerable distances despite their normally erratic flight. Both the pipistrelle, *Pipistrellus p.*, and Daubenton's bat, *Myotis daubentoni*, have been encountered at sea, miles from land. In addition, whiskered, *Myotis mystacinus*, Leisler's, *Nyctalus leisleri* and long-eared, *Plecotus auritus*, bats have been recorded from several of Ireland's largest islands.

In a way it is remarkable that the Irish hare, *Lepus timidus h.*, does not occur on Aran. Not only is it found today on most of the other large islands around Ireland but, as a relict from the Ice Age may have a uniquely unbroken history of habitation here. It is possible that hares did exist in the past and were killed off for food. The alternative scenario – that they were never there – adds substance to the theory that Aran has been more or less inaccessible to faunal colonisation other than by human involvement. There can be little doubt that rabbits, *Oryctolagus cuniculus*, were introduced to the islands as food (as indeed they were to Ireland, by Giraldus' associates). Roderic O'Flaherty referred to their abundance in the 17th century, 'In this island [Inis Mór] there be a great deal of rabbets...' . Nowadays they occupy the sandier ground where they can excavate their tunnelled homes. The largest warren appears to be in the machair at the eastern end of Inis Mór.

There is certainly enough available prey on Aran to support foxes, *Vulpes v.*, but they are unknown there. They are found nowadays on Achill and Sherkin but in these cases the barrier of the sea is not comparable to that between Aran and the mainland. The only wild carnivores on the islands today are mustelids – otters, *Lutra l.*, and stoats, *Mustela erminea h.*

Illus. 4.7. Stoat (Mustela erminea hibernica). *Diminutive size and short legs are no deterrent to Aran's stoats which often use the drystone walls as linear vantages. Here the stoat catches the eye bounding deftly along the uppermost stones, stopping occasionally to survey and take stock of its situation, then continuing on its singular route. The main prey species are rats, mice, rabbits and ground-nesting birds and their offspring. The stoats are both curious and doughty, characteristics which frequently bring them close enough to be admired by people. On such occasions their apparently benign charm and daintiness of movement belie their lethal predatory capability on rodent and bird alike.*

Given the aquatic capability of the otter and the fact that it is found commonly along the Burren's shoreline, it is easy to imagine how it could have made its way to Inis Oírr and thence to the other islands. The otter is known from Loch Mór on Inis Oírr; unfortunately one was drowned there a few years ago, in a fyke net set for eels.

The existence of the stoat on Inis Mór raises the old familiar questions concerning origins. The stoat has been in Ireland since early post-glacial times, at the latest. It may be an Ice Age survivor. It might have arrived on islands such as Aran long before man at a time when land bridges rendered them accessible to terrestrial mammals. However the stoat can also swim and may have reached Aran under its own steam, much more recently. (Sleeman points out that stoats are good swimmers capable of swimming at sea to reach islands in view). The stoat may even have been brought there (for rabbiting?); whatever the mechanism of colonisation a study of the stoat on Inis Mór could prove most revealing. It is recognised that the Irish stoat is an endemic subspecies noticeably distinct from its counterpart in Britain. It is smaller – intermediate in size between the British animal and the weasel (which does not exist in Ireland) – a development that is probably related to predatory adaptation to available prey. There are other distinctions but they are of less significance. Could the differences recognisable between the islands of Ireland and Britain, be echoed further in Aran? Probably only if colonisation was long-term. Even this does not guarantee perceptible modification but it would surely be worth the investigation.

Many of the mammals of Aran are to be found in the sea, around the coastline. Those seen most regularly are the seals. The two Irish species occur, the common, *Phoca vitulina*, and the grey, *Halichoerus grypus*, though neither have breeding colonies on the islands. The common seal has several pupping stations in Galway Bay; the grey has several along the Connemara coast. Post-breeding dispersal in search of fish undoubtedly brings small numbers of each into inshore waters around the islands. Neither species is sufficiently abundant to represent a serious additional burden to depleted fish stocks.

Cetaceans (dolphins and porpoises) are also commonly encountered around the Aran coastline and within the sounds between. As is the case along the Burren coastline, there are more sightings in the summer months probably in response to fluctuating fish stocks throughout the year. The majority of the cetaceans seen are common, *Delphinus d.*, or the larger, bottle-nosed dolphin, *Tursiops truncatus*, and the porpoise, *Phocaena p.*, but, as concentrated watching off Cape Clear over the past quarter century has shown, other species also turn up regularly in Irish waters. This has been borne out by the occasional strandings of lesser-known species on the shores of the Aran Islands. Two of the 'beaked' whales, the bottle nosed, *Hyperoodon ampullatus*, and Cuvier's, *Ziphius cavirostris*, have been encountered thus.[6] Evidence of another stranding – the seven foot long lower jawbone of a sperm whale, *Physeter catodon*, was found on Inis Oírr in 1993. In the fashion of a piece of driftwood from the shore, it was being used as a gate-barrier!

Despite these occasional hints little is known about the islands' cetacean life and in view of the fact that there was a thriving whaling industry off Ireland's west coast less than a century ago, it may yet be interesting. There are word-of-mouth reports of larger whales having been seen in recent years within a mile or two of Inis Mór's western end. Minke's, *Balaenoptera acutorostrata*, and orcas, *Orcinus orca*, have been specifically identified. A most interesting sighting occurred in the last week of May in 1993. A twenty-foot whale was seen by the crew and passengers of one of the Aran ferries as it was passing by Inis Meáin. The fact that it was jumping out of the water and splashing back again drew the attention of all

Illus. 4.8. Sperm Whale (Physeter catodon). This is the largest of the toothed whales though unlike the well-known killer Orcinus orca *which is furnished with two rows – top and bottom – the sperm is toothed only along the narrow lower jaw. The upper jaw is instead lined with a series of holes into which the teeth of the lower jaw fit when closed. The jawbone shown here was incorporated into a stone wall on Inis Oírr having obviously been found on the beach.*

The sperm is the whale immortalised in 'Moby Dick' which was avidly hunted for the commercial products such as spermaceti (for candle-wax) which could be extracted from its carcass. About fifty sperm whales were caught in a six year period (1909-1914) by two whaling companies operating out of County Mayo, seventy miles north of Aran.

Nowadays, with Irish coastal waters a declared cetacean sanctuary, these leviathans are free to come and go at will.

and pointed to it being a young humpback whale, *Megaptera novaeangliae,* a species which regularly displays such exuberant antics. (It was too large to be a bottle-nosed dolphin like 'Fungi' which also behaves thus). Young humpbacks were also seen in June 1992 off Britain's Dorset coast and along the coast of Cork.

These recent sightings of endangered species of cetaceans are most encouraging. Could they indicate a recovery in whale numbers in and around Irish waters? While it is probably too early to feel confident about such an upturn, now is the time to look for the signs. Aran would be an ideal location from which to carry out a monitoring programme on cetacean sightings. It might be possible to eventually investigate the movements of these great animals along the western seaboard using Aran as a base.

The future

Tourism on Aran has been developing at an astounding rate of late. The tooing and froing of the ferries seems almost frenetic during the summer months. While this has enabled increasing numbers of visitors from home and abroad (ten nationalities are not unusual on a ferry) to sample the islands' attractions it has been at a cost ; there is more pressure than ever on the more vulnerable of the wildlife habitats, which under stark economic scrutiny readily become viewed as 'convertible wasteland'. Temporary wetlands and coastal sand dune systems are all too often seen as such. The threat to Inis Mór's machair is ongoing; will it survive the modern trend to convert every available suitable tract into golf links?

There is no halting the inexorable rise in tourism; it is now the biggest industry in the world. Aran will have its share for better or for worse. Most of the tourist disasters seem to have occurred as a result of rampant development where vision has been relegated to a back seat. The establishment of the new visitor centre at Cill Rónáin on Inis Mór shows that the islanders are determined that this will not happen there. A natural next stage would be the establishment of a wildlife observatory with a permanent warden who would have responsibilities not only to collate data relating to all forms of Aran's natural history but would act also in the capacity of guide and educator. An important additional function would lie in vetting and countering – if necessary – developments that threaten the wildlife of the islands.

Tourism has already made its mark and the inhabitants of the main island, at any rate, have benefited materially. The conservation case is now in the emergent. There may well be imaginative possibilities for the future which combine our reawakened conservation consciousness with tourism, if we look once again at the geographic location of the islands and their maritime identity. Who is to say that, in the event of the humpback and its congeners staging a significant comeback, a new whaling industry – one based on appreciation, not exploitation – might not have its centre of operation on Aran.

Acknowledgements for Illustrations

Illus. 4.1 to 4.8, Gordon D'Arcy.

INTERLUDE

History and the 'Human Kingdom'
a context for what follows

J.W. O'Connell

With this chapter, which also is something of an introduction, we have reached the border of one territory and find ourselves about to cross over into another. As with any such territorial boundary, there are similarities and differences, continuities and discontinuities, between what is on one side, and what is on the other.

However, a little reflection shows that our analogy is not entirely accurate. For the border we are now about to cross reveals to us not simply a different terrain and a different language spoken by the inhabitants. It presents us with another dimension, a different world, a distinctively different kind of history.

The *Oxford English Dictionary* provides us with two definitions of the term *history* that will help us clarify the point we are trying to make. One defines it as *'a systematic account (without reference to time) of a set of natural phenomena'*. The second is: *'a written narrative constituting a continuous methodical record, in order of time, of important or public events, especially those connected with a particular country, people, individual, etc.'*

It is worth noting that the OED describes the first definition as 'now rare', and it is easy to see why. In each of the preceding four chapters, dealing with the *natural* history of Aran, readers will have noticed that nearly every one of the authors has felt it necessary to introduce the inter-related concepts of time, change and development. This is because since Darwin scientists have carried out their work against a backdrop of evolutionary time, where millennia are treated as casually as the passing moment is in ordinary life.

Yet when the two definitions are compared it is possible to identify an important distinction, that between *natural* history and *human* history. With human history we enter the rich and complex world of aims and intentions, carried out either by groups or individuals or combinations of both. We enter the realm of creativity, belief, dreams, hopes, desires. This kind of history describes what the poet Kathleen Raine calls 'the human kingdom'.

In the chapters that follow, each of these aspects of 'the human kingdom', as this has expressed, and continues to express, itself on the three islands of Inis Mór, Inis Meáin and Inis Oírr, will be dealt with, so that a comprehensive 'internal geography' of this particular 'kingdom' can be built up, providing travellers with the kind of guide-book that will help them find their way around.

One final point should be made. If we revert to the analogy we started with, there are certainly similarities and continuities between the *natural* history and *human* 'kingdoms', and Aran, in fact, provides an excellent example of how these overlaps operate. Humankind, in the thousands of years in which it has made the islands its home, has profoundly affected the *natural* 'kingdom' in all sorts of ways, not all of them benign.

Likewise the *natural* 'kingdom' has had a profound effect on the development and character of the *human* 'kingdom', perhaps especially so in a place like Aran. The very fact of being islands has had a dramatic effect on every aspect of human life, from the trades and occupations pursued by the people and the isolation from the events and activities on the mainland, to such things as marriage patterns and the preservation of the Irish language. The dangers and challenges of the sea, for example, have shaped the imagination of the people in ways that the folklorist, the artist and the literary historian can help to illuminate.

The *human* 'kingdom' of Aran, then, is a complex web of relationships between past and present, people and land, myth and history. The chapters that follow will examine some of the details of this unique web.

Nothing can be understood without a context. As with the ancient Irish definition of copyright: to every cow belongs its calf, so it is with history: to every fact belong its context. Before we begin examining the archaeology, history, folklore, language, artistic and literary tradition of Aran, we need a context, however brief and rudimentary, within which to situate the different dimensions of Aran that will be treated in greater detail in subsequent chapters.

It is curious that Aran, which figures so prominently in the story of early Christianity in the west of Ireland and was widely famed for the sanctity of its holy men and women, has almost no early recorded history relating to what we might describe as the secular dimension, apart from a few references in such compilations as the *Annals of the Four Masters.*

In the earliest records, the islands are first associated with a branch of the Eoganacht of Munster. This was a loose federation of about fifteen dynastic groups who, according to their origin legend, were descended from a common ancestor named Eogan Mór. However, it has been suggested that the name Eoganacht may be connected with the sacred yew tree (in Old Irish *eó* often means yew), so that an ancestral 'people of the yew', about which, of course, absolutely nothing is known, may lie lost in the shadows of prehistory.

Aran and the adjacent Burren in County Clare were ruled by the Eoganacht Aran, reputedly established here by Aengus, son of Nad Fraich, in the 5th century AD. It is this particular chieftain, described as king of Cashel in the *Annals of the Four Masters*, who allegedly gave 'that island which known as Aran' to St Enda.

The 8th century witnessed the increasing influence of the people of the Dál Cais in Clare, who two centuries later were to overthrow the Eoganachta and become the dominant power in Munster. Their most famous king was undoubtedly Brian Boru, whose children were the first to bear the name O'Brien.

We learn a few facts about the history of the islands from the *Annals of he Four Masters*, but, as that chronicle is largely concerned with ecclesiastical affairs, much of this information focuses on such things as the names of St Enda's's successors. As such, it demonstrates the continuity of the islands' religious tradition but contains little more that is relevant for purposes of tracing the early history of Aran.

So, for example, we learn that in the year 1020 a fire destroyed the church of St Enda, probably referring to the now vanished church whose stones were used in the construction of Arkin Fort in the 17th century. Again the annalists tell us that in 1081 Aran was 'plundered by the foreigners', presumably the Vikings, who, it is reasonable to assume, were also responsible for the fire recorded for the year 1020.

By the 12th century the McTeige O'Briens, a branch of the O'Briens of County Clare, were overlords of the islands, and Hardiman notes that in 1277 Galway merchants agreed to send twelve tons of wine yearly to the O'Briens as tribute for protecting the bay from pirates and privateers, by maintaining a sea-going force for the purpose.

However, in 1334 Sir John D'Arcy, with a large fleet of fifty-six ships, attacked and plundered Inis Mór. Probably in response to this raid, and to protect the islands against further attacks, the O'Briens built a fortified castle on Inis Mór near Cill Éinne, probably occupying the same strategic site where Arkin Fort was later built, and possibly another at Eoghanacht where a stone structure known as the 'old castle' exists.

The 17th century historian James Ware records the arrival of the Franciscars in 1485, who established a foundation near Cill Éinne which may originally have stood south of the village, east of a holy well called to this day the Friars' Well. Nothing remains today and we know from Roderic O'Flaherty's account, written in 1684, that it was demolished after the Parliamentarians took the island in 1652 and the stones used to build Arkin Fort.

The fortunes of the O'Briens in Aran declined throughout the 16th century. In 1565 one member of the family 'was treacherously slain in his own town of Aircin, in Aran' by his own people. Local tradition also records a murderous battle between O'Brien factions near Cill Mhuirbhigh at Fearann na gCeann, or the Quarter of the Heads, so named from the large number of skulls later dug up there.

In 1569 Queen Elizabeth appointed Murchadha na d'Tua (of the battle axes) O'Flaherty as chief of the O'Flaherty's of Connemara. In 1584 a dispute broke out between two branches of the O'Flahertys, those loyal to Murchadha na d'Tua, who had recognised the overlordship of the Queen, and the clan chieftain who had not. Murchadha na d'Tua attacked Inis Mór and defeated both the O'Flahertys who had taken refuge on the island, and their O'Brien allies, in a battle near Cill Éinne.

Shortly afterwards the islands were confiscated by Queen Elizabeth who first granted them to Murchadha na d'Tua O'Flaherty and then in 1587 granted them instead to John Rawson of Athlone on condition that he maintain a twenty-man garrison there. This was the first garrison installed by the English on the islands, an indication of their strategic importance on the wider Elizabethan stage.

In the years that followed the defeat of the Spanish Armada in 1588, the islands were granted to a succession of different individuals. Sir Robert Lynch of Galway appears to have acquired ownership from Rawson sometime later in the century, and presumably he continued to fortify them. Certainly we know that the redoubtable Grace O'Malley raided them in 1590 'with two or three baggage boats full of thieves', as a contemporary account described them.

In 1651, as the Parliamentarian army prepared to attack Galway, which had retained its traditional loyalty to the Crown, the Marquess of Clanricarde placed 200 soldiers on Inis Mór under the command of another Sir Robert Lynch, who fortified the old fort at Arkin. In December 700 more men joined the defence, but in January of 1652, 1300 Parliamentary soldiers sailed to attack the island, which surrendered on the 13th of January.

Sir Robert Lynch was declared a traitor and his lands forfeit. Aran was granted to Erasmus Smith, one of the wealthy London investors who had backed the Parliamentary cause. Smith sold them to Richard Butler, fifth son of James, First Duke of Ormonde, who was created Earl of Arran in 1662.

Paul Walsh in chapter 7, 'Arkin Fort: The Military History of a Garrison Outpost on Inis Mór', has covered the events connected with the successive garrisons there.

One of the most important and far-reaching aspects of the presence of the garrison on Inis Mór over a period of nearly 150 years was the intermarriage that took place between islanders and the men stationed in Arkin Fort. Two scientific studies, in 1955 and 1957, concluded that the long-term effect of such intermarriage was that a large proportion of islanders today are descended from these generations of English soldiers.

Richard Butler died in 1682 and the title was in abeyance until granted to a nephew, Charles Butler, in 1693. The Butler family continued to style themselves Earls of Arran until Charles, brother of the second Duke of Ormonde, died in 1758, after which the title became extinct. In 1782 it was revived and given to Sir Arthur Gore, 3rd Baronet, and continues in this family today.

In 1710 Sir Stephen Fox of London was owner of the islands, and it is suggested that he bought them while the Butler title was in abeyance. Fox sold them in 1713 to Edmund Fitzpatrick of Galway and Patrick French of Monivea for £8,200. French, a Galway solicitor, purchased his portion of the islands in trust for Simon Digby, the Church of Ireland bishop of Elphin, and the next year sold it to the bishop.

The Fitzpatricks mortgaged their half of the islands to Richard Digby of Landenstown, Co. Kildare, and in 1744 he foreclosed on the mortgage and took possession of the property, becoming sole owner of the three islands.

The 18th century was a period of relative peace throughout Ireland, a condition reflected in the very few references to the islands found in the State Papers. By the early 19th century, however, an expanding population was beginning to press on the scarce resources of land and emigration began to make its effects felt, especially on Inis Mór.

If the life of the ordinary people of the islands was hard, Aran was fortunate in escaping the worst effects of the Famine. Population figures from the years in which the potato blight was causing widespread depopulation throughout mainland Ireland actually show only a slight fall between 1841 (3529) and 1851 (3333). It was not, in fact, until the latter part of the century that emigration began to make its effect known on the islands.

What the people did suffer from, and badly, was the tyranny of the absentee landlord. At the beginning of the 19th century the islanders were obliged to try to make a limited acreage support an expanding population at the same time as paying over £2000 per annum in rent. Evictions were common throughout the century, as many, including J.M. Synge, described.

While the vast majority of islanders were Catholics, the Church of Ireland presence is indicated by the construction of a church in 1846, and in 1849 a clergyman was appointed 'competent to afford religious instruction in the native tongue'. Although converts were made, the numbers remained small, and by the mid-1930s the Protestant community had died out. The parish church, built with such high hopes, is now a ruin in the centre of Cill Rónáin.

By the late 19th century the harsh exactions of rent on land that barely served to support those who worked it exploded into a bitter land war that involved the Land League in large-scale action. Aran had its share of agitation, boycott and violence: the most violent act took place in January 1881 when some thirty cattle belonging to James O'Flaherty of Cill Mhuirbhigh were driven over the cliffs west of Dún Aonghasa. It was not until the Land Acts of 1881 and 1882 and the establishment of the Congested Districts Board in 1891 that the situation began to improve.

Domestic industries, such as knitting, were promoted, and a fishing industry, involving the building of piers and the provision of nets and boats, was actively developed.

The 19th century witnessed another important development – the opening up of the islands to the outside world. The growing interest in the antiquities of Ireland, of which the islands hold some of the oldest and most important, meant that the beginnings of a 'tourist' industry were laid. The many accounts by such people as George Petrie, Sir Samuel Ferguson, John O'Donovan, T.J. Westropp and many others, awakened interest not only in the ancient monuments of Aran but also in the lifestyle of the people.

The publication of Synge's The Aran Islands in 1907 was the culmination of the first stage of the interest, and in the decades that have followed the islands have attracted a host of writers and artists who have drawn their inspiration from the people and places of Aran.

CHAPTER 5

The Archaeology of Aran

John Waddell

'...a uniquely tender and memorious ground'

Tim Robinson

Introduction

The bare limestone landscape and the numerous ancient monuments of the Aran Islands have fascinated visitors for many years. The impression of an isolated stony world on the edge of a limitless ocean has only accentuated the attraction of the great stone forts and early churches, and much sense and much nonsense has been written about them.

The stone forts, for instance, have been variously considered as the last defences of a people driven to the western extremities of the known world by successive invaders from the east and as the remnants of a formidable barrier to a threat from a lost Atlantic continent to the west.[1] Even the very name Aran has generated woolly speculation. Fanciful suggestions include its derivation from Ard-Thuinn meaning 'height above the waves' or even from Aaron, the brother of Moses! However, the name derives from *ara*, the Irish word for kidney, which has come to mean the loins or back and the name, as in *druim*, has thus been given to a ridge of land.[2]

The three islands, Inis Mór or Árainn, Inis Meáin, the middle island, and Inis Oírr, the eastern island, lie north-west to south-east across the mouth of Galway Bay and are geologically an extension of the limestone terrain of the Burren in Co. Clare. Some writers[3] have romantically stressed the geographical isolation of the islands but it is worth noting that Inis Oírr is only about eight kilometres from Clare and Inis Mór only a little further from the coast of Connemara. Others have been struck by the sparse vegetation and great expanses of exposed limestone, and have emphasized the barrenness of the islands: 'nothing to strike the eye at first sight but a cold, hard, barren mass of sea-girt stone'.[4] But Aran is much more than bare stone. The limestone lies in clearly defined strata gently sloping to the south-south-west towards the Atlantic.[5] From the north-east, from Galway Bay, this layering appears as a series of sheltered limestone terraces descending to the sea, and it is on these terraces that the majority of the early ecclesiastical monuments are to be found (Illus. 5.1). Large areas of the upper plateau are particularly exposed to Atlantic rain and wind and here especially extensive tracts of bare limestone occur. Again, however, appearances are deceptive, a little glacial drift occurs, and, just as in the Burren, a

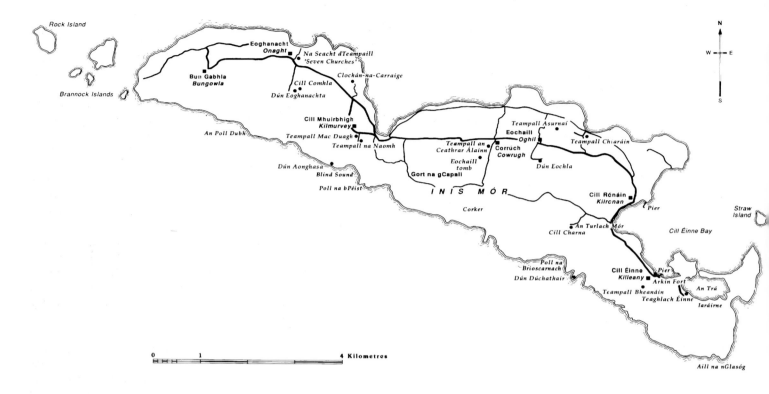

thin soil here and there on the limestone supports innumerable patches of valuable winter grazing. According to Roderic O'Flaherty in 1684: 'among these stones is very sweet pasture, so that beef and mutton are better and earlier in season here than elsewhere ...'.[6] Indeed, as in the Burren too, the early prehistoric inhabitants of Aran would probably have had to contend with a landscape rather different from that of today. The less exposed parts of the islands in particular probably supported considerable pine and hazel, as well as some oak, elm and other trees.

Antiquarian visitors to Aran

Roderic O'Flaherty, Galway historiographer and one of the last great Gaelic scholars of the seventeenth century, was the first to publish an account of the traditional history of Ireland from the earliest times for the English reader. His *Ogygia seu rerum Hibernicum chronologia*,[7] which appeared in London in 1685, drew the attention of the learned world to three of the great Aran forts including 'Dun Aengus, a great stone-work without cement which might contain in its area two hundred cows, on an

Illus. 5.1. Map of the Aran Islands showing principal sites and monuments.

amazing eminence of the sea with cliffs of a stupendous magnitude ...'. The celebrated Welsh antiquarian Edward Lhuyd visited Aran in 1700 during his tour of Ireland but, sadly, little survives of the material he gathered. He did comment on the frequent occurrence of the maidenhair fern and a sketch plan of the fort of Dún Eochla is preserved.[8]

Just over a century elapsed before there was any renewed interest in the islands' antiquities. The nineteenth century witnessed a succession of famous visitors. George Petrie studied the forts and churches in 1821 and some of the drawings he made then appeared in the revised and expanded version of his famous essay on the origin and uses of the round towers in Ireland which was published in 1845. He has been described as 'the father of sound Irish archaeology' because as one historian succinctly put it 'he succeeded in taking the subject of Irish antiquity out of the hands of the crackpots'.[9] John O'Donovan and William F. Wakeman visited Aran in the Summer of 1839 in the course of their work for the Ordnance Survey of Ireland.[10] O'Donovan's numerous notes preserved in the Ordnance Survey letters have provided many later writers with material about the islands' archaeology. William Wilde was in Aran in 1848 and discovered fragments of two high crosses there.[11] He was followed, a few years later, by Samuel Ferguson, who drew the attention of a wide audience to the major monuments of the three islands in two articles in the *Dublin University Magazine* in 1853.

The British Association for the Advancement of Science met in Dublin in 1857 and Wilde was president of its Ethnological Section. After the Dublin meeting he led a famous excursion of some seventy participants to Aran in early September.[12] Most of the great names of nineteenth century Irish archaeological studies were there, some of them already familiar with the wealth of Aran's antiquities. For, as Wilde declared, 'the Western Islands of Aran contain the greatest number of Pagan and early Christian monuments – military, domestic, ecclesiastical, and sepulchral – which can be found within the same area in Europe'. Those present included George Petrie, Eugene O'Curry, Samuel Ferguson, Margaret Stokes, and John O'Donovan. The proceedings culminated in an evening banquet in Dún Aonghasa. Among the speeches, those of Wilde, O'Donovan and O'Curry, in Irish, urged the people of Aran to protect their monuments.

It was also resolved that a book should be published on the islands' ancient remains to serve as a lasting memorial to Wilde's services as director of the expedition. Sadly this never happened though Wilde did produce a short three-page pamphlet the following year.[13]

Many subsequent visitors to the islands have commented on their extraordinary wealth of ancient monuments. Chief among these are Dunraven and Westropp. Edwin, the third earl of Dunraven, studied and photographed some of the major sites, both stone forts and churches, in the late 1860s and his work was edited for posthumous publication in 1875 by Margaret Stokes.[14] This is the first extensive photographic record of the islands' antiquities. Thomas Johnson Westropp visited Aran in 1878 and on many subsequent occasions. He published a valuable series of papers including a general account of the antiquities for the Royal Society of Antiquaries of Ireland in 1895 and a detailed study of Dún Aonghasa in 1910.[15]

George Henry Kinahan, of the Geological Survey of Ireland, was another 19th century scholar to study these ancient monuments. He was a keen antiquarian and regularly recorded archaeological sites he noticed in the course of his geological work. He collaborated with the Rev. William Kilbride, Rector of Aran, in 1866, in a study of clochans or stone huts and other settlements on Inis Mór, and Kilbride himself published an account of other monuments in 1869 in which he records one of the earliest excavations of one of the clochans.[16]

No doubt the fame of the Aran monuments and the numerous publications they prompted throughout the 19th century were the main rea-sons which encouraged the taking of many of them into State care. The fort of Dún Aonghasa, for instance, was made a National Monument in 1880 and in the following years it and a number of other forts and churches were tidied up and partly restored by the Office of Public Works.[17]

The earliest dateable traces of human occupation then known were discovered in 1885. The Rev. Denis Murphy, a visitor to Inis Oírr, persuaded the Clerk of Works engaged in the Office of Public Works' restoration of the O'Brien Castle at Formna there to investigate a low mound called Cnoc Raithní on the sea shore not far away. They discovered a Bronze Age cremation burial in a pottery urn which dates to about 1500 BC.[18]

The summer of 1895 saw the first of several excursions by sea around the coast of Ireland by the Royal Society of Antiquaries of Ireland.[19] That July they visited the three islands and it was this excursion which prompted T.J. Westropp's study published in the Society's *Journal* for the same year.

The new century, as we have seen, saw further important work by Westropp, as well as visits by noted scholars such as R.A.S. Macalister[20] and H.S. Crawford[21] who were particularly interested in the many early Christian remains there. The Rev. Dr P. Power, Professor of Archaeology in University College, Cork, courageously wrote a short guide to the antiquities of Aran in 1926 'compiled ... for most part from twenty five-years old memory'. The same year also saw the appearance of another pamphlet on the ecclesiastical remains of Inis Mór.[22] Fr M. O Domhnaill devoted considerable space to the ancient monuments in his *Oileáin Árann* of 1930. T.H. Mason, a Dublin optician and a talented photographer, published a book on *The Islands of Ireland* in 1936 and wrote a short account of the antiquities of Inis Oírr two years later.

J.R.W. Goulden, a Dublin school master and amateur archaeologist, undertook a number of visits to the islands in the late 1940s and early 1950s. He published several short accounts of some minor monuments and over a three year period from 1953 to 1955 excavated three ancient settlement sites on Inis Mór.[23] Liam de Paor published a study of the high crosses of Clare and Aran in 1956. Few general accounts of Aran have ignored the archaeology. True, John Millington Synge's famous *The Aran Islands* first published in 1907, has little or nothing to say about the remote past of Inis Meáin or the other islands, but most books have devoted some space to the islands' remarkable collection of forts and churches, often relying to a considerable extent on the work of O'Donovan and Westropp. In the 1960s and 1970s works such as P.A. Ó Síocháin's *Aran – Islands of Legend* , Daphne Pochin Mould's *The Aran Islands*, Leo Daly's *Oileáin Árann* and Antoine Powell's *Oileáin Árann – Stair na n-Oileáin anuas go dtí 1922* in the early 1980s all included accounts of the archaeological monuments.[24] The 1970s also saw some detailed archaeological survey[25] and in 1975 Tim Robinson published the first results of his cartographic work on Aran, presenting a remarkable record of settlement and monuments, and an accurate rendering of the Irish placenames. He followed this with his superb book *Stones of Aran* in 1986 which must rank as the finest evocation of the islands' past and present ever written.[26] The early 1980s saw further archaeological fieldwork on the islands, this time by the Galway Archaeological Survey under the auspices of the Office of Public Works and the Department of Archaeology, University College, Galway. This survey, under the direction of Paul Gosling, recorded over 230 ancient sites.[27] In 1992 a programme of research on the great stone forts, initiated by the Discovery Programme, began with archaeological excavations at Dún Aonghasa.[28]

The three Aran Islands comprise about 11,000 acres, or about 4500 hectares, and it is fair to say that few other parcels of land of comparable size in Ireland are so rich in ancient remains, and none has inspired so much literature, archaeological or otherwise.

Early Inhabitants

With evidence for early farming communities in the Burren of Co. Clare and in Connemara about 4000 BC, it is very likely that Aran was settled at least by that date. The coastal and island distribution of many early stone tombs shows that coastal seaways were an important means of communication in early times when, no doubt, skin boats, ancestors of the modern curragh, were widely used. No archaeological trace of these supposed earliest inhabitants have yet been identified, however, and the first certain traces of activity on the islands may date to about 2500 BC. As is often the case in the west of Ireland, it is the funerary record which offers the earliest indication of a human presence. In the Neolithic period (4500-2500 BC), early farming groups, while living in impermanent timber houses, still preferred to build durable megalithic or great stone tombs to contain the bones of their ancestors. Several examples of a late type have survived on Aran. The best preserved is in Eochaill on Inis Mór.

Illus. 5.2a. Megalithic tomb at Eochaill viewed from the eastern rear end: built about 2000 BC, it faces the setting sun.

Illus. 5.2b. Plan of megalithic tomb at Eochaill.

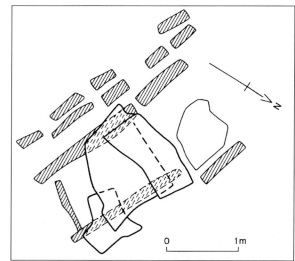

0   1m

Eochaill Wedge Tomb

This monument is situated on a low grassy ridge south-west of Teampall an Ceathrar Álainn (Illus. 5.2). What seems at first glance to be a rather roughly built box of limestone slabs is in fact carefully constructed to a plan common in the north, west and south-west of Ireland. In plan, the tomb is lower and narrower at its eastern rear end and a little wider, and higher, at its western front. This wedge-shaped plan gives the tomb type its name: it is a wedge tomb now consisting of two large slabs on either side, an end stone and three overlapping roof slabs. There is a line of outer walling on the south. It may once have been covered by a cairn of stones but little of this survives. Like most examples of its class, the tomb faces approximately west towards the setting sun.

Excavation of examples elsewhere, mainly in the northern half of the country, has revealed that the bones of a number of individuals, often cremated, were placed in these megaliths. Few objects were ever deposited with the remains of the dead: fragments of pottery are the commonest find. This pottery suggests these tombs were mainly used between 2200 and 1500 BC. Somewhere in the Eochaill area, there is presumably a small settlement of the period awaiting identification and the tomb and cairn may once have served not just as a repository for the bones of selected members of the commumity, perhaps some sacred ancestors, but also as a visible symbol of the people's territorial rights and as a focus for ritual activities some (given the orientation of the tomb) perhaps associated with a cult of the setting sun.

There may have been at least two other tombs of this sort on Inis Mór, one at Corrúch and the other at Fearann an Choirce, but no trace of them survives.[29]

Ceathrú an Lisín Wedge Tomb

A ruined wedge tomb survives near Baile an Mhothair on Inis Meáin (Illus. 5.3). It is situated on fairly bare limestone land with a view of the Clare coast to the east. The side slabs have collapsed to the south with the roof stone lying on top of them. The size of the side stones suggests that the monument was higher at its western end, so like its counterparts in Eochaill, in Clare and elsewhere, it faced westward. A line of typical outer walling is visible on the north and no trace of cairn remains. Another similar tomb may have stood some 400 metres to the west in the 19th century but nothing survives.[29]

A collapsed megalithic structure in Ceathrú an Teampaill on the north-west coast of Inis Meáin may be another wedge tomb: it was a more or less rectangular structure just under 3 metres in length and its long axis does lie east-west (Illus. 5.4).

The existence of at least half a dozen megalithic tombs on the islands is indicative of a small but significant population around and about 2000 BC. There is a large number of these wedge tombs in the Burren in Co. Clare and presumably there were close reciprocal contacts between the islands and this part of the mainland at this early date. As in the Burren, it is likely that the island subsistence of these early inhabitants was based to some degree on stock-raising: sheep and goat and cattle though sea-fishing and shell fish probably contributed to the economy as well.

There is very little other evidence of the activities of the tomb builders: it is quite possible, however, that two axeheads of polished stone date to this period. Two of these (Illus. 5.5) were found in 1961 on Inis Oírr when digging a pit for road building material near Cill Ghobnait and a third comes from a shell mid-

den on Inis Meáin. Made of various sorts of polished stone, implements such as these would originally have been mounted in a wooden haft. They were probably mainly used for felling small trees, though more lethal usage is not impossible.[30]

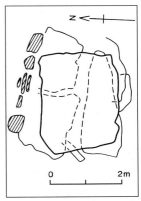

Illus. 5.3a. A collapsed megalithic tomb at Ceathrú an Lisín, Inis Meáin.
Illus. 5.3b. Plan of megalithic tomb at Ceathrú an Lisín.

Illus. 5.4. Collapsed megalithic structure at Ceathrú an Teampaill, Inis Meáin.

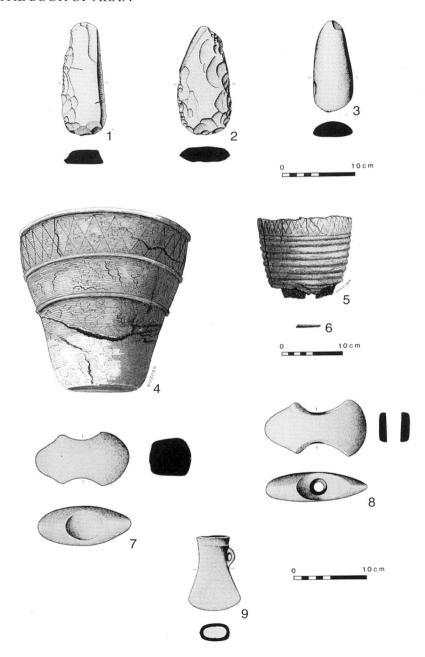

Illus. 5.5. Some archaeological finds from Aran and Clare: 1-2. Polished stone axeheads found near Cill Ghobnait, Inis Oírr. 3. Polished stone axehead found in a shell midden on Inis Meáin. 4-6. A Bronze Age cordoned urn, a second smaller pottery vessel and a bronze pin (?) fragment from Cnoc Raithní, Inis Oírr (after Wakeman). 7. An unfinished stone 'battle-axe' found near Baile an Lurgain. 8. A complete 'battle-axe' from nearby Teergonean in Co. Clare. 9. Socketed bronze axehead from Formna.

The Cnoc Raithní Burial

In 1885 a low mound close to an Trá on Inis Oírr was examined by a visiting clergyman, Rev. Denis Murphy, S.J., and the Clerk of Works who was then completing the Office of Public Works' restoration of O'Brien's Castle nearby. Only rather cursory accounts of this early unscientific excavation exist. According to the Rev. Murphy:

'a mound or hillock close to Tragh Kiera... was found to be surrounded, at a depth of some ten feet from the surface, by the foundation of a thick wall, roughly built of large stones, without any sign of mortar... When the foundations were laid bare, and the whole circle of the cashel was opened up, on digging a little into the mound inside this wall, we came on some tall stones, four feet in height set on end, and enclosing a circular space of about five feet in diameter. We set about clearing away the sand between them, and at a depth of three feet from the top of them and ten feet from the surface of the mound we came on the smaller of the two urns. We removed the sand around it very carefully, hoping to be able to raise it whole and without a break from its position. But when it was touched, ever so gently, it fell to pieces, as if it were made of sand. These we put together carefully bit by bit ... Continuing the search within the same stone circle, we soon came on another and larger urn ... The contents of both urns were bones, a substance like charred peat, and sand. The sand will have fallen in owing to pressure from above ...'.

This account is accompanied by drawings of both pottery vessels by W.F. Wakeman who also recorded the fact that a small piece of bronze about 1.6cm long (the pointed end of a pin or an awl) was found in the smaller one.[31] Judging from Murphy's description a large mound, apparently of sand, was removed, in whole or in part, to reveal a circular stone wall at a depth of 3m. Within this circular area, a circular stone-built grave about 1.5m in diameter and about 90cm deep contained two pots each containing fragments of cremated human bone. The larger of the two is a fine example of a Bronze Age Cordoned Urn dating to about 1500 BC (Illus. 5.5). They are so named because they invariably have two or more raised mouldings or cordons around the exterior of a somewhat bucket-shaped body and one broad zone of simple geometric ornament below the rim. A few examples are known elsewhere in Co. Galway and in Co. Mayo but urns of this type are mainly found in north-eastern Ireland and in Scotland. It is possible that individuals accorded this sort of burial were privileged in some way – a large pottery urn may have been some mark of status and only certain members of the community may have been honoured with formal burial and a ritual which demanded the building of a large cremation pyre somewhere on Inis Oírr three and half thousand years ago.

A low mound known as Cnoc Raithní, the hill of ferns, is usually identified as the location of these two Bronze Age cremations. It is a roughly circular mound surrounded by a drystone wall some 21m in diameter. The mound is flat-topped and has, in its southern half, a number of protruding slabs which seem to be traces of a couple of long slab-lined graves. To the north of these possible graves a small sub-rectangular mound with a drystone kerb sits on top of

Illus. 5.6a. Cnoc Raithní, Inis Oírr: burial mound. The circular mound has several stone settings in it which may be pre-Christian graves. It may have produced a Bronze Age burial dating to 1500 BC. The site was restored in the 19th century.

Illus 5.6b. Plan of Cnoc Raithní burial mound.

the oval mound. What appears to be a rectangular setting of slabs protrudes from the flat top of this feature and two upright slabs stand near its western end (Illus. 5.6). This is a puzzling monument, there is certainly no trace of the circular cremation grave and how much of either the large mound or the small rectangular mound is due to 19th century restoration work is uncertain. Long slab-lined graves are often dated to the early Christian period and it is possible that Cnoc Raithní is a complex multi-period structure, a prehistoric site re-used at a later date.[32]

One stone object from Inis Oírr may be probably contemporary with the Cordoned Urn burial. This is an unfinished stone 'battle-axe', a casual surface find in 1970 near Baile an Lurgáin (Illus. 5.5). If finished it would have resembled an example from Teergonean townland on the nearby Clare coast. Highly polished, with a relatively slender perforation for a wooden haft, these objects were hardly offensive weapons as their fanciful name implies. It is generally believed that they had some ceremonial role and were possibly symbols of prestige.

Activity on Aran in the later Bronze Age, around and about 800 BC. is indicated by one other Inis Oírr find. This is a bronze socketed axehead (Illus. 5.5) found just 20cm below the surface in a field at Formna.[33] It would originally have been mounted in a bent wooden haft and the loop may have served to take a leather thong to bind the two together. Early occupation on the site of the great fort of Dún Aonghasa on Inis Mór dates to this period as well.

The Stone Forts

The half a dozen great stone-built forts on the Aran Islands are splendid examples of their kind and they have captured the imagination of numerous visitors since at least the 19th century. This type of fort is well known in western Ireland in particular, from Donegal to Kerry, and quite a few fine examples occur in Co. Clare, but the special attraction of the Aran monuments lies in great measure in their dramatic and relatively remote location.

Two of the forts stand apart from the rest, for Dún Dúchathair and the famous Dún

Aonghasa, both on Inis Mór, are situated on the cliffs of the inhospitable Atlantic coast and seem to many to confront the unknown hazards of an immense ocean.

Dún Aonghasa
'...the most magnificent barbaric monument in Europe'

George Petrie

The great fort of Dún Aonghasa stands on the edge of a sheer sea cliff nearly 100m high and also dominates the lower lands of Cill Mhuirbhigh to the north-east (Illus. 5. 7-8). Today the eye of the visitor is caught at once by the imposing stone wall of the inner fort, an almost semi-circular enclosure on the cliff edge. But the monument is much more complex than that, it has outer defences enclosing a

Illus. 5.7. General plan of Dún Aonghasa (after Cotter).

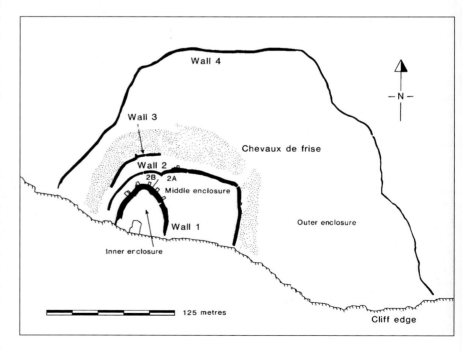

total area of 5.7 hectares (14 acres) and may have been modified more than once in ancient times as well as being restored in the 1880s. The crude buttresses which now support the ramparts at various points are recent additions.

Illus. 5.8. Dún Aonghasa: 'the most magnificent barbaric monument in Europe'. The great wall of the inner fort and two of the three outer ramparts are visible, as is the stone chevaux-de-frise.

Illus. 5.9. Rampart of inner fort with sidelong flights of steps to the right of the mural chamber.

Illus. 5.10 opposite page. Entrance to inner fort viewed from the interior with vertical flights of steps to the right.

Illus. 5.11 opposite page. Westropp's sketch plan of the rampart of the inner fort showing the terracing and the presence of internal faces.

Inner Fort

The stone-built rampart of the inner fort is about 4m high at present but in the 1830s parts of it were up to 5.5m high. It has a slight external batter, that is it slopes inwards from base to top to give greater stability and has a maximum thickness of over 5m. The low, narrow, lintelled entrance is on the north-east; its innermost section is an unroofed passage.

The interior is of irregular U-shaped plan, with an average diameter of about 47m and now open to the Atlantic at the southern cliff edge. Presumably the enclosure was once an oval or

at least D-shaped with a wall or rampart on this seaward side. No written records survive to testify to its original shape and it seems likely that part of the fort collapsed into the sea in the remote past. The inside of the rampart is terraced and, in the northern half of the enclosure, half-a-dozen sets of stone steps give access to the two levels of terracing below the parapet (Illus. 5. 9-10).

Here we are confronted with the problems posed by the 1880s restoration, for no records seem to have been kept of what was then found and what actually prompted the construction or reconstruction of the features visible today. That there were terraces and steps is not in doubt, however. Though the monument was very dilapidated and the walls ruined (as Dunraven's pre-restoration photographs show[34]) internal features were visible. Petrie who first visited it in 1821 refers to 'a level terrace at the height of 6 feet from the ground' and O'Donovan noted that this rampart 'is made up of three distinct walls built up against each other, each wall faced with stones of considerable size ... The two external divisions are here raised to the height of 18 feet, but the internal division is at present only 7 feet high ...'.[35] The construction of the rampart in sections, with several internal wall faces (Illus. 5.11) may reflect various phases of additional walling. The purpose of such internal facing in ramparts is not clear: some may be an attempt to give greater stability but some may indeed be due to the addition of extra walling just to give a more massive appearance to the structure. In any event the fort we see today is the result of a number of refurbishments in ancient times, long before the restoration work of the 19th century. Samuel Ferguson, writing in 1853, has offered the clearest of the all-too-brief pre-restoration accounts of the interior: 'At the right, on entering, are the remains of a flight of steps conducting to the lower banquette, the form of which is with difficulty traceable among the masses of fallen stone. One or two other indications of stairs may be detected, but were it not for the very distinct construction of the rampart in three concentric sections, one would be at a loss to understand the principle of the construction. On ascending the mound [of stones], however, the three concentric walls are seen in perfect distinctness, the middle one rising through the ruins of the other two, save in one or two points, where the exterior envelope still stands to near its original height'. Thus the two internal terraces visible today are likely to be approximate representations of what there once was.[36]

The original number of stone steps is problematical.[37] Clearly the short straight flight of steps to the right of the entrance (to the north as the visitor enters) is original, Ferguson noted it as we have seen. Both straight and sidelong flights of steps were noted in 1878,[38] and the pair of sidelong flights of steps on the northwest is probably original too.[39] To what extent the other straight flights of steps, the one on the north leading from the lower to the upper terrace, and the pair to the south of the entrances (running from ground level to the lower terrace and from there to the second terrace) reflect original features is not known. They may have been figments of the restorers' imagination, perhaps even built just to facilitate the modern visitor. This seems unlikely, however, because what little evidence there is, from pre-restoration accounts of Dún Aonghasa as well as from other restored Aran monuments, be they forts or churches, suggests that while walls may have been rebuilt and consolidated and some much ruined flights of steps may not have been recognised, few, if any, invented features were added.[40]

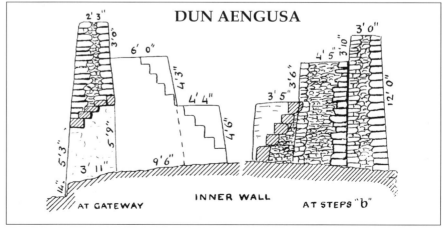

DUN AENGUSA

AT GATEWAY   INNER WALL   AT STEPS "b"

The only visible feature in the enclosure is a natural rectangular platform of limestone about 60cm high abutting the edge of the cliff, its purpose is unknown. There is also a small rectangular chamber in the western wall at ground level just south of the lower sidelong flight of steps.

On the outside there are several vertical joints in the rampart, these are usually considered to represent the construction of the wall in sections by different groups of labourers and have been identified in other stone forts elsewhere.

Outer Defences

Some sort of modification seems to have been done to some of the outer defences. These outer works now comprise two stone ramparts, a fragment of a third and a stone *chevaux-de-frise*.

Beyond the inner fort, the middle enclosure is formed by a long irregular rampart with one terrace and one internal medial facing. The terrace of this middle rampart is an original feature, it was recorded by Petrie and Ferguson, for instance, neither of whom record steps or more than one entrance.[41] Westropp noted no steps either in 1878 so the flight of steps by the north-eastern entrance may not be ancient. It does not follow that every terraced stone rampart had to have stone steps, the former presence of wooden steps and walk-ways is a possibility. On the north there is a lintelled entrance and another unroofed passage-like entrance on the north-east. A third occurs on the north-west and faces an entrance in the fragment of rampart which survives some 14m away at this point.[42]

The fragment of rampart is roughly similar in

Illus. 5.12. 'Like infinite head-stones of the dead': the stones of the almost impenetrable chevaux-de-frise impede the approach to the middle and fragmentary ramparts.

construction to the middle rampart, it has one terrace in places, one surviving entrance and no surviving steps. Petrie, however, records '2 flights of steps'.[43]

Chevaux-de-frise

Immediately outside this fragment on the west and north and beyond the middle rampart on the north and east is one of Dún Aonghasa's most noteworthy features. This is the stone *chevaux-de-frise* which more or less extends in a great band 15 to 38m wide around the fortifications from cliff to cliff; some of the stones are up to 1.75m high (Illus. 5.12). The name *chevaux-de-frise* is used to describe wooden stakes or upright pointed stones placed in the ground outside a fort to hinder attackers and it is said to derive from spikes used by Frisians to impede enemy cavalry in the late l7th century.[44] Though now much ruined in places this defensive work is an impressive sight and must once have formed an almost impenetrable obstacle to anyone approaching the outer defences: when first erected the limestone pillars must have been a razor sharp deterrent to any attacker and since the terrain in any event precluded mounted assault their purpose must have been to impede an attack on foot on the middle rampart. Today they stand, a relic of a long forgotten threat, and, in the words of Samuel Ferguson, 'arranged round the base of the fortress, like infinite head-stones of the dead'.[45]

The outer wall at Dún Aonghasa is a modest and dilapidated structure which was originally at least 2m thick and still has, on the north, a lintelled gateway; it may have had a medial facing and possibly a terrace.[46]

A glance at the plan of the fort as it is today clearly shows that the middle rampart falls into three sections. The length on the west and north-west is concentric both with the inner rampart and with the fragment. It is possible that these two sections once continued east and south to form a great oval trivallate fort. But there is no trace whatever of such a continuation on the ground and no one knows, of course, how much of the cliff has disappeared into the sea over the centuries. The existence of the fragment and the abrupt change in direction in the middle rampart do indicate some modification.[47] At a guess the original fort may have been a D-shaped cliff fort like the well-known stone fort at Cahercommaun, in the Burren, in Co. Clare.

Excavation

Excavation in the inner enclosure has demonstrated that the site was first occupied in the later Bronze Age about 800 BC. The foundations of circular huts have been found along with fragments of plain pottery vessels and broken pieces of clay moulds for the casting of bronze swords, spears and axes have been found (Illus. 5.13): the bronze casting in particular implies that this may have been a settlement of some importance at the time suggesting as it does the presence of specialised craftworkers such as weapon smiths. Other objects found date to the early Christian period 500-1000 AD. Traces of several circular hut foundations have also been discovered as well as animal bones (mostly sheep and some cattle) and bones of birds and fish. It is also possible that the site was occupied through the Iron Age, a brooch of this period was discovered in the last century, but other evidence for this is scanty. It is likely that the earliest settlement in the later Bronze Age was enclosed by a stone rampart, this being eventually superceded by the later walls visible today (for at least part of the inner wall overlies this early occupation).

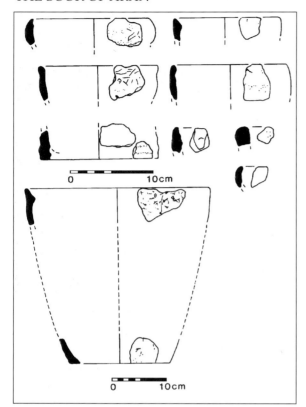

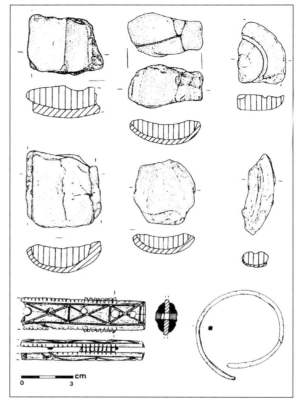

Illus. 5.13. Left: sherds of plain pottery vessels of later Bronze Age date found at Dún Aonghasa. Right: fragments of clay moulds for various bronze objects including a spearhead, swords and rings or bracelets. The bronze bracelet on the lower right is probably of prehistoric date but the bone comb dates to the early Christian period occupation at the site (all after Cotter).

Dun Angeus

Many of these strange dry-stone structures are to be found on the West coast and on the islands. Dun Angeus is the most important. It is a half-circle which rises in tiers around an arena where the rock has been levelled out and which has been exactly cut in half by the cliff edge. The drop is sheer and breathtaking. Splinters of basalt set into the ground at an angle form a chevaux de frise which bars access and which has given support to the theory that this is a military monument. Dun in Gaelic does in fact mean fortress. This seems absurd: whoever is inside can see absolutely nothing of what may be going on outside. There are no loopholes or crenellations to give a view of the approaches. To climb the outside wall without making a sound would be child's play. It would be equally simple to throw the defenders, taken by surprise from behind, into the void. I am more inclined to think that this is an amphitheatre for solemn inaugurations, seasonal rituals, or for those druidic gatherings where a concert of lamentations accompanied the plunging of the setting sun into the ocean. Since textbooks are as slow to die as myths, people persist in describing these structures as 'forts'. A Professor from Galway who shares my doubts and who I had questioned about this simply told me that it takes a long time to get something into the head of an Irishman and even longer to get it out.

Translated (with original spelling of 'Dun Angeus') from Nicolas Bouvier, *Journal d'Aran et d'autres lieux* (1990).

Dún Dúchathair

Just 3.5 miles away is another remarkable stone fort on the Atlantic cliffs. This is a promontory fort known as Dún Dúchathair or 'the black fort'. Here a much eroded promontory is heavily defended on its landward side by a stone rampart and *chevaux-de-frise* (Illus. 5. 14-15). As in other forts of this promontory type a neck of land is cut off by a rampart, in this instance a massive curving stone construction over 6m high and 5m thick now with two main terraces and several sidelong and vertical flights of steps. Early pre-restoration accounts are brief and unsatisfactory and it is difficult to be certain if terraces and steps are all original.[48] There was probably at least one terrace and there are the last traces of an entrance through the rampart near its eastern end but almost all evidence has disappeared with the collapse of parts of the cliff.[49]

If questions about the number of terraces, the doubtful presence of steps and the position of an entrance still remain, there is no doubt about the existence of some stone huts in the interior of the fort for several can still be seen today. The stone foundations of at least four conjoined and roughly oval huts lie just inside the central part of the rampart. It is debateable how ancient these are but they were probably remodelled or partly rebuilt in the 19th century restoration. There were others in one or two lines running the length of the promontory but only faint traces of them exist today. O'Donovan recorded in 1839: 'inside the wall are rows of stone houses of an oblong ... form but now nearly destroyed, one row extending along the wall and built up against it, another running from north to south for a distance of about 170 feet where it originally branched into two rows, one extending south-west as far as the margin of the cliff, and the other to the

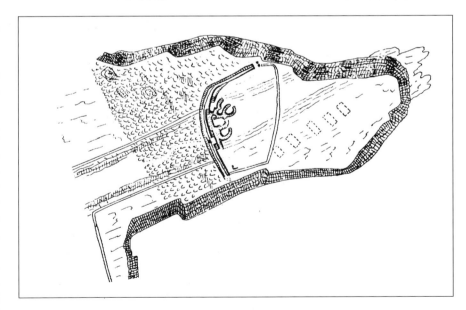

Illus. 5.14. Both the aerial view and Westropp's sketch plan of Dún Dúchathair show the ruined chevaux-de-frise *on the left and a series of different forms of hut sites on the promontory within the fort.*

south-east to the opposite margin, these two rows thus branching from the main row are nearly washed away by storms...'. There is also a small chamber in the rampart recalling the similar one in Dún Aonghasa.

Outside the rampart are the remains of a very ruined *chevaux-de-frise*. Many stones are fallen and its full extent is difficult to determine. It seems to have been built of lower and less closely set stones than that at Dún Aonghasa.

Illus. 5.15. Dún Dúchathair: a classic example of a promontory fort.

Dún Eoghanachta

Like the remaining forts on Inis Mór, Dún Eoghanachta is situated on one of the limestone terraces overlooking the north-eastern and eastern parts of the island. It dominates both a wide area west of Cill Mhuirbhigh and the much ruined early ecclesiastical site of Cill Comhla on the terrace below. The fort is an imposing example of a relatively common type of circular stone-built cashel (Illus. 5.16). It has an internal diameter of about 27m enclosed by a massive rampart some 5m high and over 4m thick built of large limestone blocks many laid transversely. It is a triple wall with two internal faces and one terrace below the parapet.[50] The entrance, on the south-east, was 'nearly destroyed' in 1839 when O'Donovan visited the monument. It was rebuilt in the restoration of the 1880s. Five sets of straight steps give access to the lower terrace and one set of straight steps and three sets of pairs of lateral flights lead to the parapet. Three of the lower steps were recorded by Petrie who noted only one set of steps leading from the lower terrace to a second terrace. O'Donovan noted four sets of lower steps. It seems probable therefore that most, if not all, of the lower straight steps visible today are original features. The sidelong flights now running to a parapet were not noted by Petrie or O'Donovan but the former's plan suggests two terraces below a parapet.[51]

In the interior there are the remains of three sub-rectangular stone huts against the western rampart and the largest of these has two niches in one wall.[52]

Dún Eochla

Dún Eochla is a fine oval stone fort with an outer rampart located in a commanding situation on the north-eastern limits of the highest

Illus. 5.16. Aerial view of Dún Eoghanachta and Westropp's sketch plan.

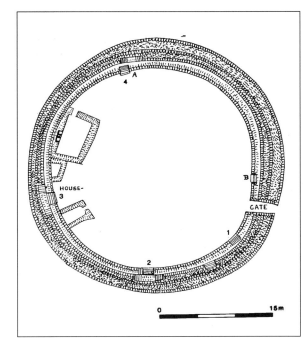

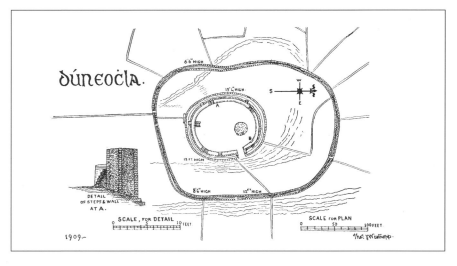

Illus. 5.17. Dún Eochla: oval stone fort with an outer rampart. The drum-shaped pile of stones in the interior is the result of 19th century restoration. Westropp's sketch plan shows the terracing and steps.

ground on Inis Mór. The great inner fort stands on a natural terrace but its smaller outer rampart, some distance away, runs irregularly along a low ridge on the east and through more low-lying grassy ground elsewhere (Illus. 5.17). The inner enclosure is similar in size to Dún Eoghanachta with internal diameters of about 28m by 23m and with a rampart up to about 5m in height and 3.5m in thickness. Again the rampart is a triple wall with two internal faces recorded by several earlier writers.[53]

As at Dún Eoghanachta there is now one terrace below a broad parapet and several straight flights of steps (some with a lateral flight) give access to the terrace. A number of straight flights also lead to the parapet from the terrace. It is difficult to reconcile these various steps with the very few earlier accounts of this rampart in pre-restoration days. According to O'Donovan, only three sets of steps were visible in 1839: on the south-west a straight flight of steps leading to the terrace, on the south a lateral flight of steps running from the terrace to the top of the parapet (this flight is described as running to the left), and finally on the northeast, within 6m of the entrance, a straight flight up to the terrace from the ground.[54] The rampart was nearly destroyed on the north-east but reasonably well preserved in other places; the inner wall segment was apparently much damaged on the east. The oldest known sketch plan of Dún Eochla (and indeed of any Aran monument) suggests that much of this destruction may have occurred in the 18th century. The complaint of O'Donovan and Wilde that rabbit hunters were primarily to blame for the dilapidation of forts like Dún Aonghasa in the early 19th century may hold good for the preceding century as well. One sketch plan dating from Edward Lhuyd's visit to Aran in 1700 is preserved (Illus. 5.18)[55] and shows that at that time the inner fort had two terraces below a parapet with three straight flights from the ground to the lower terrace and two pairs of opposed lateral flights of steps leading from the lower to the upper terrace. There was a possible hut against one wall in the interior and the outer rampart had one terrace and one straight flight of steps leading to it.[56] The differences between the measurements of the rampart in 1700 and those taken by O'Donovan in 1839 and the respective descriptions suggest that most of the parapet had collapsed in the intervening period.[57] In its original condition the inner fort at Dún Eochla must have been an imposing sight indeed.

Today there is no trace of any hut in the interior. A large drum-shaped pile of stone is the result of some tidying-up in the last century.[58] The outer rampart retains traces of its terrace but no steps survive and the original entrance is destroyed.

Dún Chonchúir

Dún Chonchúir is the largest of the two stone forts on Inis Meáin and occupies a prominent position overlooking a large part of the island. The fort is a great oval enclosure about 69m north-south and 35m east-west internally with a low cliff on its western side providing some natural defence. A large outer enclosure on the east with a further smaller outwork on the north-west offer additional protection[59] (Illus. 5.19).

The oval enclosure is defended by a massive rampart which, with a maximum height of some 6m. and a thickness in places of over 5m, is larger than that of the inner fort at Dún Aonghasa. Again this is a triple wall with two

Illus. 5.18. The earliest depiction of any Aran monument is a sketch plan of Dún Eochla dating from Edward Lhuyd's visit to Aran in 1700. Now in the British Library, it shows that the outer rampart had at least one flight of steps and that the inner fort had both vertical and sidelong flights plus two terraces below the parapet.

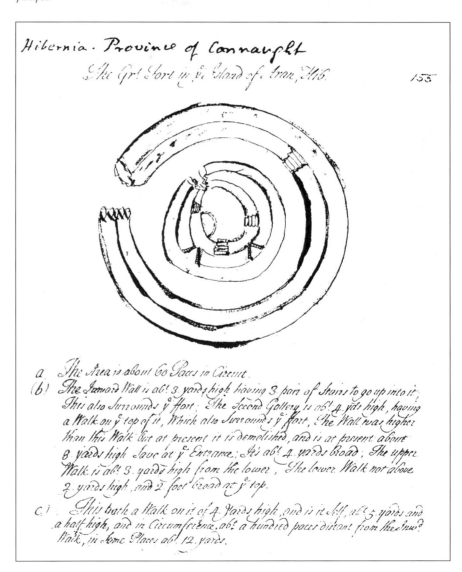

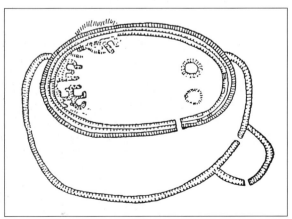

Illus. 5.19. Dún Chonchúir, the largest stone fort on Inis Meáin, has two additional out-works protecting the east-ern side of the massive oval enclosure. These and the remains of various hut sites in the interior were recorded by Westropp in a sketch plan.

internal faces recorded by earlier writers. Before restoration there were two terraces below a much ruined parapet with traces of several straight flights of steps leading to both terraces. At least one of the flights was a lateral one from the lower to the upper terrace. Today it is obvious that the rampart has been quite irregularly reconstructed with different levels only occasionally reflecting the original three-fold construction with two terraces. In some places the outer segment of the rampart is lower than the middle section and this reflects the greater collapse of parts of the outer section in the last century.[60] While some vertical and lateral flights of steps are original features it is impossible to determine how many of the three dozen or so different sets of steps now to be seen should be so considered. The entrance on the north-east was quite ruined in the last century and has been rebuilt.

In the interior there are the remains of a num-ber of stone huts partly rebuilt on their old foundations, they were greatly ruined in 1839.[61] Outside the oval enclosure a number of vertical divisions are visible in the rampart's outer face; there is one joint to the right of the entrance. Joints of this sort are generally believed to reflect the building of such walls in separate sections; as already noted they are to be seen at Dún Aonghasa and elsewhere.

The eastern outer enclosure may have been a later addition to the fort. Though early sketch plans show the wall of this crescent-shaped area joining the fort's rampart on the north-west and south-east, there is no indication that they were ever bonded together. The outer wall was much collapsed in the last century but has traces of a terrace.[62] Attached to this enclosure on the north-east is a fairly substantial addition of sub-rectangular plan.[63]

Dún Fearbhaí

Dún Fearbhaí is the smaller of the two stone forts on Inis Meáin (Illus. 5.20). On the south-eastern side of the island, it is situated on a low sloping hill commanding the area of Baile an Mhothair.[64] One rampart, almost straight on the east and west and more rounded on the north and south, encloses an area of almost sub-rectangular plan measuring about 27 by 23m. According to O'Donovan the rampart was a triple one, as he put it, having 'three distinct divisions built up against eact other, and faced with stones of considerable size'. It is difficult to be certain but it seems to have only two sections with an average total width of just over 3m and an external height varying from 3 to 5m. The inner section forms a narrow parapet approached by four sets of steps in the west, north, north-east and south-east; these are combinations of vertical and lateral flights. There are several lateral flights on the south including one running from the terrace to the top of the parapet. O'Donovan only records three sets of steps however, all seemingly giving access to the terrace on the west and on either side of the entrance on the north-east and on the south-east. The entrance was virtually destroyed at this time and, like some of the flights of steps, was reconstructed some fifty years later.

Dún Formna

O'Brien's Castle on Inis Oírr is surrounded by a stone rampart (and there may be the remains of a second outer wall): it has been suggested that this is a much modified earlier stone fort.

Who built the great forts?

The half dozen large stone forts are by no means the only forts or enclosures on the islands: a number of other smaller monuments of this sort also survive. However, the great forts have naturally attracted the most attention, and beg the obvious questions about purpose and date.

Early legend attributes the construction of some of these forts to a group of defeated *Fir Bolg* who, along with others of their kin, were driven westwards to Connacht in pre-Christian times. Aonghas and Conchúir, two of the sons of Umor, are credited with the great forts on Inis Mór and Inis Meáin respectively which bear their names. Some scholars have thought that these *Fir Bolg* were related to the *Belgae* of Gaul and southern Britain and thus a date in the second or first century BC for these forts seemed a reasonable possibility.

Illus. 5.20. Dún Fearbhaí on Inis Meáin is a small sub-rectangular fort with terraced rampart and steps.

The romantic legend of a dispossessed people forced to the western limits of the known world has inspired more than one passage of purple prose. For instance: 'Granted that stones are the commonest objects of the bare, rocky Aran islands, and that ample material for the building of these gigantic constructions twenty times over is there available for the picking up, the question still remains, why did any company think it worth their while to build them in such a desolate place? And the only reasonable answer which presents itself is, that the essential germ of the story transmitted to us by the medieval scholastic historians is true, whatever we may think of its specific details: they were the last shelter of expelled refugees, fleeing from some rapacious conqueror. Driven, step by step, back to the western coast and to the islands beyond, they here made their final stand, by no mere conventional metaphor but in grim, literal reality, "between the devil and the deep sea". Nothing but massacre, or drowning in the Atlantic deeps, awaited them outside their island fortresses: in desperation they heaped them up these vast walls, to shield them from the fury of the tempest that had burst upon their country and their kindred'.[65]

Legend, romantic or otherwise, is no sure guide. An inextricable mix of fabricated or mythologised history and historicised myth has bequeathed us a story of a *Fir Bolg* colonisation of Aran cast in terms of a traditional migration model, a recurring feature of early origin tales. Even if the existence of a *Fir Bolg* people is conceded, something that is by no means certain, then this migratory tale may be just as much a literary invention as the account of the journeying of the Sons of Míl from Spain.[66]

The archaeological evidence is more helpful, though not as informative as we would wish. For a number of reasons the forts have often been labelled Iron Age, the *Fir Bolg* legend being but one factor in this dating. The presence of a *chevaux-de-frise* at Dún Aonghasa and Dún Dúchathair is another significant feature. Stone and wooden versions of this unusual defensive measure have been sporadically recorded in late prehistoric times in parts of Central and Western Europe. A small number of stone forts of irregular plan in north-central Spain and in northern Portugal have stone *chevaux-de-frise* usually around just part of their defenses. Dating evidence is meagre but dates from the 6th century BC or earlier to the 4th century BC have been suggested.[67] Seven examples are known from Wales and Scotland and traces of what may have been a wooden one have been excavated outside a hill-top fort on the Isle of Man.[68]

Archaeological excavation at Dún Aonghasa has demonstrated that at least one of the Aran forts was lived in and possibly strengthened in early Christian times and that their beginnings may, at least in the case of this fort, lie in the later Bronze Age.

It is a reasonable supposition that the great forts at least were planned and built by chieftains of wealthy communities. Considerable labour was involved in their construction, whether by slaves or freemen. The reasons for building them may have been complex. Necessity may have been partly responsible: some may have been intended to serve as defended settlements or even as general refuges for use in times of danger (and since prolonged siege warfare was probably neither customary nor practical, questions of internal water supply are irrelevant). If, as seems possible, sheep, cattle and fishing were the basis of an economy supplemented to a significant degree by the fruits of piracy, stout defences may have been all the more necessary. It is not impossible that they were also the focus for some occasional ceremonial activities though it is unlikely that this was ever their primary function.[69]

The imposing scale of the great forts, however, may indicate another equally compelling necessity: they may in part be expressions of social self-assertion by the chieftains who built them, a necessary demonstration of rank. Indeed, in early Ireland, one of the duties due to a chieftain was help in the construction of the rampart of his fort and the size and complexity of its construction might be a reflection of the numbers of a lord's clients or vassals and certainly was a reflection of his status. As an early law tract says: 'It is then that he is king when ramparts of vassalage surround him'.[70]

Here we may have an explanation for the vertical joints visible in the ramparts of some Aran forts (and stone forts elsewhere in the country), perhaps they were built in sections over a period of time as part of the fixed amounts of manual labour due to a lord. This sort of situation might encourage the construction of additional facings to thicken ramparts and even encourage the proliferation of forts, some for habitation, others perhaps for other purposes such as cattle enclosures or centres for craftsmen for example.

The occupants of forts like Dún Eochla and Dún Eoghanachta presumably derived some of their wealth from the limited pasture the islands had to offer but it is hard to imagine that this was a sufficient basis for the wealth and tribute implied by one or more great forts. It seems likely that the interests of the island's chieftain or chieftains extended into Co. Clare (where similar stone forts are well known) and, more significantly, to the coastal seaways of the west coast. The strategic location of the Aran Islands, controlling coastal traffic northwards and southwards, must have added to their economic and political importance. Two thousand

or more years ago large sailing currachs were probably a common sight on this western coast. Wooden galleys with oars and sail were probably known as well. It may not be too far fetched to see some of the Aran forts, at least, as the stony memorials of long forgotten chieftains who once exacted tribute along part of the western coast and who, perhaps occasionally, indulged in a little profitable piracy.

Minor Forts and Other Settlements

Aside from those great forts with traces of clochans in their interior, there is abundant other evidence for ancient settlement on the Aran Islands, notably on Inis Mór. This evidence is much less imposing, however, consisting for the most part of a few ruined, small enclosures and a number of collapsed houses or clochans.

Dún Beag

The small enclosure south-west of Corrúch aptly called Dún Beag is a good example of the former. It is situated on a fairly prominent

Illus. 5.21. Many low oval grass-covered mounds of stones on Aran are the remains of collapsed dwellings. This is a large example north-west of Dún Beag.

hillock overlooking Fearann an Choirce and Port Mhuirbhigh to the north-west. Of sub-rectangular plan, it measures about 70 by 36 metres overall and is enclosed by a rampart surviving only in places and then as a low stony bank now obscured by field walls. On the north-east a roughly quadrilateral annex is enclosed by another wall in an even more ruined condition which is also obscured by a more recent field wall. A blocked-up entrance with a stone lintel now incorporated in the field wall may be an original feature.[71] Within the large oval enclosure there are two small circular depressions on the west and a low oval mound on the south-west which may be the remains of huts or collapsed clochans.

Baile na mBocht

The area in Eochaill townland, south of Corrúch, between Dún Beag and Dún Eochla is littered with ancient remains. The name Baile na mBocht, village of the poor, has been given to at least part of this area for many years.[72] The Eochaill wedge tomb is situated just east of Dún Beag but east of this again lie dozens of grassy mounds many of which may be the remains of collapsed houses or clochans of uncertain date. Over twenty examples have been recorded here (Illus. 5.21) along with a number of enclosures. A maze of field walls now make access to this area very difficult. These walls often run across the surviving mounds and it is possible that many mounds have been removed in field clearance and the stones of many others have been used for wall building.

This ancient settlement was first recorded in 1866 by G.H. Kinahan of the Geological Survey.[73] Among a range of miscellaneous monuments he noted a number of cnocans (or hillocks) which he considered to be the col-lapsed remains of clochans or beehive cells covered with clay. These were often low, somewhat oval mounds with a depression in the centre. Sometimes they were almost kidney-shaped or had the appearance of two conjoined mounds. A few triple mounds are recorded.

Small circular mounds could be prehistoric burial mounds and indeed a conjoined pair on Inis Oírr were tentatively identified as such in the 1930s.[74] In fact some archaeological excavation in Baile na mBocht in the 1950s has demonstrated that some (if not all) of these mounds are the remains of collapsed dwellings. J.R.W. Goulden, a Dublin school teacher with an interest in archaeology, excavated three sites which he labelled 'Oghil I', 'Oghil II' and 'Oghil III'.[75]

The first of these, 'Oghil I', was a roughly oval, stony, grass-grown cairn about 14m across and just over 1m high. Excavation revealed an area of stone paving, traces of a fire, several arrangements of upright slabs, and a low stone wall beneath the cairn but no clear traces of hut foundations were discovered. Fragments of animal bones, of cattle and sheep, and large quantities of shells, notably limpet were found. A few stray pieces of human bone were also recovered but the general impression was that this was a settlement site of some sort where meat and shell fish were consumed.

Clear and unambiguous evidence for dwellings were found, however, in the two other mounds. 'Oghil II' (Illus. 5.22) was another oval, stony, mound about 17m in maximum dimensions and 1.40m in maximum height. The foundations of two circular huts were found beneath this pile of stone. In Goulden's opinion a later hut has been constructed inside the remains of an earlier one. The larger hut circle had a diameter of 6.40m internally. A hole in the centre of the floor was probably for a timber post to give support to a conical roof which was almost certainly thatched. The small rectangular and circular structures on the east may have been additions for storage purposes. Numerous animal bones and sea-shells were found, discarded on the spot by the inhabitants. Some small shells of the sort which attach themselves to the edible sea-weed, dulse, suggest that this may have been part of the diet too.

Nothing was found to give a clear indication of date: finds included tubular antler handles (presumably for metal knives or awls), a stone spindle whorl (evidence for spinning), a broken hammer made of sandstone, and a chipped and partly polished piece of stone. Another discovery on top of the mound of stones was part of a granite bullaun stone probably used like a mortar for grinding or pounding.

Excavation at 'Oghil III' was a little more informative. Before work began this site appeared to be a low triple mound of stones about 21 by 16m and some 90cm in maximum height. As the stones of the mound were removed the lower levels of a complex three-roomed structure were revealed (Illus. 5. 23-24). Goulden's

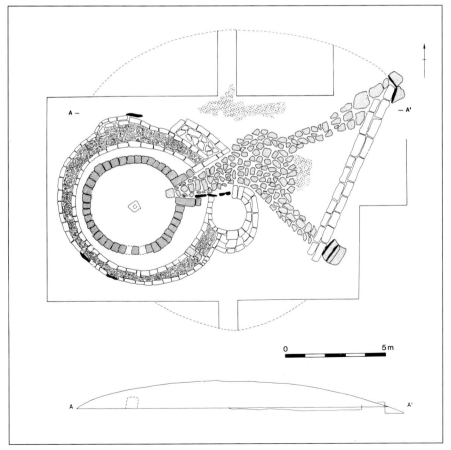

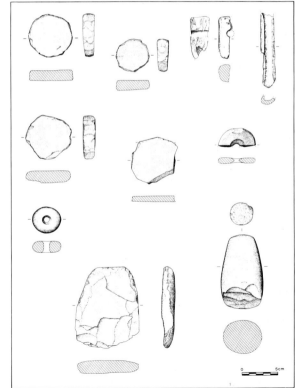

description was brief:

'The dwelling consisted of three almost circular rooms placed roughly like the leaves of a shamrock. Extending eastward like a stem was paving which for much of its length was composed of two layers. The mounds consisted of broken stone and midden material of many kinds. In it there was little stratification except in the lower levels where the only food remains were limpet shells. It would appear that in the earliest period of occupation the inhabitants had either no cattle or insufficient to warrant slaughter. In the later midden material the bones of ox and sheep (or goat) were plentiful and there were some pig bones... one skull, that of a very young pig, was found (the only skull in three excavations). It was possible to show that the two small rooms near the entrance were earlier than the large room which lay to the west. The roofing of the smaller earlier rooms may have been some form of corbelling but the large room or house must have been thatched. In Oghil II a central hole had been broken in the middle of the floor of the large circular room. In this case a large triangular hole had been broken in the rock. Each of the sides measured almost exactly eight feet in length and it can be assumed that instead of a single pole some sort of tripod was used. The hole had been filled afterwards with rubble and flagged with flat stones. Just inside the door of the western room two rotary quern-tops of sandstone were found. These may have been used to hold the pivots on which the door turned ...'.

Illus. 5.23. 'Oghil III': ground plan and possible reconstruction of an ancient house site excavated in the 1950s in Baile na mBocht.

0   4m

Other finds included some fragments of plain hand-made pottery, a small iron ring, bone skewers, part of bone handles, a small stone amulet, and several stone pounders. None of these items provide a clear indication of date, though the quern stones, if contemporary with the use of the house, might suggest occupation of the site in the first millenium AD.

Even though many questions remain unanswered about when and how the inhabitants of these house-sites lived, the animal bones, the quern stones for grinding corn, and the sea shells indicate a varied subsistence. More significantly these excavations have demonstrated that some at least of the stony mounds on Aran were dwelling places and not burial mounds as had been thought. These investigations also suggest that not all of these sites are collapsed clochans. Some may have been completely built of stone with beehive-like corbelled roofs, but others like 'Oghil II' and 'Oghil III' probably had low stone walls surmounted by timber-supported thatched conical roofs.

Clochán na Carraige

Completely stone-built examples do survive and the best known is the exceptionally well-preserved clochan in Cill Mhuirbhigh townland called Clochán na Carraige.[76] Externally this appears to be an oval, stone-built hut, roofed in beehive fashion (Illus. 5.25). Internally, however, its ground plan is almost a rectangle (about 6m by 2.35m) and it has two opposing doorways, one in the middle of the north-west wall, the other in the south-east wall. Each of these doorways is just over 1m high. A narrow window occurs at the south-western end. The walls are well built and over a metre in thickness. The beehive construction or corbelling with its over-sailing slabs is neatly and regularly executed particularly on the interior.

Opposed doors are a feature of the traditional thatched house of the west and north of the country. It is commonly believed that the doorways of this sort were made to allow one or other to be used depending on the direction of the wind. It is also possible that they had a role in indoor milking, a cow entering via the front door and exiting in the same direction via the back door. Whatever the explanation for the origin of this feature, it precludes a central open hearth as Goulden found at Eochaill. It is likely that the hearth was placed near one end, possibly the south-western with its narrow window. If this area was the living quarters,

Illus. 5.24. 'Oghil III' during excavation: the foundation wall of the main structure is exposed; the low rear doorway is visible in the foreground.

Illus. 5.25. Clochán na Carraige: the best preserved of the island's clochans has an intact corbelled 'beehive' stone roof.

the north-eastern end may have been for storage or animals. No smoke-hole is visible but with or without one, smoke would have collected in the upper part of the clochan above the level of the lintels of the doors. Here some foodstuffs could have been smoked or fuel stored and dried. This sort of cosy smokiness, though inimical to insects and pests, did not impress one 17th century commentator on the Irish scene, who may have been just a little biased:

> 'Their cabbins full of Dirt, and Smoak
> Enough an English Man to Choake.
> Of which themselves doe take up halfe,
> The rest serves Cow, Sow, Goat and Calf,
> Who round the Fire doe in Cold Weather,
> Both eate their Meat, and lie together.
> Each cabin with two Dores is graced
> Like squirrills 'gainst each other placed.
> One still is stopp'd with Straw, and Wattle,
> When wind on that side House doth rattle,
> And when to th'other it is shifted,
> Then Dore to th'other side is lifted'.[77]

Well made clochans, like Clochán na Carraige, are stone versions of a widespread and much less permanent type of dwelling more often than not constructed of wattle and daub, or even of sods or turves, with a thatched roof. The date of this and other Aran clochans is unknown. The discovery of a whale's vertebra in Clochán na Carraige is recorded but obviously offers no clue as to date.[78] Traces of similar houses of oval plan externally and rectangular plan internally have been found at Keem on Achill Island.[79] Their date is also unknown but, like Clochán na Carraige, they could have been build in Medieval times or even later.[80]

Only a few other Aran clochans are sufficiently well preserved to give an indication of their original plan. Some are similar in design to Clochán na Carraige. Two, west of Dún Eoghanachta, also have more or less rectangular internal ground plans and opposed doorways.[81] The southern example (Illus. 5.26) is the smaller and has two small niches for storage purposes in its southern and eastern walls respectively, and a small window in its western end wall. A sketch published by Kinahan in 1867 shows that the roof had a hole in it at that time but was otherwise intact.[82] The larger northern-most clochan (Illus. 5.27) was half collapsed in the last century but had at least one window (in the northern wall) and at least one niche (in the western wall).[83]

Of the other double-doored clochans on Aran, one example deserves mention. This is Clochán an Phúca, the clochan of the ghost, which according to an 1840 drawing had an intact corbelled roof, opposed doors and a usual internal partition just over a metre in height.[84]

Other forms of clochans do occur on Aran: a roofless and more or less rectangular example with just one door lies south-west of Cill Ghobnait on Inis Oírr. Some of the mounds in

Baile na mBocht may represent the remains of collapsed circular examples of the sort commonly found in places like the Dingle peninsula, but evidence for a corbelled roof is usually lacking.

These various types of ancient settlements on Aran raise many questions. At present it has to be emphasised that both corbel-roofed structures like Clochán na Carraige and the circular huts excavated in Baile na mBocht are of uncertain date.

Illus. 5.26. One of two clocháns near Dún Eoghanachta is now ruined and has one or two external walls added to it It was nearly intact in 1867 when sketched from two angles by George Kinahan.

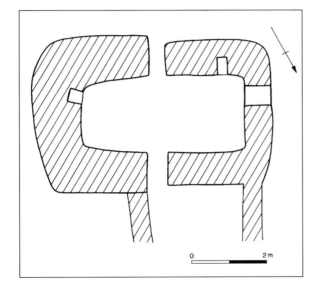

Illus. 5.27 below. A second ruined clochán near Dún Eoghanachta is now partly surrounded by collapsed stone-work but the opposed doors and traces of a window in the north-western wall (sketched by Kinahan) are still visible.

Early Christian and Medieval Aran

A remarkable number of ancient ecclesiastical remains is testimony of Aran's importance as a centre of religious ritual and learning in early Christian times from the fifth century AD. The introduction of the Christian religion to Ireland had profound cultural repercussions: new developments in art and architecture and the inception of writing were just some of the consequences. All are represented in the archaeology of early Christian Aran where Christianity may have been first established by Eanna or Enda some time around 500 AD. Reputedly trained in the famous monastery of Candida Casa, Whithorn, in south-west Scotland, he was probably the first to introduce monasticism, in the strict sense, to Ireland.[85] His monastic rule was one of great severity, a fierce regime of prayer, learning, austerity and mortification. Many disciples were attracted to this ascetic life style and among the more famous followers of Enda were Ciaran of Clonmacnoise and Jarlath of Tuam. Historical facts are few but as with many other early saintly persons legendary and superstitious details are commmoner.[86] It is claimed, for example, that Enda once crossed from Gorumna in Connemara to Inis Mór in a stone boat, a feat which had a somewhat damaging effect on the confidence of a local pagan chieftain named Corban.[87] Legend also has it that no less than 120 saints lie buried in Enda's foundation near the village of Cill Éinne. Tales like these are a mark of the religious significance of 'Aran of the Saints' for as well as being one of the great centres of early Irish monasticism, it was to endure as a centre of religious activity and popular pilgrimage for over a thousand years.

Cill Éinne

Little survives of Enda's famous monastic establishment. There were once six churches in and about the village of Cill Éinne. Four of these, including a 15th century Franciscan friary, were demolished to provide material for the Cromwellian fort at Arkin. The friary probably stood somewhere south of the village in a sheltered area of good land, perhaps just east of a holy well now called the Friars' Well. To the south irregular grassed-over traces of walls are visible and beyond these there stands the remains of a high cross (see below) and the stump of a round tower, the only one on the islands. Just the lower three metres of the tower survive, standing on a narrow plinth; no trace of a doorway is visible and, as was customary, it presumably was several metres above ground level. To the south is Tobar Éinne, a stone-roofed holy well at the foot of a low limestone outcrop with a crudely built altar or leacht surmounted by a modern cross slab beside it.

The two churches which do remain, Teampall Bheanáin and Teaghlach Éinne, probably owe their survival to the fact that they are located quite some distance from Arkin Fort possibly at the limits of the monastic complex.

Teaghlach Éinne

The simple rectangular church known as Teaghlach Éinne is located in a large graveyard near the sea-shore. Here was the monastic cemetery and an early oratory, perhaps of 9th century date, which was extended and modified many centuries later. The eastern gable and part of the northern wall are early; two typical and peculiarly Irish features of these primitive stone churches can be seen on its

regions of the west the impression of great size was usually achieved by placing large flat slabs on edge. The simple round-headed window in this wall is original too and the early church may have had an internal length of about four metres with its doorway in the western gable. At some late date, possibly in the 17th century,[89] it was extended westwards by almost three metres and a window and doorway constructed in the north wall, which also incorporates, on its exterior just below the window, a large early grave slab laid on edge. This 1.14m long sub-rectangular slab bears an early Irish inscription in two lines which reads OROIT AR SCANDLAN ('Pray for Scandlan') and it presumably once marked the grave of a person of some significance (Illus. 5.30).[90]

Illus. 5.28-9. Teaghlach Éinne is a two-period church: the eastern altar end and part of the northern wall are early, the rest and the doorway are later.

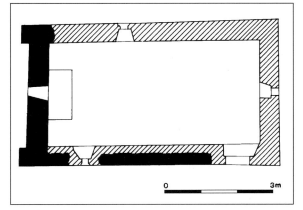

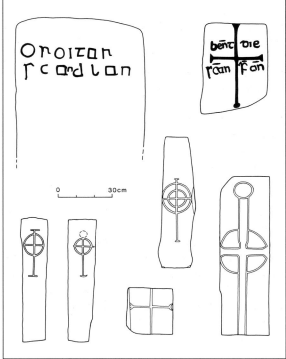

exterior (Illus. 5. 28-9). Firstly, the side walls project to form *antae*, these projections supported roof timbers and may themselves be translations into stone of the corner timbers of wooden prototypes. Secondly, the wall appears to be built of exceptionally massive masonry. Indeed, nineteenth century writers often referred to this use of roughly dressed large stones as Cyclopean.[88] In fact in the limestone

Illus. 5.30. Grave slabs at Teaghlach Éinne: two are inscribed and ask for prayers for Scandlan and for Sanctan.

A second inscribed grave slab is now incorporated, along with some other fragments, in a modern altar in the church: an Irish and Latin inscription BENT DIE F AN SCAN is cut in the four quarters of a simple Latin cross with expanded terminals. Several words are contracted as indicated by horizontal lines; expanded the wording reads (moving almost superstitiously *deiseal* or sunwise around the cross) BENDACHT DIE FOR AINM SANCTAN ('The blessing of God on the soul of Sanctan').[91] History has long forgotten Scandlan and Sanctan of Aran.

Some Medieval carved fragments are also incorporated in the makeshift altar, as are two cross-inscribed stones, a third such stone is now cemented into the wall near the door and a fourth, with a cross on two opposing faces was found in recent excavations.[92] These were probably simple grave markers.

Among the other objects in Teaghlach Éinne are two granite bullaun stones (presumably for grinding and pounding foodstuffs) and three cross fragments now cemented together.

According to tradition the grave of Enda the founder lay north of the church but today it is obscured by wind-blown sand and by more recent graves. The limited excavations undertaken in the 1980s to clear the accumulated sand from around the church did reveal a possible slab-covered grave but it was not investigated further.

High Crosses

There were at least two limestone high crosses in the ecclesiastical complex. Both were smashed to bits, probably in Cromwellian times, but one fragment of one and five pieces of the other have been found. Where they originally stood is unknown. The first cross is represented by part of its head: the upper member, the central portion and one arm. It was discovered by Conleth Manning in the 1980s excavation just beyond the eastern gable of the church. The cross head is made of a thin slab only 11cm in thickness and one segment of a thinner ring survives (Illus. 5.31). One face bears part of a crude crucifixion scene: a Christ figure with extended arms wearing a long sleeved garment pleated below the waist has a small hollow in the surviving hand perhaps indicating a nail. On the arm below this hand is a bent figure holding a pole and representing Stephaton the sponge bearer. The head and spear of Longinus are visible on what there is of the opposite arm. The other face of the fragment is decorated with a pattern of knot work within a double frame.

The second cross comprises both the three pieces cemented together in Teaghlach Éinne and two now cemented to a plinth near the remains of the round tower. It is possible to offer a tentative reconstruction of this cross on paper (Illus. 5.32).[93] One face bears the enigmatic figure of a hooded and caped individual on a horse which is mounting a step or a slab. Above this there probably was a human figure encircled by a ring of knot-work but only a pair of feet and the hem of a long pleated garment are visible. Below this is a marigold pattern, some knot-work, and a complicated design of interlaced beasts. The other face had a larger human figure carved on it (and this may have been a crucifixion scene). Above and below are various rectangular panels of knot-work, fretwork and, at the base, a design of interlocking C-shaped scrolls. The narrow sides of this cross below the arms were also decorated.[94] This cross, and the other at Teaghlach Éinne and those at Teampall Bhreacáin beyond Cill Mhuirbhigh, were possibly painted in contrast-

Illus. 5.31. Part of the head of a high cross discovered by Conleth Manning during excavations at Teaghlach Éinne in the 1980s.

Illus. 5.32. Reconstruction of several fragments of the one high cross now located at Teaghlach Éinne and near the remains of the round tower at Cill Éinne.

ing colours in ancient times, and must have been striking features of the Aran landscape.

Teampall Bheanáin

The churches of Aran are generally situated in sheltered and relatively fertile locations on the lower limestone terraces of the north-eastern coast. However, the small oratory of Teampall Bheanáin is an impressive exception. It is believed that it was dedicated to St Benignus, a disciple and successor of Patrick at Armagh.[95] It stands conspicuously on top of the hill above Cill Éinne and presumably because of its windswept position it is orientated in a north-south direction instead of the usual east-west axis (Illus. 5.33). The simple slab-lintelled door, narrower at the top, is in the northern gable wall and is a type characteristic of early stone churches. Teampall Bheanáin also has the characteristic massive masonry already seen at Teaghlach Éinne; it is one of a number of simple churches without the projecting *antae*, but

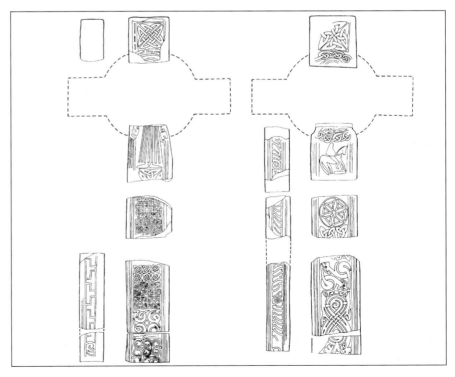

probably once had corbels at the corners to support the timbers of the steeply pitched roof. It may have been built in the 11th century.[96] There was one narrow window not in the gable opposite the door but in the eastern wall maintaining the tradition of an eastward window. One of the corner stones on the south-east exterior has the inscription CARI carved on it.

A tiny building like this could not have been used for congregational worship of any size and, at most, it could perhaps have held half a dozen people. Perhaps it was the oratory of an anchorite or hermit, or given the importance of the cult of relics in the early church it is conceivable that one of the roles of Teampall Bheanáin may have been to contain a relic of the holy Benignus. The remains of two small stone reliquaries have been found elsewhere on Aran, at Cill Comhla, below Dún Eoghanachta, and at Cill Cheannannach on Inis Meáin. Excavation in the immediate vicinity has led to the suggestion that a stone-built terrace to the east and just down hill from the church is part of a tiny double rectangular enclosure around the east, south and west of the church.[97] Part of an early cross slab was found to the south and a rectangular structure immediately to the north was used if not built in the seventeenth century. Pilgrimage activity may be the explanation for some of this occupation.

Cill Charna

Little remains of this church site north-west of Cill Éinne and nothing is known of its history. There are the featureless remnants of a small rectangular church, only the foundations surviving in places. A large cross slab once stood nearby (Illus. 5.34) and there is a blocked up holy well in the vicinity.[98] It was recorded in the last century that the water in this well was

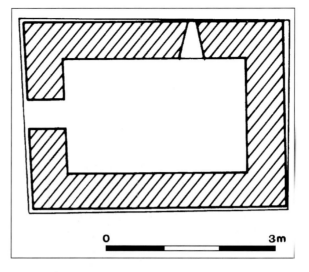

Illus. 5.33a. Plan of Teampall Bheanáin.

reputed to be unboilable and had curative properties; it was also claimed that if dead fish were put in it, they would come alive again.[99]

Cill Rónáin

Nothing is known about Rónán and if there ever was a church site here, nothing survives today. There is now a small rectangular stone-walled enclosure known as an atharla just north of Cill Rónáin, the modern village. The unusual name atharla (of which there are three or four on the Aran Islands) means a grave or a burial place and this was certainly the purpose of one such site near Mainistir Chiaráin. The Cill Rónáin enclosure was featureless in the last century[100] but today it has a small altar in it.

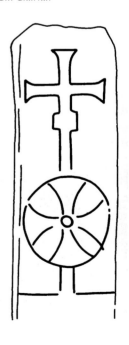

Illus. 5.34. John O'Donovan's 1839 sketch of a large cross-inscribed slab at Cill Charna.

Illus. 5.33b. Teampall Bheanáin.

TEAMPUL BENIN, ARANMORE, R.W. 2166.

Mainistir Chiaráin

An interesting collection of monuments does survive at Mainistir Chiaráin, Ciaran's monastery or church. Also known as Mainistir Chonnachtach or Connacht Monastery, it was, according to tradition, founded by Ciaran in the 6th century before he established the great monastic foundation at Clonmacnoise. The principal feature at Mainistir Chiaráin is a well preserved but very simple Medieval church. It is a rectangular structure with a lintelled or trabeate doorway in an archaic style at the west end: the door jambs are chamfered externally and the lintel is decorated with three engraved lines, a vertical line flanked by a diagonal line. There is an arched late Medieval doorway in the north wall. The finely wrought east window is an example of a western version of the Transitional style of architecture in which the round-arched Romanesque gave way to the Gothic with pointed arches and distinctive mouldings. The tall, narrow, round-headed window is widely splayed internally and framed by prominent mouldings.[101] Externally and internally the arches spring from corbels or capitals with low relief foliate decoration.

There are the remains of a small square building immediately to the north of the church, a rectangular structure to the south, and another more or less square structure to the south-east (Illus. 5.35). Several interesting cross-inscribed slabs stand nearby. One, a few metres to the north-east of the church, has a small hole near its top: according to one report this 'holed-stone' had curative properties, 'when women are sick their linen clothes are sometimes pulled through the hole. It seems to possess more of a sacred character to the peasantry than the other crosses on the Island'.[102] This may once have been the case but its original

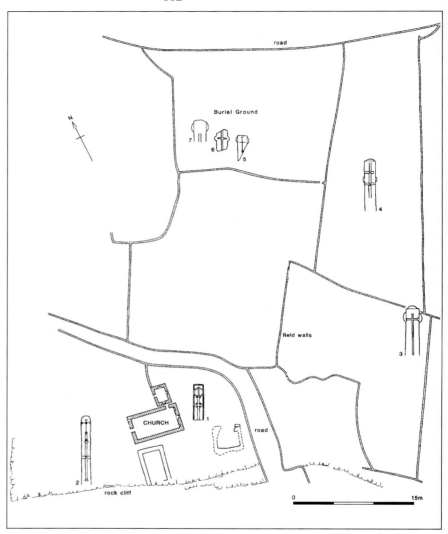

Illus. 5.35. General plan of Mainistir Chiaráin showing the approximate location of a series of cross-inscribed pillars. The three examples in a field to the north are in a small burial ground.

purpose was probably more functional. It has been plausibly suggested that the slab was really a sun-dial: 'the hole is meant to receive a stick thrust into it to serve as a gnomon and mid-day would be marked by the shadow running down the vertical diameter of the circle beneath. It is quite possible that the other hours, or at least certain other divisions of the day, were marked on the circumference by means of paint ...'.[103] The incised cross below does imply a liturgical purpose for this early time-piece (Illus. 12.6).

A remarkably tall cross-inscribed pillar stone stands in a field wall to the west of the church: it has two crosses carved on its eastern face, one above the other. Two unusual slabs stand some distance to the east and north-east: the eastern example has a Latin cross carved on its western face, the north-eastern has a double-armed cross carved on its eastern face; both slabs have bosses protruding from the top and sides giving them a rudimentary cross-like shape. These three stones may have been

boundary markers delimiting the monastic sanctuary to ensure that the limits of the holy ground were clearly marked.

Other upright cross-carved pillar stones may have stood in the general area. A small burial ground some distance north of the church contains fragments of three further cross-inscribed slabs, each with lateral bosses or arms; they have ben re-used as grave markers.[104]

The southern limits of the church site are formed by a low limestone cliff. To the west of the church at the base of this cliff is a holy well, a water-filled natural hollow in the rock, dedicated to Ciaran. John O'Donovan in 1839 claimed that it was this well which according to legend produced a fish large enough to feed 150 monks.[105]

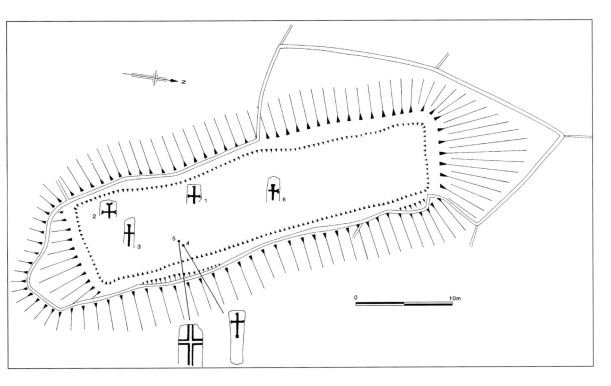

Illus. 5.37. General plan of an Atharla: a burial place for unbaptised children with a number of cross-inscribed stones of possible early date.

An Atharla

A small burial ground on a hillock near the shore, overlooking Port na Mainistreach, the bay of the monastery, is known as the Atharla. It is long, narrow and rectangular in shape and enclosed in part by a grass-grown collapsed stone wall (Illus. 5.37). A number of small stones protrude through the grass in its southern half – these may mark the graves of unbaptised children for local tradition records that this was its purpose at least in relatively recent times. However it may have a more ancient history for a number of these stones are cross-inscribed (Illus. 5.37:1-6). The simple form of the crosses makes dating difficult but they could conceivably be early. Apart from one small standing pillar stone (4) and one flat slab (5), the stones are all small rectangular blocks of limestone.[106]

Teampall Asurnaí

The small ruined church, Teampall Asurnaí or St Sourney's Church, is situated on a more or less level terrace overlooking a series of fields not far from the coast. According to tradition, Sourney was a female saint who retired to Aran from Drumacoo, near Kilcolgan, Co. Galway.[107] The church is a small rectangular structure with traces of a west door and an east window: the slightly convex shape of the external side walls is an unusual, and seemingly original, feature (Illus. 5.38).[108]
Other remains in the vicinity include traces of a featureless, stone built, rectangular structure a short distance to the west of the church. A smaller stone-built rectangle some distance to the east is reputedly the grave of the saint and is traditionally known as 'St Sourney's Bed'; the interior is featureless. Nearby is a slender rectangular pillar stone with a Latin cross on one face, and fragments of three other cross-inscribed slabs have been identified (Illus. 5.38). St Sourney's Well, to the north-west of the cross-inscribed pillars, is a large granite bullaun stone, not a natural well. It has been said that it is never empty of water though not fed by any spring.[109] A nearby thorn tree has been revered as the saint's holy bush. Sacred trees of various sorts are associated with a number of church sites and holy wells elsewhere in Ireland and there is some evidence to suggest that holy trees may have been a regular feature on early church sites and may reflect the practice of the christianisation of pagan sacred woods or groves.[110]

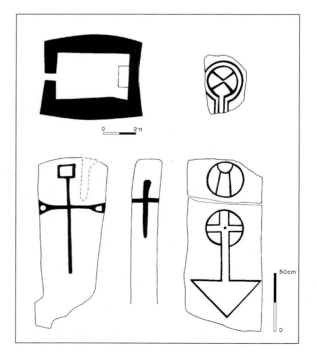

Illus. 5.38. Teampall Asurnaí (plan) and cross-inscribed grave slabs.

Teampall an Ceathrar Álainn

The small 15th century church known as Teampall an Ceathrar Álainn, the church of the four beautiful saints, lies south-south-west of the village of Corrúch. The four beautiful saints after whom it is named were Fursey, celebrated for his missionary work in Britain and on the Continent, Brendan of Birr, Conall and Bearchán. Why these four virtuous persons were commemorated on Aran is not recorded. The church itself is a ruined, simple rectangular building constructed of carefully selected limestone blocks; it has been partly restored (Illus. 5. 39-40). There is a simple window and a pointed door in the northern wall and a narrow ogee-headed window in the eastern gable above the altar. Outside and attached to the eastern end of the church is a rectangular stone-built 'leaba' which contains five plain grave slabs laid almost contiguously. This grave plot is the traditional 'bed' of the four saints and in the past people slept in it in the belief that diseases would be cured.[111]

Illus. 5.39. Teampall an Ceathrar Álainn viewed from the south-east: the leaba or grave of the four beautiful saints is attached to the end wall of the church.

A few metres south-east of the church is a holy well surrounded by a low stone wall. This apparently is Tobar an Ceathrar Álainn and even up to recent times contained the occasional token offering such as pious medals, rosary beads or buttons. Fish-hooks, iron nails, shells and pieces of crockery have also been noted.[112] The playwright J.M. Synge recorded that this well cured blindness and epilepsy and that the blind son of a Sligo woman regained his sight here.[113] It was this miraculous well which inspired his play *The Well of the Saints*.

North-east of the church and half hidden under a field wall is a bullaun stone designated a holy well on the early Ordnance Survey maps. Another bullaun stone is to be found a few fields west of Teampall na Ceathrar Álainn, here too are two tall and quite plain pillar stones and a number of small irregular mounds with smaller associated slabs. These features

possibly mark the western limits of the ecclesiastical complex.

Teampall Mac Duagh and Teampall na Naomh

Two churches are situated just south-west of Cill Mhuirbhigh. The larger, and more complex, is named Teampall Mac Duagh and dedicated to Colmán Mac Duagh who in the sixth century founded one of the most famous monasteries of Connacht at Kilmacduagh, Co. Galway. The original part of the church has the characteristic features of primitive stone churches (Figs. 5. 41-43): a lintelled or trabeate west doorway with inclined jambs, a pair of *antae* clearly visible at the western end, and the characteristic massive masonry. Like Teampall Bheanáin, this part of the church may have been built in the 11th century.[114] At a somewhat later date, possibly in the 13th century, the eastern gable was demolished and a chancel with an arch was inserted between the *antae* here. A stone now lying outside the eastern end of the chancel may be the head of the original east window. The chancel has a tall narrow east window and a smaller southern one. The final phase of alteration occurred in the 15th century when defensive parapets were added to the tops of the chancel side-walls.[115]

One of the stones of the outer northern wall (near the north-western corner) bears a puzzling low-relief carving of an animal which seems to have a bushy tail, a disproportionately long body and a small head. It has variously been described as a horse, pine-marten or fox: it is most likely a horse.[116]

A tall cross-inscribed pillar stone stands just west of the church. It is a massive slab over 2m high and it has a simple and fairly crude Latin cross carved on its rougher western face. On its eastern face, however, there is a large, well-

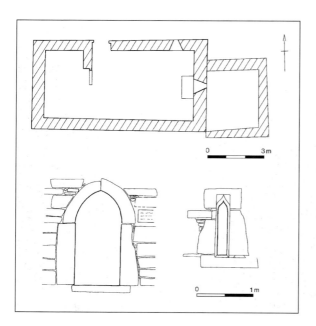

Illus. 5.40. Plan of Teampall an Ceathrar Álainn with details of north door and east window.

carved two-line, ringed, Latin cross. The ringed cross finds its finest expression, of course, in the famous series of High Crosses, and the inspiration for the ringed form of cross head has been much debated. The shape of the Teampall Mac Duagh example is a reminder that the cross within a wreath may have been one of the formative influences. It has also been suggested that this cross with its circular base is a version of the Medieval representation of a cross on an orb perhaps symbolizing the rule of Christ on earth.[117]

Not far from the church is a walled holy well, Tobar Mac Duagh, and a short distance to the south-east is Teampall na Naomh, the church of the saints. Nothing is known of this very simple rectangular oratory and only the lower levels of the walls survive. East of the church, a curving line of collapsed stone may be the remains of an enclosing wall; on the south a low limestone cliff may have formed part of the

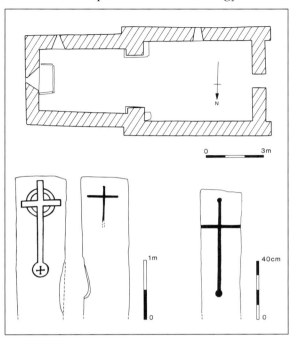

Illus. 5.43. Teampall Mac Duagh: plan of church. Below left: cross-the inscribed pillar. Below right: an early pillar stone in modern grave-yard near Cill Mhuirbhigh (after Higgins).

Illus. 5.42. A strange carving of a horse is to be seen on one of the stones of the north-west wall of Teampall Mac Duagh.

Illus. 5.41. An imposing cross-inscribed pillar stone stands in front on the west end of Teampall Mac Duagh whose simple lintelled door-way and antae are visible.

enclosure. This limestone bluff continues west and north-westwards. A 20m long section of a stone rampart of massive construction sits on top of this bluff just south-west of Teampall Mac Duagh: its original line cannot be traced. When George Petrie visited Aran in 1821 about half of this great enclosure survived, the rest having been destroyed when some of the houses of Cill Mhuirbhigh village were built.[118] The modern graveyard near the village contains an early pillar stone with a simple Latin cross on it (Illus. 5.43).[119]

Cill Comhla

Cill Comhla is a small and very ruined ecclesiastical site to the north of the stone fort of Dún Eoghanachta. The remains of an irregularly shaped enclosure, now just a low stony bank of U-shaped plan, lie just below the bluff on which the fort stands (Illus. 5.44).[120] The full extent of the enclosure is not clear, but it probably surrounded at least two collapsed clochans and, possibly, a small stone church of which only one low wall remains. It certainly enclosed the most significant surviving feature – part of a stone-built shrine or monumental reliquary. The broken remnants of two side-stones and one triangular end-stone are visible, and originally the shrine would have resembled a ridge-tent about 1m high. These slab-shrines are an essentially Irish type of monumental reliquary and they were built to house the bones of some holy person. In some cases a circular hole was even cut in one of the stones to allow the faithful to touch the relics or the sacred earth within. A perforated end-stone of this sort is to be seen at Cill Cheannannach on Inis Meáin.

Who Comhla was is not recorded and no one remembers why his or her bones were venerat-

ed. The relics of a revered saint or the grave of the founder of a monastery were often marked in a special way. One form is the rectangular leaba or saint's bed or grave so often recorded on Aran, the slab shrine is another distinctive form, and both may have been important focus points in the rounds of the Medieval pilgrim.

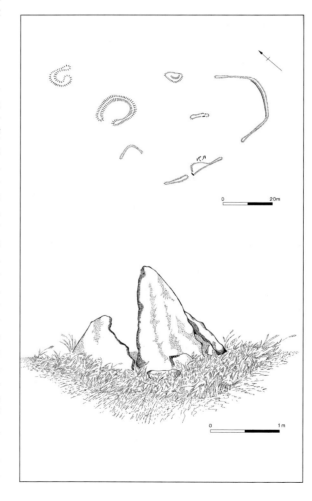

Illus. 5.44. Cill Comhla: plan (above) of the remains of an enclosure with irregular structures. The remains of the slab-built shrine (below) are situated at the south-west limits of the site.

Na Seacht dTeampaill and Teampall Bhreacáin

The complex of buildings known as na Seacht dTeampaill, or the Seven Churches, near the village of Eoghanacht, probably provides the best illustration of how important the combination of church, well, saint's bed, holy graves, high crosses and cross-slabs may have been for the devotions of both the ecclesiastical community and the visiting pilgrim (Illus. 5. 45-47). Despite the popular name, there are only two churches here, one is Teampall Bhreacáin or St Brecan's Church, the other Teampall an Phoill, the 'Church of the Hollow'. The other buildings which survive all seem to be domestic dwellings.[121]

Very little is known about Brecan, he is probably the same person commemorated in the name of Kilbrecan townland, near Quin, Co. Clare.[122] According to an anonymous 15th century poem, which may be a versified version of a lost life of the saint, he was originally named Bresal and was the son of Eochaidh, king of the Dál Cais of Clare.[123] As a bishop his first mission was to Aran perhaps late in the fifth or early in the sixth century. Here he is said to have destroyed a pagan idol, Brecán, taken his name, and converted the pagan sanctuary into a Christian diseart or monastic retreat. In his words:

'I came to Iubhar [of Aran] and established my settlement, everyone was pleased in turn when I expelled the devils.
Fierce Brecán Cláiringneach was in Iubhar before me, I undertook to expel him and I sanctified his place'.

Some other verses of this poem, which is addressed to his kinsman and pupil Toltanach, give a fascinating picture of the activities and preoccupations, saint-like and not so saint-like, of an early holy man:

'I got my seven requests, God was satisifed with my offerings, not least of them was that on an enclosed piece of land He created a sanctuary for pilgrims.
I left this dísert and went on a circuit with Ciarán when I performed the functions of my calling at Dooras and at Durlas of the sunny rooms.
A dispute arose between me and Ciarán of good understanding, along this boundary wall as far as Durlas I left Dooras without water.
Boldly I cursed the cows of Dooras when they would feel the torment of thirst at the onset of bulling and lactation . . .

My blessing and my lasting blessing on the family of brave Mael Domhnaigh, may their enemies not destroy them provided they pay my taxes.
May the great related family not lack leading men. I am entitled to a full grown pig from every herd from the Clann Mael Domhnaigh. If they give them every single year I will ward off every robber from them . . .

A blessing on the O'Hallorans, over me their power is great, I bequeath well-being to their cows and excellence of entertainment.
If the stately people of Mael Domhnaigh fail me may their herds of pigs be depleted and their leading men the fewer for it . . .

I am the prophetic Brecán, accomplished son of a king of Munster, telling the story of the western world. Arise, O Toltanach'.

Illus. 5.45. Aerial view of Teampall Bhreacáin: 'the Seven Churches'.

Illus. 5.46. General plan of Teampall Bhreacáin: despite the popular name of 'the Seven Churches' there are only two churches here, one dedicated to the saint, the other known as Teampall an Phoill.

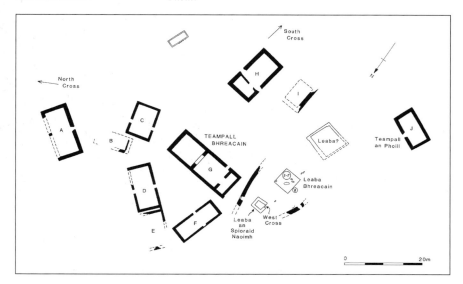

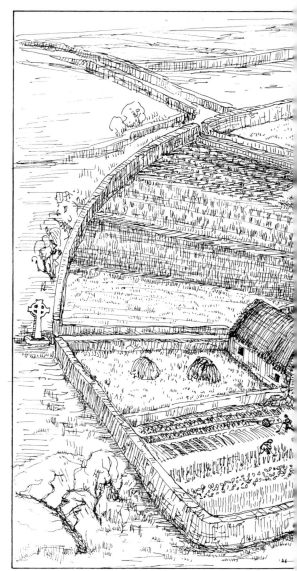

Illus. 5.47. An artist's reconstruction of Teampall Bhreacáin as it may have been in or about the 16th century when it probably was an important pilgrimage centre. Some of the stone houses which survive were probably for the use of visiting penitents and pilgrims.

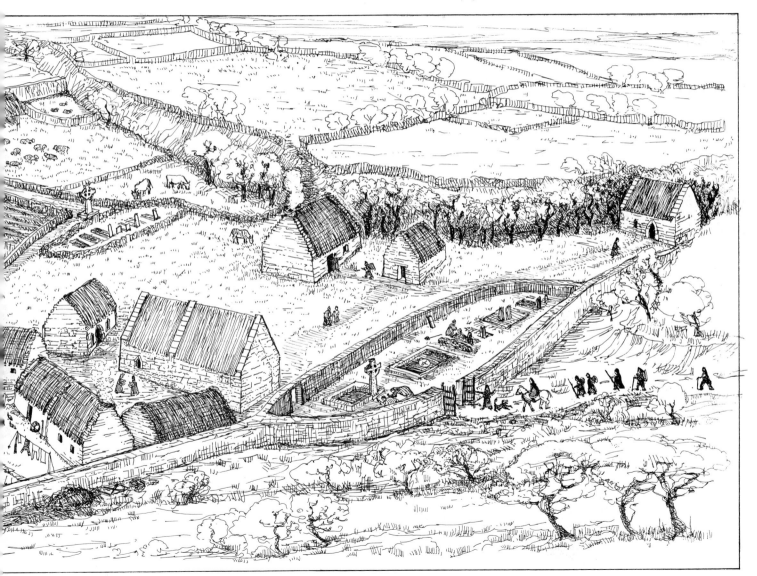

The church called Teampall Bhreacáin is the largest building on the site and is of various dates (Illus. 5.48). The earliest remains are to be seen in the north and west walls with massive limestone masonry and one of a pair of *antae* surviving. Its original doorway was, presumably, in the south wall. This part of the church predates the 13th century and its stonework is clearly distinguishable from the smaller masonry of the rest of the building. The church was more than doubled in size in the 13th century with the addition of a chancel, chancel arch and a slender Transitional window in the east gable. Minor modifications, in the fifteenth or sixteenth centuries, included an internal partition wall and the doorway and window now in the south wall of the nave. A stone set in the inside wall of the western gable bears the inscription OR[OIT] AR II CANOIN (Say a prayer for two canons).

The second church on the site lies to the south-west. The unusual name, 'Church of the Hollow', was its popular name in the 17th century. It is a small, simple rectangular structure with a narrow trefoil-headed window in the

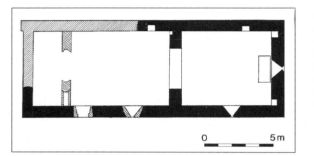

Illus. 5.48. Teampall Bhreacáin, the church of St Brecan, dates to various periods: the earliest part is the north-west corner with one of the antae *still in place. Most of the building is a 13th century extension.*

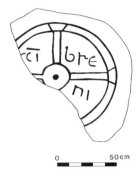

Illus. 5.49. Teampall an Phoill is a simple rectangular church of 15th or16th century date.

Illus. 5.50. The probable grave of St Brecan is a small rectangular enclosure with part of a large grave slab inscribed with the saint's name.

east gable, a doorway with a pointed arch and a simple window, both in the north wall (Illus. 5.49).

The rest of the buildings in the complex seem to be domestic dwellings of one sort or another. The ogee or trefoil-headed windows and pointed doorways in Buildings C and H indicate that these at least are of later Medieval date. Several (C, D, F, H) have opposed doorways as in clochans like Clochán na Carraige and the more recent traditional thatched houses of the west. Some of these unusually substantial structures may have been the dwellings of the religious community, others may have served as guest houses for pilgrims. These pilgrims would probably have participated in a prayerful circuit of various penitential stations, or leabaí or saints' graves, and indeed other sacred features such as holy wells, trees and high crosses.

The grave of the founder was certainly one important focus of religious activity. A small rectangular setting of stones south-west of Teampall Bhreacáin may be the grave of the saint for among the grave slabs which lie on it is the greater part of a particularly large sub-rectangular grave slab with rounded corners: it bears a Greek cross within a double circle and the remains of an inscription which reads SCI BRECANI (that is Sancti Brecani: [the grave or slab] of St Brecan: Illus. 5.50).[124] Several other grave slabs are nearby: two bear traces of inscriptions; one which may read ORAIT AR ANMAIN SCANDLAIN (Pray for the soul of Scandlain) is now virtually illegible,[125] the other reads OR[OIT] AR MAINEACH (Pray for Maineach).

Another rectangular setting of stones to the south may be a second leaba or penitential station. According to one 19th century account 'when any member of a family falls sick, another member makes a promise, that if the sick one recovers, the person promising will sleep one, two or three nights in one of the saints' beds. One bed at the Seven Churches (probably St Brecan's Bed) is said to be occupied pretty regularly'.[126]

To the east, beyond the domestic buildings a rectangular setting of limestone slabs set on edge encloses what appear to be five slab-covered graves with an approximately east-west orientation (Illus. 5.51). Four interesting cross-inscribed slabs stand on its western side but one of these has been moved to this spot since the 1930s. The others are probably in their original positions: one is a slender pillar with a Latin cross with splayed terminals and a base shaped like a pair of bent legs. This may be a representation on stone of a processional cross (perhaps a metal one) set into a stand of some description.

The second is a cross-inscribed slab with the Latin inscription VII ROMANI (Seven Romans). This stone has provoked many theories and some have suggested that it marks the last resting place of seven Roman pilgrims. It has also been argued that it might be dedicatory rather than funerary and erected in honour of the seven martyred sons of Symphorosa who are named in the Irish martyrologies of Oengus and Gorman. Another interesting hypothesis is that it commemorates seven people who favoured the Roman or Continental church in a famous 6th century controversy about matters such as the date of Easter and the proper form of clerical hair-style. Peter Harbison has offered the plausible suggestion that this stone was erected by seven people who had made the pilgrimage to Rome and who had also come to Teampall Bhreacáin.[127]

Illus. 5.51. Four cross-slabs now stand near a grave plot on the south-eastern side of the site. One of these (second from the left) bears the famous VII ROMANI inscription, another is dedicated to Thomas the Apostle.

It is also possible that this slab commemorates the Seven Sleepers of Ephesus. Their story was one of the most widespread and popular legends of the early Christian and Medieval world: seven young noblemen of Ephesus concealed themselves in a cave to escape the persecution of the Roman Emperor Decius. They fell into a miraculous sleep and awoke several centuries later in the reign of the Christian Emperor Theodosius II. The legend originated in the 5th century and was popular because it affirmed the belief in the resurrection of the dead. It figures in Anglo-Saxon and early Irish literature.[128]

A third slab bears a representation of another processional cross set in a stand and has an inscription, which may read CRONMAOIL, carved on it.[129] The fourth has a finely carved and elaborate ringed cross with the dedicatory inscription TOMAS AP (Thomas the Apostle);[130] this slab was moved here from the church Teampall Bhreacáin some years ago.[131]

History does not record why this particular apostle should be commemorated on Aran.

A number of other cross slabs, are to be found on this site (Illus. 5.52) and several holy wells are also recorded. Tobar an Spioraid Naoimh, a well dedicated to the Holy Spirit, was venerated in the 19th century; as were Tobar Bhreacáin (dedicated to St Brecan) and a third well to the north of the site.[132]

The remains of three high crosses have been found here.[133] All were smashed to pieces centuries ago, but in every instance sufficient survives to give a clear idea what they originally looked like.

The shaft of the West Cross stands at one end of the rectangular walled structure known as Leaba an Spioraid Naoimh near Teampall Bhreacáin. Several pieces of the head lie nearby but part of the middle of the cross and one arm are missing (Illus. 5.53). Originally it was just over 2m high with a ringed head, deeply cusped at the angles of arms and shaft. A cruci-

Illus. 5.52. A range of cross-inscribed slabs of different sizes and dates are preserved at Teampall Bhreacáin: some are dedicatory, others may have marked graves

fixion scene is carved on the west face, the figure of Christ being flanked by a pair of smaller figures. Two further human figures are placed horizontally below the outstretched arms. Above is a panel of crude interlace forming a cruciform design, below a panel of thick knot-work and near the base a design comprising a spirally twisted pair of biting animals, possibly snakes. The other face is decorated with panels of interlaced knot-work and one panel of rectilinear fret-pattern.

The basal fragment of the shaft of the North Cross stands at one end of a small rectangular enclosure some distance north-east of Teampall Bhreacáin. Fragments of this cross lie nearby and these were apparently collected among the ruins of the complex in the 19th century. A little of the shaft and the arms are still missing but it is clear that originally this cross, with a height of over 4m and carved from one great limestone slab, must have been one of the most imposing of the Aran high crosses (Illus. 5.54). The figure of Christ is flanked by two figures and there is a poorly executed panel of interlace forming a cruciform design above and a panel of fret design and two panels of interlace below. The other face bears a series of panels of interlaced knot-work.

The crucifixion scenes on both of these crosses are fairly rudimentary: the legs of the figure of Christ, for example, are shown but no clothing is indicated. Presumably a painted short tunic or loin-cloth was added and indeed the various decorative panels may have been painted too. The pairs of flanking figures may be representations of the two thieves, or of Longinus the lance-bearer and Stephaton bearing a cup of vinegar. It is impossible to be certain given the absence of detail but the latter pair are more common on Irish crucifixion scenes.

Illus. 5.53. The shaft of the West Cross stands at one end of a leaba near Teampall Bhreacáin; the fragments of the shattered head lie nearby.

Illus. 5.54. The North Cross at Teampall Bhreacáin was broken into over ten pieces not all of which have been recovered. When it stood over 4m high and when it was painted in contrasting colours (as may well have been the case), it must have been a striking feature of the pilgrims' circuit.

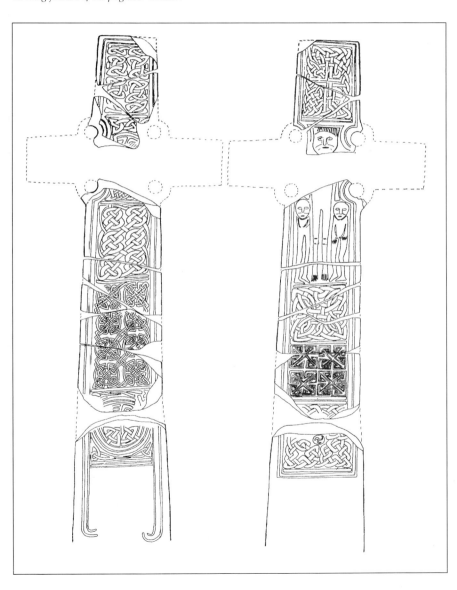

The original position of what is now called the South Cross is not known. Its fragments were collected amongst the ruins in the 19th century and cemented to a plinth of limestone blocks on top of a low limestone bluff, above and to the south of Teampall Bhreacáin (Illus. 5.55). This unfortunate treatment obscures one entire face. The cross itself is broken into at least seven pieces. It has an asymmetrically ringed head and the greater part of the exposed face is ornamented with panels of interlaced knotwork and fret patterns.

These three high crosses were probably erected in the 12th century; they may well have marked the limits of the ecclesiastical sanctuary and were very probably significant focal points in the circuit of the Medieval pilgrim. The number of stone buildings, cross-slabs and crosses here are eloquent testimony of the former importance of the site, important enough, perhaps, to attract pilgrims who had also been to Rome. But historical references are very few: Aran was one of more than half a dozen holy places which a certain Heneas Mac Nichaill was obliged to visit to atone for having strangled his son in or about 1543. He very probably did his penitential rounds here at Teampall Bhreacáin as well as elsewhere. Aran also figures in a list of places of popular devotion to which Pope Paul V granted papal indulgences about 1607 and this was no doubt a considerable encouragement to both the devout and the superstitious participants in the pilgrimage trade of the period.[134]

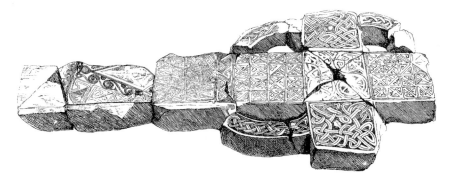

Illus. 5.55. The South Cross at Teampall Bhreacáin (after Margaret Stokes.)

Illus. 5.56. Cill Cheannannach, Inis Meáin.

Inis Meáin: Cill Cheannannach

The principal church site on Inis Meáin is Cill Cheannannach. It lies close to the eastern shore and is protected on the west and south by rocky cliffs. A modern sub-rectangular enclosing wall surrounds a simple rectangular church of sizeable limestone masonry with a lintelled west doorway and a small triangular-headed east window (Illus. 5.56). Projecting corbels, a rare feature on early Irish stone churches, occur at either corner and these (like *antae*) would once have supported the wooden barge boards of the gables. Much of the enclosure is filled with 18th, 19th and 20th century grave slabs

Illus. 5.57. Triangular end-stone of a slab-built shrine at Cill Cheannannach: the hole was made to allow the faithful to touch the relics within.

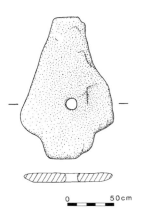

0   50cm

and these graves have probably obliterated other early features.

There was once a slab shrine here, for one end stone survives, but where it originally stood is not known (Illus. 5.57). The surviving stone is interesting, like the Cill Comhla end-stone, it is a flat slab of triangular shape but it has a circular hole near its base and just above a tenon which must once have slotted into a basal piece. The shrine probably held the holy bones of the church's founder. The Northumbrian story of Ultan, 'a blessed priest of the Irish race' who could 'ornament books with fair markings' illustrates what may well have happened here: when the earth had eaten his body, Ultan's bones were disinterred, washed and carried in clean vestments to dry in the sun and then placed 'in the inside of a prepared tomb which stood on the floor of the blessed church'. Who Ceannannach was is uncertain: the son of a Leinster king according to one tradition, a female saint according to another.[135]

It is possible that the name may be a reference to Gregory the Fairheaded, Gríoir Ceannfhionnadh, after whom Gregory's Sound between Inis Meáin and Inis Mór is named.[136] A holy well, Tobar Cheannannach, lies some 30m north-west of the church.

Very little survives of other church sites on Inis Meáin: only some of the foundations of Teampall na Seacht Mac Rí (the church of the King's seven sons) remains and they are obscured by more recent walling. Atharla Chinndeirge is close by, it is the rectangular leaba of a female saint of this name, and is surmounted by a relatively modern stone cross. Her holy well is a short distance to the southwest.

Teampall Mhuire was a small 15th century church but nothing remains of it except a granite bullaun stone (used as a font) and one or two other fragments now in the modern church nearby.[137]

Inis Oírr: Cill Ghobnait

The church site of Cill Ghobnait on Inis Oírr (Illus. 5.58) is dedicated to St Gobnait of Ballyvourney, Co. Cork, who is still venerated on her feast day there on the 11th February. Why there should be a connection with Aran is not clear though one tradition has it that Gobnait came from Clare, fleeing an enemy and, having spent some time at the Cliffs of Moher, came to Aran.[138] Even though she is considered to be the patron saint of beekeepers, she obviously cannot be credited with having anything to do with Aran's peculiar bumble bee, *Bombus muscorum smithianus*. The church

Illus. 5.58. Plan of the church site of Cill Ghobnait, Inis Oírr, showing church, clochán, graves and bullaun stones.

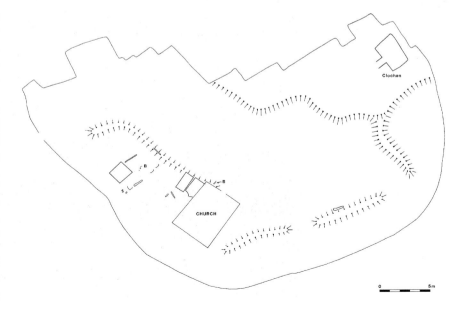

Illus. 5.59. The church of St Gobnait and the nearby roof-less clochán.

at Cill Ghobnait is a small rectangular building with lintelled west doorway with inclined jambs and a simple east window (Illus. 5.59). It was probably built in the 11th century.[139] Several stone-built graves lie to the south of the church and there are two bullaun stones nearby. Traces of low stony banks both to the south and north indicate that the ecclesiastical enclosure may have been sub-divided but no trace of an original enclosing wall survives. To the west below a low cliff is a small ruined clochan of sub-rectangular plan; its corbelling survives only to a height of 1.50m and the interior measures a mere 3 by 2 metres. If this was a hermit's cell, of man or woman or both, it was probably one of warm smoke-filled sanctity.

Tobar Éinne, a holy well dedicated to St Enda, is situated almost three quarters of a mile to the south-west. In the 1930s religious emblems were still to be seen there, it was said to never run dry and was noted for its miracles.[140]

Teampall Chaomháin

At first glance Teampall Chaomháin or St Cavan's Church appears to have sunk deep into a sandy hill close to the north shore of Inis Oírr. In 1684, according to the historian Roderic O'Flaherty, this church and, to the north of it, the saint's tomb with 'a square wall built about it' were situated 'on a plain green field in prospect of the sea'. Since then the church, which must have stood on a low flat knoll, has been inundated by blown sand and surrounded by an accumulation of graves (Illus. 5.60). There are traces of a midden of shell fish in the sand nearby.

The sand has now been cleared away from the walls of the church which is of somewhat more complicated form than usual: it is essentially a nave and chancel building with a trabeate door in the west end, and a pointed south door and chancel arch. Westropp thought that these two late features were insertions into a nave and chancel structure of the one date,[141] but it is clear that the narrower chancel and the chancel arch are additions, a century or two later, to a smaller rectangular oratory of 11th century date.[142] The west door is now the entrance to a small late annex which is usually considered to have been a sacristy.

The saint's bed or grave is just north-east of the church: originally it was a rectangular arrangement of stone slabs which enclosed a fine cross-slab (Illus. 5.61). These have now been incorporated in a small, modern roofed building. It was here, in the saint's grave, that Roderic O'Flaherty recorded that 'sick people use to lie over night, and recover health of God, for his sake'. He went on to declare: 'I have seen one grievously tormented by a thorn thrust into his

Illus. 5.60. Teampall Chaomháin, Inis Oírr, has been inundated by sand in the past. Today a stone wall surrounds the church in an attempt to exclude the encroaching sand.

Illus. 5.61. The saint's grave north-east of Teampall Chaomháin is marked by a fine cross-inscribed slab now protected by a small building.

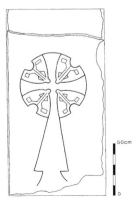

eye, who by lying so in St Coeman's burying place, had it miracuously taken out, without the least feeling of the patient, the mark whereof, in the corner of his eye, still remains'. According to O'Flaherty this grave also had the power of adapting itself to the size of every person who lay in it and cures were still being reported here at the beginning of the twentieth century.[143]

The recumbent cross-inscribed slab on which the faithful lay is the most ornate example on the Aran Islands. A Latin cross, with a splayed shaft on a narrow base, has the four quarters of the cross-head decorated with an unusual and intricate pattern of rectilinear and C-shaped motifs. Various writers have argued that encircled cross designs like this are based on the *flabellum*, a liturgical fan, though why the symbols of fan and cross should be combined is not clear.[144]

Cill na Seacht nIníon

Cill na Seacht nIníon, or the church of the Seven Daughters, is a puzzling site almost lost in a rocky landscape of small fields in Ceathrú an Chaisleáin south of O'Brien's Castle. The site seems to have been a circular cashel or stone fort modified as an ecclesiastical enclosure. Traces of a substantial cashel wall (with a north-south diameter of about 27m) survive for almost three-quarters of its circumference; this is not traceable on the south and on the east where various walls and small enclosures occur beyond the presumptive line of the original enclosing wall. In the southern part of the cashel there is a rectangular pile of dry masonry presumably a leacht or altar, or penitential station; several stones protruding through the grass nearby may mark graves.

Three conjoined rectangular walled structures

lie outside the line of the cashel wall on the east and the easternmost of these contains a tall cross-inscribed slab sadly broken into three pieces in or about the late 1970s (Illus. 5.62).[145]

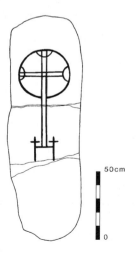

Illus. 5.62. Cill na Seacht nIníon seems to have been a stone fort modified as a church site of which little survives. A fine cross-inscribed slab is now broken into several pieces by vandals.

50cm

0

The cross itself is a simple two-line Latin cross with a ringed head, but it is represented as standing on a more or less rectangular base, the sides of which are formed by two small crosses. This may be an echo of the custom of flanking a large cross with two smaller ones representing those of the two thieves.

Almost nothing is known about the Seven Daughters though there is a tradition that they were the daughters either of a British or a Leinster king: the memory of their collective name and these stony remnants are all that survives here. However, their cult was fairly widespread in Connemara where a number of holy wells bear the name Tobar na Seacht nInÍon.[146] One other site on Inis Oírr with female associations is the so-called Cathair na mBan ('the fort of the women') which is located near the late 18th century signal tower (one of a number on the western coasts built to warn of a French invasion) south of O'Brien's Castle. Far from being a fort Cathair na mBan appears to be a ruined circular cairn about 13m across; it may possibly be a prehistoric hill-top cairn.

O'Brien's Castle

The most conspicuous monument on Inis Oírr is O'Brien's Castle or Caisleán Uí Bhriain, also known as Dún Formna, formna meaning the top of a hill. The substantial though irregular stone wall which surrounds the castle may be a prehistoric or early historic stone fort modified in the Middle Ages: a sort of bastion of rectangular plan and uncertain date occurs on the west (Illus. 5.63). The entrance is on the northeast and about 17m outside of this entrance some very large stones are clearly visible (for a stretch of almost 25m) in the lower levels of a modern field wall. This may be the remains of an outer wall: perhaps an out-work protecting

Illus. 5.63. O'Brien's Castle (Dún Formna), Inis Oírr. The late 18th century signal tower (built to warn of a French invasion) is visible on the lower left.

the entrance but possibly once surrounding the hill.[147] Only archaeological excavation will tell whether there was once an ancient stone fort on this spot.

Little is known about the history of the castle which commands both the shore below and extensive views to the north and east. It was probably built in the 14th or 15th century by one of the Clann Thaidhg Uí Bhriain, a branch of the O'Briens of Clare, who held Aran since at least the 13th century for it is recorded in 1277 that the merchants of Galway paid this family a tribute of wine to keep the bay free of pirates. For a century or two this and other

O'Brien castles, and O'Brien galleys, must have had an important role in controlling the seaward approaches to the town of Galway.

The castle itself is a small rectangular two-story structure, now ruined particularly on the south; much of this destruction took place in 1652 when Galway (and Aran) surrendered to Sir Charles Coote of Cromwell's Parliamentary forces. Some restoration work was undertaken here in the last century.

The door, in the north-east wall has been modified, but gave entry to a window-less vaulted ground floor chamber with another vaulted chamber on either side: only the side room on the south-east had a narrow window, and it may have been a guard room. As in tower houses elsewhere, the ground floor, ill-lit if lit at all, was used mainly for storage, the living quarters were above. Stairs would have given access to a first floor hall which had windows in all but the north-west wall. From this floor a mural stairway, the steps still to be seen in the ruined south-west wall, led to a wall-walk and parapet and, possibly, to further quarters in an attic below a steeply pitched roof. Whether slated or thatched, this roof was protected by a high crenellated parapet with one narrow opening surviving on the south-east. Alternating slabs of the wall-walk formed gutter and spout and projected externally through the base of the parapet. Though especially necessary in the wet Aran climate this drainage system also served to weaken the parapet and is one reason for its ruinous condition.

The living quarters were not large, the first floor area measures only about 10 by 4.5m and a room above would have been considerably smaller; however, it should not be forgotten that various other structures such as flimsier timber buildings probably stood nearby.

Indeed the remains of several clochans were reported in the enclosure in 1877.[148]

Two further minor details are worth noting: apart from the small trefoil-headed south-west window on the first floor, the only carved stones are two projecting corbels each carved with a primitive human face (Illus. 5.64). One stares out towards Galway and Connemara from the north-east wall, the other looks

Illus. 5.64. A protective ritual at O'Brien's Castle? Two primitive stone heads stare blankly from its walls towards Connemara and towards Clare. Were they meant to ward off evil?

blankly out from the south-east wall towards Clare. Their purpose is unknown but they can hardly be just decorative; the schematic depiction of just eyes, nose and mouth is possibly a deliberate primitivism recalling ancient, pre-Christian representations of human heads. Were they placed here as ritual protection to guard some unknown O'Brien from ancient evils far beyond the holy shores of Aran?

Acknowledgements

I am grateful to Jane Conroy for the translation of the passage from Nicolas Bouvier's work (reproduced by kind permission of Editions Payot). My thanks too to the many students of archaeology who studied the ancient monuments of Aran with me throughout the 1970s.

Acknowledgements for illustrations (all John Waddell and Angela Gallagher unless otherwise stated)

Illus. 5.1. Ordnance Survey of Ireland permit no. 5878.
Illus. 5.2-3. Plans, DeValera and O Nualláin 1972.
Illus. 5.5. Drawing, Angela Gallagher courtesy of National Museum of Ireland (nos.4-5, W.F. Wakeman).
Illus. 5.7. Photo, Office of Public Works.
Illus. 5.8. Plan, Claire Cotter, Discovery Programme.
Illus. 5.11. Drawing, T.J. Westropp.
Illus. 5.12. Photo, T.H. Mason.
Illus. 5.13. Drawing, Claire Cotter, Discovery Programme.
Illus. 5.14. Photo, Office of Public Works.
Illus 5.15-16. Plans, T.J. Westropp, Photos, Charlie Byrne.
Illus. 5.17. Plan, T.J. Westropp, Photo, Cambridge University Collection of Air Photographs.
Illus. 5.18. Plan, British Library, Stowe Mss.
Illus. 5.19-20. Photos, Cambridge University Collection of Air Photographs.
Illus. 5.23 Drawing, John Waddell and Anne Korff.
Illus. 5.25. Photo, Office of Public Works.
Illus. 5.26-27. Drawing, G.H. Kinahan.
Illus. 5.29. Plan, Con Manning, Photo, Office of Public Works.
Illus. 5.30. Drawing (cross slabs), Con Manning.
Illus. 5.31. Photo, Jim Bambury, Office of Public Works.
Illus. 5.33. Plan, Con Manning, Photo, T.H. Mason (courtesy of Ulster Museum).
Illus. 5.34. Sketch, John O'Donovan.
Illus. 5.43. Drawing (pillar stone), Jim Higgins.
Illus. 5.45. Photo, D. Pochin Mould.
Illus. 5.47. Drawing, Anne Korff.
Illus. 5.49. Photo, Office of Public Works.
Illus. 5.54. Drawing, John Waddell.
Illus. 5.55. Drawing, Margaret Stokes.
Illus. 5.60. Photo, T.H. Mason.
Illus. 5.61. Drawing, William Walsh.
Illus. 5.63. Photo, Cambridge University Collection of Air Photographs.

Ilus. 6. 1. St Enda (some-times Eanna), the saint most closely associated with the Aran Islands, especially Inis Mór, flourished towards the end of the 5th and the beginning of the 6th centuries. Ryan, in Irish Monasticism *(1931), described him as the founder of Irish monasticism and many stories exist that tell of other early Irish Christians, among them St Colmcille, St Jarlath of Tuam, and St Ciaran of Clonmacnoise, spending time under the direction of St Enda before returning to the mainland and establishing their own monastic settlements. Most of these stories are probably legendary, but they attest to a strong tradition that was later to make the Aran Islands a popular place of pilgrimage. According to a 12th century life of St Ailbe, who, according to one version of St Enda's life, secured Inis Mór for the saint, 'No one but God alone knows the number of saints buried there'. St Enda's Feast Day is March 21st. The illustration shows a window from the stained glass studio of Sarah Purser of St Enda in the beautiful parish church in Spiddal (built in 1904), designed by William A. Scott.*

CHAPTER 6

St Enda of Aran : Tracing an Early Irish Saint

J.W. O'Connell

'The isles of Aran are fameous for the numerous multitude of
saints there living of old and interred, or there trained in religious
austerity, and propogating monasticall discipline in other parts;
venerable for many sacred churches, chappells, wells, crosses,
sepulchres, and other holy reliques of saints still there extent, as
monuments of their piety; reverenced for many rare priviledges of
sacred places therein, and the instant divine punishments inflicted
on such as dare violate or prophane them; frequently visited by
Christians in pilgrimage for devotion, acts of pennance, and miraculous virtues there wrought'

Roderic O'Flaherty
Description of West or H-Iar Connaught

If Ireland has become famous as the land of saints and scholars, then the three islands of Inis Mór, Inis Meáin, and Inis Oírr – traditionally known as Ara na Naomh (Aran of Saints) – have a strong claim to be the resting place of the highest concentration of these champions of early Irish Christianity. Indeed, the 12th century author of the life of St Ailbe describing the part played by this saint in gaining Inis Mór for St Enda, calls it 'an island of saints', and declares: 'Nemo scit numerum sanctorum qui sepulti sunt ibi, nisi solus Deus' (No one but God alone knows the number of saints buried there).

The trouble is, lacking any means of questioning God about the lives of these early Aran saints, patient inquirers find themselves echoing the words of Sir Thomas Browne who concluded, after considering the ironies of fame in his *Hydriotophia, or Urn Burial*, that 'the greater part must be content to be as though they had not been, to be found in the Register of God, not in the record of man'. A melancholy conclusion, and certainly a frustrating one for the historian. Just how frustrating can be seen if we focus our attention, as I intend to do in this chapter, on the best known saint connected with Aran, St Enda. Often described as the patriarch of Irish monasticism, St Enda's closest associations are with Inis Mór, the largest of the three islands.

Ryan, in *Irish Monasticism*, summarizes the most important contribution made by the saint to the early Irish church: 'With Enda, as far as can be ascertained, monasticism in the strict sense (of embracing vows, complete seclusion from the world and a stern system of discipline) began in Ireland'.

In beginning our search for this early saint we may begin by noting the chief sites on Aran associated with his name. All of these, with one exception – Tobar Éinne on Inis Oírr – are on the largest island.

Even before we set foot on Inis Mór we encounter St Enda in the name given to the bay, Cill Éinne Bay, on whose north-western shore lies Cill Rónáin, the principal town of the island. On the south-east shore is the village of Cill Éinne (the church of Enda), and the same name also has been given to the townland division that includes the entire south-east portion of Inis Mór.

In this same area, situated among the sandhills at the eastern end of an Trá Mhór, we find the ruins of a small stone church called Teaghlach Éinne (St Enda's house or, perhaps, household), and a graveyard which tradition identifies as the final resting place of St Enda and over a hundred other nameless saints. Two high crosses, some of the pieces of one now cemented together and standing close to the ruined round tower, while a fragment of a second was only discovered during an excavation in the 1980s, belonged to the monastic settlement but date from a period long after the time of St Enda.

This round tower, now only a low stump but reported by Petrie to have been some sixty metres high before being blown down in a storm, also belongs to a later period. A small, roofed holy well dedicated to the saint lies to the south, but this too is almost certainly a later attribution.

The ruins of an exceptionally small church, Teampall Bheanáin, believed to be dedicated to St Benignus, one of St Patrick's disciples, stand on a hill overlooking Cill Éinne, and historians and archaeologists have argued that this church originally marked the western perimeter of the monastic 'city' that possibly dates back to the time of St Enda himself.

Unfortunately, when the Cromwellians fortified Inis Mór in the middle of the 17th century, and built Arkin Fort to defend the harbour, St Enda's church and a later Franciscan friary, were, according to O'Flaherty, 'both demolished for building the cittadell with their stones'.

In c.1645, shortly before the Cromwellians arrived, Dr. Malachy O'Kealy, Archbishop of Tuam, compiled a list of the churches of the three islands and gave a description of two churches associated with St Enda:

'1. The parish church (to wit of the first island) commonly called Kill-Enda, lies in the county of Galway and half barony of Aran; and in it St Endeus, or Enna, is venerated as patron, on the 21st of March. (In his description of Teampall Bheanáin, O'Kealy adds that it is 'situated near the parish church, which is called sometimes Kill-Enda, that is the cells or cell of St Endeus, and sometimes Tempull mor Enda, or the great church of Endeus').

'2. The Church called Teglach-Enda to which is annexed a cemetery, wherein is the sepulchre of St Endeus; with one hundred and twenty seven other sepultures, wherein none but saints were ever buried'.

These are the sole physical traces of St Enda on Inis Mór – Teaghlach Éinne, a holy well which tradition associates with the saint, and a village that preserves the general location of the long vanished 'great church of Endeus'. However important these things may be for determining the age of Christianity on the island, they do not aid us greatly in coming any closer to the saint we are trying to trace.

Can we get any closer to the saint through the documents that tell us of his life?

Before we answer this question, we should first note that most scholars place St Enda at the end of the 5th and the beginning of the 6th centuries. These dates, even if only roughly accurate, confront us with a difficulty at the very start of our search. For the fact is, there are very few authentic or historically reliable documents from this period of Irish history.

The earliest life of St Enda we possess, which O'Donovan dates to c.1390, is attributed to Augustine MacGradin, an Augustinian canon who was born in 1340 and died in 1405 at Clonmacnoise. It is sobering to consider that this first life was compiled nearly eight hundred years after the period in which the saint is alleged to have lived.

One of O'Donovan's observations indicates another difficulty. 'It is to be regretted', he writes, 'that no older life of the archimandrite is now accessible. For MacGradin does not appear to have been well acquainted with the topography of Aran, and it is obvious (from an incorrect reference made by MacGradin to another early saint) that he mistook the text of the old writer from whose work he compiled the life of St Enda. Either this is the case or Colgan has not given his words correctly'. O'Donovan also draws attention to a further difficulty affecting the reliability of MacGradin's life of the saint: the stages by which it has reached us.

A little background information will be helpful in explaining this.

After the defeat of Hugh O'Neill in 1603 an ambitious plan was put in train by a dedicated group of Franciscan scholars at the newly founded College of St Anthony in Louvain. Faced with the threat that knowledge of the early history of Ireland was in danger of disappearing in the wake of the English conquest, a herculean task was undertaken to preserve in written form whatever could still be gathered together from the extant sources, themselves scattered far and wide throughout the country and in religious foundations on the continent.

Out of these labours came one of the most important historical compendiums we have for early Irish history, the *Annala Rioghacta Eireann*, more commonly known as the *Annals of the Four Masters*. This remarkable work, under the general direction of Michael O'Cleirigh, is a compilation, year by year, of the most notable events, heavily slanted towards those with an ecclesiastical significance, in early Irish history. The final recension of the *Annals of the Four Masters*, completed in 1636, was undertaken by John Colgan, whom we have already met in O'Donovan's comment on MacGradin's Life of St Enda. Colgan was a member of the family of O Colgain, hereditary erenaghs (lay custodians) of the church of Donaghmore in Inishowen north of Derry.

In 1645 Colgan, described by O'Flaherty as 'this learned and laborious compiler of the lives of our national saints', pub-

Illus. 6.2. John Colgan (c.1590-1658) was a Franciscan friar and Professor of Theology at Louvain whose best known work, a six-volume compendium of early Irish history and the lives of the Irish saints, remained unfinished at his death. Colgan was also responsible for the final recension of the Annals of the Four Masters, *to which he also gave the title by which it is known today.*

The third volume of his projected six volume compendium, which was in fact the first volume to be published, appeared in 1645 under the title Acta Sanctorum Veteris et Majoris Scotiae seu Hiberniae. *In it are recounted the lives of the Irish saints whose Feast Days fall during the first three months of the year. It is here that we find Colgan's version of the life of St. Enda, which was compiled out of Augustine Mac Gradin's 14th century life, as well as other sources that are now lost. Although John O'Donovan regarded Colgan's life as of little historical value, according to more recent scholars it is possible to detect at least some authentic material about the saint.*

lished the first volume of his major undertaking *Acta Sanctorum Veteris et Majoris Scotiae seu Hiberniae*, in which are recounted the lives of the Irish saints whose feast days fall during the first three months of the year, including St Enda, whose feast day was March 21St

Colgan followed this in 1647 with *Trias Thaumaturgae*, in which he published all the known texts relating to the lives of Saints Patrick, Brigid and Colmcille. Unfortunately, the death of his colleague, Michael O'Cleirigh in 1645, who had returned to Ireland in order to make copies of all manuscripts in the Irish language relating to church history, removed one of the Colgan's chief co-workers. Colgan himself died in 1658, leaving in manuscript three works on the early Irish saints of the continent.

The Life of St Enda as printed by John Colgan is, as the historian James Kenny points out, undoubtedly a late production, worked up from several different sources, now lost and therefore impossible to date, as well as MacGradin's 14th century life. Kenny agrees with O'Donovan's assessment that this life is of little historical value. This is hardly surprising given the considerable scale of time involved, and the complicated and altogether obscure circumstances of its transmission. As M.R. James indicates in *The Wanderings and Homes of Manuscripts,* early texts, whether in manuscript form or as bound books, are prey to an almost limitless number of dangers as they make their way through the centuries.

Leaving aside for the moment consideration of the internal evidence in our early texts and manuscripts, which will be considered in the next part of this chapter, it is clear that Colgan's life can only be seen as the *end result* of a lengthy process of transmission that possibly goes back to an originally oral tradition about the saint that presumably began shortly after his death.

Who first committed this oral tradition to manuscript is not known. Nor can we have any idea how long a time passed before it was set down in this fashion. Was the earliest life of Enda composed by a disciple? Was it composed on the island, or years, possibly centuries, later, and on the mainland? We don't know.

Manuscripts are fragile and, before the advent of printing, sometimes unique.

We cannot know how many copies were made of a supposed early life of the saint, nor have we any 'control' text that would enable us to assess textual variants that almost certainly crept into the early manuscript over the centuries – copyist errors, small changes designed, perhaps, to harmonise disparate accounts of the same events, additional passages introduced by a scribe in order to explain some aspect of the original story that, by the time he came to transcribe his material, had become confused or no longer possible to understand.

We cannot know where our supposed early life of the saint was housed. We cannot know if portions of the early text were lost of mutilated in some way, and the missing or destroyed material supplied by the ingenuity of a later transcriber, who may have misunderstood or even invented material in order to fill out the blanks.

By the time O'Donovan was writing in the mid-19th century these problems were clearly recognised. He questioned, we recall, whether MacGradin was familiar with the topography of Aran, and also whether Colgan correctly transcribed MacGradin's own manuscript.

To sum up, we do find ourselves with a source for the life of St Enda, but it is one which is hedged round with problems both as to the nature and reliability of the original materials used in its composition, and the tangled and mostly obscure process by which these materials have been transmitted to us over the centuries.

Yet even if these difficulties did not exist, there still remains the problem of what kind of documents these saint's lives are supposed to be. Why were they composed? And what purpose or purposes were they intended to serve?

To begin with a fundamental point, they cannot in any way be described simply as biographies, written to present their subjects as clearly and accurately as their sources permit. Biography, in the sense that we can speak of Richard Ellmann's biography of James Joyce, makes use of critical methods of source evaluation that would have been altogether foreign to the authors of these 'sacred' lives.

For the motivation behind these lives was specifically religious. They were intended to edify those who read them by demonstrating clearly, through incidents and reported words, the sanctity of the person being written about. Furthermore, they often had a propagandising function in that they aimed to demonstrate the antiquity of a particular religious practice or a specific monastic foundation.

And this is not all. Because they were the lives of holy men and women, touched by God in all the details of their existence, they partook liberally of the supernatural. In fact, as Kenny points, 'the essential proof of an individual's sanctity was his power to work miracles'. For example, the hagiographers (a much better term for these authors, who were writing 'sacred' and not secular lives) often borrowed freely from already existing lives of saints when an incident seemed appropriate for the saint they were dealing with.

This practice, which sounds like plagiarism to the modern mind, was not seen as such by these authors; rather it was 'the exercise of an equal right to draw on a common stock of hagiographical lore'. From the earliest account of a Christian martyr, Stephen, in the Acts of the Apostles, it was common practice to use prototypes from the Old Testament and the life of Christ as patterns for giving shape to the incidents of any particular saint's life in this way assimilating their activities to the divine plan.

Furthermore, in a fashion similar to what Gospel scholars now recognise operates in reports of Jesus' activities, 'there cannot be the slightest doubt that the monastic hagiographers themselves provided a large portion of the anecdotes of the miraculous set forth in their compositions, in the pious belief, perhaps, that a saint must necessarily have performed such wonder-works'. Writers of saint's lives wrote to emphasise the importance of their particular saint, and they would assume quite naturally that they were capable of any suitably miraculous event.

In the specific Irish context we also have to allow for the strong tendency towards the magical. The saint, in the eyes of these authors, was a man of power, and the early saints were seen as inheriting the magico-religious associations of the druids. It is remarkable that in many of these early lives little attention is paid to the specific moral dimension, and the saints often behave in a manner more nearly akin to that of the wonder-worker and shaman than the more conventional picture of sainthood we are familiar with in, for example, St Bonventure's Life of St Francis.

As we will see when we come to examine the material belonging to the life of St Enda, these early saints exhibited a kind of holy cantakerousness. It is a quality that did not escape the attention of Gerald of Wales in the 12th century who concluded that 'the saints of this land ... are more vindictive than the saints of any other region'.

That it was not only foreigners who noted this trait can be shown by the remark attributed to Cuimmin Condeire about the 6th century St Ruaddan, that 'he loved cursing'. An even more direct parallel with the notion of an uncanny and potentially dangerous power belonging to these early saints which links them to the druids, we have the distinctly nervous response made by the teacher of the 6th century St Senan who, when told that his pupil had just performed a miracle, observed 'It would be wise to be careful with him – woe to the one who crosses him'. There is more of Merlin the magician than Mother Teresa in these early Irish saints. Kenny provides a useful summary of these points:

'The mind of the Irish people during the early Christian era was, fundamentally, the product of countless ages of paganism. The popular legends moulded under a pagan, or semi-pagan, attitude of mind contained a large amalgam of 'magic' and 'superstition', those survivals of primitive religion. So far, therefore, as the *acta sanctorum* depend on popular legend they are, in some degree, records of primitive and, superimposed thereon, an upper section of mythology. Myth and magic were ejected from their positions of supremacy by the coming of Christianity, but the evidence does not indicate that the sphere of operation of either was extensively diminished'.

All of these factors operate much more strongly when the figure being written about, like St Enda, belongs to the early centuries of Irish Christianity. We can expect to find little of historical value, and a great deal that belongs to a strange world, where magic and folk-belief and the still surviving motifs of the pre-Christian pagan world keep rather uneasy company with the new, and no less fabulous, impulse of early Irish Christianity.

St Enda is recognised as a saint by the Roman Catholic Church. This might seem an unremarkable statement until we realise that there were literally hundreds of 'saints' who do not share this distinction. As Farmer points out, 'place-name evidence and the number (and obscurity) of Celtic saints seem to indicate a far greater proportion of the inhabitants of Ireland, Scotland, Wales and Cornwall were more holy than those of any other area'.

The explanation for this otherwise curious state of affairs, he argues, 'is due to the extended use of the term 'saint'. It appears, in other words, that the word had a much wider reference in Celtic areas, and could refer simply to pious church-founders or even learned ecclesiastics.

In the *Vita Sanctorum Hiberniae*, three orders of Irish saints are distinguished. To the first order belong the saints of the time of Patrick – 'all bishops, eminent and filled with the Holy Spirit, numbering three hundred and fifty'.

It is to the second order that St Enda belongs: 'In this second order there were in fact few bishops but many priests, to the number of three hundred. They had diverse liturgies and diverse rules of life, but they celebrated one Easter (this refers to the dispute over the date of Easter between the Celtic Church and Rome which was settled at the Synod of Whitby in 664 in Rome's favour), and they practised one tonsure, from ear to ear'.

St Enda, in the list that follows is in the exalted company of other well-known saints of the Irish church – Finnian, Abbot of Clonard; Colman Mac Duagh of Kilmacduagh; Comgall, Abbot of Bangor; Ciaran of Clonmacnoise; Columba of Iona; and Brendan of Clonfert, celebrated for his legendary voyage.

St Enda's feast day, as already noted, is March 21St This was probably the traditional date of the saint's death, which would have been celebrated as the occasion of his entry into heaven and the company of the saints who have gone before. Whoever St Enda may have been, the Catholic Church has given him its seal of approval.

Roderic O'Flaherty, who is given high marks by the notably sceptical O'Donovan, presents a brief summary of St Enda's life in his *West or H-Iar Connaught* written in 1684:

'St Enda, son of Connal Dearg of the notable Orgiellian family of Ulster, and brother-in-law, by his sister, to King Engus of Munster... followed the evangelicall precept of forsaking a rich patrimony for Christ, and this merit brought him to be abbot beyond seas in Italy, before he came with one hundred and fifty religious persons to Aran, where he lived to his decrepit age, upwards of fifty-eight years'.

It is clear that O'Flaherty in this account relies almost entirely on MacGradin's life of St Enda, although he demonstrates a degree of critical control in dispensing with the more fabulous aspects included in his primary source.

When we turn to MacGradin we suddenly find ourselves almost overwhelmed with the kind of specific information that lends itself to the development of a full-scale life of the saint. However, as we have seen this is just the kind of detailed account that arouses suspicion that other than historical considerations are at work.

St Enda's (in Irish: Éinne or Ende; in Latin: Endeus or Enna) birthplace is given as County Louth, and he is said to have been born sometime in the middle of the 5th century (the date 461 has been suggested), the son of Connell Dearg, the king of Oriel, a territory some historians have identified with the modern diocese of Clogher but which others have extended to include not only Louth but Monaghan, Armagh and Fermanagh.

On the death of his father, Enda succeeded him and proceeded to behave in a manner typical of the pre-Christian (and we might add, the post-Christian) Celtic chieftains of the time, warring against his enemies.

Three of Enda's sisters are said to have been nuns and one of them, Fanchea, was in charge of a convent in the neighbourhood of Enniskillen. Returning from battle to the convent, Enda tells his sister he has been avenging the death of his father. Fanchea tells her brother that their father is in hell, presumably because he died ignorant of the message of Christ.

One of the young postulants had caught Enda's eye and, exercising a kind of Celtic *droit de seigneur*, he demands she be given to him. Fanchea, telling him to wait outside, approaches the girl and asks her if she would rather love the spouse Fanchea loves, that is, Christ, or an earthly spouse.

The young postulant declares, of course, that she desires to be wed to Christ. Fanchea leads her to a chamber where she bids her lie on a bed, whereupon the girl piously dies. After covering her face with a veil, Fanchea admits Enda who is struck to his very soul when he discovers she is dead. Fanchea, in the manner of these saint's lives, immediately begins to tell Enda that this will be his fate if he does not repent and accept Christ.

As MacGradin writes, 'And then St Fanchea discoursed to him of the pains of hell and of the joys of heaven, until the young man's tears began to flow. O! the wondrous mercy of God in the conversion of this man to the true faith! For even as He changed the haughty Saul into the humble Paul, so out of this worldly prince did he make a spiritual and a holy teacher and pastor of His people. For having heard the words of the holy virgin, despising the vanities of the world, he took the monk's habit and tonsure, and what the tonsure signified, he fulfilled by his actions'.

After founding a monastery at Killanny in Louth, Enda is encouraged by his sister to complete his spiritual education at the famous monastic foundation of Candida Casa (the White House) at Whitethorn, Galloway in Scotland, where he is said to have studied under St Manchan or, alternatively, St Ninian, the apostle to the Picts.

As St Manchan is said to have flourished in the 7th century and St Ninian in the 5th century, the later makes more historical sense. St Manchan was probably favoured by MacGradin because he was known to be an Irish abbot.

MacGradin next has Enda make his way to Rome where 'attentively studying the examples of the saints, and preparing himself in everything for the order of the priesthood, having at length been ordained priest, he was pleasing to the most high God'.

While it is not impossible that Enda, like many other Irish clerics over the early centuries, may have actually gone to Rome, there was a definite ecclesiastical motive in associating him with the spiritual capital of Christendom, which was to emphasise that from the very beginnings of the Irish Church, the see of Rome was regarded as pre-eminent in matters of doctrine and discipline.

While we may doubt this visit, and the monastery Enda is said to have founded in Italy, we next find him in Drogheda (a return to this area from Scotland would be more likely), where he established several more churches on either side of the Boyne.

Next we are introduced to another of Enda's sisters, Darenia, the wife of Aengus, king of Cashal (the *Annals of the Four Masters* give his death as 489). At this point MacGradin's life is supplemented by the 12th century life of St Ailbe. According to this life, it was through the intercession of St Ailbe that Enda was granted 'that island which is known as Aran', which the king said he had never even heard of! In MacGradin's version, the king's hesitation is said to be due to his reluctance to give any land for God's use that was not 'good and fertile and easy of access'.

In any case, Aengus eventually granted Aran to Enda, but the fact that the 12th century life of Ailbe makes no mention of the relationship MacGradin says existed between the king of Cashel and Enda, and that he has to rely on Ailbe's help in gaining the island, raises the suspicion that this relationship is a later pious fabrication.

Enda soon discovered that Aran was under the control of a Fir Bolg chieftain named Corban. But first Enda had to get to the island (the sources are silent as to the travel arrangements of his one hundred and fifty followers) and he apparently decided that a demonstration of his powers was in order.

So Enda took ship in a stone boat, the kind of transport that only saints in the making would chance to use. As this unusual craft approached Inis Mór, Corban's subjects were seized by panic and headed for the coast of Clare.

Our sources dispute what happened next. According to one account Corban, 'a second pharaoh, *obduratus in malicia*', fled along with his people but proposed a further test of Enda's powers. Safely ensconced near Corcomroe in Clare, he had a cask filled with corn placed near the shoreline. If, he declared, the cask was transported to Enda on Inis Mór by itself, he would surrender the island to Enda. Of course, the cask arrived safely, and the spot where it landed, a small bay adjoining on the east side an Trá Mhór, is known to this day as Port Daibhche (the port of the cask) and a stone, reputed to be the saint's boat, is still pointed out.

Illus. 6.3. Teaghlach Éinne is situated at Cill Éinne and stands in a large graveyard near the shoreline. According to tradition the grave of St. Enda lies to the north of the church, although it is impossible to say if this tradition is accurate. The drawing shown was done by William Wakeman (1822-1900), a skilled artist and antiquary who recorded hundreds of monuments for the Ordnance Survey undertaken in the 1830s. In an article published in Duffy's Hibernian Magazine *in 1862, Wakeman described Teaghlach Éinne 'as a perfect example of the oldest Christian work to be found in western Europe'. Wakeman was also the author of* A Handbook of Irish Antiquities *(1848), as well as other local and general guides, all illustrated by him.*

Illus. 6.4. Teampall Bhreacain or St Brecan's church, stands not far from the village of Eoghanacht, and is associated with St Enda's famous adversary. St Brecan is said to have destroyed a pagan idol, taken his name, and established his church on the site of a pagan sanctuary. The saint was not happy with St Enda claiming primacy on Inis Mór and proposed a contest to settle the matter. Both men would begin saying Mass at the same time and then set out walking, and where they met would establish the ecclesiastical division of the island. However, Brecan started Mass earlier than the agreed time and started walking. St Enda, meanwhile, learned of the deception and prayed for assistance. Accordingly, St Brecan's feet stuck in the sand at Cill Mhuirbhigh and St Enda got the lion's share of the island. This drawing is by T.J. Westropp, a pioneer archaeologist/antiquarian often described as the 'father of Burren archaeology', and comes from one of his note books, now in the Royal Society of Antiquaries, which show him to have been a talented artist as well as a patient recorder of early Irish antiquities.

Illus. 6.5. Mainistir Chiaráin, or St Ciaran's monastery or church, was founded, according to tradition, by the saint before he set up the great monastic foundation, with which his name is intimately connected, at Clonmacnoise. An attractively simple medieval church, referred to by Roderic O'Flaherty as 'Mainistir Connachtach, that is the Connaught Monastery', Wakeman, whose drawing of it is shown, described it as 'the finest church on the island'.

Another account of Corban's vacating of the island has the unfortunate chieftain agreeing to take a forty days visit to Corcomroe to see if God wanted Enda to have possession. Enda proceeded to round up all Corban's horses and drive them over a cliff, after which the poor creatures were swept first to Inis Meáin and finally to Inis Oírr. What this was supposed to prove is obscure.

In any case, Corban caused no more trouble. However, it would appear from some accounts that Enda's claim to the island was not immediately accepted even by his holy companions. Enda divided the island between nine other monks, but kept half for himself.

Quite justifiably we may feel, the others grumbled and decided to go on hunger strike – a well documented pre-Christian method of protest – but then two doves flew in from Rome, one dropping a missal into Enda's lap, the other dropping a cape around his shoulders to indicate his primacy. This timely miracle seemed to settle matters, but Brecan at Eoghanacht refused to accept this as the final word.

So Enda proposed a means to resolve the jurisdictional logjam. He and Brecan would say Mass, each beginning at the same time, Enda at Cill Éinne and St Brecan at Teampall Bhreacáin, and when they were finished they would start walking towards each other, and where they met they would divide the island. Brecan, perhaps recalling the doves and the stone boat, started saying Mass before the agreed time, finished, and set out walking. He should have known better. For Enda got wind of the deception and prayed for assistance. As Brecan and his monks reached the sea at Cill Mhuirbhigh their feet stuck fast in the sand, and Enda got the lion's share of the island.

The only problem with these colourful stories of St Enda and St Brecan is that many scholars question whether the latter saint ever existed because we are told in another early document, a poem put into the mouth of Brecan, whose original name was Bresal, that Brecan was originally the name of an idol on the island destroyed by Bresal. So it is possible that Brecan started his literary life not as an early Christian saint, but a pagan god who was Christianised and given a fictitious identity.

Illus. 6.6. St Brendan of Clonfert (c.484-577 or 583), is the subject of one of the most popular saints' lives of the Middle Ages, the Navagatio Sancti Brendani (The Voyage of St Brendan). In c.558 St Brendan founded the monastery of Clonfert in County Galway. The saint's fame rests on the Navagatio, said to have taken place between 565 and 573. As a literary production it belongs to the early Irish genre of the imram, the story of an adventure at sea, of which the Imram Maelduin (The Voyage of Maelduin) is perhaps the best known example and from which the Navagatio itself borrows incidents.

With its colourful account of sea monsters, talking birds, islands made of glass, and even an encounter with the demon-tortured Judas Iscariot, the Navagatio was long thought to be wholly legendary. But in 1976 the writer and traveller Tim Severin, in a wooden-ribbed leather skinned boat modelled on the kind that would have been used by the saint, showed it was possible for St Brendan to have sailed from Ireland to Newfoundland by a North Atlantic route.

The illustration shown is an ink and watercolour representation of St Brendan by Wilhelmina Margaret Geddes designed in 1924 for Curraun Church on Achill Island, Co. Mayo.

Having settled the question of who was in charge on Inis Mór, Enda's monastic city flourished and, as the years passed, a host of other holy men (and the occasional woman – St Urnaí or Sourney, for example) made their way over the water to submit themselves to the stern rule of the saint: St Finian of Clonard, St Finian of Moyvilla, St Jarlath of Tuam, St Kevin of Glendalough, St Carthach of Lismore, St Colman of Mac Duagh, and St Brendan of Clonfert who apparently stopped off for a blessing before setting off into the unknown (possibly the fictitious unknown unless we accept the result of Tim Severin's voyage).

Two of the most famous early saints, St Ciaran of Clonmacnoise and St Colmcille, also spent time under the discipline of St Enda, but their stories could not be more different. While St Ciaran's departure was attended with tears and St Enda's moving words – 'O my brothers, good reason have I to weep, for this day has our island lost the flower and strength of religious observance'. St Colmcille was driven away.

Evidently St Colmcille had fallen in love with the island, and he requested permission from St Enda for some land on which to build a church. St Enda refused, so St Colmcille persuaded St Enda to grant him as much land as his cloak could cover, to which the saint agreed. However St Colmcille had prayed for divine assistance and his cloak miraculously grew in size until it had covered an extensive piece of ground.

Furious at being bested by methods he must have believed were his alone to use, St Enda declared St Colmcille an outlaw and ordered a strict penance of fasting. Finally, when the emaciated saint was ready to leave the island, St Enda refused permission for anyone to carry him to the mainland. So Colmcille set off on a marathon swim that eventually brought him to Kerry. A poem attributed the saint, which probably dates from at least the 10th century, laments his departure from Inis Mór. Another version of Colmcille's story has the saint laying a terrible curse on the island in response to his rough treatment.

St Enda's fame and the austerity of his rule – to test the sanctity of his disciples he had them go naked into the frame of a currach and if water came in they were in a state

of sin – ensured that his name would endure. He died, full of years, in 549 and was buried, according to tradition at Teaghlach Éinne.

What can we salvage from the hectic efflorescence of legend, myth, and magic? What are the facts that we can take with a reasonable degree of certainty? They do not amount to very much, and we must even treat this bare minimum with caution.

After we have wielded the critical scalpel, we are left with a few facts that would seem to pass the test of authenticity. Enda was born in Louth, but according to the great Celtic scholar Heinrich Zimmer, Connell Dearg was a fictitious figure. According to David Hugh Farmer, in his authoritative *Oxford Dictionary of Saints*, Enda's father was named Ainmure. It is likely that as a young man Enda, like many young men of his time, followed the profession of a soldier for a brief period.

At some point he embraced Christianity, though the circumstances will probably never be known . That he then went as a postulant to the monastery of Whithorn in Galloway under the direction of St Ninian, traditionally the apostle to the Picts of Scotland, is also among the facts that seem plausible. There was, we know from Bede, the historian of the early English Church, much contact between Ireland and Scotland, which had been heavily colonised by the Irish of Ulster in an earlier period.

The tradition that connects Enda with Drogheda is strong, though the exact nature of this connection is, again, unclear. The story of Enda using his family connections to gain a foothold on Inis Mór seems unlikely. Yet, given the tremendous importance of kinship in early Irish society, this is something about which we should keep an open mind.

Nonetheless, we must recall the remarkable fact that Aenghus seemed unaware even of the existence of the island he is supposed to have given to his brother-in-law. The alternative version which has Ailbe interceding on Enda's behalf sounds more likely. But this too could have been motivated by the desire to associate Ailbe with such a famous monastic site as Enda's had become in pious memory by the 12th century. On the other hand it might just be a bit of ecclesiastical oneupmanship.

That Enda certainly did establish a monastic settlement on Inis Mór seem undeniable. That his rule, along with the well known inclination of the early Irish saints to seek out isolated places in which to pursue sanctity, it is not unlikely that other monks spent time on Aran. But exactly who they were, and if they included the list of famous saints found in the Enda tradition must remain open. What is also undeniable is that those who did spend time on the island returned to the mainland where they spread the fame of St Enda and the spirituality of Inis Mór.

And that is about all that is left when the historians and philologists have finished their labours. And, as we must again stress, even this rests on no authentic first-hand sources and so may be inaccurate in part or altogether. The association of other famous saints, such as Ciaran of Clonmacnoise and Colmcille, probably rests on nothing more than the desire on the part of later hagiographers to bring the principle saints of this period into contact with one another.

Before concluding we should glance at an interesting theory that meets head on the problems raised by our paucity of reliable information about the saint.

Recognising how insecure the foundation for even the few things we can claim to know about St Enda, the late Hubert Butler drew what he regarded as the obvious conclusion – that he never existed as an historical personage at all. In a delightfully speculative essay entitled 'Influenza on Aran', Butler declared, 'My guess would be that the saints were the fabulous pre-Christian ancestors of pre-Celtic and proto-Celtic tribes and amalgamations of tribes'.

Referring to other Celtic tribes of the earliest period, he argues, 'We know that the Esuvii had Esus as ancestor, the Lepontii had Lepontius, the Salassi had Salasus'. Who was the ancestor of the Eneti-Veneti the tribe Butler's argument concentrates on? Surely someone like Enetus or Venetus. 'But we know these proper names only in their Romanized form where the singular ended in -us, the plural in -i. The Gaulish form could easily have been, or become after several generations in Ireland, something like Enna or Enda...'.

It is an ingenious theory, and this brief summary does not do justice to the very plausible arguments Butler marshals to support it. But common sense utters a strong protest. Granted that the secure facts about St Enda are meagre in the extreme, and that they are hopelessly entangled with legendary material, to take the step of denying the very existence of the saint seems an unnecessarily extreme way of dealing with the problem.

St Enda existed in the 6th century and was associated with the earliest Christianity in the remote outpost of Inis Mór. Our records for this early Irish saint are certainly more precarious than we would wish them to be, but, even allowing for all the intervening difficulties, that they point back, through who knows how many layers of legend, to a real individual, is something about which we can feel confident. Yet if we are obliged to reject Butler's theory, we can enthusiastically endorse another point he makes. 'For the Irish people to forget their saints is for them to forget their childhood. We are emotionally and intellectually committed to them. They beckon us along a private road that leads not only to the Irish past but to the past of Europe. It is through them that we can learn about the youth of the world and the infancy of religion'.

Acknowledgements for Illustrations

Illus. 6.1. Photo, A.Korff.
Illus. 6.2. Drawing, After Fra Emmanuello da Como, National Gallery of Ireland.
Illus. 6.3. Drawing, W.F. Wakeman.
Illus. 6.4. Drawing, T.J. Westropp.
Illus. 6.5. Drawing, W.F. Wakeman.
Illus. 6.6. Drawing, Wilhelmina Margaret Geddes, National Gallery of Ireland.

*Illus. 7.1. Arkin Fort at the
end of the 19th century.*

CHAPTER 7

Arkin Fort:
the military history of a garrison outpost on Inis Mór

Paul Walsh

Arkin

Towards the south-western end of Inis Mór stands the village of Cill Éinne. Prior to the 19th century, this small settlement had been the administrative centre and principal harbour of the islands. The seaward side of the village is dominated by a massive stone wall and rectangular tower, remnants of the fort built by the Cromwellians, in 1652-3, on the site of a pre-existing castle.[1] In the medieval and early modern periods the village – or town as it was then called – at Cill Éinne was known by the name Arkin, variously spelt Arkyn or Ardkin. The Irish form, Aircín, signifies a natural creek or harbour, a name also fairly common along the Connemara coastline,[2] and the presence of such a feature may well have influenced the initial choice of location for the Early Christian settlement and subsequent castle. However, it is not known when or by whom a castle was first constructed here. It is possible that the sept of the O'Briens, who effectively controlled the Aran Islands from, at least, the late 13th to the mid-16th century, had some form of stronghold on this site. The earliest reference to Arkin castle as such dates to the later 16th century.[3]

The Commonwealth Fort

The military history of Arkin properly begins in the middle of the 17th century when Ireland became engulfed in that calamitous eleven-year conflict which devastated the whole country. In the folk memory of the native Irish one individual alone stands condemned for the resultant catastrophe: Oliver Cromwell. And he has become immortalised in the very name by which the remains of Arkin fort were traditionally known: Ballaí Chromwell, Cromwell's walls.[4]

With the execution of Charles I, in 1649, and the triumph of the Parliament in England, attention was turned to the subjugation of Ireland. In that year, Cromwell began his devastating campaign in the eastern half of the country and thereafter the Irish armies were beaten one by one until the war was brought to a close in 1652. On the 12th April in that year the Cromwellian forces entered the town of Galway. The articles of surrender, signed a week earlier, included terms for both the 'soldiers of the garrison of Galway and Isles of Arran'. A detachment of soldiers and some ordnance had been ordered to be sent to the islands, during the previous April[5] and it is likely that many of these would have been stationed at Arkin castle. The Cromwellian authorities recognised the importance of having a garrison on the islands and immediately began constructing fortifications at Arkin. The nearby Franciscan friary and St Enda's church were pulled down and the stone used to build the new works.[6] In late November or early December of that year, before the fort was finished, it was captured by the Irish with the help of some of the islanders. The blame for the loss of Arkin was laid firmly at the door of the commanding officer, Captain Deyas, whose 'supine carelessness and negligence' were deemed to have caused this disaster.[7] The capture of the fort so alarmed the Cromwellian commissioners, perceiving it as some manifestation of God's displeasure, that they ordered a day of fasting and humiliation to be observed throughout all the precincts.[8] Nevertheless, not relying on providence alone, they immediately sent a large force by sea to retake Arkin which surrendered on 15th January 1653. It appears that the fort was then completed and a full company of foot soldiers (one hundred men) was garrisoned there.[9] In October 1655, a large boat and five men were ordered to be provided to fetch firing for the soldiers there. A small garrison from Galway had been placed in the castle at Lettermullan specifically for this purpose. From here the black Connemara turf was brought over to the islands.[10] It should be noted, however, that the commissioners did not simply cater for the physical welfare of the army, but were ever zealous in providing for their spiritual needs as well, and we can be sure that they appointed an 'able, pious, and orthodox minister of the gospel' to serve with the soldiers on Inis Mór, as had been done, in 1656, for the garrison on Inishbofin.[11] When it came to burying their dead the Cromwellians did not use the local cemetery but, instead, chose a site by the seashore about 450 metres west of the fort; just east of the roadway which leads to the airstrip. Nothing now remains to identify this place as hallowed ground.

Inis Mór and Inishbofin: Island Prisons

In February 1657, the government decided that the islands of Aran and Inishbofin were to be used as holding-camps for the numerous priests and religious who were then incarcerated in various prisons around the country.[12] In 1653, all Roman Catholic priests were declared to be guilty of high treason, and it was a felony to harbour or relieve one. It has been estimated that as many as 1,000 priests may have been forced into exile. Nevertheless, numerous priests remained in the country and others who had initially gone abroad returned to minister to the people. A bounty of five pounds on their heads, they were hunted down, imprisoned and many were sent to the West Indies to be sold into slavery. However, pressure from foreign governments compelled the authorities to reconsider this practice. The establishment of prison camps off the west coast must have seemed like the ideal temporary solution. Both Inis Mór and Inishbofin served as such from 1657 until 1662.

Initially, fifty clerics were sent to the islands and we know that a further thirty-six were transported there in 1659. From time to time various monies were allocated from the public purse for their upkeep and towards 'the building of cabins, and the prisons for the said Popish priests'.[13] Very little of this money, however, appears to have found its way to them for contemporary accounts record that they were almost starved, being forced to live on 'herbs and water'.[14] It was not until after the collapse of the Commonwealth and the restoration of Charles II to the throne, in 1660, that the lot of the clergy in Ireland began to improve. Those imprisoned on Inis Mór and Inishbofin had to wait until 1662 to be liberated; it is said this was done as a gesture to the new English Queen who was a Catholic.[15]

The Restoration

Many who had supported Charles II or who helped bring about the Restoration – including some shrewd Cromwellian veterans – received commissions in the new Irish army which was completely remodelled at this time. One of these, Robert Deey, mayor of Dublin in 1659-60, was commissioned as captain of a foot company, in October 1660, and was posted to Arkin fort in 1662. From this period forward the forts at Arkin and Inishbofin come under the one command. We can only guess as to the thoughts which passed through Deey's mind when he first sailed into Cill Éinne Bay and saw the ruins of Teampall Bheanáin silhouetted on the skyline above the fort. This was a man accustomed to the hustle and bustle of the capital city and used to the pomp and trappings of high office. Now he was arriving as commander of what the authorities considered was a remote island garrison. How did he view this appointment? On this, as indeed on most personal matters, however, the records are unfortunately silent.

Deey's company comprised one hundred men including the commanding officer. The captain resided at Arkin with half of the company and sent his lieutenant to Inishbofin with the remainder. Each fort also had a 'gunner' whose job was to look after the ordnance.[16] Arkin contained seven guns but these were of little use, however, as they were all unmounted. It appears that the foot company were not the only soldiers stationed on Inis Mór. Part of a troop of horse were also quartered at Arkin during 1662 and 1663.[17]

Because of the remoteness of the islands the company was allowed an advance of one month's pay so that they could buy provisions. They had already spent their previous allocation on 'beef, butter and oatmeale' and they needed the additional money to pay the islanders who had 'trusted the soldiers beyond their abilities'. Captain Deey's lieutenant was also given funds to repair the houses in and adjoining both forts.[18] Deey continued in charge at Arkin for about a year, until the summer of 1663; by then there were only sixty-four men remaining in his company.

A New Commander

Deey's company was replaced by one under the command of Nicholas Bayly who was to govern both forts for the next eighteen years. Captain Bayly was a veteran soldier and had held the rank of major in the army in England during civil war. Like Deey, he too petitioned the King at the Restoration and received a commission in the Irish army.[19] On his arrival at Arkin he lost little time in organising his new quarters and immediately sent a detailed report on the 'necessaries wanting in the garrisons of Arran and Buffin' to the Duke of Ormond.

He requested two large guns to defend the harbour at Arkin, a new boat to fetch the turf from Connemara (the old one being in very bad repair), a larger vessel to carry the various supplies to both Inis Mór and Inishbofin, and various guns for the fort on Inishbofin. He also drew attention to the fact that he had but twenty-eight men at Arkin and as it took five men to man the turf-boat, and these could often be absent for six or eight weeks at a time due to bad weather, he could not in all safety release them for that task. Accordingly, he sought additional personnel. It appears that the company did not buy all their provisions locally for Bayly requested the larger vessel because supplies were purchased where they 'may be cheapest had, which is sometimes in the year no nearer than Galway, Sligo or Derry'.

Captain Bayly's requests were granted and he appears to have carried out various repairs to the forts. He was promoted to the rank of major, allocated two men 'skilled in marine affairs' to serve as masters of the boats and the strength of his company was gradually increased so that, in 1665, he had some two hundred men under his command. These new arrivals were on secondment to the islands from the other foot companies around the country. Bayly was sent additional ordnance, ammunition, powder, uniforms, swords, muskets and two drums with drumsticks – the 17th century equivalent of a modern communications system.[20] The necessity of strengthening the island forts, as indeed the other forts throughout the country, was occasioned by England's war with France and the Low Countries. The government were fearful of an enemy landing in Ireland, but apart from reports of Dutch privateers operating off the coasts, little of consequence happened. In 1667, Bayly received a commission to be governor of both the Aran Islands and Inishbofin and, in August of that year, the war with the French and Dutch came to an end.[21] Those men who had been posted to the islands, in 1664-5, presumably returned to their companies.

Now that the threat of war had passed Major Bayly appears to have settled down to carrying out the duties of both commanding officer and island landlord; he was tenant to the Earl of Arran who owned the Aran Islands. Life for the garrison must have been fairly routine and much of their time was probably spent in getting on with the normal day-to-day business of living on an island. Fuel and supplies had to be imported though we can be sure that they also availed of local produce. Likewise it is inconceivable that the soldiers followed the celibate lifestyle of their monastic predecessors. More than likely some of them married local girls and settled permanently on the island. It was customary for officers and soldiers alike to have their wives and families with them and we know that Captain Bayly was married and had, at least, one son. These, undoubtedly, resided in the fort or in a house nearby, for little, if any, money appears to have been spent on the upkeep of the fortifications in the decade following the war. In 1677, Arkin is described as having an adequate wall 'but ye buildings therein are fallen downe'; it was estimated that the whole would cost £150 to repair.[22] Whether or not the necessary works were carried out is unknown and Bayly is now recorded as moving, from time to time, between Galway, Inishbofin and Inis Mór.[23] He appears to have become dissatisfied with his lot for, in 1681, we find him in London on business. He evidently considered that his best prospects lay outside the army for he sold his commission in that year to one Amyas Bushe, who in the words of the Earl of Arran, had 'never bore arms before, and his whole business hitherto has been towards the pen' and, as he pointed out to his father, the Duke of Ormond, 'your Grace had better take one that has a mind to learn than keep one who has forgot'.[24] Accordingly, we find Captain Bushe listed as being quartered at Inis Mór until 1685. It seems that his company provided only a token military presence on the island for the fort's gunner and ordnance had been transferred to Charles Fort, Kinsale, by 1682. Likewise, the fort on Inishbofin appears to have been abandoned at this time.[25] In 1684, the Irish army was completely reorganised and it was probably as part of this that Bushe's company was withdrawn from Inis Mór in the following year.[26] The fort at Arkin had been garrisoned for some thirty-three years. As far as the authorities were concerned the island forts had served their purpose and were of little further use.

Williamite Garrison

The Aran Islands did not play any part in the struggle between James II and William of Orange over the kingship of England. According to the Williamite governor of Galway, writing shortly after its surrender, in July 1691, the fort on Inis Mór was in ruins and he was considering sending a foot company there.[27] There is no doubt that a garrison was subsequently maintained on the island from time to time, as the occasion demanded. In 1710, Sir Stephen Fox (who had purchased the islands from the Earl of Arran) petitioned Queen Anne seeking protection for his property. He pointed out that for a number of years the islands had been raided by French privateers during the summer months. He had spent a considerable sum of money in providing quarters for the soldiers who were sent out there from the garrison at Galway, but these were withdrawn in September, and did not return until the following summer. In the meantime, the bedding and other items had been 'spoiled and embezzled'. He requested that the fort should be repaired and a foot company sent there. Fox appears to have received no satisfaction, however, and, in 1713, he sold his interest in the islands.[28] The history of the fort effectively draws to a close here, in as much as there is no further record of any significant military presence within its walls.

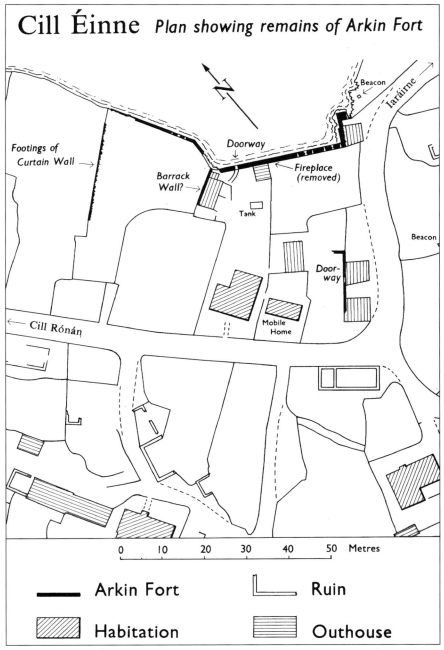

Illus. 7.2. Plan of part of the village of Cill Éinne showing the remains of Arkin Fort (March 1993).

Illus. 7.3. This rough pencil sketch-plan of the fort at Arkin was drawn by Colonel Robertson, in February 1797, and formed part of proposals which he compiled for the defence of Galway Bay (Oireachtas MS 8.H.21). It is very difficult to reconcile his plan with the remains that survive today.

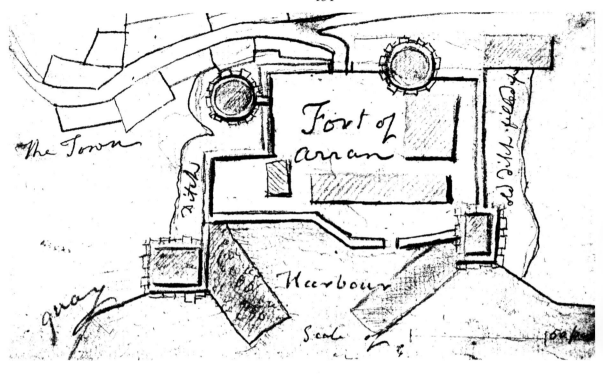

Irish Coastal Defences

Throughout the 18th century, the government were ever alert to the possibility of an invasion of the country and from time to time various plans were prepared in expectation of such an attack. During the years 1796-8, a Colonel W. Robertson drew up proposals for the defence of Galway Bay.[29] He visited Inis Mór, in February 1797, and drew a rough, pencil sketch-plan of the fort; the only known plan in existence (Illus. 7.3). It is titled 'Old fort at N[orth] Arran [i.e. Inis Mór] where a company of infantry m[igh]t be quartered & the barracks repaired'.

His plan indicates that the fort was protected by a fosse on the east and west sides, though he does note that the former was then 'filled up'. It is very difficult to reconcile his plan with the remains that survive today. Even allowing for artistic licence, Robertson's plan represents an unusual layout for a fort constructed in the mid-17th century. It is atypical in having two round towers as part of its defences. One of these is represented as almost free-standing with the curtain wall set back to accommodate it; a most unusual arrangement. By the middle of the 17th century round towers had long ceased to be used by military engineers for defensive purposes and their place was taken by a variety of angular bastions; the fort on Inishbofin being a typical example of the style of military architecture employed at this period. It is reasonable to suggest that these round towers may once have formed part of the original Arkin castle or its bawn and that the Cromwellians simply incorporated them into their new works. Indeed, the free-standing tower could be interpreted as another example of the cylindrical medieval tower house, three of which survive in the Burren region of northwest Clare.

Colonel Robertson records that in Cromwell's time 'no enemy was expected to attack Ireland from the west, in the manner we now have so much reason to apprehend'; prophetic words indeed which were to be realised in the following year when the French landed at Killala, Co. Mayo. Times were changing and the new attitude towards the defence of Ireland is reflected in the construction of numerous Martello towers and signalling stations around the coast in the early 19th century. The ruins of two of these signal towers – the tattered remnants of the slate cladding still clinging to the walls to keep out the Atlantic storms – stand on the highest point of Inis Oírr and at Eochaill on Inis Mór testifying to the part played by the Aran Islands in this grand scheme.[30]

The Passage of Time

And so the wheel had come full circle. Just as the Franciscan friary and St Enda's church had served as a quarry for the fort, so too did the fort become a source of stone for the many cabins which were built within it and against its walls. Within forty years of Robertson's visit most of the fortifications appear to have been pulled down or were incorporated in the various habitations and sheds built on the site. The remains received only a passing glance from John O'Donovan when he visited the island, in July 1839, collecting information on the placenames and antiquities for the Ordnance Survey. Fortunately, William Wakeman, the artist who accompanied him took a slightly greater interest and made two sketches of the fort (Illus. 7.4).[31] It appears that one of the round towers depicted on Robertson's plan then survived. This was subsequently pulled down and, unfortunately, its location is unknown.

Illus. 7.4. Two sketches by William Wakeman of the fort of Arkin, drawn in July 1839; (RIA OS Letters, Co.Galway, Vol.3, p.403). The upper sketch depicts the seaward curtain wall and defences; very much as they survive today. The lower sketch shows one of the two circular mural towers which formed part of the landward defences. In 1821, the Donoughoe family lived in one of these; probably this one. The tower was pulled down sometime during the nineteenth century and its location is unknown.

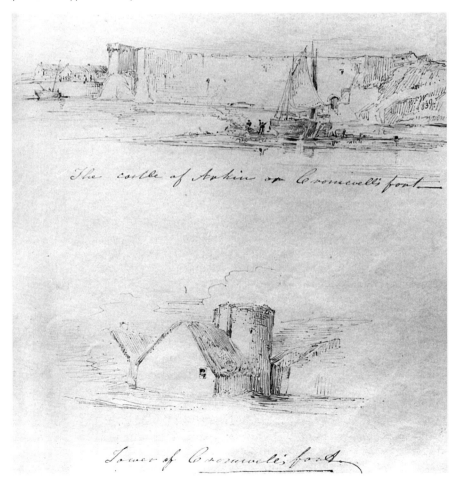

The castle of Arkin or Cromwell's fort

Tower of Cromwell's fort

Ballaí Chromwell: Cromwell's Walls

Without doubt, the best view of the remains of Arkin fort is to be obtained by standing on the quay-side near the beacon (Illus. 7.5) or, better still, waiting until low tide and walking along the foreshore below the cliffs. From here it is possible to see the full extent of the surviving wall on the seaward side. The most eye-catching feature is the rectangular corner tower which projects from the main curtain wall by the roadside. Its parapet wall is carried on corbels or stone brackets whose curving profiles and sharp angular edges further enhance the castle-like appearance. It is pierced with a number of small gun loops. In the curtain wall beside this tower are two double-splayed embrasures for cannon. These are flanked on either side by gun loops. Though blocked up with dry-stone walling their jambs can be readily traced in the interior masonry. Access to the fort from the sea was provided by a doorway at the foot of the curtain wall. From here a passage-way leads upwards into the interior. Though the jambs have been removed and the passage and doorway blocked up its round-headed arch of cut stone testifies to the skill of the mason's craft (Illus. 7.6). This entrance was protected by a device called a machicolation which projects from the top of the wall directly above the doorway. It allowed the defenders to drop rocks or other missiles on would-be assailants below.

Illus. 7.5. Photo of fort from quayside showing the corner tower and curtain wall. The blocked doorway gave access to the fort from the sea and was protected by a machicolation at the top of the wall directly above it.

Illus. 7.6. This round-headed doorway in the curtain wall gave access from the sea to a passage which led upwards into the fort. The stones are decorated in typical 17th century style with rows of punch-dressing along the edges. The jambs have been removed and the doorway blocked up; the blocking is represented in the illustration by finer pen-work.

Illus. 7.7. Photo of the curtain wall taken prior to reparations carried out by the Office of Public Works. The large ragged gap in the masonry indicates the position of the fireplace. A small chimney projects from the top of the wall above it. The cross is carved on the lintel of the gun-loop nearest the roadway.

If we move our vantage point to the roadway beside the tower (Illus. 7.7) we should note the small chimney which projects from the top of the curtain wall about mid-way along its length. At its base the masonry bears the tell-tail signs of having being repaired. From here a large fireplace was removed. It is not likely that this was an open-air fireplace and it must have formed part of a barrack building which was built against this section of the curtain wall. Part of another building or curtain wall forms part of the two old houses which now serve as roadside sheds. A blocked-up round-headed doorway, similar to that already described, survives in the interior of the northern-most shed (Illus. 7.8). In fact, two vertical breaks in the exterior masonry of the shed wall indicate its position. It is not possible to determine the original position of the south-eastern curtain wall. It may be that the present roadway marks this boundary and Col. Robertson's plan would support this hypothesis.[32]

In late morning, when the sun begins to illuminate the landward side of the curtain wall, it is possible to make out a simple equal-armed cross with expanded terminals on the lintel of the gun loop nearest the road. This carving is very similar both in size and style to another cross which was carved on the bare vertical rockface above a holy well on Inis Oírr. The latter is accompanied by the date '1818' and the name 'J' or 'I Healy' (Illus. 7.9). Such crosses are a special feature of Galway city and its environs and are to be found carved on both public buildings and private dwellings alike. The carvings sometimes incorporate the religious monogram IHS and many bear the same 'Healy' name: most are dated 1816. Who Healy

Illus. 7.8. Photo (taken in 1952) showing the blocked-up round-headed doorway which forms part of the wall of a roadside shed.

Illus. 7.9. Below (a) Cross carved on the interior lintel of the western-most gun-loop in the curtain wall; (b) Cross carved on the rockface above a holy well north of the old coastguard station on Inis Oírr.

was or why he chose to be remembered in this way is a mystery.[33] Mystery too surrounds the section of broken pillar with square base and octagonal shaft which lies among the boulders on the foreshore below the fort: it is now covered in seaweed and visible only at low tide. This is probably part of the shaft of a late medieval cross.[34] The fragment serves to remind us of the earlier history of this site. The fort was but one in a succession of buildings, both religious and secular, which formerly stood at Cill Éinne and those who dwelt within them are no less deserving of being remembered than the soldiers who were garrisoned here in the 17th and early 18th centuries.

Acknowledgements for Illustrations

Illus. 7.1. T.H. Mason.
Illus. 7.3. Oireachtas Library.
Illus. 7.3. Royal Irish Academy.
Illus. 7.5, 7.7, 7.8, Office of Public Works.

Acknowledgements
I wish to thank the Director of Operations, Ordnance Survey, for permission to publish this paper. The survey would not have been possible without the generosity of the people of Cill Éinne who allowed me access to the remains. To Patrick Melvin, in the library of An tOireachtas, the staff of the library in the Royal Irish Academy, and to Aideen Ireland and Frances McGee in the National Archives, my special thanks for assistance with source material.

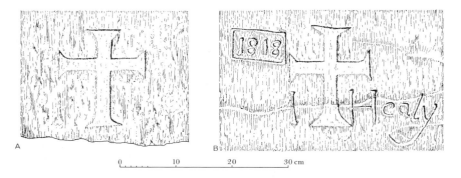

A

B

0   10   20   30 cm

CHAPTER 8

The Maritime History of the Aran Islands

John de Courcy Ireland

Introduction

Vivid indeed is the memory of my first visit to the Aran Islands. It set fire to an interest in island history that had been accumulating for a number of years, and has kept it burning fiercely ever since.

The visit took place in January 1939. I was not very long married and a chance acquaintance with a young Galway woman who had worked as a deck-hand in one of the ships of the last fleet of long-distance sailing merchant ships, owned by Ericsson of the Åland Isles in the Baltic Sea, aroused our interest in Aran. She introduced us to one of the many remarkable characters then resident in the islands, Dr O'Brien, the Aran doctor, whose strange genius has, I feel, never received the tribute it deserved in the ocean of words that has been written and spoken about distinguished Aran islanders of the 1930s.

The doctor urged us to come and spend a few months in the islands. He could acquire us a cottage in Cill Éinne for £5 if we did not mind 'roughing' it, and was sure our sojourn would open for us innumerable magic doors. My wife persuaded me to go ahead and have a look.

Until 1939 my acquaintance with islands had been a matter of vision rather than visits. I had once set foot on Dalkey Island, which has been visible from wherever I have been living for most of the past half-century, and my wife and I had recently spent a day on Lundy Island in the Bristol Channel – romantic enough and deservedly giving its name to a whole area in the regular British weather-forecasts for mariners. Beyond that there had been my unforgettable first sight of America, when the beautiful island of Fernando de Noronha slowly heaved itself out of an oily tropical sea off the coast of Brazil, to salute an elderly cargo ship in which I was working, and glimpses of the Canaries and a number of Caribbean isles from the decks of banana ships. The fascination of islands had begun to operate, and now I was about to visit probably the most talked-of islands in my own country.

I met the doctor in Galway and we embarked in the Dublin-built *Dun Aengus*, already over thirty years old, as fine a seaboat as ever was launched and one of the great characters in the maritime history of Aran. A searing westerly wind was blowing, the worst, people said, and one of the worst, I do not doubt, for the past twenty years. It took a little over eight hours to get to Cill Rónáin, during which the doctor had comforted a multitude of sick and scared passengers, and I had gazed transfixed at the Aran sea showing its tumultuous might.

time we accompanied the doctor on his visits to the smaller islands. O'Brien was quick to interest me in the islands' maritime history so far as he knew it – O'Briens had played a dominant role therein – but was even more eloquent about the history of polar exploration, on which he owned the largest private library I have ever seen. Where, oh where is it now?

The inadequacy of the local fishing fleet, in

Illus. 8.1. The 'Dun Aengus' leaving Cill Rónáin.

Illus. 8.2. Embarking the 'Dun Aengus' off Inis Meáin.

A few weeks later both my wife and I embarked at Galway in the redoubtable *Dun Aengus*, having left most of our furniture in the care of the Limerick Steamship Company in Galway. The doctor arranged the transport of ourselves and the little we had brought with us to our little cottage, and so our Aran sojourn began.

I was at once overcome with admiration for the extraordinary skill of the islanders with their currachs and the noteworthy sea-going qualities of the Aran currachs in which from time to

spite of the quality of the men who manned it, was only too obvious. In the 1930s our fishing industry had been so neglected that it was able to land only 10,000 tons (some 240,000 now) per year, a lot less than the country was *exporting* before the 1914 war. I saw evidence of the efficiency of the local lifeboat station, belatedly opened only twelve years before, and the sight of an Irish Lights tender flying, as they were still to do for many years, a British ensign drove me to write a letter to the *Irish Press* pointing out that it looked as if a world war was approaching and we had no ships of our own to guarantee our national survival. This was one of my earliest ventures into what became a lifelong campaign for the development of a strong national maritime economy.

The Islands' Early Maritime History

There is evidence that the Aran Islands have been inhabited for at least four and a half thousand years. There were certainly people on Aran in late Neolithic times if not earlier and habitation continued through the Bronze and Iron Ages and into the period when the arrival of Christian missionaries brought literacy and the misty beginning of genuine historical records.

There is little doubt that the first Aran folk arrived in skin-boats, ancestors of the present-day currachs. These evolved very slowly down the centuries – seafarers have, historically speaking, been very conservative. Once convinced that something worked they were reluctant to innovate for fear of inviting disaster. Islanders above all have traditionally developed a profound and ineradicable respect for the fathomless treachery of the sea. Many books on Aran comment on the rarity of fatal currach accidents off the islands, and cite years when the few occurring were undoubtedly the result of too much drink taken. This trait is one of many shared by islanders, as a consequence of being islanders, the world over. For all the differences of speech, dress, habitation and culture generally, I have been made forcibly aware of the similarity in attitudes and reactions of island people in all the islands I have become closely acquainted with in the long years since I first visited Aran, whether on the Isle of Lewis, or Orkney, or Shetland, or Ushant or Noirmoutier (physically so very different)

Illus. 8.3. The coracle was almost certainly the original type of skin boat used in Europe from Mesolithic times, from which in time the various kinds of currach derived. It is possible that Aran's earliest inhabitants arrived in coracles.

Illus. 8.4. A currach propelled by paddles as all primitive currachs were, from an early Christian stone pillar at Bantry, Co. Cork.

Illus. 8 5. A currach with a single simple square sail off Inis Oírr.

off the coast of France, or Korčula in the Adriatic, where Marco Polo was born, or indeed islands in the Aegean.

The earliest skin-boats were undoubtedly paddled – in some parts of the world they still are. The similarities between Irish, Iberian and North African skin-boats, to my mind, reinforces the much disputed *Atlantean* theories of Bob Quinn: that the pre-Iron Age inhabitants of the coastal fringe of North Africa and Western Europe were one and the same people. There are several elements in the maritime history of Aran that remain mysterious and the introduction of the oar is one of them; its invention was a major revolution. No less mysterious are questions such as when and how the use of the sail was introduced, and when did the west of Ireland first become acquainted with wooden-built vessels. It may be that the version of the Brendan story that has him coming back to Ireland in the skin-boat in which he began his adventures, to build a wooden ship to ensure their successful conclusion, echoes a controversy in the fifth or sixth centuries AD on the relative excellencies of the skin-boat in its most sophisticated form and the new-fangled wooden vessel for long-distance voyaging.

Regarding the sail, there is fierce controversy among maritime historians about when it first began to be used in northern Europe, with a recent tendency towards acknowledging priority to boat-designers of the Celtic-speaking world, among whom the most celebrated were the Veneti of southern Brittany, whose oaken-hulled vessels, with leather sails and anchors secured by iron chains instead of rope cables were immensely sophisticated for the time (1st century BC) when Julius Caesar wrote his description of them. And Ireland certainly, and Aran probably, had maritime relations at the time with Brittany.

The saintly scholars of the late fifth century who settled in Aran and transformed its appearance with their imaginative building skills and the ideas of its inhabitants by their teaching almost certainly will have come in currachs propelled by oar and sail, that were slowly developing towards the high point in sophistication reached by the 17th century, as we know from the famous sketch of a currach

Illus. 8.6. A currach propelled by typical bladeless oars. Such currachs have been in use for probably some 2,000 years, the only change being that tarred canvas replaces the original skins stretched on a wooden frame.

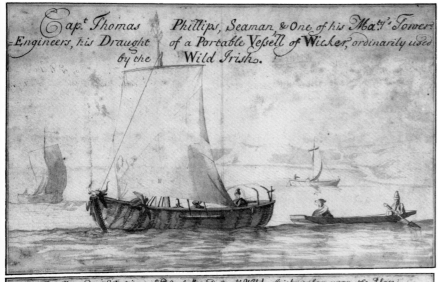

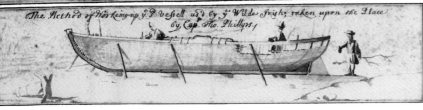

Illus. 8.7. A currach sailing and a currach under construction as sketched by Irishman Thomas Phillips, sea captain and engineer employed by the English Admiralty, in or about 1685. This shows the currach at the most sophisticated stage it ever reached.

is in the sea and your pathway upon the great waves'.

To the early centuries of the Christian era can be ascribed the remarkable mythical voyages westward over the ocean described in the *Imrama*, out of which grew the long-held (and oft-attested) belief that with luck looking westward from Aran you could see the fabled Island of Hy Brasil, the search for which was one of the triggers that fired off the passion for oceanic exploration that grew in Europe in the 15th century and was destined irrevocably to change the course of world history.

Illus. 8.8. Early map showing the legendary island of 'Hy Brasil', in 1513 by Martin Waldseemuller. Most early maps show the island further out in the Atlantic. This map shows it just about where various claims have been made in the past century or so of the sudden appearance of an island through or after mist off the Kerry coast. Waldseemuller multiplied the Aran Islands.

capable of carrying up to thirty aboard, with a sail made of strips of canvas, a kedge-anchor and a stern-rudder, made by the Irish-born seaman and engineer Thomas Phillips in 1685.

The story that St Enda came to Aran in a stone boat need not be taken seriously, but that the saintly scholars used them is a widely-diffused belief. This can best be gathered by perusing *Santos e Barcos de Pedra* written in 1991 in his native Galician by Professor F. A. Romero, who quotes numerous cases, including several in Brittany where, in at least two places, the rocks alleged to have been saints' boats can be seen, and recalls the famous song said to have originated with the rowers of the stone boat that brought the body of St James to Compostela, beginning 'O teu camiño está no mar e o teu sendeiro sobre as grandes ondas' – 'Your road

Illus. 8.9. Historical sailing craft such as sailed past Aran to and from Galway in the 14th, 15th and 16th centuries.

From the era of the Saints to that of the 'final' English conquest

Illus. 8.9. (i) A cog, the typical north European merchant ship of the 13th to 16th centuries, the first ship-type after the much older Chinese junk to be steered by a stern rudder rather than a steering oar.

Illus. 8.9. (ii) A carrack, the typical European trading vessel of the 15th and 16th centuries, used particularly in the trade between Galway and Portugal.

Illus. 8.9. (iii) A caravel, a ship-type developed by the Portuguese about 1400 and used extensively in the first great European voyages of discovery. Caravels appear occasionally in records of Irish-Portuguese maritime relations in the 15th century.

From perhaps as early as the seventh century for hundreds of years the MacTeige O'Briens, from Co. Clare, controlled the Aran Islands as a largely independent entity. The early monasteries continued to operate, and of course depended, like the O'Briens, on maritime transport for connection between the islands and with the mainland. The survival of the currach down the centuries and a comprehensive record of early 16th century European shipping surviving in the Bibliothèque Nationale in Paris recording the prevalence of skin-craft off our west coast lead to the supposition that both monks and O'Briens went about their maritime business in currachs, depending no doubt to a large extent on fish for sustenance. It was apparently in these centuries that the use of seaweed began in the rudimentary agriculture possible on the rocky island soil.

Those great seamen, the Norse, are recorded as having paid at least two visits in the 11th century but seem to have left no lasting influence comparable to what they did elsewhere round our coasts. Cill Éinne was then and for long after the islands' principal port. The Normans had settled in a considerable area of Ireland in the 12th and 13th centuries and gave intermittent allegiance to any king of England able to enforce it. They also were fine seamen, who came in wooden ships of the latest design, and soon introduced (to develop the trade relations with the Continent which they fostered through the seaport towns to which they gave charters) the cog, the chief European merchant ship of the 13th to 16th centuries and the first European ship-type to be steered by a stern rudder, long used in China instead of a clumsy steering oar. Cogs were also used for fighting. They probably made up the greater part of the

56-ship fleet of Lord Justice d'Arcy who occupied the islands temporarily in 1334 in the name of the far-off king in London. The O'Briens were soon back in control. When late in the 15th century St. Enda's original monastery at Cill Éinne was replaced by a Franciscan foundation (suppressed in 1586) there seems to have been an upsurge in island trade. Back in 1939 I found hops growing wild on the site, which suggests that the Franciscans brewed beer and perhaps shipped it to the mainland or even farther.

But the great importance of the Aran Islands throughout the 14th and 15th and well into the 16th centuries was as the maritime outpost of the fast-growing commercial city of Galway. Galway, virtually in fact an independent maritime republic, a miniature Pisa or Amalfi, built up powerful trade links with Portugal (where Galway cloth and cloaks from Ireland were the height of fashion in the 15th century) and also with ports in what is now Spain, with Brittany, the Netherlands, Germany and as far away as Polish Gdańsk. In return for its cloth and cloaks and other commodities such as hides, salt fish and wolfhounds, Galway imported great quantities of wine and also iron and honey and spices, and, after the Portuguese began growing it, first in Madeira and then São Thomé, sugar, hitherto a very rare luxury.

As this rich trade required protection from piracy, carried on principally by the O'Malleys from Mayo, and the O'Flahertys, but also on occasion by English and Breton sea-robbers, the O'Briens were given annually by Galway 12 tuns of wine (a tun was 146 litres or 252 gallons) for protecting Galway trade from pirates. The growing importance of the Aran Islands for European shipping can be traced by examining the growing accuracy of their depiction by the new but ever more important breed of European map-makers – from Portuguese

Illus. 8.9. (iv) A galleon, an evolution from the carrack, used for trading but primarily as a fighting ship, the first stage in the process of differentiating war ships from trading ships. In 1588 several galleons, returning from Philip II of Spain's failed expedition against England, sailed southward past the Aran Islands.

Illus. 8.9. (v) A Hebridean-type galley as used by Grace O'Malley and other west of Ireland chiefs to patrol the seas claimed by them off the coast of Connacht.

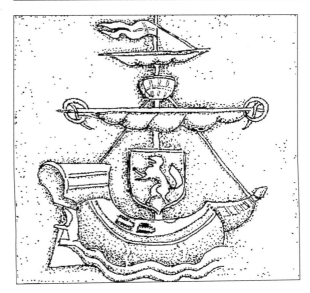

Illus. 8.10. Galway City arms in the 17th century emphasising the city's dependency on the sea-trade, which the Aran islanders were paid to protect from local pirates.

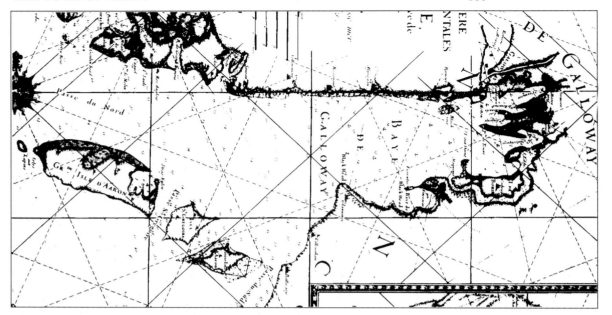

Illus. 8.11. After the Dutch, the French became Europe's leading hydrographers and this French chart (section) of 1690 reflects the excellence of the hydrographic service recently inaugurated by Colbert. It was made in the year of the Battle of the Boyne when the French were using Galway as their base for continuing their campaign in Ireland on behalf of the exiled King James II of England.

Illus. 8.12. This early 18th century map (section) by H. Moll makes clear the importance at the time of Cill Éinne as the leading port in the islands. Gregory Sound was then and had for a long time been called St Gregory's Passage.

Reinel in the late 1400s, who had three islands all right and quite accurately shaped, but no named sounds, through Genoese Maggiolo of 1512, who knew of the Gregory Sound, by way of Mercator's *Angliae, Scotiae et Hiberniae Nova Descriptio* of 1564 and a group of mid-16th century Breton charts produced at Le Conquet, to much more exact 17th century maps.

O'Flahertys, who had played their part in 16th century piracy off our west coast, defeated the O'Briens in 1584, and took over the islands. Then in 1587 the increasingly powerful government of England annexed the islands and proceeded to grant them to an English settler from Athlone, after which they passed into the hands of a succession of owners, of whom much the most eminent was a son of the first Duke of Ormond, made Earl of Aran (hence Arran Quay in Dublin), till the end of landlordism in Ireland. In 1588 the islands witnessed the passage by of a number of ships of Philip II of Spain's disastrous Armada, several of which were wrecked further south on the Irish coast.

The 17th to the 19th centuries

During the Kilkenny Confederation war, 1642-52, recently built Arkin Fort was strengthened and Inis Mór garrisoned in hope that an expedition from France in support of the Confederation would reach Galway, but Cromwell's forces seized the islands temporarily (the English navy, rapidly becoming one of the world's strongest, supported Cromwell in the English Civil War), lost them to Confederates from Inishbofin arriving in vessels of types not described, but retook them with the fleet's backing in 1653. From then on the islands have been spared the need for mention in the annals of naval history.

It was during this period that the traditional skin covering for the currach's wooden frame-

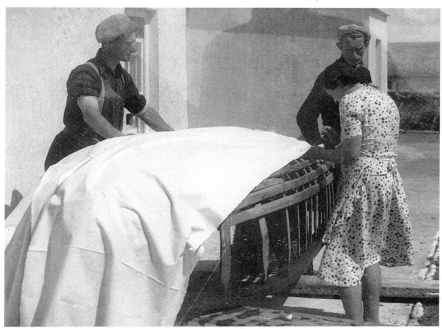

Illus. 8.13. Putting canvas on a currach, 1940. Originally currachs were made of skins stretched over a wicker structure, not tarred canvas on laths as now.

Illus. 8.14. Nailing the tarred canvas on to a currach frame. Inis Oírr 1959.

Illus. 8.15. A new currach is being made by Rory Concannon on Inis Meáin, 1993. The long laths (bow to stern) shown in the picture are temporary timbers placed so as to ensure that the hoops are lined up exactly right. When the permanent laths are put on they will be nailed to the hoops (at each intersection) with copper nails. There are three important qualities which make the currach a safe boat in rough seas, when properly handled of course, the first being lightness which makes it lift over the waves. The second is the high bow which prevents on-coming seas from flooding the boat, and finally the smooth roundness of the bottom which causes waves coming from the side to pass under the boat without causing it to roll. A keel would give such seas a 'grip' on the boat and might over-turn it. The basic design of the currachs used in the Aran Islands does not seem to have changed for many years (perhaps for hundreds of years). Materials have changed somewhat, notably the use of glass fibre instead of canvas for the covering.

work was replaced by tarred canvas. Fishing continued to be a vitally important occupation, but it would have flourished more with larger boats. Access to the main market in Galway and subsidiary markets such as Doolin in Co. Clare was made difficult by the eternal uncertainty of conditions at sea.

This was also the period when the first shipment of potatoes to the island occurred, to become a stock crop, and when the Galway hooker became the standard vessel involved in the lively if not very remunerative trade in passengers and goods along our west coast, and occasionally in fishing.

For the islanders, hookers became very important as conveyors of turf for fuel from Connemara, chiefly to Cill Mhuirbhigh, whose little port grew in importance. It is notable that, unlike in the case of say Ushant or Shetland, there are only a few records of Aran islanders going off as merchant seamen.

The 19th Century and up to Independence

This was the century of the Great Famine, but though the islanders' potatoes were affected by the blight other crops and above all an abundance of fish prevented starvation. The invention of the steamship, leading eventually to the establishment of a regular service between Galway and Cill Rónáin (replacing Cill Éinne as the principal island port from the 1850s) made communication with the mainland easier, increased the meagre variety of goods available for island consumption, and facilitated emigration, which became an important factor of island life. The islanders will have seen passing the big (for then) paddle-steamers, already obsolete, of the gallant but short-lived Galway Royal Mail Line between 1858 and 1863, and heard rumours early in this century of Galway

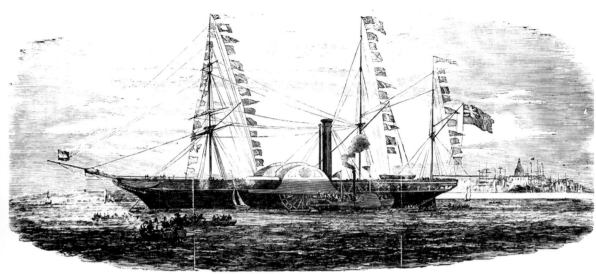

THE "VICEROY," AT ANCHOR IN THE ROADS IN GALWAY BAY

Illus. 8.16. Paddle steamer 'Viceroy' at anchor in Galway roads, 1850. The ocean-going paddle steamer was a novelty in 1850. Twelve years before, the Cork-owned and manned 'Sirius' had made the very first Atlantic crossing by a ship driven by steam-power alone. Galway Royal Mail used ships a little bigger than 'Viceroy'.

being developed as the then United Kingdom's chief Atlantic port to facilitate the flow of supplies to England from North America in case of war in Europe.

The second half of the 19th century saw many improvements for life on the islands of a maritime nature, but, as everywhere for islanders, the improvement in their life-style was less rapid than that for the average (though not for a big minority) among mainlanders. This century, especially after the establishment of the Commissioners of Irish Lights in 1867, saw an efficient coast lighting system put into operation all round Ireland, including Rock Islet Lighthouse and Straw Island Light Tower in Aran. (There had been one from early in the century on the high ground above Eochaill, but it was badly placed). Proper charts were made (new ones are now needed) that greatly assisted navigation through the North, Gregory and Foul Sounds and round the islands. A Coast Guard was set up, partly, it is true, to check

Illus. 8.17. 'Citie of the Tribes' – shown here from Nimmo's Pier with Galway's mid-19th century docks as background – was a paddle steamer that greatly improved communications between Aran and the mainland.

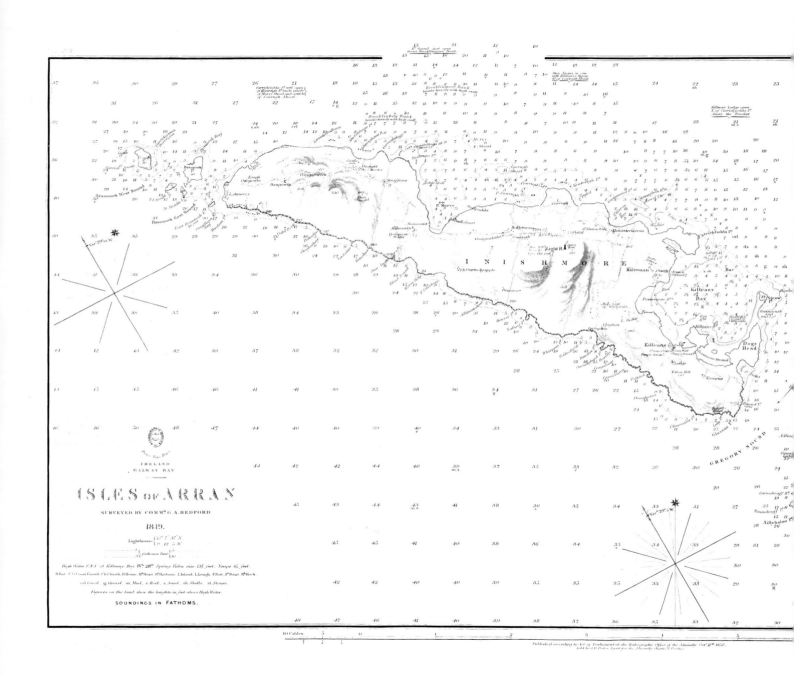

ISLES of ARRAN

SURVEYED BY COMMᴿ G. A. BEDFORD

1849.

SOUNDINGS IN FATHOMS.

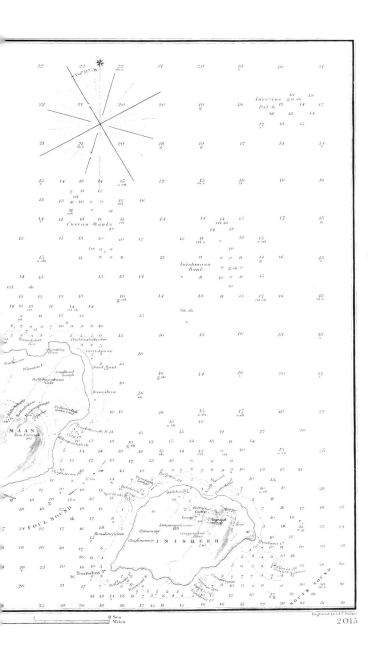

Illus. 8.18. This is an early chart of the Aran Islands made when Navan-born Francis Beaufort was hydrographer for the British Admiralty. Known for his wind scale, he was acquainted with Galway and was the most thorough organiser of chart work round the globe till that period.

smuggling, to which the islanders were not averse, but also to give help when life was in danger at sea. The kelp industry flourished, bringing a relatively sizeable income to the islands. With the opening of top class seaweed research at the Martin Ryan Marine Research Centre at University College, Galway, there is now hope of a revival, in modern form, of sea-

Illus. 8.19. Connemara hooker with turf sailing to Aran, 1943. A ship type famous for our west, and in a different pattern, our southern coasts, dating from around 1700, first as a fishing and later as a cargo vessel.

ARRAN ISLAND, GALWAY. 5051.W.L.

Illus. 8.20. Cill Rónáin pier at the beginning of this century. Apart from hookers, a nobby and zulu can be seen on the far left of the pier. Nobbies and zulus were introduced to the islanders for fishing by the Congested Districts Board at the end of the last and start of this century; they were much more manoeuvrable than hookers or currachs for fishing.

Illus. 8.21 far left. The Connemara nobby 'St Colmcille' sailing out of Lettermullen bound for Aran, 1939-40.

Illus. 8.22 left. A late 19th century fishing ketch of zulu type.

weed collection in Aran.

But the greatest boon to the islanders was the setting up of the Congested Districts Board by act of the British parliament in 1891. The Board's inspector reported on Aran in 1893 that 'larger and better-manned boats' were required to develop the islands' great potential as a fishing centre. He found '116 currachs, 12 small sailing boats, third class, and four large trading boats' [hookers] engaged in fishing (there had been in 1837, 120 craft in all, almost a third of them small sailing craft, the rest currachs). The harbour facilities were poor, the inspector reported.

Improvements at once followed, with the development of a successful net-making industry, the start in 1905 of construction in the islands of new and better-type vessels (zulus), the encouragement of lobster-catching, harbour improvements, and the formation of the, for a time, very successful Aran Fisheries Cooperative Society. Gone were the days of fifty years earlier when visitors complained that there was not a decked boat to make the stormy passage to the mainland in, and when Aran and Claddagh fishermen fought pitched battles at sea and jealousy between drift-netters and trawlers led to bloodshed.

S S. DURAS. GALWAY. 4082. W.L.

Illus. 8.23. Steamer 'Duras' at Galway Pier about 1900. The 'Duras' was specially built for Galway Bay SB Co. at South Shields, 1893. Iron hull 96 feet long. Compound steam-engine; and took the place of 'Citie of the Tribes', the first Galway-Aran Steamer (1872).

The screw-driven steamship had ousted the paddle-steamer, whose paddle-boxes were frequently damaged by high seas. The 'Duras' was called after the residence of J. Lynch chairman of the Congested Districts Board. She also ran to Ballyvaughan (one class only). There were two classes to Cill Rónáin (3/- or 2/6). She was supplemented by the 'Dun Aengus' in 1912, and scrapped in 1916.

Illus. 8.24. The 'Duras' approaching Ballyvaughan pier.

Illus. 8.25, 8.26, 8.27. Screw-steamer 'Dun Aengus', built by Liffey Dockyard, Dublin, in 1910. The most celebrated of the ships that linked the islands with Galway, carrying passengers, goods and cattle in all weathers in a career of half a century. Where necessary, on Inis Meáin for example, horses and cattle were towed by currach to the off-shore steamer and then winched aboard.

During the 1914 war, helped by the growing availability of motor engines, Aran fishing did well, but, as already noted, the achievement of national autonomy in 1922, though a boon in most respects, led to total neglect of our maritime possibilities with the death that same year of Arthur Griffith, the only one of our founding fathers that had understood the opportunities offered by our maritime situation.

Since the founding of the State

The biggest developments in Aran's maritime history between the two world wars were the opening of Kilronan Lifeboat Station in 1927 (a list of its achievements, many of them outstanding, is appended) and the brief flourishing of the basking shark fishery which led to Robert Flaherty making 'Man of Aran', in 1934, one of the greatest films ever screened. The rise, progress and second demise of this industry was described in a memorable paper to the Royal Irish Academy in 1966 by the chief scientific adviser to the Department of Fisheries, Dr. A.E.J. Went.

During the 1939 war islanders exercised what had been their right under Brehon Laws but forbidden since Elizabethan times of collecting the wrack thrown ashore from ships lost at sea by act of war (or, for that matter, by stress of

Illus. 8.28. Loading cattle on to SS. 'Dun Aengus' at Cill Rónáin pier, 1956.

weather). They always had, probably will always try to, and certainly did in 1950 when the wreck of the SS. *Plassy* occurred on Inis Oírr, the crew having been most efficiently rescued by the Coast Life-Saving Service, set up here and elsewhere by the new state to perform some of the duties formerly incumbent on the Coast Guard. Dramatic photos of this rescue are among the exhibits at the National Maritime Museum in Dun Laoghaire.

Bord Iascaigh Mhara, founded in 1952 and refashioned ten years later, did much to encourage and help Aran fishermen to develop their natural talents for fishing. Probably the start of the modern Aran fishing industry and rise to importance was the handing over by her Killybegs builders in September 1966 to Ciaran Gill of Cill Éinne of a new 56-foot trawler, *Ard Scia*, and another landmark, seven years later, was the launching for another Aran skipper of the largest wooden trawler ever built in Ireland (also at Killybegs), 78 feet long. By 1977 the Aran fishing fleet consisted of 21 modern vessels, six of them classified as large and nine as medium-sized trawlers, the rest half-decked lobster boats, all power-driven. It has grown further since then, and so has the number, then 17, of local fishermen trained as skippers at the National Fishery Training College at Greencastle, Co. Donegal.

Meanwhile, the *Dun Aengus* (so heartily welcomed when she replaced the first regular Galway link, *SS. Duras*, more than 20 years old) had been herself replaced by the *Naomh Eanna*, also Dublin built, which in its turn has been replaced by a multiple service, both from Galway and from Rossaveal, supplemented by occasional day-trip vessels, and also a regular (when fine) air service. The evolution of Aran's connection with its mainland has been curiously paralleled by the evolution of Breton Ushant's with its. Some Aran folk still unconsciously echo ancestral concern about the probable length and certain psychological shock of the trip to the mainland by talking of going 'as Arainn go hEirinn'. But it seems to me that Aran at least has, for the time being, banished the fear, so constantly expressed in this last half-century, that the next century will early on see the final desertion by their inhabitants of all Ireland's offshore islands. The recent continuous influx of leisure seagoers, a new feature of Aran's age-old maritime history, will probably alone be enough to keep a goodly population in the islands (even if their lighthouses are now automatic), hoping perhaps still for the day when paradisical Hy Brasil will heave itself above the western horizon as Fernando de Noronha long ago did for me.

Illus. 8.29. Seventy eight feet long wooden trawler 'Azure Sea' built at Killybegs for an Aran fisherman in 1973, part of Aran's contribution to the great renaissance of the Irish fishing industry sponsored by An Bord Iascaigh Mhara in the 1960s and 1970s.

Illus. 8.30. Motor vessel 'Naomh Eanna', called after Aran's most famous saint who, it is claimed, came there in a stone boat. She was the first diesel driven vessel to serve the islands; built in Dublin, owned by C.I.E., which took over the Aran-Galway link from the defunct Galway Bay Company.

APPENDIX

Galway Bay Lifeboat Station

Before Galway Bay Lifeboat Station was opened in 1927, lifesaving at sea around the Aran Islands had, since its establishment at strategic points round Ireland in the 1820s, depended on the Coast Guard. This was a multi-purpose body intended to watch for possible infiltration of foreign agents or native subversives, to report sightings of possibly hostile ships in time of war, to assist in combating smuggling, to signal local disasters to regional Coast Guard headquarters, and to save life and property in cases of shipwreck.

The organisation that soon took the name Royal National Lifeboat Institution was founded in 1824, and at once instituted a system of awards, the Gold Medal very rarely, the Silver, rarely, and the Bronze, not very often, and Scrolls and Certificates, to honour all acts of exceptional skill and courage, saving life at sea round Britain and Ireland, whether by lifeboatmen or others. Four Silver Medals were won by Coast Guards stationed in the Aran Islands. The winding up of the Coast Guard Service, when our State was set up in 1922, led the Lifeboat Institution to consider the possibility of establishing a lifeboat station for Galway Bay. Its investigation persuaded the Institution that such a station was a necessity now the Coast Guard had gone, and the first Cill Rónáin lifeboat was brought to the islands and a crew trained in 1927.

From RNLI records

1830 Voted Silver Medal to Bartholomew Hynes, Coast guard, for the rescue by boat of five men from the brig *Lillies*.

1837 Voted Silver Medal to Lieutenant James H.M. Robertson for the rescue by boat of two persons from a small Irish hooker which sank off Trout Rock.

1847 Voted Silver Medal to James McKenzie, Coast guard, for the rescue of a man from the *Seahorse*, the sole survivor.

1851 Voted Silver Medal to John Hein, Master, and Thomas Larkin, Mate, for the rescue by longboat of the Russian barque *John* of the crew of 14 of the yacht *Owen Glendower*.

1927 Station established by the Royal National Lifeboat Institution.

1938 Voted Bronze Medals to Coxswain John Gill, Mechanic Joseph Doyle, Bowman P. Flaherty and crew members W. Gorham, P. Gill, J. Flaherty and T. Flaherty for the rescue of 12 men from the trawler *Hatano* on 16th August: On the night of August 16th, 1938, the trawler *Nogi* of London ran aground 300 yards north west of the lighthouse on Straw Island just off Inis Mór. The wrecked trawler lay exposed to strong winds and very heavy seas. The crew launched a small boat manned by the boatswain and one crew member, but the painter parted and the boatswain was thrown out. Luckily, he managed to clutch the trawler's anchor and was hauled on board. The boat containing the other man was carried away.

A sister trawler, the *Hatano*, radio'd for help and launched a boat with four men aboard. In the heavy seas the boat got into difficulties and was carried toward

Illus. 8.31. Coxswain John Gill and Fr Keane SJ, on lifeboat, photographed by Fr Browne, August 1938.

Illus. 8.32. The wreck of the 'Nogi' on Straw Island off Inis Mór. Photographed by Fr Browne from the 'Dun Aengus' when leaving Cill Rónáin.

the rocks. The message from the *Hatano* was picked up by another trawler which contained two members of the Galway Bay lifeboat, the *William Evans*. Twenty minutes after the SOS was received, the lifeboat was launched.

On her way to the *Nogi*, the *William Evans* picked up the four members and took their boat in tow. On arriving at the *Nogi*, the coxswain was unable to run the lifeboat alongside the trawler. The bowman, P.Flaherty, with four crew members, W.Gorham, P.Gill, J.Flaherty, and T.Flaherty boarded the small boat which had been in tow, Fastening a line to the lifeboat they rowed to the *Nogi*. Two lines were thrown from the trawler and the boat was pulled alongside. With heavy seas breaking over the trawler six of the eleven crew men were taken off and put on board the lifeboat. The remaining five men were rescued in the same way.

Then began an eight hour search for the crewman who had drifted away in the small boat. He was eventually found dazed and exhausted after his ordeal. The lifeboat then returned to her moorings more than fifteen hours after she had first put out.

For their courage and great skill in the execution of this rescue, Coxswain John Gill, Motor Mechanic Joseph Doyle, Bowman P. Flaherty, W.Gorham, P.Gill, J.Flaherty and T.Flaherty were all awarded the Bronze Medal for gallantry. The other four members of the crew, Michael Hernon, second coxswain, Michael Dirrane, assistant motor mechanic, Colman Flaherty and Thomas Beatty, lifeboatmen, received the thanks of the Institution inscribed on vellum.

Illus. 8.33. Survivors and crew of lifeboat coming from the wreck of the 'Nogi' arriving at Cill Rónáin, August 1938.

Illus. 8.34. Survivors of the 'Nogi' and crew of lifeboat at Cill Rónáin pier, August 1938.

1962   Voted Bronze Medals to Coxswain Coleman Hernon, Assistant Mechanic B. Mullen and crew members T. Joyce and P. Quinn for the rescue of eight men and a dog from the mv *June* of Groningen on 16th January, who had taken refuge on Mutton Island:

In a SW wind force 7 gusting to force 9, with a rough sea and visibility much reduced by squalls of hail and rain, the Coxswain manoeuvred the lifeboat as close to Mutton Island lighthouse as possible. Using a boarding boat, made fast by line, B. Mullin, T. Joyce and P. Quinn took turns at rowing to the lighthouse in order to rescue the eight survivors of the mv *June*. The boarding boat was swamped on several occasions and altogether seven attempts were made before the rescue was successfully completed. Throughout the rescue the lifeboat was manoeuvred by Coxswain Hernon with considerable skill in broken water and strong gale conditions which added a considerable element of danger. This led to the boat being chosen as 'heroine' of George Morrison's Gold Medal lifeboat film *3000 miles of peril*.

1967   Awarded framed letters of thanks, signed by the Chairman, to each member of the crew in recognition of their courage in boarding the lifeboat on 25th October to rescue eight men from the Greek motorvessel *Razani* of Piraeus. It took two hours to board the lifeboat and three times the 18ft 6in boarding boat was driven back on to the beach by the south-south-westerly storm and very rough sea. An additional monetary award was also made to each man.

1987   The thanks of the Institution inscribed on vellum were accorded to Coxswain/

Illus. 8.35. Coley Hernon, Cill Rónáin, Lifeboat coxswain, chief character in George Morrison's Gold Medal film of the Irish Lifeboat service, '3000 Miles of Peril'.

Mechanic Bartley Mullin in recognition of the seamanship and determination displayed by him when the lifeboat landed 21 crew from the fishing factory ship *Cornelis Vrolijk*, which had run aground on Lower Gorumna Island in a south-south-easterly storm and very rough seas on 9th November 1986.

1990   The thanks of the Institution inscribed on vellum were accorded to Coxswain Padraic Dillane and crew members Seamus O'Flaherty and Mairtin Fitzpatrick for the rescue of two skin-divers in difficulties off Doolin Point in winds gusting to storm force and very rough seas on 14th August 1989:

Coxswain Dillane skilfully manoeuvred the lifeboat close inshore and launched the Y boat. Crew members S. O'Flaherty and M. Fitzpatrick manned the Y boat and with courage and skill successfully rescued the two skin-divers and transferred them to the lifeboat.

Illus. 8.36. Cill Rónáin lifeboat's rescue of the crew of the Dutch fish-factory ship 'Cornelis Vrolijk' off Gorumna Island, November 9th, 1986.

Acknowledgements for Illustrations

Illus. 8.1. Photo, G.A.Duncan.
Illus. 8.2. Photo, G.A.Duncan.
Illus. 8.3. Photo, National Museum of Ireland.
Illus. 8.5. Photo, National Museum of Ireland.
Illus. 8.6. Photo, National Museum of Ireland.
Illus. 8.7. Drawing, Magdalene College, Cambridge.
Illus. 8.8. Map, National Library of Ireland.
Illus. 8.9. Drawing, Anne Korff.
Illus. 8.10. Drawing, Anne Korff.
Illus. 8.11. Map, Galway County Library.
Illus. 8.12. Map, Galway County Library.
Illus. 8.13. Photo, Bord Fáilte.
Illus. 8.14. Photo, Bord Fáilte.
Illus. 8.15. Photo, Rory Concannon.
Illus. 8.16. Drawing, The Illustrated London News Picture Library.

Illus. 8.17. Photo, Maurice Semple.
Illus. 8.18. Map, Galway County Library.
Illus. 8.20. Photo, National Library of Ireland.
Illus. 8.21. Photo, Bord Fáilte.
Illus. 8.22. Photo, T.H. Mason.
Illus. 8.23. Photo, National Library of Ireland.
Illus. 8.24. Photo, National Library of Ireland.
Illus. 8.25. Photo, National Museum of Ireland.
Illus. 8.26. Photo, G.A.Duncan.
Illus. 8.27. Photo, G.A.Duncan.
Illus. 8.28. Photo, Bord Fáilte.
Illus. 8.29. Photo, The Irish Skipper.
Illus. 8.30. Photo, Galway Advertiser.
Illus. 8.31, 8.32, 8.33, 8.34, Photo, Fr Browne S.J. Collection.
Illus. 8.35. Photo, John de Courcy Ireland.
Illus. 8.36. Photo, John de Courcy Ireland.

Illus. 9.1. One of William Wakeman's (1822-1900) drawings,
'Teampal Chiarain', done during his visit, along with John
O'Donovan, to Inis Mór in 1839 as part of work for the
Ordnance Survey. In his memoir of that visit, contributed to
Duffy's Hibernian Magazine *in 1862, Wakeman observed,*
'No district in Europe, whether on island or continent, contains,
in the same space, so many architectural monuments of the early
Christian Church, as are encompassed by the shores or cliffs of
Aran'.

CHAPTER 9

The Rediscovery of the Aran Islands in the 19th Century

J.W. O'Connell

In 1900 the Aran Islands, with a total estimated population of some 2,400 people, was emerging from a century for which there is so little documentary material it is almost impossible to say anything about what was happening at all. Irish historians sometimes refer to the 18th century as the 'silent century' because, compared to the turbulent 17th century, for which there is abundant documentary material, this particular century was, relatively speaking, a peaceful one, a calm after the political and social upheavals of the Parliamentary and Williamite wars.

If this is the case for the country at large, it is even more so for the three offshore islands of Inis Mór, Inis Meáin and Inis Oírr. Because of this lack of information it is a simple task to summarise briefly the few documented facts there are.

We know, for example, that by the middle of the 18th century the Digby family of Landenstown, Co. Kildare, owned the islands, but as they were absentee landlords their impact was mainly felt only in the form of the high rents their tenants were obliged to pay.

The small garrison at Arkin Fort on Inis Mór was probably withdrawn around 1685, although during the early years of the 18th century small detachments of soldiers were occasionally sent out from Galway to protect the islands against French privateers.

Fishing and small-scale farming continued to be the main occupations of the islanders, whose chief contacts were with the town of Galway and Connemara and, to a lesser extent, the southern coastline of Clare.

Yet by the end of the 19th century and the early decades of the 20th century, the people and culture of Inis Mór, Inis Meáin and Inis Oírr were becoming known not only throughout Ireland but throughout the Western world, inspiring writers and artists like John Millington Synge and Jack Yeats, while the superb archaeological heritage of the islands, stretching back thousands of years had captured the imagination of Europe.

How can we account for this dramatic change? How is it that these three islands, to which it has always, until recently, been difficult to travel, became by the turn of the 20th century one of the favoured destinations of writers and artists, naturalists and social scientists?

Before we suggest an answer it will be helpful to set the scene with a few observations on why these distant islands, lashed by Atlantic storms and sustaining a culture that to the self-consciously 'cultivated' imagination of the 18th century would have appeared close to the barbaric, should have begun to attract the attention of educated people as the 19th century began.

Thirty years before the end of the 18th century Dr Samuel Johnson, best known for his work on the first English Dictionary, travelled with his future biographer, James Boswell, to the Western Islands of Scotland. Johnson was a man of an inquiring mind and many of his remarks on the people and culture of this isolated part of Scotland reveal a sympathy that sets him apart from most of his contemporaries in England, whose taste in natural scenery was largely limited to the meticulously planned gardens and parklands designed by men like the famous 'Capability' Brown.

Yet Johnson was still very much a man of his times, and the times he lived in held, almost as an article of faith, that the city was the motivating force of civilisation, that neatly ordered plots of land, worked by industrious farmers, were evidence of the outward spread of 'rational' improvement, and that only those countries and peoples who exhibited the characteristics of this view of civilisation were worthy of serious or prolonged consideration.

So we find Johnson writing of the 'dreariness' of the landscape, that the 'uniformity of barrenness' he observed on his journey 'can afford very little amusement to the traveller', and that such regions as he found himself passing through must wait 'long before they are civilised'.

Visiting a 'dun' on Skye, Johnson remarks only that 'edifices, either standing or ruined, are the chief records of an illiterate nation', and that the islands in general 'afford few pleasures, except to the hardy sportsman, who can tread the moor and climb the mountains' 'Of the Erse language', he writes, 'it is the rude speech of a barbarous people, who had few thoughts to express, and were content, as they conceived grossly, to be grossly understood', and he concludes, 'Hopeless are all attempts to find any traces of Highland learning'.

Yet even as Johnson was travelling through the Highlands and Western Islands of Scotland, a change was beginning. Cultural historians refer to this change as the Romantic movement and the main, indeed the decisive, difference between the perspective it elaborated and that of the 18th century was a new tendency to see a positive value and interest in cultures and peoples very different from those of Western Europe, especially those previously dismissed in contemptuous terms as 'barbaric'.

In practical terms, this change in perspective meant that older and more 'primitive' civilisations were seen as having a value of their own, and that the study of the language, the folklore, and the manuscripts of these cultures not only had an intrinsic value, but that much of importance could be learned through such study.

Seen from this angle, the Aran Islands offered a perfect example of a people and culture that had remained apparently untouched by what many were now starting to describe as the 'defects' of a too-cultivated civilisation.

Furthermore, along with the new perspective went in many cases a renewed sense of national pride in the past, and an increasing awareness that every nation had its share of literary, architectural and archaeological glories that were crucial in defining the identity of the nation.

In the particular case of the Aran Islands, a crucially important factor focusing attention on the islands was the decision taken by the English Parliament in 1824 to recommend a complete survey and valuation of the entire country. Accepted by Parliament, the Ordnance Survey, a branch of the British Army, was instructed to undertake the task of mapping Ireland on a scale of six inches to the mile.

It was the constellation of remarkably talented men – scholars and artists and antiquarians – who came together under the auspices of the Ordnance Survey that was to play a decisive part in ending the isolation of the islands and opening them up to the world.

Before presenting some of these 19th century accounts, we should at least consider the 17th century beginnings of antiquarian interest in the Aran Islands as represented in the work of Roderic O'Flaherty.

Roderic O'Flaherty (1629-1718) was one of the most learned scholars of the 17th century, an age that witnessed the first, tentative beginnings of a disciplined, scientific study of the past, based on the collection of primary source material and its assessment.

Apart from *A Chorographical Description of West or H-Iar Connaught*, written in 1684 but not published until 1846, O'Flaherty's most important work is *Ogygia seu Rerum Hibernicarum Chronologia*, published in London in 1685. It was translated into English by the Rev. James Hely and published in Dublin in 1693.

The full English title reads like a programme of 17th century antiquarianism: *Ogygia; or, a Chronological Account of Irish Events collected from Very Ancient Documents faithfully compared with each other & supported by the Genealogical &*

Chronological Aid of the Sacred and Profane Writings of the Globe. The significance of O'Flaherty's *Ogygia* rests on the fact that it was the first history of Ireland available to English scholars, written in the language of international scholarship, Latin, and it is clear that it was read by other antiquarians with interest and appreciation.

O'Flaherty, even though he was writing from the west of Ireland, was part of a wider movement of scholarship that included such figures as John Aubrey, the first to draw attention to Stonehenge and the virtual 'discoverer' of the remarkable late Neolithic 'temple' at Avebury in Wiltshire, Elias Ashmole, assiduous collector of manuscripts and author of the *History of the Order of the Garter,* and Anthony A'Wood, the cantankerous author of *Athenae Oxioniensus,* a history of Oxford from 1500 to 1690.

O'Flaherty was educated at the famous Galway school (its site is now occupied by the Customs House on Flood Street) run by Alexander Lynch, who numbered among his teachers the genealogist and antiquarian Dubhaltach Mac Firbisigh, and among his pupils John Lynch, whose books include a translation of Keating's *Latin History of Ireland,* as well as a refutation of Gerald of Wales' 12th century account of the country.

One of those who read *Ogygia* was Edmund Lhuyd (1660-1709), a Welsh antiquarian, naturalist and keeper of the Ashmolean Museum in Oxford who visited O'Flaherty at his house at Parke, between Furbo and Spiddal, in 1700 to collect material for his *Archaeologia Britannica.* Published in 1707, it is also important for containing the first Irish-English dictionary. Lhuyd visited Aran and sketched a plan of Dún Eochla on Inis Mór and also commented on the prevalence of the maidenhair fern. O'Flaherty was also in contact with William Molyneux, founder in 1683 of the Dublin Philosophical Society.

Although evidence is entirely lacking, it is hard not imagine that other travellers and antiquarians, stimulated by O'Flaherty's writings, visited Aran in the 18th century. The 18th century built on the foundations laid by the great 17th century antiquarians, and in such journals as *The Gentleman's Magazine* learned papers were regularly printed from contributors in both Britain and Ireland.

O'Flaherty's *Ogygia* and *West or H-Iar Connaught* were certainly highly regarded by scholars, and, so far as the Aran Islands are concerned, the latter book remained the only description of the antiquities of the three islands until their 19th century 'rediscovery'.

Illus. 9.2. John O'Donovan (1809 - 1861) is one of the most important scholars and antiquarians of the 19th century. In the course of his work for the Ordnance Survey he visited every parish in the country, and his Letters, preserved in the Royal Irish Academy, are an invaluable source of information. O'Donovan was one of the first scholars to apply a scientific approach to the cataloguing of Irish manuscripts. With Eugene O'Curry he founded the Irish Archaeological Society in 1840. His many translations include his landmark six volume edition of The Annals of the Four Masters, *with the English and Irish texts on facing pages. In 1850 he became Professor of Celtic Languages at Queen's College, Belfast. Among his last projects was his work in translating the Seanchas na hEireann, the ancient 'Brehon' laws of Ireland.*

The decision by the English Parliament to map both England and Ireland resulted in the appointment in 1827 of Lieutenant Thomas Larcom of the Royal Engineers as supervisor of the ambitious project's work in Ireland. Larcom's intention was not merely to map the country but to provide what he described as 'a full face portrait of Ireland'.

In practice this meant that the history, topography, antiquities, customs and traditions of each area were to be meticulously recorded, as well as correct spelling of Irish place names. To this end he decided to learn Irish.

Illus. 9.3. George Petrie (1789 - 1866) was an artist, musician and pioneering antiquarian. He paid his first visit to the Aran Islands in 1822, and was the first, after Roderic O'Flaherty, to describe the principal monuments. In 1833 his famous essay on the 'Round Towers of Ireland' won the Gold Medal of the Royal Irish Academy. In the same year Petrie was employed by the Ordnance Topographical Survey where he had as his assistants John O'Donovan and Eugene O'Curry. The plan to produce a series of Memoirs that would present, in Thomas Larcom's words 'a full face portrait of Ireland' was declared too costly by the Government after the publication of the first and only Memoir, but Petrie and his assistants continued to gather material. Petrie was a fervent champion of Ireland's monuments and culture, which he urged his fellow countrymen to preserve for future generations.

James Hardiman, author of the *History of the town and county of the town of Galway* (1820), recommended a young scholar named John O'Donovan who was, at that time, copying Irish manuscripts for Hardiman and laying the foundations for his later invaluable work on the Irish manuscript tradition.

In 1830 Larcom appointed O'Donovan to the staff of the Ordnance Survey to advise on the correct rendering of place-names that would be printed on the maps. O'Donovan quickly got to work on the question of place-names, but it was not until 1834 that he began field work.

From 1834 until 1840 O'Donovan travelled the country, taking lodgings in each area to be surveyed, questioning locals on Irish pronunciation of places, and patiently visiting and recording the nature of the antiquities that happened to be in a particular area. He brought to bear on his fieldwork his considerable knowledge of original Irish manuscripts that might shed light on the history of the regions he surveyed.

Larcom's plans for 'a full face portrait of Ireland' included the publication of a series of Memoirs that would collect all this information. To that end a group of scholars were employed by the Ordnance Survey under the direction of George Petrie (1789-1866), one of the most important antiquarians of the 19th century.

Working with Petrie were John O'Donovan, his brother-in-law, the great scholar Eugene O'Curry, the poet James Clarence Mangan, and several others employed in the copying and transcription of relevant material.

Also on the staff was the talented young artist William Wakeman, who has left a colourful account of the trip he and O'Donovan made to Aran in 1839, when, as he puts it, 'those islands were as yet almost a *terra incognita*, the place having been examined by only one true antiquary'.

This was George Petrie, who, Wakeman continues, 'some twenty year previously had visited the islands, and filled his sketch books with drawings and measurements of many of the principal objects of interest then to be found'.

William Stokes, in *The Life and Labours in Art and Archaeology of George Petrie* (1866), writes that 'Of these singular islands, though previously described by O'Flaherty, Petrie may be said to be the discoverer – at least in an antiquarian point of view'.

Petrie, who made his trip in 1821, was interested not only in the antiquities but the people as well, and describes them as 'a brave and hardy race, industrious and enterprising ...strangers to bigotry and intolerance'. His narrative contains a moving account of a scene he witnessed when 'a great number of islanders had determined to emigrate to America'.

They had been accompanied to the ship, which lay at anchor off Galway, by a Mr O'Flaherty, an islander regarded, says Petrie as 'the *pater patriae* of the Araners . . . the reconciler in all differences, the judge in all disputes, the advisor in all enterprises, and the friend in all things.' As the emigrants took their leave of him:

'Men and women all surrounded him – the former with cheeks streaming with tears, and the latter uttering the most piercing lamentations – some hung on his neck, some got his hands or arms to kiss, while others threw themselves on the deck and embraced his knees'.

Roughly twenty years later O'Donovan and Wakeman set sail on St John's Day, 1839, from Galway on 'a fine old Claddagh hooker, of about 16 tons...named the Saint Patrick'. After a night journey, they spotted the big island:

'The light had been seen for several hours...at length, after some very lengthened tacks and other nautical manoeuvres, we were safely landed at the little quay of Kilronan, the principal village on the Great Island. This happy deliverance took place about six o'clock in the morning, and we were very glad, shortly afterwards, to find ourselves in Mrs. Costello's little cottage.'

Wakeman gives a vivid account of their visit to Dún Aonghasa which gives not only an amusing account of the unabashed enthusiasm of these pioneer antiquarians but also a good idea of how the two men – artist and antiquary – dealt with the sites they visited elsewhere:

'Fired with a desire to visit the great Figbolgian Fort of Dún Aonghasa, we made but little delay at Mrs Costello's. Armed with measuring tapes, note-books, and sketching materials, we started over the rocks, in the direction of the western cliffs, upon the highest of which the great Acropolis of Aran stands.'

Wakeman, better than O'Donovan himself, who, in his

Ordnance Letters on Dún Aonghasa writes with scholarly detachment, wonderfully captures the impression made on the great antiquarian by the first sight of what is still regarded as one of the finest ancient monuments in Europe.

'A smart walk brought us in sight of the object of our day's pilgrimage; and I shall never forget O'Donovan's burst of enthusiasm when the old palace fortress of the days of Queen Maeve first met our view. He literally shouted with delight, and, after launching his umbrella a marvellous height into the air, threw himself on the ground, and shouted again and again.'

As the two men got down to work, Wakeman recalls that 'not a sound was to be heard but the booming of the ocean amongst the inaccessible caverns many fathoms below, or the screaming of the birds, who seemed clamorously indignant at our intrusion upon their dominion'.

O'Donovan returned to Galway after finishing his work, but Wakeman remained on the island ' to complete some work which, owing to stress of weather, we had but poorly finished'. His return voyage nearly ended in disaster, 'for when off Black Head, our hooker was struck by a squall, which came so suddenly that not a stitch of sail could be taken in. For a moment our gunnel was under water. The squall passed away almost as quickly as it had come upon us, and the only remark our hardy helmsman made was (referring to the boat), "begor, she got a drink".'

Unfortunately for O'Donovan and the others employed in the Topographical Department under George Petrie, the decision was taken by the Government to dispense with the series of Memoirs. However, the Ordnance Survey Letters of John O'Donovan along with the sketches by William Wakeman are preserved in the Royal Irish Academy. The material on Aran is extensive and extremely valuable as providing a record of the monuments of the islands as they were in the early part of the 19th century.

Sir Samuel Ferguson (1810-1886) was another scholar and antiquarian who visited the Aran Islands in 1853. Ferguson, who was Deputy-Keeper of the Public Records in Dublin, was elected President of the Royal Irish Academy in 1881. His most important work is *Ogham Inscriptions in Ireland,*

Scotland and Wales (1887, edited posthumously by his widow), but he was also a poet who utilised the stories found in such ancient manuscripts as the *Banquet of Dun na nGedh and the Battle of Magh Rath* for epic poems like 'Congal' (Yeats used the same source for his play 'The Herne's Egg').

Ferguson's account of his visit to the Aran Islands appeared in the *Dublin University Magazine* in 1853. It forms part of a two-part article that traces his journey from Clonmacnoise to Aran, which he reached not from Galway but Doolin.

'A row of two hours, against an unfavourable wind and through a rough sea, brought us to a little creek on the south side on Inishere. Here the canoe was drawn up, inverted, and carried on the backs of two of the crew, to one of the country dry-docks. Half a dozen other corraghs (sic) were already laid up within the little enclosure, resting with their gunnels on stone props, so as to clear their curved prows of the ground'.

Ferguson stayed with 'the respectable Widow O'Flaherty, to whom I am indebted for the rites of hospitality' in 'a little bed-room, not to be despised by one accustomed to sea-side lodgings'.

Ferguson's fascinating account is full of careful observations on the life of the inhabitants — their methods of thatching, the quality of the soil and 'the practice of forming artificial fields by the transport of earth', and, of course, descriptions of the monuments he had come to see.

On Inis Mór Ferguson took lodging with Mrs Costello at Kilronan, possibly the same Mrs Costello who had taken in O'Donovan and Wakeman when they had visited in 1839. Patrick Mullen, 'the guide and antiquary of the islands', showed him around, taking him to Dún Aonghasa and the ruins of the many Christian churches on Inis Mór. From his account it sounds as if the going was rough: 'It were tedious to enumerate the various minor ecclesiastical sites pointed out on Aran; nor shall I task the patience of the reader, by following Mr Mullen on his tour of all the *teampuls* and *man-isters* which the venturous antiquary may still trace through their coverings of bramble and nettles'.

However, he does provide a careful account of Cill Éinne and noted that 'Enda's original church has disappeared, and the blowing sands have quite obliterated the cemetery famous for its one hundred and twenty inscribed tombs of saints, adjoining it'.

Before leaving Inis Mór for the coast of Clare, he passed through the village of Cill Éinne. 'This luckless spot suffered about a year since a terrible calamity. The men and youths of the village, to the number of fourteen, had repaired to a flat, projecting rock to fish, and were engaged in angling from this natural platform, when one of those sudden waves which sometimes start up capriciously in the Atlantic, rolled in an swept them all away. There was scarcely a house in the village that had not lost a father, a son, or a brother'.

A few years after Ferguson's visit Inis Mór witnessed a remarkable spectacle, which it would not be too fanciful to describe as the first influx of 'tourists', when seventy members and associates of the Ethnological Section of the British Association made an excursion to the island in September, 1857, under the supervision of Sir William Wilde, father of Oscar and at that time Secretary of the Royal Irish Academy. The high point of the visit was a banquet held inside the walls of Dún Aonghasa. Among the distinguished company were George Petrie, Eugene O'Curry, and John O'Donovan, old friends from the Ordnance Survey days, as well as Sir Samuel Ferguson.

Martin Haverty, one of the party, has left us a detailed account of the visit, which must have astonished the inhabitants of the island. The *City of Tribes* and the Trinity House steam yacht, *Vestal*, dropped anchor in Cill Éinne Bay three hours after leaving Galway and the ships' boats, assisted by the coastguard boat, landed the party at Cill Éinne village.

Wilde, the 'cicerone' of the group, blew a whistle and proceeded to give an impromptu lecture on Arkin Fort after which the party headed for the round tower near St Enda's church. At the 'beautiful cyclopean Oratory of St Benan or Benignus', the group was treated to an account of the monument by Petrie, who observed that 'when he was in the island, thirty-five years ago, the round Tower they had just visited was much higher than at present; and he then met an old islander who remembered when it was 82 feet in height'.

Illus. 9.4. Samuel Ferguson (1810 - 1886) had a varied career, that brought him from Belfast, where he founded the Protestant Repeal Association in support of the Young Ireland movement, to the position of President of the Royal Irish Academy in 1881. Knighted in 1878 for public services, Ferguson's literary output was as varied as his career. His most important antiquarian work is Ogham Inscriptions in Ireland, Scotland and Wales *(1887, edited by his widow), but he also wrote poems, both serious and comic, and humorous stories like 'Father Tom and the Pope', contributed to* Blackwoods Magazine.

On the second day, the party visited Dún Eoghanachta, where Mr Thomas Thompson, the agent to the property, addressed the people on the necessity of preserving this and the other memorials on the island from dilapidation, after pointing out that the activities of 'idle boys for several years past' led him to fear 'that antiquaries at some future time will have few specimens of them left to ground their conjectures upon' – a curiously modern and prophetic warning!

At last the large party arrived at Dún Aonghasa, the 'culminating point of interest – the chief end and object of our pilgrimage'. Despite the clear exhaustion of some of the party, Haverty observes that 'to have seen this would have amply repaid any of the party for the whole fatigue and trouble of the expedition'.

This ancient monument, which Petrie had described in 1843 as 'the most magnificent barbaric monument now extant in Europe', was transformed into 'our banqueting hall' under the supervision of Wilde. The scene Haverty describes must be given in his own words: 'The stewards commenced their duties; the hampers were unpacked; and the company were arranged in a spacious circle on the grass in the centre of the fort, separated from the overhanging brow of the terrific precipice by a wide, low ledge of limestone, which formed a sort of table, upon which a part of the viands were laid: the waves of the great Atlantic breaking all the while on the rocks below, yet, at such a distance beneath us that their roaring only sounded like the gentlest murmurs'.

As the stewards cleared away the remains of the banquet, Wilde called upon the Rev. Dr MacDonnell, Provost of Trinity College, to preside as a number of those in the party addressed the assembled company. The Provost introduced the various distinguished speakers, among them Petrie, who recalled his first visit in 1822. Eugene O'Curry delivered an address in Irish to the islanders who had accompanied the party, in which he praised the 'gentlemen of great learning, who devoted their time for many a year to study and write about Ireland' (this was greeted with cries in Irish from the islanders, 'Musha, they're welcome!'). Finally John O'Donovan made a brief speech in which he also reflected on the present dilapidated state of the monuments he had originally seen twenty years ago.

Illus. 9.5. This sketch by F. W. Burton shows (left to right) the great Irish scholar, Eugene O'Curry (1796 - 1862), a peasant woman, and Samuel Ferguson. Dated September 6th, 1857, the sketch was done during the famous visit of the members and associates of the Ethnological Section of the British Association to the Aran Islands. Eugene O'Curry was, like Petrie and O'Donovan, one of the finest Irish scholars of the 19th century. Born in Clare, he was self-educated and was one of the young men who worked under Petrie on the Ordnance Survey of Ireland. His work cataloguing Irish manuscripts in the British Museum, Trinity College and the Royal Irish Academy gave him an unsurpassed knowledge of the subject, finding expression in two publications – Manuscript Materials of Ancient Irish History *(1861) and* Manners and Customs of the Ancient Irish *(3 volumes, 1873).*

After Patrick Mullen, who had been Ferguson's guide a few years earlier, added his support to what O'Donovan had said, 'a musician with a bagpipes, then played some merry tunes, and the banquet at Dun Aengus terminated with an Irish jig, in which the French Consul joined *con amore'*. At the end of the third day the party boarded ship and 'made a prosperous voyage to Galway, where we landed in time to enjoy our dinner previous to the starting of the special train for Dublin'. Clearly these eminent antiquarians knew how to order their priorities!

The second half of the 19th century witnessed an increasing number of visits by many more people, among them writers like Mary Banim whose account of her visit appeared in the *Weekly Freeman* in 1896; Lady Augusta Gregory, who collected material for her *Visions and Beliefs in the West of Ireland*; Padraig Pearse, who visited Inis Mór and Inis Meáin in 1898; and the poet and critic Arthur Symons who visited Aran in 1896 with W.B. Yeats.

Thomas J. Westropp (1860-1922) was probably the last of the great antiquarians to follow in the footsteps of men like Petrie, Ferguson and O'Donovan. A member of the Royal Society of Antiquaries of Ireland from 1886 and President in 1916, Westropp wrote hundreds of articles on different aspects of Irish antiquities, especially those found in the Burren, and many of his notebooks, containing his first-hand observations as well as accomplished water-colours and pen and ink sketches of what he visited over the years, are now in the Royal Irish Academy in Dublin.

Again, like Petrie and Ferguson before him, Westropp was fascinated by the people as much as the monuments they lived among. In 1878, on his first visit to Inis Meáin, he noted: 'This island is an extremely primitive place. We saw women grinding meal with querns & weaving the cloth which dyed red or brown forms the staple female dress. The men usually wear blue cloth clothes & scotch caps & 'pampooties' or raw hide shoes of untanned skin laced up the heel & instep, the wooden home made vessels are of the earliest type and very like the ones in the RIA museum'.

On Inis Mór 'stands the fine church of Temple Manistir Kieran where tradition says Columkille remained for some years studying with Kieran the carpenter, here a boy sold us two crown pieces of Queen Elizabeth found in a neighbouring field'. Westropp returned to the islands on several occasions with members of the Royal Society of Antiquaries. By now the islanders must have grown used to these groups of tourists disembarking at Cill Rónáin and spreading out to visit the monuments that were their daily companions as they went about their ordinary lives.

Over the space of a century the Aran Islands went from being isolated places rarely visited by outsiders, to becoming the destination of many different kinds of people with every kind of motive: writers looking for inspiration, social scientists eager to study a unique society that had preserved a way of life almost unchanged over centuries, antiquarians examining the historical monuments whose origins extended into the distant Christian and pre-Christian past; patriots seeking the primordial 'soul' of the Celt; and the curious, whom we today would describe as tourists.

A picture had been constructed by those who visited the islands, a picture of a people and a culture that seemed to embody all the virtues of the unspoiled Irish peasant. However, it was in many ways a caricature, since poverty and hardship were never far away, even as the 19th turned into the 20th century.

Illus. 9.6. Two drawings by Lady Augusta Gregory (1859 - 1932) showing (on left) Cill Ghobnait, an 11th century church on Inis Oírr dedicated to St Gobnait of Ballyvourney, Co. Cork, and (on right) what she calls 'the tree of Inisheer', which is probably the same 'one tree of the island' mentioned by Samuel Ferguson in his 1853 account of his visit to the three islands, that stood near Cill Ghobnait.

Inisheer - May 5- 1898 -

'Some Pagan thing' -

Illus. 9.7. Described by Lady Gregory as 'some Pagan thing' and dated 5th May 1898, this is, in fact, a prehistoric burial mound, Cnoc Raithní, on Inis Oírr.

It was to be part of the achievement of John Millington Synge, who is, ironically, partially responsible for the romantic image of the Aran Islands that persists even today, to graphically describe these hardships, along with the violence of evictions and other less savoury aspects of island life.

The rediscovery of the Aran Islands by the great antiquarians of the 19th century – Petrie, O'Donovan, Ferguson, Wakeman, and Westropp, to name some of the most important – laid the foundations for much of what was to follow in the 20th century. They were pioneers who opened up the riches of a place and a culture that continues to fascinate us as we head towards the turning of another century.

Illus. 9.8. Another drawing by Lady Gregory of a typical Aran hearth, with the large black kettle suspended from the chimney, a bench to sit on near the fire, and several alcoves used to keep things warm. It is at a hearth like this that we can imagine Lady Gregory sitting while she collected some of the material for her Visions and Beliefs in the West of Ireland *(1920).*

Illus. 9.9. A trio of visionary voyagers – (clockwise) J. M. Synge, George Russell (AE) and W. B. Yeats are depicted in this charming sketch by Harold Oakley. Yeats first visited the Aran Islands in 1896 in the company of Symbolist poet and critic, Arthur Symons, who wrote about his experiences in Cities and Seacoasts and Islands *(1897). Yeats recalled being introduced to an old man who fixed him with a penetrating eye and spoke two enigmatic sentences to him: 'If any gentleman has done a crime, we'll hide him. There was a gentleman that killed his father, and I had him in my own house six months till he got away to America'. Repeated later to Synge, these words provided the inspiration for* The Playboy of the Western World.

Yeats met Synge in Paris later in 1899 and advised him to 'give up Paris...Go to the Aran Islands. Live there as if you were one of the people themselves; express a life that has never found expression'. Synge's The Aran Islands, *his brilliant account of his time there, was published in 1907.*

Acknowledgements for Illustrations

Illus. 9.1.   Drawing, Royal Irish Academy.
Illus. 9.5.   Drawing, National Gallery of Ireland.
Illus. 9.6, 9.7, 9.8. Drawings, National Library of Ireland, by
           kind permission from Colin Smythe.
Illus. 9.9.   Drawing, Hugh Lane Municipal Gallery of
           Modern Art.

Illus. 10.1. As there was no turf on the islands it was imported from Connemara by hooker until recent decades. Considerable commerce based on the turf trade grew up between the islands and Connemara during the centuries and turf remained one of the most important imports until coal and gas replaced it in the 1960s and 1970s. It was deposited on the quay by the boatmen and transported to the home by the woman of the house in a wicker shoulder basket, the cliabh gualainne.

CHAPTER 10

Resources and Life:
aspects of working and fishing on the Aran Islands
Anne O'Dowd

Visitors and Trade

Island life is generally depicted in a nostalgic and traditional way intimating the survival of age old practices to a modern time and depicting a slow and unhurried way of life. Writers, artists, linguists, photographers and film-makers attracted to the Aran Islands over the centuries have certainly portrayed in their chosen medium the traditional ways they observed on these islands with a sense of capturing in print, on canvas or in film, aspects of a way of life on the verge of oblivion.

Ironically, despite all the attention devoted to the islands over the years from Roderic O'Flaherty in the late 17th century, to the 19th and early 20th century observers – including Oliver Burke, Samuel Lewis, John O'Donovan, Haddon and Browne and the Congested Districts' Board – folklorists, linguists and novelists from Lady Augusta Gregory to John Millington Synge and Holger Pedersen, photographers and film makers including Thomas Mason, Robert Flaherty and Muiris Mac Conghail and artists from Jack Yeats to Gwen

O'Dowd, very little description of everyday life was recorded in detail sufficient to reconstruct, for example, the day to day working and living habits of the communities of this island group. The native writers, Mairtín Ó Direáin and Liam O'Flaherty especially, have redressed this imbalance somewhat. Haddon and Browne's account at the end of the 19th century is probably the best observer's precis of the life of the islands. They titled their work 'The Ethnography of the Aran Islands' and essentially they documented in an academic fashion everything they saw. Synge's views of the islands, on the other hand, are particularly romantic; in his eyes the islanders were practising a 'simple life' which had elements of the 'artistic beauty of medieval life'.

Throughout the 19th century and certainly until after the second World War the life of the people was far from one of pleasantly existing in a romantic setting of stone and sea and sky. Times were hard as they were for so many, not only in other island communities, but through-

Illus. 10.3. A turf carrier near Cill Rónáin in the 1940s.

out the mainland as well. Synge's views could not contrast more sharply with those of Peadar Ua Concheanainn, a native of Inis Meáin, who described the people in the early 20th century as sglábhuighthe agus fátalaighthe (labourers and hunters), who every day of the year, early and late, wet or dry, were out seeking a living from their patches of land, or out on the sea fishing. They were obviously very hard workers,

Illus. 10.2. A young woman from Inis Oírr poses in this photograph to show the cliabh gualainne *loaded with seaweed for kelp.*

evidenced strikingly in the stone walls seen everywhere – the visual remains of some of their labours, the making of which, judging by their size and quantity, might indeed seem to an outsider to have been an addiction.

The way of life during the 19th and early 20th centuries could not be described as a subsistence economy, trade and social links having been established with the Galway and Clare coasts for many generations. Exports in the 18th and 19th centuries would have included kelp, fish, limestone, seabirds' eggs and feathers, and livestock, including pigs and sheep, but more especially, cattle. Imports in the earlier years included turf, boats, tools and poitín and later on staple foodstuffs such as flour, tea and sugar. Nor was it an isolated lifestyle as French, Spanish and English fishermen had fished in the waters offshore from at least the 16th century. There would have been more isolation between the nucleated settlements of early 19th century Aran than between the island group as a whole and the outside world.

Natural Resources and Clothing

Synge's observations on the peoples' clothes, furniture, furnishings etc. being 'full of individuality', fashioned from materials both common and, to some extent, peculiar to the islands, are more astute in that these objects do show the links between the islanders and the world immediately about them. Their use, for example, of natural materials – rye straw to thatch their houses and to make sheep fetters, tethers and donkey spancels, straw door liners and food containers; horsehair for ropes; sally rods for cradles and the range of wickerwork containers used for transporting sand and seaweed, for straining potatoes and for holding the long spillet lines; animal skins – bullock and heifer – and to a lesser extent, seal, for the rawhide shoes, cow skin for the currachs and

Illus. 10.4. A cuingir chao-rach for tethering two sheep together. It is made of rye straw and consists of two rope rings joined by a short length of rope. The rings are c. 18cm in outside diameter and 2cm thick. The rope joining them is 17cm long and 1 cm thick.

Illus. 10.5. A basketmaker on Inis Oírr shows the first stage in the making of a scib, a small circular basket of unpeeled rods used for straining the water from boiled potatoes. The finished basket measures c. 40cm in diameter and 9cm deep.

Illus. 10.6. left. George Gillen (Seoirse Ó Giolláin), the weaver, at his loom in his workshop at Fearann an Choirce. Weaving was the traditional trade of the Gillen men, learning from one another through the generations since their arrival on Inis Mór from their native Leitrim. The weaver would weave about 20 metres of cloth in a day, his arms and legs working furiously all the time while his eyes kept track of the numerous warp threads. His charge for a metre of plain cloth was four pennies (4d).

sheepskin for the buoys for the fishing nets and lines. Providing fuel for the islands' fires was a constant worry and a solution was found when it was discovered that dried cow dung, set alight, gave a moderate amount of heat. Fish oil, especially oil from the liver of the sunfish or basking shark, provided light.

The most visible expression of this utilisation of the natural resources to visitors to the islands up to the 1940s and the 1950s was, of course, the traditional clothing made from flannel woven from the wool of the island sheep. The natural browns and whites, and the blues and reds had particular appeal to artists and photographers thanks to whom we now know more about the traditional clothing on the Aran Islands than anywhere else in the country.

Illus. 10.7. Having started the wheel spinning with a strenuous movement of her hand the spinner feeds one end of the roll of carded wool onto the swiftly whirring spindle which the wheel has set in motion. Holding on to the other end of the roll she draws it out while simultaneously she moves backwards from the turning wheel. Women and girls traditionally carded and spun the wool – the cards or combs being bought in Galway. From about the 1920s the sacks of wool were sent to Lydon's woollen mills in Dominick Street to be spun into rolls in preparation for spinning.

There was great uniformity in the clothes worn by women throughout Ireland for most of the 19th century and country women simply wore a skirt and blouse or jacket buttoned to the neck. On Aran the skirts, or cotaí as they were called, were generally made from flannel or fleainín, a heavy woollen tweed woven locally. The skirts were very wide and often contained a width of 4-5 metres of material which was dyed red, black or dark blue. They were gathered into the waist with a chequered cotton waistband known as a fad and were often worn with two or three white flannel underskirts. A combed or raised pile on the surface of the skirt gave it a luxurious finish. The jacket or bodice was worn either inside or outside the skirt and might have been made from breidín or frieze, a rougher woollen cloth than the fleainín, or any variety of materials including linen, cotton and calico. A jacket or deaicéid of fleainín, with a velvet collar and velvet cuffs, was a popular fashion among the women of Aran in the 1930s and 1940s. An apron worn over the skirt had been a additional item of women's dress, both inside and outside the house, during the centuries and may be seen as a diminutive of the original outer cotton or wolsey gown. The naprún seicear, or check apron, as it was known, was made from a generous width of black and white or blue and white check cotton. Next to the skin women wore a shift or léine of cotton or fine linen but, it was their outer clothes which were especially distinctive.

In most of Ireland during the 19th century women wore the hooded cloak to keep themselves warm. It seems that the cloak never became popular or fashionable on the Aran Islands, the women there preferring to keep themselves warm with the red or black plaid shoulder shawl – the seáilín pleaid. Shoulder shawls or wrappers of light woollen weave were also worn and the colourful crocheted and knitted shawls, still to be seen on Inis Meáin, became popular in the 1930s. A still warmer outer garment was the heavy woollen shawl with a wide patterned border and cotton fringing, known to many as the Galway shawl because of its popularity throughout that county. The shawls were made in Scotland and began to make an appearance at the turn of the century. Like the hooded cloak in parts of Cork, women were to be seen wearing the Galway shawl with its distinctive brown and fawn colours as recently as the 1960s. On Aran the Galway shawl replaced an older form of cloak or shawl which the women themselves invented by sewing a crios or woollen belt for decoration to a spare cóta or skirt. This they placed on their head allowing the full width of the skirt to drape over their shoulders and down their bodies, back and front, thus giving

Illus. 10.8. Unlike the men, who donned knitted and crocheted tam-o'-shanters, and later broad rimmed hats and tweed caps, the women generally went bareheaded. The imported tartan or plaid shawl with its red patterns and the finely woven black woollen shawl protected their upper bodies.

Illus. 10.9 below. A group of women coming from mass. The woman on the right is wearing the so-called Galway shawl while her three fellow travellers wear the older traditional form of cloak – a skirt or cóta decorated at its edge with a crios.

the appearance of a cloak. A woman would describe this covering as 'cóta ar mo bhráid' and some of the older women continued the tradition for wakes and funerals only until the 1940s.

A man from the Aran Islands wore a suit of clothing which included an inner shirt of a light blue woollen cloth, the léine ghlas, which was essentially a tunic with set in sleeves and a narrow neck band. The bástchóta, or sleeved waistcoat, was worn over the léine ghlas and it was made from white flannel. It had a V-shaped neck opening and was closed at the front with 3 to 4 buttons. For extra warmth the man might have worn a second and heavier woollen shirt, the léine ghorm, which was in style similar to the inner shirt but more ample

Illus. 10.10 left. In the late 1940s the islandman's suit of clothing would have cost him £9.2s for the bheist, bástchóta, treabhsar *and* léine, *an increase of more than three-fold on pre-war prices. Brand new, the clothes weighed close on 5 kilograms. Being made from hardwearing materials they lasted for many years.*

Illus. 10.11 right. Unlike other countrymen, Aran men did not wear an outer coat. The sleeveless waistcoat or bheist *was the outer garment worn over layers of shirts,* léinte, *and a* bástchóta *or sleeved waistcoat of undyed white wool. The wide brimmed felt hat, an import from Dublin, made its appearance at the turn of the century.*

in width allowing it to be worn over both the léine ghlas and the bástchóta. The waistcoat or bheist was generally the only outer upper garment worn by the older men. The front of it was made from undyed brown or grey frieze which was lined with white flannel, while the back was of blue frieze, corresponding to the material in the trousers. The more common

type of trousers, treabhsar, worn by Aran men at the beginning of the 20th century had wide, loose legs ending well above the ankle with a slit some 7cm long on the outer side of each leg. In more recent times the more close fitting trousers, or bríste, were made from a brown or grey frieze similar to the cloth in the front of the waistcoat. The underpants, or drár bán, were made with full-length legs from white flannel and both they and the outer trousers were secured around the waist with a colourful woven belt or crios.

Men, women and children wore simple moccasin style shoes of untanned leather. People nowadays call these shoes pampooties, a name which seems to have been given to them by one of the many visiting observers of the 19th century. On the islands they are known as bróga úrléir, i.e. bróga úrleathair, and while they were at one time made from seal skin, they were in recent times always made from cow hide. A penknife was used to cut the hide and make the holes for toe and heel seams which were secured with fishing cord. The life of a pair of bróga úrleathair was only 4 to 6 weeks. They became hard and dry with use and had to be left soaking in water to restore their flexibility. They were worn over hand knitted socks which were generally dark blue in colour with a pattern of triangles in blue and undyed white wool at the toe end.

Children, both boys and girls, wore clothes similar to their mothers until they were well into their teens. A dress or frock, the cóta cabhalach, was a black, red or white flannel skirt sewn to a cotton or linen bodice. Over the cóta cabhalach the toddlers wore a beibe or bib of cotton, young boys a frieze jacket of grey or brown cloth and, in later years a knitted jumper, and young girls a shoulder shawl or hug-me-tight similar to their mothers. The shoulder shawl was worn by folding it into a triangular shape which was placed over the shoulders and across the breast. One point of the triangle hung loose down the back while the other two were secured at the waistband or tied in a knot at the back.

Knitted ganseys or jumpers did not form part of the traditional clothing on the Aran Islands

Illus. 10.13 below. Weaving a crios in 1952.

Illus. 10.12 above. Weaving the woollen belt or crios was the work of the woman of the house. The coloured warp threads were first arranged in the desired pattern and length by tying their ends to the legs or backs of chairs in the kitchen. The woman tied one end of these threads in a loose knot to her left pampootie. She held the other end of the warp threads in her left hand and started weaving. The principle was that employed when using a loom and a band of wool was tied around the upper and lower threads to keep them apart. The warp threads were wound around a small piece of stick, a fiteán, held in the woman's right hand.

until the beginning of the 20th century. The raised pattern knitting, which has become so popular world-wide in the last fifty years or so, was probably primarily influenced by the ganseys worn by the visiting English fishermen. The earlier patterns consisted of simple rope and moss stitch designs on the yoke and upper sleeves only. The Aran style jumper, with its complicated set of patterns, which we know today, is a 20th century development of the simpler form. The patterns developed over the years through a combination of inventiveness on the part of the knitters and the growth and spread of various beliefs about the individual stitches. While the stitches may reflect elements of the local landscape including field patterns and stone walls, they are basicallly geometric shapes.

House and Hearth

The older thatched houses, few of which now remain on the islands, are one storey high, rectangular in ground plan and built of limestone with walls some 60-80cm thick. The inner and outer surfaces of the walls are constructed of dry stone walling with a rubble core in between, while the gables are stepped and project over the thatch at each end. The roof is supported on a frame of couples resting on the tops of the side walls and the roof itself is a thatch of rye straw over a complete cover of scraws. The thatch is kept in place with a network of ropes tied to rows of pegs driven into the walls of the house just below the eaves and into the tops of the gable walls. This thatch would be renewed every two years. The ground plan of the houses consists of either two or three rooms with a kitchen and a bedroom, or a kitchen in the centre and a bedroom at each end. Most of the houses have two outside doors placed one opposite the other in the kitchen and the wind direction decides which one is left open during the day for light and ventilation. Generally, the kitchen was supplied with only one window and this was placed on the front wall of the house.

Illus. 10.14. Young boys wore a flannel frock and jacket or knitted pullover or gansey until their early teens. Fooling the fairies or daoine maithe *into thinking that they were little girls, and not boys whom they preferred, has been given in many parts of Ireland as an explanation for this custom. The real explanation has probably more to do with household economy. The woman of the house made her own and her children's clothes from her own cut down cast-offs. The longer she could provide for both her daughters and sons in this way, the more she saved on otherwise expensive weaver's and tailor's bills.*

Illus. 10.15 above. Traditional house at the end of the 19th century.

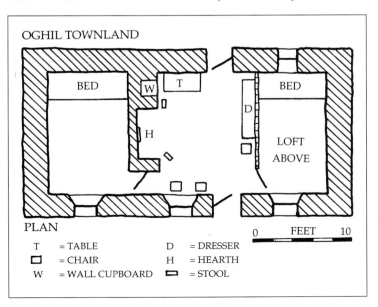

Illus. 10.16 below. The walls of the traditional houses were built of irregular stones and generally both the inside and outside were whitewashed. The ground floor plan shows the arrangement of the rooms and the two doors opposite each other in the kitchen. The roof is thatched with rye straw, the straw being tied on to the scraw or sods of turf laid on the rafters. Straw ropes form a net on the roof to keep the thatch secure. The houses were lightly thatched every one to two years and each had an outhouse placed near it in which potatoes were stored.

Illus. 10.17. The rye straw is stacked in preparation for thatching. Inis Mór, 1993.

In these houses every household activity was centred in the kitchen especially around the hearth which was a large arched recess with a crook for hanging the pots and skillets over the open fire. All the cooking for animals and humans was done over the open fire – potatoes were boiled in the pot, soda bread was baked in the pot oven and thin cakes of oaten bread were baked on the griddle, a flat iron pan. The position of the furniture in the kitchen was similar from one house to the next. The dresser

Illus. 10.18. The fire-place, a large recess on either the left or right hand side in the kitchen on entering the house, had a hook or crook hanging down over the fire for the suspension of the pot-bellied cooking pot. The kitchen floor was rarely boarded and was generally the bare rock or clay. The houses varied in size with an average kitchen measuring some 3m x 4 m. Artificial light in this view was provided by a paraffin lamp hanging on the wall to one side of the hearth. Several pieces of cut hide for pampooties, bróga úrleathair, are hanging on a line over the fire. In the 1960s £4-5 was paid to Galway butchers for a bullock skin (croiceann bulláin) from which the shoes were made. The group of holy pictures on the side wall next to the hearth was a feature of many houses on the islands.

was placed at the partition wall between the kitchen and the small bedroom, or seomra beag, as it was generally called – the larger bedroom at the other end of the house being the seomra mór. The small bedroom was supplied with two windows one on either side wall as it seems generally that two rooms were made out of this space as the family grew. A small table might have been placed by this partition wall also with a second table by the door leading to the other side of the house. In some houses a long form was placed beside the second table and a selection of holy pictures was hung on the wall above. The only remaining furniture in the kitchen included a few low stools by the fire and a couple of chairs. Storage areas for pots not in use, fishing gear and various baskets etc. were also to be found in the kitchen, in a wall cupboard to one side of the hearth, for example, or in the lofts over the bedrooms. In the 19th century the beds were described as 'tent' beds, i.e. with boarded ends and pitched roofs which made them warm and draught proof. At the beginning of the 20th century such beds were deemed unhealthy by the medical profession and they were gradually replaced with simpler plank beds without the canopy.

The type of traditional house described above, the central hearth house, was the most prevalent traditional house on the islands. However, some other traditional types are also to be seen

Illus. 10.19. A dresser with its delph in a house in Gort na gCapall, Inis Mór. The seomra beag or small bedroom often had a wooden partition between it and the kitchen and to save timber the dresser was used as part of this partition.

Illus. 10.20. A wicker cradle, cliabhán, made of unpeeled sally rods. The body is 91cm long, c 45cm at its widest and the hood is made in one piece with the body. The wooden frame of the cradle, into which the warp rods are set, has a rocker at each end and two side rails. Four transverse rails are nailed across the top of the side rails to support a mattress.

such as the two-roomed thatched houses with the hearth placed at one gable wall and a few examples of the hearth lobby type house. This latter has its front door in line with the hearth and in place of entering the kitchen directly one goes through the front door into a small lobby or porch area. Both the Land Commission and the Congested Districts' Board introduced improvements to the dwellings on the islands at the end of the 19th century. The traditional houses were provided with tiled roofs from this time and the walls of many houses were raised. In the process extra space for sleeping accommodation was provided and the houses became one and a half storeys with a dormer window in the roof. New house plans were introduced by the CDB in the 1920s such as the one storey house which was similar in plan to the traditional type with its hearth in the centre of the house. However, it also had bigger windows, a porch and a tiled roof. The CDB also introduced the two-storey

Illus. 10.21 below left. A shell lamp made of a large scallop shell with a wick of twisted strands of wool. Oil from the liver of fish provided the fuel. Such lamps were used on the Aran Islands in the 19th century and were to be found placed on a projecting stone or wooden bracket near the fireplace.

Illus. 10.22 top right. Wooden canna used when milking cows. It was also used to take dinners to men working in the fields by carrying it in a cliabh on the back. These stave built vessels were made in a choice of sizes and this example from Inis Oírr is 30cm high and 23cm in base diameter.

Illus. 10.23 right. Ciseán, a container of lipe work, i.e. the cylindrical coils of rye straw are secured with strips of bramble bark. It is from Aran and was presented to the National Museum in 1918. It measures 27cm in height and 24.5cm in base diameter. Two lugs of twisted bramble are inserted in the sides of the ciseán and attached to these is a handle of hard 2-strand cord. These containers were used on the three islands to bring hot dinners to the men working in the fields. They were preferred to wicker baskets as they kept the food warmer.

farm house, which remained a popular house plan until the middle of this century, and the asymmetrical two storey, three bedroom house which has its door near one gable end.

Grants for new house construction in the Gaeltachtaí began in 1929 when more house plans were introduced to the islands. Standard designs up to the early 1960s included the two-storey farm house, which had been introduced by the CDB, and a single storey tiled house which was provided with a porch, a central kitchen and three bedrooms. In the 1960s Roinn na Gaeltachta devised a selection of almost thirty house plans which would comply with planning regulations. The range included the modern two-storey, chalet and small house types to be seen today along side spacious bungalow designs introduced in the 1970s and the 1980s.

Illus. 10.24. The thatched Telephone Exchange on Inis Meáin.

Work and Economy

The islanders were particularly fortunate in the mid-19th century in that the potato blight did not reach the islands. There had been a famine in the early 1820s, but the potentially disastrous consequences of this were contained due to the scale of the relief operations. They lived chiefly in the early 19th century by fishing and kelpmaking, sowing their patches with potatoes and rye, using seaweed as their only fertilizer. They fished during the summer months with spillet and hand lines and drift nets for cod, ling, haddock, turbot, gurnet, mackerel, bream and herring; they had lobsters, crabs, cockles and mussels in abundance; they fished in May and June for the basking shark, the commercial value of which in the 18th and 19th centuries was so high that shark fishing was second in importance only to the herring fishery. There were plenty of hares and rabbits on the islands; they were visited by gannets, pigeons and plovers, and puffins lived in the cliff faces.

While geologically the islands can be treated as a unit, linguistically and economically they are quite different. Inis Meáin is the least accessible of the three and the island with the smallest population. This island was able to meet much of its food needs from the land which may explain the smaller numbers of fishermen living there than on the other two islands. In contrast, Inis Oírr, the smallest island had a higher population than Inis Meáin and, consequently, more fishermen. Inis Oírr's main contacts have traditionally been with the Clare coast and the Irish spoken there has a number of affinities with the Munster dialect of Clare. Inis Mór had a garrison established near the village of Cill Éinne in the reign of Elizabeth I when the strategic importance of the islands at the entrance to Galway Bay was realised. Cill Rónáin became the administrative capital and, as a consequence, largely English speaking because of its direct contacts with Crown representatives over the years. A commercial fishing industry was also established in Cill Éinne before it was transferred to Cill Rónáin at the end of the 19th century. Most heads of households on the three islands were farmers/fishermen and an extraordinarily high proportion of the population, almost a quarter for the islands as a whole and nearly a third for Inis Meáin alone, were engaged in making cloth and clothes for the islands' own use. The importance of this latter occupation had changed perceptively by the century's end when the young people, especially on the big island, had begun to purchase large amounts of shop tweeds and fashionable clothes. The locally woven flannel and frieze were still extensively worn on Inis Meáin and Inis Oírr until the 1940s.

Emigration was high, the traditional destination being south Boston, an area even today inhabited by a high proportion of Irish speakers from the Aran Islands. Inexplicably, the islanders did not practise seasonal migration which, elsewhere along the west coast, added much needed cash to the household economy. Synge does mention that the fluency of English of Pat Dirrane, the storyteller, was due to the months he had spent as a harvestman in England in his younger days. However, recorded numbers of seasonal migrants from the three islands are so low as to be insignificant. This is particularly surprising considering the relative closeness of the Achréidh, an area in east Galway around Athenry where men from Connemara traditionally found work every year. As a result, aside from emigrant remittances and, in more recent decades, government subsidies, the islanders were totally dependent on the resources of the islands for

The estimated cash receipts and expenditure of families in poor and ordinary circumstances in the 1890s							
RECEIPTS		£	s.	d.	**EXPENDITURE**	£	s.	d.
Sale of 5 pigs		10	0	0	Rent	3	0	0
" " cattle		7	0	0	Clerical dues	0	10	0
" " sheep		5	0	0	Clothes	6	0	0
" " 1 foal		5	0	0	Meat and flour	12	0	0
" " kelp		9	0	0	Groceries	6	11	0
" " eggs		1	0	0	Tobacco	2	12	0
" " butter, wool and seaweed		2	0	0	Spades	0	10	0
" " fish		3	0	0	Extras	2	0	0
					Turf	3	4	0
		£42	0	0		£36	7	0

RECEIPTS		£	s.	d.	**EXPENDITURE**	£	s.	d.
Sale of 2 pigs		4	0	0	Rent	1	10	0
" " sheep		2	0	0	Clerical dues	0	5	0
" " fish		4	0	0	Clothes	5	0	0
" " 1 calf		4	0	0	Meat and flour	9	0	0
" " kelp		9	0	0	Groceries	3	10	0
" " seaweed		1	0	0	Tobacco	2	12	0
" " eggs		1	0	0	Turf	3	4	0
					Extras	1	0	0
		£25	0	0		£26	1	0

Source: Congested Districts' Board, *Baseline Reports*, 1892-1896.

their livelihoods.

The economic base of the islands had changed very little by the end of the 19th century. Major Ruttledge-Fair, the Congested Districts' Board inspector, was a visitor in the early 1890s and reckoned the cash receipts and expenditure of families in both, what he termed, ordinary and poor circumstances.

Apart from the combined income from the sale of livestock and fish, income from the sale of kelp was proportionally high for the majority of the islanders. The glass and soap making industries in the early 18th century initially produced a demand for kelp which was supplied by the coastal dwellers around Ireland for generations and, in later years, demands for iodine revived the flagging industry and provided the much needed income once again. In more recent years the fine powder produced by burning sea rods, slata mara, has been used in the ice cream, paint and cosmetic industries. Dozens of types of seaweed grow around the

Illus. 10.25 opposite page. Women did not do much work in the fields other than weeding potatoes. Outside of housework, childminding and spinning and dyeing, they did their share of backbreaking work helping the men during the season of drying and stacking kelp. Gathering carrigeen moss from the rocks was a task which was almost exclusively their own.

Illus. 10.28 opposite page. A racán or seaweed hook which is a smith-made 3-pronged iron rake used to gather loose seaweed floating near the shore. It is from Inis Mór and when in use it would have a wooden handle some 3-4 metres long attached to the tang. Each of the long prongs is round in section, some 48cm in length and 1.2cm in diameter.

Illus. 10.26 above. Up to the beginning of this century there were no roads as such – other than path or trackways – on either Inis Meáin or Inis Oírr. As a consequence there were no wheeled vehicles and goods such as seaweed for kelp and seaweed and sand for making land were carried in panniers of wood and sally rods by donkeys and horses.

Illus. 10.27 below. Gathering seaweed with a racán, *a seaweed hook. The sheepskin tied to the man's back will prevent water from the weed soaking into his clothes when he piles it on his back to take it from the shore to dry land.*

Illus. 10.29. There was no constant wage labour in former times on the islands but there were opportunities for earning some extra money at both seaweed gathering and kelp burning. Prices per ton of kelp fluctuated greatly. In the opening years of the 19th century kelp was selling for £13 a ton but the price had dropped to £4 a ton by 1820. A century later it was fluctuating around £4 and it is estimated that some two thirds of the population were engaged in kelpmaking at this time.

coast but the main distinction was made between the black (feamainn dhubh) and red (feamainn dhearg) seaweeds – the former growing above the low water mark and the latter below. The red weed was potentially more valuable, yielding the salts containing iodine, and the red weed known as coirleach was particularly favoured for kelp. The seaweed was collected in late spring for fertiliser and early summer for burning into kelp. It was harvested from the sea with a seaweed rake known as a racán and loaded into the baskets (cliabh gualainne) and panniers (cliabh feamainne) with a seaweed hook, the bacán. The seaweed for kelp was burned in a low rectangular kiln (tornóg), and a long handled iron poker, the bod raca, was used to turn the seaweed while it was being transformed. In the 1890s also, land, i.e. dúrabhán, was still made by spreading layers of seaweed, sand and the available scarce

soil and animal manure on the bare limestone to produce the main crops of rye and potatoes. Earlier in the century, in 1855, William Wilde had reckoned that of the total acreage of the islands – some 11,000 acres – 740 were under crops and nearly 700 of these were sown with potatoes. Judging by these figures alone it would not be correct to view the islands as nothing more than unproductive, bare rock. While the sandy nature of the soil made it unsuitable for oats, it did produce good pasture and the cattle and sheep reared on the islands have for long had a good reputation. Roderic O'Flaherty wrote in 1684 that 'among the stones is very sweet pasture so that beef, veal and mutton are better and earlier in season than elsewhere', and Samuel Lewis, who visited Aran in 1837, noted that while the prevailing crops then were potatoes and rye with small quantities of barley, their most profitable

Illus. 10.32. A wooden stave built vessel used for carrying water from the well and to the animals in the pastures. It was known as an ancard. This example from Inis Oírr has 13 staves. It is 41cm high with a bottom diameter of 36cm and a top diameter of 28.5cm. The ancard is bound with four iron hoops and for carrying it two lugs of hoop iron are placed on opposite sides. The lugs are kept in place by inserting their ends under the two middle hoops. Through the lugs a length of thick 3-ply rope, 2cm in diameter, is inserted and the ends of the rope are roughly spliced together to form a continuous band. The ancard was either carried on the shoulder or secured by the rope to either side of the straddle on the back of a donkey.

Illus. 10.30. The work in the fields was all spade labour and the islanders' hardiness, strength and activity in the early 19th century was attributed to the quality of the air along with their 'sobriety and industrial habits' by John O'Flaherty who visited Aran in 1825. Only a small portion of the land on the islands was naturally fit for crops. A considerable percentage of the existing soil was made by carting seaweed and sand from the shore and spreading this in layers on the bare limestone.

Illus. 10.31 right. A harvest scene below Dún Aonghasa photographed by Fr Browne, August 1938.

stock was their breed of calves, much sought after by the Connacht graziers. Stock rearing retained its position as the basis of agriculture into the 20th century and buyers from Clare, in addition to those from Connacht, also bought livestock during the summer months. Much of the surface area of the islands is made up of limestone pavement with pockets of a light fertile soil especially in the north eastern parts; the bare limestone at the 'back' of each island produces good grazing between the limestone slabs. Due to the porous nature of soil and limestone, however, watering the cattle remained an annual and constant problem. This was alleviated greatly by the building of water troughs in the 1920s. Up to this time the cattle were watered by hand mainly with stave built vessels manufactured on the islands.

Illus. 10.33. Most of the fields are small by any standards with the high walls of stones piled loosely one on top of the other providing protection for the crops and animals from the biting wind which might otherwise sweep everything away. In some places the walls are of considerable height and wooden and metal gates were introduced in recent decades. Traditionally access to a field was made by removing the smaller stones piled between larger flags placed at intervals around the field.

Illus. 10.34. A water trough or tank for catching rain water for cattle. They can be seen scattered throughout the islands and this example is on Inis Meáin. They each consist of a sloping platform down which the rainwater flows into a limestone trough. The platforms are constructed of a formation of stones over which are laid rough limestone slabs. Many of the pastures are some distance from a natural spring and to obviate the need to carry water in the ancard over rough terrain, the water troughs were dispersed throughout the islands once the initial idea was introduced in the first decade or two of the 20th century.

Illus. 10.35. The light sandy soil did produce excellent crops of potatoes which were an important export. The currachs were used to deliver the sacked potatoes to the steamer.

Fishing

Fishing on the islands remained undeveloped and essentially primitive until recent decades. Cliff fishing with handlines baited with periwinkle and crab was widely practised and fish caught included ballan wrasse (ballach), gurnet (cnúdán), pollock (mangach), coal fish (glasóg) and mackerel (ronnach.) There was an art to fishing from the cliffs; sitting up to hundreds of feet above the sea required immense sensitivity to react swiftly to the movement of the fish below.

Irish fishermen generally had to watch on during the centuries while Ireland's coastal waters were being fished by outsiders – in the 15th and 16th centuries by the Spanish who frequently had hundreds of vessels fishing around the coast; in the 17th century the French and English took over and throughout the 19th century the Aran fishermen had to contend with the tyrannical attitude of the Claddagh fishermen until at least after the mid-century famine when death, poverty and subsequent loss of the fishing gear saw the beginning of the end of the Claddagh fishermen's dominance of Galway coastal waters. In the 1890s the Royal Dublin Society investigated the seas off Galway and Mayo and in their report stated that 'no place seems so admirably suited for a fishing station as the Aran Islands'. In 1892, the Congested Districts' Board established the spring mackerel fishing and a mackerel curing station at Cill Rónáin. Spring fishing for mackerel lasted for about two months, from mid April to mid June and it was mainly a big boat occupation. During the autumn fishing season the mackerel generally were lying too close to the shore for the big boats, and the small boats were able to avail of the catch. The later season began in August and was widespread along the west coast. The CDB made many efforts to assist the expansion of the industry in the following years but a decline in the catches and the uncertainty of the market by the end of the century hindered the development. Sailing boats of any kind – currachs or yawls – could not compete with large steamers and motor trawlers and because the islanders remained traditionally farmer/fishermen, being described as boatmen rather than sailors, they did not tend to fish until the fish went to shore. There was some development of the industry during the first World War years but the main effort to organise the industry came in 1931 when the Irish Sea Fisheries Association was established. Its functions were taken over in 1952 by Bord Iascaigh Mhara. The successful development of the islands' fishing industry is a very recent feature of the islands' economy and it is not surprising that many of the old fishing methods and the gear remained as late as the 1950s and 1960s, to be collected by the National Museum and the Department of Irish Folklore at University College, Dublin.

Illus. 10.36. Currachs survive all along the west coast and it is possible to see the craft's development from the most primitive of the Rosses and Donegal islands paddling types to the refined elegance of the Kerry naomhóg. The Aran currachs vary in size depending on the number of rowers – 2, 3 or 4 – to be accommodated. In plan it has a low, narrow hull, a low transom and sheered bows. Each man rowed two oars and the larger Aran currachs carried a small lug sail hoisted on a mast set in the bows.

Illus. 10.37. Bringing currachs to the sea, Inis Meáin
1952.

Illus. 10.38 right. Two
glionda or hand lires used
for catching bream and mackerel. Each consists of a square
wooden frame made of 4
pieces of timber 1.8cm thick.
That on the left is 22cm
square while the example on
the right is 23cm. The lines
are wound onto the frames
and each line has a lead
weight attached. One of the
weights is half oval in section,
12cm long, flat at one side
and tapering at both ends,
while the other is bell-shaped
with a base diameter of 5cm
and a height of 6cm.

Probably the most ancient method of catching
fish was by hand or by spear. For catching fish
in any quantity, however, it was the use of net-
ting which marked the industry's main development and one which can be compared to the
effect of the introduction of steam trawling to
the industry in the mid-19th century.
Throughout the 19th century line fishing was
particularly important to the fishing industry
along the west coast and, being essentially part-
time fishermen fishing in rocky waters, longline

or spillet fishing was especially suited to the
needs of the Aran fishermen. Fish caught by the
longlines included cod (troisc), ling (langaí), ray
(roic), turbot (turbaird), hake (colmoirí), haddock (cadóga), dogfish (freangaigh) and large
halibut (bóleathaí). The fishermen began
preparing their gear as early as November and
this would have included the long line itself,
the droim an spiléid, a strong line 3-5mm in
diameter, tied to which at regular intervals
were approximately 120 snood lines, consisting
of lighter line about 2mm in diameter, each one
from c. 30cm - 260cm long and with a hook tied
to its end. The hooks were bought in Galway
and the fishermen distinguished between the
large and small spillet lines – the hooks and
snood lines on the latter being smaller in size.
They depended in the early 19th century for
herring to bait the long lines and up to the end
of the 1840s there was great herring fishing all
along the west coast. The herring shoals had
virtually vanished after the mid-century famine
when the fishermen began to use lugworm and
ray in addition to herring for baiting the lines.
A spillet or spiléid was considered to be a
man's share in a boat and each fishing team
generally consisted of three men. They made
the snoods themselves, and formerly the longlines also, using a wooden framed device
known as a cairt with which it might take four
hours to make 400-500 snoods. As soon as the
weather was fine enough in the springtime, the
nets were set for catching herring to be used as
bait. Each net had a strong back rope with
corks attached to keep it afloat. It was not
moored, but was allowed rather to drift with
the tide and the fish, in trying to get through it,
got their heads in past the gills and were then
caught. The drift nets were set in the evenings
and taken up the following morning and the
catch, in addition to herring, might also include
pollock, mullet and whiting.

Illus. 10.39. Twisting the snood line required two people. The cairt *was tied to the side members of a ladder at a distance of about 2.5m from the ground. When the threads were set up on the* cairt, *one man pulled the* dorú *which set the* smólanna *turning – twisting the threads into one.*

Illus. 10.41 right. Scoilteán, *cloving stick, which held the hooks of the spillet while drying the line and baiting the hooks. It consists of two pieces of wood, one of which is larger and is provided with a channel into which the other fits. In this example from Inis Oírr, the larger piece is 41cm long, circular in section and 3cm in diameter. One end of the smaller piece of wood, which essentially forms a rod, is nailed into the channel and further secured by tying it with a string binding. The hooks of the spillet line were slipped on to this rod and the whole* scoilteán, *with attached hooks and lines, was placed in a hole in the wall to keep it secure.*

Illus. 10.42 right. When the fishing is over and the catch removed from the hooks by the women, the long line is hung to dry. Here the scoilteán is set into the gable wall of the house and the hooks are placed on its narrow rod.

While drying the lines, the hooks were held on a cloving stick, scoilteán, to avoid becoming entangled in the line. Fishing was primarily a male occupation, the women being involved in taking the fish from the currach and cleaning them, in drying the nets and lines and baiting the hooks. As the hooks were baited they were placed side by side at the shallow end of the holding basket, or ribh, while the longline, or droim an spiléid, to which they were attached was coiled at the deep end. Each scoilteán held about 120 hooks and three scoilteán composed each man's spillet held in his own ribh. If there were three men in the team each might have a long line of some 540 fathoms. When the three were stretched together along the seabed, it could comprise a couple of miles altogether.

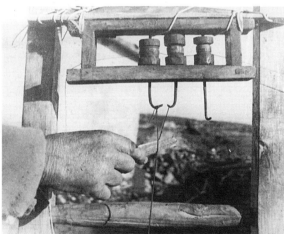

Illus. 10.40. *A close up view of the* cairt *secured to the ladder. The small wooden stick in the man's hand helps prevent the two strands of the snood line overtwisting and tangling. It was placed at the point where the strands wrapped around each other in order to ensure firm and even twisting.*

Shooting the line was a highly skilled job requiring great dexterity and it was the responsibility of the oarsman at the stern helped by the middle oarsman, while the bow oarsman continued to row the currach into the wind. When he got the order, the stern oarsman threw the first buoy, which was either made of cork or sheepskin (pucán), with its line attached, into the sea, followed by the first main anchor stone (cloch chinn), the baited spillet lines and the middle (cloch chinn láir) and second main anchor stones and buoys. The lines were left out for a couple of hours before being hauled. In the event of the line breaking the scríobóir, or scraper, was dragged along the seabed to retrieve it. The stern oarsman also hauled the line and used a stick known as a slúdán to release the hooks from the fish. The slúdán was a deal stick c. 45cm x 4cm at its wider end. A V-shaped notch at one end was passed down along the shank of the hook into the stomach of the fish and a quick, forceful jerk of the stick freed the hook.

Illus. 10.43. Baiting the long line hooks and coiling the line in the ribh was work usually done by the women in the house. In this ribh some 540 hooks will be laid in the basket's shallow end at the front of the photo while the long line will be coiled carefully in the basket's deep end.

Illus. 10.44. Ribh, the basket used to hold the spillet lines. It is flat bottomed and made of unpeeled rods. It is 104cm long and 49cm across at the widest end which is also the shallowest end at 6cm, compared to 22cm at the rounded end. The baited hooks of the spillet were placed at the shallow end, while the line of the spillet, the droim an spiléid, was carefully coiled in the deep end.

Illus. 10.45 right. Scríobóir, line recoverer, which was trailed along the seabed to recover lost fishing lines. It is a bar of iron 30.5cm long and 2cm in diameter. The line by which the scríobóir was trailed was secured in the hole at one end. At equal intervals the bar is pierced transversely to take four iron rods the ends of which are bent upwards to form 8 hooks. In this example one of the hooks of the lowest pair is missing and it has been replaced by binding a large fishing hook to the end of the bar with string.

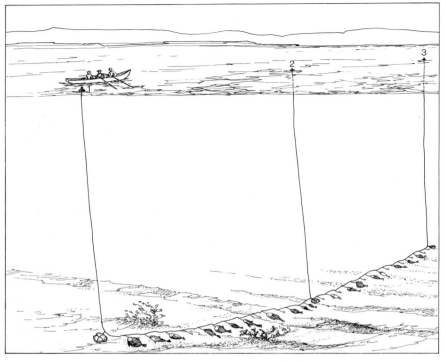

Aran bream, which achieved a fame and noto-riety of their own being exported far and wide, were fished in both deep and shallow water from the beginning of June and the fishing con-tinued all through the summer months. The 3-man team fished from the currach in rocky spots with rough seabeds with hand lines (gliondaí), trolling at sunset and again just an hour before sunrise, and fishing while the cur-rach was anchored in either shallow water (from 6-12 fathoms) with unweighted lines at night time or in deep water (from 12-24 fath-oms) with weighted lines during the day. On

Illus. 10.46 above. A cross-sectional view of fishing with the spillet line (an spiléad) off the Inis Oírr coast. The buoys 1, 2, 3, at water level indicate the position of the line on the seabed where it is weighted with stones. It was the stern oarsman's job to reach out for the buoy to pull in the fish laden catch.

(Drawing after H. Becker by kind permission)

Illus. 10.47. A pucán, *sheep skin buoy, used on the spillet lines. The sheep skin has been formed into a bag and tightly bound with a rag around a wooden plug at the top of the buoy to form an air-tight bag. The wooden plug is pierced through with a hole at a*

distance of c. 3cm from its top; this hole accommodates the mooring rope. The wooden plug is pierced with a second hole just above the rag bind-ing and this hole slopes through the plug's thickness into the interior of the buoy. It is through this hole that the buoy is inflated and it is sub-sequently plugged with a piece of timber wrapped around with a piece of rag. The buoy is c. 32cm high and c. 29cm at its widest. Its whole outer surface has been covered with tar.

Illus. 10.48 below. A stone anchor for anchoring currachs and used on the three islands. It was known as a cailleach. *It is made of two wooden boards set in a* V-*shape between which is wedged a large flat stone and below which is a transverse piece of wood piercing the side boards. The perpendicular height of the anchor is 61cm.*

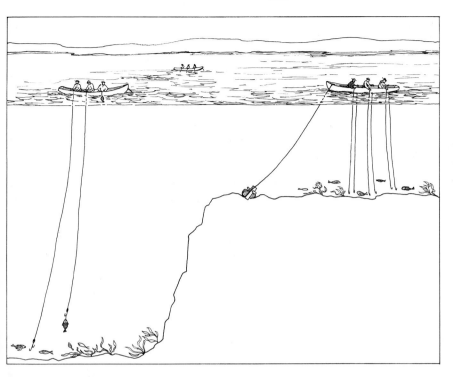

Illus. 10.49. In this cross section, fishing for bream in shallow and deep water is illustrated. When fishing in shallow water, from 6-12 fathoms, the boat is anchored and each man in the crew operates two unweighted handlines – one on either side of the boat. The double hooked lines for deep water fishing for bream were weighted with small lead weights.

(Drawing after H. Becker by kind permission)

At the end of the autumn the bream swam to shore and were caught with drag nets. There was very little art to this type of fishing other than to drag the net through the soft sand and remove the fish caught in the mesh.

When the catch was landed another member of the crew was assigned to draw lots for the equal division of the catch between the three crew members. The fish were separated into three relatively equal heaps and the lots used to draw the heaps included three miscellaneous objects picked from the shore, eg. a shell, a piece of stick and a piece of seaweed. The man assigned the task put two of these objects in one hand, eg. his left hand, and the third in the other hand. One of the others would announce which lot he wanted, eg. he might decide on the shell, while the other would take the stick. The man with the objects in his hand was left with the seaweed as his lot and he would then assign the heaps of fish to the lots according as they were placed in his hand, eg. the shell at the front part of his left hand being the heap furthest from him on his left side, the piece of stick at the back of his left hand being the heap nearest to him on his left side and the piece of seaweed in his right hand being the pile lying on his right side.

Some of the fish were salted and dried, especially bream, mackerel and wrasse – there being a market for dried wrasse from the Aran Islands as recently as the 1970s. To salt the fish they were put on a clean surface and the scales were scraped off. They were then gutted with a sharp knife and washed well with fresh water. After they were allowed to drain each fish was split along its side, salted with rough salt and placed skin side down in a clean barrel. Each barrel would hold from 300 to 400 fish, and they were left curing for 3 to 4 weeks. After this time they were taken from the barrel, again

their way to the fishing spot, guided by landmarks, they might cast the handline to catch mackerel for bait although bream would take most baits including lugworm (lugaí), mackerel guts (putóga ronnach), sand eels (scadáin ghainimh), dug from the sand with three-pronged forks, and shelled limpets (bairneacha). The limpets were shelled the previous evening by placing them in a pot of water over the fire, which caused the fish to come out of their shells, at which moment they were removed from the heat and thrown into a wicker basket. Spraying them immediately with cold water prevented them from going too soft. A favoured bait was crab, bream being especially attracted to the smell of crab roe tied to the shank of the hook and one member of the team was assigned to make the crab pots.

washed in clean water, drained on a wicker basket and spread on the stone walls to dry for a couple of days. Some of the fish were kept for the islanders' own use, but most were sold to the boatmen from Connemara and to buyers from Galway.

A proverb from Inis Oírr runs

Carraigín, sleabhcán agus sú na mbairnigh,
Cuir i do bholg é agus beidh tú láidir.

'Carrageen, shore food and the juice of limpets, Put it in your stomach and you will be strong'

and aptly describes the uses to which some of the islands' resources were put by the people in their daily lives. Today such natural resources are bringing in much welcome revenue from tourism and providing a livelihood which will ensure the future of the islands for generations to come. It should never be forgotten that it was these same resources, especially of sea, stone and soil, which, in former times, tested the capabilities and capacities of the islanders to the limit.

Illus. 10.50. The cured fish are laid out on a stone wall or even on a thatched roof to dry. They have already been salted and stored in a barrel for up to three weeks to cure. They were left to dry for a day or two before being sold to the buyers from Galway. The money from the sale went towards buying provisions such as turf, tea, flour and sugar.

Acknowledgements

The National Museum's Irish Folklife Division holds an extensive collection of photographs many of which were taken at the turn of the century and from about 1910-1930. Most of the Aran photographs are in the Mason Collection and several others were taken by F.E. Stephens, Synge's nephew. Efforts are being made by the National Museum to identify the people in the photographs. Any information concerning the dates and persons in the views in this chapter which will help with this project will be gratefully received and acknowledged.

The publishers are very grateful to the Director of the National Museum of Ireland for his generosity in allowing the reproduction of the wide selection of photographs from the Irish Folklife Division's collections.

The author would like to thank Valerie Dowling, Photographer, National Museum, Máire Bean Uí Fhlaithearta, Michael Gill, Máirtín Ó Conghaile, Brian Ó Catháin and Bairbre Ó Floinn for their help and advice in the preparation and writing of this article.

Acknowledgements for additional illustrations

Illus. 10.3, 10.37, photo, Bord Fáilte, Illus. 10.13, 10.50 (lower) photo, G.A.Duncan; Illus. 10.15, photo, T.H. Mason; Illus. 10.16, 10.17, 10.24, 10.33, 10.34 photo, 10.46, 10.47 drawing Anne Korff; 10.39, 10.40, 10.42, 10.43, 10.50 (upper), photo, Heinrich Becker; 10.31. photo, Fr Browne S.J. Collection.

My Early Life in a Thatched Home.

Dara Ó Conaola

People nowadays no longer have the same feeling towards their homes as they used to have in times gone by. The ancient dwellings were the centre and focus of everyday life. Many changes have taken place since then. 'All human life was there', one might say, because the home was the scene of births, romance, weddings, work, entertainment and deaths. Ordinary chores like raking over the fire at night were treated with respect. The old people recited a special folk prayer on such occasions.

I was born in a thatched house on the Aran Islands. My early life was spent there, and I remember it well. It is this house I intend to describe.

Thatching

The thatching day was a great event. Help would be already organised for the occasion. The youngsters had a great time. Thatching usually began at the beginning of Autumn – before the rough, blustery weather of winter set in.
'The house thatched, the turf brought and the rent paid' – when those three requirements were fulfilled by the old people they no longer bothered about how the winter would be. Those things are not all that important today. Thatching, along with other old crafts, is fast becoming a lost art.

Solid Stones

> *'May the fort we are in be a solid castle*
> *The enemies pursuing us be blind*
> *The Holy Ghost among us*
> *May He put His shield above us...'*

I often heard my mother say this prayer as she blessed the little house we lived in on Aran. And a solid castle it was – well able to withstand the winter wrath of the Atlantic storms and driving rain. No rain ever came through its thatched roof and no damp ever rose along its sturdy walls. There were no better building materials than the dry stones and the locally quarried cement-like mud called 'dobe'.

Building the House

The year of the big wind – 1839 – was when the house was built. That was the year my great grandfather came from Connemara to settle here. He was the man who built the house. According to the old people he was about to build it in another place initially. I know the spot well: 'beyond the Clifftop', as the place is called, on the south side of the main road. He was digging the stones on the site one day. Who should happen to come along but a travelling man.

'God bless the work', says he, employing the traditional greeting.

'Would you mind my asking why you are getting the stones ready.'

'I'm building a house'.

'Now,' said the man of the roads, 'If you take my advice you'll put up no house in this spot'.

'Why shouldn't I'?

'Just know this much. There was a fairy palace going through here and if you build here you'll never again have a day's peace in your home'.

'Maybe, you're right, indeed...'.

And so my grandfather had second thoughts. He followed the travelling man's advice and built the house in another place. I often heard it said that there were certain places where it wouldn't be right to build a house. There were houses, according to local tradition at any rate, which were supposed to be haunted. This was said to be the reason for it.

Old Customs

The old people were very superstitious and they were reluctant to interfere with anything that would bring misfortune. They would not tamper with traditions. Nothing was built on to the west of a house because:

'Fear níos fearr ná Dia – a man better than God,
A chuireadh fad ar a theach siar – that would build to his house towards the west'.

The person who would put an extension to the west of the house was considered to be demonstrating his disregard of God and he was considered not to be lucky as a result. I never heard how that belief began. It is my personal opinion that one time people associated God with the west, because in pagan times they used to worship the setting sun. Perhaps this tradition came down from those far off days?

Nestled Together

The house I was born in was attached to another one, and that one to yet another one – all three in one line – snugly terraced together. Ours was the furthest east of the three. This meant that the other two were built earlier, as I wouldn't say, indeed, that our neighbours thought themselves better than God.

It was common then for two or three houses to be attached to one another in this way and this brought the community closer together. It was an advantage also when putting up the house, as one gable end, that of the existing house, would be already built. Another reason for houses to be built in twos and threes was as one unit they would be able to stand up better to the storms. It also saved a lot of building time and labour.

This layout had a few drawbacks, although they didn't apparently bother the old people a lot. The centre house was completely stuck between the other two. The people who lived there had no path around the house itself. They had to cross a path belonging to someone else. To go to the back of the house they had to go the long way around. I'm certain this wouldn't please the people of this generation! In those days there were far more serious things than Planning Permission causing concern.

The people in the centre house, between us and the other house, could have chosen a more suitable site to build. They had one in another village and, in fact, when they finally built a new house it was in the other village they built it. When we built a new house it was also in a better location from all angles. We had plenty of space. It was just as close to our land, the shore and church, as well as being built on higher ground. But it would appear that our forefathers didn't bother much about sites or locations. All they wanted was a strong house built with the least amount of trouble and delay possible.

There was another old house in our village and I often heard it said by the old people that it took only one week to build it. There must have been a lot of help involved in its construction – because it contains an almost countless amount of big strong stones. It is still standing today.

Construction Design

Those houses were no palaces, but they were comfortable enough. They were adequate for the times and blended well with their surroundings. Indeed, this is more than can be said about some of today's architect-designed buildings.

The design was simply a rectangle with two walls and two gable ends. There was a door in each wall. There weren't many windows because at that time even sunlight was taxed!

When our house was built it had two windows. The larger one was not quite three feet high by less than two feet wide. One of the doors was usually left open for ventilation and also for light. It was called the open door or sheltered door. The wind door or closed door was the name of the other door. Our house faced south and most of the houses faced either south or north. But the occasional one faced east or west. There was a front and back garden which we called sráideannaí (streets). Sometimes people had an enclosure at the gable end which was called the pen: Buailín thóin na binne.

If the house was a little distance in from the main road or from the Kings Road, as people used to call it, there would be a boreen going down to it.
There was only the occasional gate. Gaps along the road were the usual thing. Steps arranged for getting over the stone walls were called stiles. If there was not a gate a gap would be left in the stone fence instead. The gap was built with smaller stones, gap stones, and it was easy to set it up or to take it down, depending on the circumstances.
Straw, of course, formed the thatched roof of the house. The rafters were usually of bog oak which was brought from Connemara. A layer of scraw, which was a strong topsoil,

also from Connemara, was spread over wooden laths to carry the thatch.
The walls were stone, cemented with yellow clay or mortar. The stones were visible on the outside of the house. The walls and gable ends were white washed. Sometimes on the gable the lime didn't go to the top; it might only be the same height as the wall or just above it.

Interior Layout

The front door in our house led straight into the kitchen. From there a door led to the big room, and another door to the small room. There were three rooms in the house, with the kitchen at the centre; the big room was off the kitchen at the back of the hearth, to the west, and the small room was to the east. Another window was added later. There were three windows in all, as I remember it; one on the south side and two original ones on the north side.

The kitchen was about 12' square. It was small enough, I suppose, but as the old man who lived in the house with us used to say to anyone who came to the door: 'Come in. If you can find room for yourself, you're welcome'.

The hearth was laid down between the big room and the kitchen. A door to the right of the fireplace went to the big room. Over that door and under the roof beside the chimney, there was access to the small loft, which was just over the big room. It was a black hole, its only light was the amount that leaked into it from the kitchen. It was a place where things were stored or even hidden.

On the Loft

On the opposite side of the kitchen over the small room was the loft. Compared to the small loft it was spacious and bright. It was open all the way up to the rafters. It stuck out a few feet from the wall of the small room to give it extra width. The loft ledge was the name given to that area. There was a beam running across the house under the edge of the loft. It was there to support the loft, of course, but it had other uses too. Pork or lamb could be seen hanging from the beam on occasions. Items like fishing gear or a basket of salted fish were kept in the loft. But, in fact anything could be found there, particularly implements that were stored there for safe keeping.

Around the Fire

The fireplace was big and wide with two nooks on either side of the fireplace where people sat. The hearth or hearth-stone, as it was also called, was made from mud. Yellow mud or 'dobe' is a type of clay obtainable in certain places on the island. It was ready for moulding when it was wet. The old people recommended it highly and made mud floors from it.

A stone arch was over the fire. Those stones were not visible because they were covered and dashed with mortar, as was every part of the house on the inside. It was a pity they couldn't be seen because the arch was indeed a lovely piece of craftsmanship.
There's many a new house which has a stone arch in it, also. A timber support keeps the arch up while it is being built. The stones are expertly chosen and shaped. They lie against one another in such a way that when the timber is removed the arch is able to stand firmly in position. The centre stone in the arch is called the key.

An iron crook hung down over the fireplace and this was used to suspend pots over the fire. There were two sections to enable you to lower or raise it, depending on the type of pot on the fire. 'Who is in the nook, with a hook in the eye, fidgeting and fumbling' was a riddle referring to the crook, and an accurate description it was too. One part goes up, the hook, inserted in a hole in the other part. There was a series of holes to fix it at whatever height you needed. At the lower end it was so arranged that it can go backwards and forwards to take pots of any size.

There were two types of pots around the fire: the potato pot and a large pot for pig potatoes. It had a circular mouth and a round bottom. It had three short legs, and two 'ears' to lift it and also to hang it over the fire.

The pot-oven was used for baking bread in the open turf fire. It was a lot like the potato pot but the base was flat. The lidded pot was placed in the centre of the fire and covered over with sods of burning turf to form a closed hot oven. Thin cakes were baked on the griddle. This was only a flat iron plate that used to hang over the fire.
All the pots were made of iron. There was an iron lid for each pot. They were hung on the crook by special iron handles which folded together when they were not in use.
There was an iron pan and an iron kettle also. Each was given the same consideration, as the old saying had it: the kettle calling the pot black.
Usually if there was never anything on the fire, the kettle would be hanging down, boiling and singing, so that it would be easy to make a pot of tea. Usually an earthenware teapot was beside the fire.

The tongs were usually left in the nook and were used to put a sod of turf on the fire or an ember under the teapot, or to light one's pipe. Often, however, it was laid across the embers to roast mackerel or herring. They called this the gridiron, although a proper gridiron existed as well. 'Roast mackerel from the gridiron, It was great sport and plenty of it', as the song has it.

There was a timber hatch in the floor in front of the fire. It served well to put the iron pots on when they were taken from the fire. It was easy to break the pots legs, and putting them on timber gave them a better chance. It was also likely that people put their feet on this hatch when they were seated at the fire doing light work and entertaining themselves. There was usually a stool to sit on in each nook. Those two corners were good and warm.

Cleaning the Chimney

It was thought that there was never any comfort in a house when the chimney did not draw properly. People did their best to keep it as clean as possible, but sometimes despite their best efforts the chimney did not draw too well. When this happened nobody was blamed but the wind. Two men were needed to clean the chimney. One man on top and the other man below, inside, who used a rope tied round a bunch of strong bushes to scrape off all the loose soot.

Kitchen Furniture

Our table was against the south wall and there was a chair at the end of the table just beside the front door. On the wall above the table pictures hung, holy ones, for the most part. Against the north wall was a big stool or form. Above it there was a cubby-hole. It was just a hole in the wall with threads, pins and knitting in it. There wasn't a single window in the kitchen. There were no complaints though, as enough light and fresh air came through the open door.

Facing the fire at the other side of the kitchen stood the dresser. Cups, mugs, plates, jugs, dishes and every kind of useful utensil for the house were on the dresser, while the food was stored in the bottom section. A row of coloured jugs was on the dresser counter. Usually the clock was put in among the delph on the shelves.

The door to the small room was next to the dresser. Between it and the back door was a little table. The bucket of fresh water, milk cans and other vessels were left on it. In the south corner on the other side of the dresser were some small shelves. Utensils needed in the kitchen were spread out on them.

The Doors

Laid against the closed door was a traditional type of draft excluder. It was made from straw and woven somewhat like a floor mat. Also placed against the closed door were stools or any other pieces of furniture not in use. Often a whole lot of things were put there out of the way.

If the wind came in the open door they used to 'change the door'. A person would often be heard to say: 'The door has been changed in M's house'. That was the same as saying that the wind had changed, there was probably a weather change coming. There was a half-door also in the front door.

I suppose people thought there was no need for the complete door to be opened at times. There was enough to see and plenty of air available above the top of the half-door.

I heard it said that in places there used to be sally lengths hanging in the door to keep flies out. Door shade it was called. But I never saw it on the islands. Above the south door, on the rafters and on the few boards under the roof, there were a lot of St Bridget's Crosses. The custom was to put up a St Bridget's Cross on the eve of St Bridget's feast day in honour of the saint. St Bridget was one of Ireland's first saints and her feast-day falls on the first day of Spring, that is, the first day of February each year.

The Big Room

The kitchen was the principal room. The fireplace could be described as the heart of the house. But the big room had an importance all its own. In our house two generations were born in this room and many members of our family died there. It wasn't exactly as big as the kitchen and it had one window to the north. There was a fireplace too, in the big room. We used to call it 'the little fireplace'. It backed on to the big fireplace. There was a wooden mantel-piece over the fire. It was rather plain but well finished.

In the corner there was a press or dresser set into the wall, near the fireplace. 'Muifid', we called it. Glasses and ornaments of any kind would be stored in it. Medicine would also be there, and perhaps a drop of 'the hard stuff'.

Opposite the door in the north corner there was a board to hang clothes on. It was attached to the wall and it had pegs to put clothing items on. Underneath on the floor was the 'córa' or chest, which was the strongbox of the house. It was a wooden box, 2'6" long and 1'6" wide and deep. Between the córa and the bed stood the room table.

We also had a typical, traditional Aran cradle, which was made from sally reeds, which are to be found in swampy places near spring wells on the island. There were two shaped pieces of wood underneath to rock it. It was made like a basket with a cover over it at the top end.

The Small Room

There were two beds in the small room and there wasn't much room in it for anything else. It had two windows, one to the north, and the other to the south. There were some of the old houses which had two little rooms, the north and the south room. Those houses were somewhat longer than ours. With the passage of time indeed, the design of the thatched houses was changed considerably. There was one type which had no gable end to it but was rounded and was built in the form of a hive.

There was only one of those in my neighbourhood. Yet another type had the fireplace next to the gable and there was a kind of an open chimney going up to a hole in the roof which allowed the smoke out. A wooden frame was fixed in the ridge and the thatch arranged around it. I never saw one of those on the island but I've heard of them.

Traditional Household Items

Fáideog (a wick used as substitute for a candle) was the name given to the lighting facilities in the past. This was a little tray of oil with a wick in it. There were also candles which the people themselves made. They used to melt sheep and cattle fat and put a cotton wick through it. The oldest form of lighting I remember, however, was the oil lamp that used to hang from the chimney. An image of the Sacred Heart was hung in every household, with a small red oil lamp always burning before it.

Square shoulder baskets were used to carry potatoes and turf. They were also used to carry seaweed up from the shore to the roadside where the seaweed would be loaded into other baskets, straddled across a donkey's back. A ciseog (a round, shallow basket) was a special basket for potatoes. Boiled jacket potatoes were emptied into this flat basket from the cooking pot. The water draining into a keeler tub underneath. In olden times the family would then sit around the basket to eat their meal. Smaller versions of the round and square Aran baskets were used for holding eggs, bread and other foods.

A 'Keeler' tub was used until recent times for washing potatoes and for other household purposes. An essential item was the hand-operated spinning-wheel used for spinning the wool for the knitting of Aran sweaters. Most householders on the island would have used these locally-made wheels.

We had a milk churn of the type which was commonly used by island women in making their own butter. This was a wooden, stave-built, vessel with a lid. The handle of the wooden dash passed through a hole in the lid.

Numerous other implements and objects of daily life were in use in the days of the thatched cottages. Since then many a change has taken place. It won't be long before nobody will know the purpose of half of the things which were so precious in the old houses.

Perhaps Tomás Ó Criotháin of the Blasket Islands off the Kerry coast said it all when he ended his great classic *The Islandman* with the words: 'Ní bheidh ár leithidí arís ann – Our likes will never be again'.

CHAPTER 11

The Yearly Round on Inis Mór – Árainn:
calendar custom and belief in an island community

Padraigín Clancy

The story of the yearly round on Inis Mór – Árainn – is the story of the people of Inis Mór and how they live on a rocky island on the edge of the Atlantic at the end of the twentieth century. It is a story which embraces the whole of Inis Mór, tracking from earliest times to the present day. For as the eminent Irish ethnologist, Caoimhín Ó Danachair, so aptly put it in the opening lines of his definitive account *The Year in Ireland — A Calendar,* 'If one were to ask which branch of folk tradition most widely reveals the panorama of the whole it would undoubtedly be Calendar Custom'.

The many festive days and feast days which comprise the yearly round on Inis Mór open as windows for us onto this island's story. Each occasion, in its own way, brings alive an aspect of tradition. The whole is essentially a tale of sea, sky, earth and rock. The landscape and the elements and an island people's response to them. It is a story of hard work and endurance. It tells of family, community and social tradition, the natural bonding and rivalries of a people anywhere, perhaps all the more intensely experienced in the small space of an island. It is a story which can proudly and uniquely boast of an unbroken Gaelic civilisation, language and culture. A story of faith, religious custom and belief from 'Pagan past to Christian present'. Above all each festive occasion is a time of celebration. Whether it be through music, ritual, prayer, song or dance, each event is a celebration of 'life' itself on Inis Mór and its continued existence and survival there from earliest times to the present day and beyond.

Each occasion carries within it a note of remembrance and of hope and is a time of regeneration. For those who do the 'Turas' or Pilgrimage at Teampall an Ceathrar Álainn on the 15th August each year, do so in the footsteps of their ancestors, with the children of today in the assurance and hope of tomorrow, the 21st century and beyond.

Two parts to the year

Just as the old Celtic calendar was divided into two parts – a dark half and a bright half – so too may the year on Inis Mór be divided. The division is a fundamental one rooted in the natural circumstances of weather and seasonal change and its effects are complete and dramatic on the entire fabric of island life.

The Dark Half

The dark half begins with the onset of the long dark winter nights and is marked by the celebration of Oíche Shamhna or Hallowe'en on October 31st. This is one of the most significant festive occasions in the yearly round on the island and certainly the most significant turning point. For from Oíche Shamhna onwards the great wave (which brings brighter days and calmer seas with thousands of visitors) ebbs. Suddenly winter has arrived. Seas begin to swell, passenger boats become less frequent and the island returns to the possession of the islanders.

Women and men take a much needed rest from the constant hard work and industry of the visitor orientated summer months. Many Bed and Breakfasts close, restaurants are less busy, and minibus tours diminish. Down go the hot coal fires and out come the knitting needles as many a long winter night is passed by women in preparation for the coming summer's retailing. Men too, traditionally, draw indoors from this date. Currach fishermen stop fishing, securing their boats on shore from the anticipated winter gales. The larger trawler activities are similarly curtailed as the Atlantic weathers become more furious.

In former times, according to the memory of older islanders, full preparations were made by Hallowe'en to safeguard family and home for the winter. As one elderly neighbour of mine tells me, tradition had it – 'dá mbeadh do dhothain móin istigh agat – fé Shamhain – agus tuí ar an teach, nach mbeadh aon ghá imní dhuit' meaning 'if one had enough turf in stock and the house rethatched before Hallowe'en there would be no cause for worry during the coming winter'. Hence, traditionally, on Inis Mór the potato crop is harvested by this date and rethatching on older dwelling houses and outhouses is completed.

In the area of entertainment the contrast with brighter days is considerable. From Hallowe'en the visiting bands and groups which frequent the island in calmer weathers, cease to come and the islanders rely on their own creativity and resources for entertainment and survival. Winter bonding begins as local talent is used to sustain one another, keep the 'craic' going and the spirits up. Classes recommence for young and old in traditional 'sean nós' singing, set and céilí dancing, art and creative writing. Card parties begin as do dart competitions and pub quizzes. Women's groups reform, Christmas pantomime preparations commence, youth group activities resume, sales of work and various fund-raising events for local and world-wide charities are organised.

The high point of all is the monthly lifeboat night. An evening of music, song and dance held in an island pub to raise money, in support of the lifeboat service which operates out of Cill Éinne Bay on Inis Mór and provides an essential service for the peoples of the west coast.

The Bright Half

With the coming of St Patrick's Day, followed closely by Easter, the dark half of the year passes — the bright half has arrived. Longer hours of daylight, better weather conditions, and calmer seas change the dynamic of the island, once again, dramatically. The island turns from itself and opens up to the visitor. Bed and Breakfasts re-open as women begin their long season of catering. Craft shops and restaurants return to full business.

Men move outside once more, building and redecorating. Traps receive a fresh coat of paint and bicycles and minibuses their seasonal service. Currach fishermen move back onto the sea preparing pots and nets for the coming season. Vegetables and potatoes are sown as

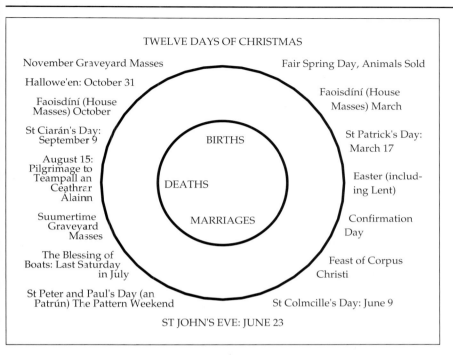

TWELVE DAYS OF CHRISTMAS

November Graveyard Masses

Hallowe'en: October 31

Faoisdíní (House Masses) October

St Ciarán's Day: September 9

August 15: Pilgrimage to Teampall an Ceathrar Álainn

Suumertime Graveyard Masses

The Blessing of Boats: Last Saturday in July

St Peter and Paul's Day (an Patrún) The Pattern Weekend

ST JOHN'S EVE: JUNE 23

Fair Spring Day, Animals Sold

Faoisdíní (House Masses) March

St Patrick's Day: March 17

Easter (including Lent)

Confirmation Day

Feast of Corpus Christi

St Colmcille's Day: June 9

BIRTHS

DEATHS

MARRIAGES

Illus. 11.1. The Yearly Round in Inis Mór, late 20th century, includes fixed and movable festive days and feast days.

spade work and planting commences. The winter entertainment schedule ceases abruptly and visiting bands provide much of the entertainment.

By the annual June Bank Holiday weekend the island is once more in full swing as the first of several thousand visitors arrive, among them many hundreds of Irish language students. The focus is on the visitor and remains that way until the great wave ebbs, once again, at Hallowe'en.

Oíche Shamhna - Hallowe'en

The custom of celebrating Hallowe'en or Oíche Shamhna as it is termed in the Irish language is an ancient part of the Celtic calendar. That tradition survives all over Ireland in various forms. On Inis Mór, as already outlined, this night is a key event in the calendar. Its celebration involves the whole island in a unique way.

Hallowe'en on Inis Mór – What Happens?

A visit to the island at Hallowe'en and what greets one's eyes and ears is mysterious indeed. Gone are many of the normal human beings of everyday life and in their place are masked cloaked 'otherworld' creatures termed Taibhsí and Púcaí (Ghosts and Fairies). These are island men and women in complete disguise. Cill Rónáin becomes a ghost village as they prowl about in 'total' silence creating mischief and mayhem.

For here is the living custom of Hallowe'en Guisers on Inis Mór today with its own distinct elements. In contrast with other parts of Ireland where the custom of disguise is practised at Hallowe'en not only do the children of the island dress up but so too do the adults. Furthermore, the disguise adopted is total, as weeks of carefully concealed preparations go into ensuring one is not recognised. Hands are gloved, rings removed, body shape altered and postures changed. Nothing is revealed and all is concealed as one becomes an effective ghost, witch, or 'otherworld' creature. Nowadays some also assume the guise of a notable political figure and it is not uncommon to find a Charlie Haughey, Ian Paisley or Margaret Thatcher lookalike prowling about on Inis Mór of a Hallowe'en.

Silence is maintained throughout the night by those in disguise and it is this practice which

Illus. 11.2. Hallowe'en guisers, 'House visiting'!

Illus. 11.3. 'Traditional strawman'.

gives the tradition on Inis Mór its own unique and tangible eeriness. In other parts singing and chanting are often a regular part of the nights entertainment, but not so on Inis Mór, where all is done in silence.

Guisers begin their night's activities by house visiting. Doors are traditionally left open to allow the silent otherworld creatures to enter freely. Undisguised friends puzzle and laugh over their visitors, providing them with the traditional Hallowe'en festive fare of apples, nuts and brack.

Guisers then move on to the pubs where beverages are consumed by use of straws in order to avoid removing the mask, and fatal detection! The usual chatter of pub life is replaced by a cloak of silence which is nothing short of astonishing.

The nights entertainment comes to a close with a 'Céilí Mór' in Cill Rónáin Village Hall. Here disguised and undisguised enjoy high merriment and much frolicking. A special dance called 'Damhsa na Taibhsí' (The Dance of the Ghosts) is announced and all guisers take to the floor in a competition to select the most successful disguise. The decision having been made, an award is granted to the winners. The last dance is called, after which those in disguise slip away into the dark of the night – still undetected. The night of mysterious revelry has ended for another year. The 'otherworld' and this world have come together yet again on Inis Mór on Oíche Shamhna in a very real way.

St John's Eve
Oíche Tine Chnáimh – Bonfire Night

If Hallowe'en is a key event of winter time on Inis Mór, St John's Eve is a key event of summer. Traditionally on this eve, which falls on the night of June 23rd, fires are lit in every village throughout the island, in honour of St John and to mark mid-summer. Fires are also lit on the neighbouring islands of Inis Meáin and Inis Oírr as well as in many other parts of Ireland.

Preparations for the lighting of fires on Inis Mór begin well in advance of the night, with tyres, old furniture and goods being stacked up for the occasion. As the sun sets on the eve of the feast, villagers make their way to the fire area. The fire is traditionally lit in the same spot from year to year, hence some fires may be as old as the custom on Inis Mór itself which could be of some antiquity indeed, possibly even dating back to pre-Christian times.

As the fire is lit and tended, traditionally by the men and boys, all villagers, young and old, gather about for a night of entertainment, song and dance. The customary words – 'Go mbeirmid beo ar an am seo arís' – 'may we all have life this time next year'— can be heard as the flames spring to life against the night sky and the continued life of each village is celebrated. Fires across the sea in Connemara are observed as islanders wonder can theirs be seen as clearly.

As the night goes on younger people often move from fire to fire in search of the biggest fire and the best 'craic'. Older folk tend to retire earlier and some traditionally bring home a 'splainc' or 'ember' from the village fire which they add to their own. This it is believed will bring a blessing to the home, family, and produce for the coming harvest season and year.

Illus. 11.4. Tending the fire in Bun Gabhla Village on June 23rd, 1991.

Illus. 11.5. Tom Ellen Hernon in the village of Corrúch on St. John's Eve, 1992.

An Patrún – The Pattern

Following closely on St John's Eve is the traditional festive event known as 'An Patrún' or 'The Pattern'.

This event takes place over a few days and is held in honour of St Peter and Paul's feast day, June 29th. St Peter and St. Paul have a special connection with the monastic site known as na Seacht dTeampaill or the Seven Churches to the west of the island. Traditionally, a pilgrimage was made to this site on their feast day. Nowadays, however, this is no longer practised and instead the celebration of the occasion is focused in Cill Rónáin village to the

Illus. 11.6. Traditional dancing during the Pattern weekend in Cill Rónáin, 1991.

east. A 'pattern' Mass starts the occasion and this is followed by three days of sporting activities for young and old, including road races, field sports and fun sports. Much enjoyment is had by all as islanders get their opportunity to test their mettle. Weight throwing, tug-o-war and donkey-back races, add to the spirit of the occasion.

The highlight of the weekend comes on Sunday afternoon when traditionally the 'currach' boat racing competitions are held. Three-man rowing teams come to Inis Mór from all over Connemara and the nearby islands to compete in these events. Ancient rowing skills and inherited strength and understanding of the sea are displayed by the participants as the races get underway. There is much cajoling and lively conversation as observers cheer on their favourite teams. Nowadays, too, the event has taken on a new spirit with a special women's event, allowing the 'fairer' sex to show their prowess on the sea.

As it is the month of June the weather is generally fine and there is no shortage of open air entertainment at 'The Old Pier' in Cill Rónáin with plenty of music, song and dance.

Pilgrimage on Inis Mór: an Turas

The tradition of doing 'an Turas' i.e. making a pilgrimage to a sacred place is an intrinsic part of Irish folk tradition. Scholars tell us that many sites date back to early Christian times and some may be even older still. On Inis Mór the tradition of pilgrimage is a strong and living part of island custom and belief.

There are three important occasions of pilgrimage in the Inis Mór calendar. A pilgrimage is made on June 9th in honour of St Colmcille, another is made on August 15th in honour of Our Lady's Feast and one is made on September 9th in honour of St Ciarán.

Inis Mór has a long historical connection with many famous Irish saints. In folklore the island is sometimes referred to as 'Árainn na Naomh' or Aran of the Saints. According to hagiography, St Colmcille and St Ciarán are both said to have spent time on Inis Mór training at St Enda's monastic foundation.

Today each pilgrimage brings together islanders of all generations, as both young and old walk in the footsteps of their ancestors around holy well or altar, praying and giving thanks for good health and prosperity.

Pilgrims traditionally arrive at the holy place at 3 pm. The community is then led by a priest in saying the rosary. When this is completed pilgrims gather seven stones in their hands and do the 'Turas'. That is, they walk seven times around the holy well or altar area in a clockwise direction, casting a stone aside as they complete each round.

The 'Turas' is done in silence — pilgrims praying quietly the traditional Ave Maria and Pater

Noster as they pass. The occasion is one of reverence and respect, not only for community and tradition but also for landscape. Done outdoors amongst the ancient rocks of the island, against a blue-green back-drop of sea and sky, one cannot fail to be touched by the tangible sanctity of 'Árainn na Naomh'.

These are just some of the key events in the Inis Mór calendar. Looking at them we glimpse the story of an island people. Having resided on this island for a number of years now, I can say with great personal gratitude that it is undoubtedly a story of life, pride and vitality, a tribute to the tenacity and survival of a Gaelic civilisation and people. Long may we continue to celebrate, Árainn. Go mba fada buan sibh!

Illus. 11.7. Extract from the Schools Manuscript Collection 1938, in which a young school girl in Inis Mór describes the festivals of the year.

Acknowledgements for Illustrations

Illus. 11.1. to 11.6., Padraigín Clancy. Illus. 11.7, Manuscript, published by kind permission of the Head of Department, Department of Irish Folklore, University College, Dublin.

One of a group of four road-side cenotaphs near Eochaill. The inscriptions ask for mercy for the souls of Julia Derrane (1868) and Bridget Dirrane (1811). (Photo, Galway Archaeological Survey.)

Lord hae mercy on the soul of Julia Derrane died in the 26 year of her age 1868 Erected by her Father Daniel Derrane

O Lord have Mercy on the Soul of Bridget Dirrane alis O Brien Who departd this life 9th of Nov. 1811 aged 48 Years this monument was erectd by her beld. husband Patk. Dirrane

To the Memory of the Dead

One of the many unusual features of Aran is a series of monumental cenotaphs. They are confined to Inis Mór and most of them stand on the side of the main road from Cill Éinne to Eoghanacht.

Three examples, conspicuously sited on the high ground behind Cill Éinne Bay, are the earliest: the two largest are tall rectangular pillars with pyramidal tops surmounted by a cross and were built about 1754. The smallest, a pillar with a stepped top, is the oldest, dating to 1709. All three bear inscribed slabs commemorating various members of the Fitzpatrick family who were landlords of Aran in the earlier 18th century.

The twenty eight roadside cenotaphs are flat-topped pillars built of limestone blocks with some mortar. They usually have two inscribed slabs facing the roadway. Many of these bear simple geometric decoration or sun-bursts and commemorate families such as Wiggins, Dirrane, O'Flaherty, McDonogh, Mullen, Gill, Naughten, O'Donnell, Coneely, Hernan and Folan. All date to the 19th century ranging from 1811 to 1876 with one or two additional inscriptions up to 1892.

Tim Robinson, who has studied these leachtaí in his 1991 monograph *Mementos of Mortality*, believes their real puzzle lies in the fact that, unlike the early Fitzpatrick examples (and a few of similarly early date in Co. Galway) dedicated to landowners or gentry, the Inis Mór roadside monuments were built in memory of ordinary members of the tenantry in times of considerable hardship. What prompted their construction is far from clear but the custom of halting in the course of funeral processions and the practise of building small funeral cairns at such spots may have been a factor as was the existence of a 19th century craft of gravestone making which meant that Inis Mór had craftsmen who though unlettered were capable of reproducing the repetitive formulas of memorial English in memory of the dead.

CHAPTER 12

Fáilte roimh thorann do chos ní amháin tú fhéin!
The sound of your footfall is as welcome as yourself

Lelia Doolan

Tunnelling out through lattices of stonework, light flings a reserving shadow. Step echoes step. The clay answers back in lonesome conversation. Nothing intrudes, but you can feel the heartbeat of the earth on your foot. The shadow is a veiled form, striving within the labyrinth. Slowly, it rises to daylight.

Illus. 12.1. 'Tunnelling out through lattices of stonework...'

O God, bless the step that I am taking
Bless for me the clay beneath my foot.

A Dhia, beannaigh an chéim a bhfuil mé ag dul
Beannaigh dom an chré atá fé 'm chois.

Above the vast tillage of the sea, a needlework of walls hems in the island's frugal bounty. It modestly stitches a human edge to the encroaching halter. Animal and human, and everpresent birdsong, make their way among the immortal elements. Fragments of this primal discourse linger at ruined temple or by shrine, by the sweet water of a blessed well, urgently seeking benevolent intercession.

May God bless, you, Cinndearg, bright darling!
May the angels and saints bless myself
It is to you I come, telling my story
To you I make my complaint, asking your aid
That you help me for the honour of God. Amen.

Go mbeannaí Dia dhuit, a Chinndeirge, geal gléigeal!
Go mbeannaí mé fhéin na naoimh is na n-aingeal
Is chugatsa a thagaim ag insint mo scéil dhuit
Is ag déanamh mo ghearáin leat ag iarraidh do chú-
naimh
Le go gcabhrófaí liom in onóir Dé. Amen.

(Prayer before making the rounds at the Well of St Cinndearg, Inis Meáin).

'Giortann beirt bóthar', Nora says. Two shorten the road. She bends her knee uphill, heaving a sack of fodder towards the distant beasts. Amalgamate of life and afterlife, the Creed and Coronation Street find easy comradeship in her. The islands' ancient life includes the present: airstrip and currach, stars and the electric light, cashel, factory and modern dwelling, seanchas and slang and central heating and the telephone; Stations and the Credit Union; making the land and making fun; accepting sudden death — and hurricanes of visitors. Shawls and red skirts (ringed with black velvet for marriage), tweed and pampooties endure in remnants, to the stranger's eye, of coloured scarves and geansais.

Nora unmakes the wall, climbs up and steps across the crag, crooning a salutation. Later, we carry buckets to a waiting trough under the Easter sunlight. All the while, the sea croaks within its subterranean halls. The cattle munch serenely.

The engine of work drives the days forward – hauling, digging, sowing, trawling, reaping, making and re-making, tramping in all weathers, playing, praying:

> O sweet heart of Jesus
> We praise you!
> With the strength of our minds
> With the gladness of our hearts
> Early to our work
> Late to repose
> O loyal sweet heart
> Do not part from us forever.

> *O Chroí mhilis dhílis,*
> *Molaimid thú!*
> *Le láidreacht ár n-intinn*
> *Le haoibneas ár gcroí*
> *Go moch ag an obair*
> *Go mall ag an só*
> *A Chroí dhílis mhilis*
> *Ná scar linn go deo.*

Illus. 12.2. Nora (left) as a young woman, enjoying life with her sister, Saile Pháidín Saidhbhín (now Bean Uí Fhathartaigh).

A walk with Nora is in no way linear. It is a pilgrimage of enquiry, instruction, declaration. 'O, I was *aerach* in my youth!': light-hearted, merry, giddy, frolicsome. The fellows lined the schoolyard, I've no doubt, intrigued and captivated. Her father was a knowledgeable man and gave his children lore, like all the islands' elders, to set down in copybooks at school – 'and all forgotten now', she shakes her head, pointing to wayside plants, naming their curative powers:

Copóg rua (dock) against chilblains breaking out on the shin, or the sting of a nettle. The selfsame nettle, good for health when eaten young – or older, boiled up, bottled and rubbed on to ease the suffering of arthritis.

The soot of a turf fire in hot milk for a cold, or
an onion boiled in sour milk.
Carageen for the cough or shortness of breath.
Cow parsley for kidneys.
Moss or cobwebs (however musty) to stop a
flow of blood.
Meacan an leonadh (probably elecampane or
comfrey) scraped and mashed to form a
plaster for sprain or fracture.
Póirín seangán (stonecrop) mixed with unsalted
butter to make a green ointment for closing a
deep cut.

*Illus. 12.3. Nora at home
today. Her stories and notes
on island life are among those
collected in the late thirties by
the school children of Inis
Meáin for the Irish Folklore
Commission. It was Nora
who first welcomed me with
the greeting that forms the
title to this chapter.*

The juice of *Buachaill tí* (houseleek) squeezed
on the eye, will ease it.
Bainne bó bleachtáin (cowslip) or the milk of
dandelion for curing warts.
Garlic eaten raw to clear the blood and mend a
sore throat.

Recital brings her memory back – 'but now',
she smiles, 'they go to the nurse for antibiotics

and the flu injection'. The word for flower is
bláth but Nora employs a word still used on the
smaller islands – *pabhsae* or *posae*: posy. The
scholars' copybooks of almost sixty years ago
were full of stories and reports: field names,
the potato, games, superstitions, special days,
clothes, holy wells and meals and the feast of
St Brigid.

Nora pauses and settles herself on the path to
tell the story of why Brigid's day comes on the
first day of February: 'Mary and Brigid were
walking out together and Brigid went ahead to
protect and hide the Virgin. So Mary said: "I
can give you no help in return but I will give
you the day before my own day". So February
1st is St Brigid's Day and the second day of
February is the feast of Mary of the Candles'.
Earthly and heavenly goddess stand at the
threshold of the season of fertility:

Brid by my lying down
Brid by my rising up
Brid on my every side
Mary to help me
On water that would drown me
On fire that would burn me
In the night that would distress me
In the troubles of the year
From tonight to this night's year
And tonight itself.

Bríd ag luí dhom
Bríd ag eirí liom
Bríd gach taobh dhíom
Muire do mo chumhdach
Ar uisce do mo bhá
Ar thine do mo dhó
Ar urchóid na hoíche
Ar anachain na bliana
Ó anocht go bliain ó anocht
Agus anocht fhéin.

Illus. 12.4. Tobar na mBráthar (Friars' Well). Handwritten on the reverse of this old photograph: 'Station of the Cross on St Eany's Walk or terrace, Great Isle of Aran. Never cultivated, as the Saint walks on this terrace at night'. The well is overgrown now, and the station is not to be seen but the place is marked on Tim Robinson's Map (no.9).

On St Brigid's day, if it were fine, it was customary to gather periwinkles and limpets, and to bring fresh fish into every house so that fish would be plentiful and increase the island's harvest in the coming year. The diet of olden times has changed a little; now there is flour for bread and cake and biscuits alongside the omnipresent potato, and more meat – and tea, taken in the hospitality of Nora's kitchen. And other changes: the children's recreations of old – Tip and Tig or Blind Man's Buff, and gathering sloes and blackberries in Autumn take place now alongside Star Trek and computer games.

'I am an awful gambler' Nora announces, pausing on the path to let that sink in. Playing cards

twice a week, relishing the cut and thrust of it, and the diversion. We amble on, me with my hesitant Irish, Nora nimble and reflective: 'Faigheannn cois ar siúil rud éigint ach ní fhaigheann cois ar cónaí tada' – the one who goes out gets something but the one who stays in gets nothing – 'did you ever hear that?'

We are on our way to Tobar Isleamáin, named for the saint who came sailing by and landed here in search of water. He found a well by the shore and left the print of his hands and his two knees there.

I have walked the islands' other blessed wells. On Árainn (Inis Mór), the Friars' Well at Cill Éinne is not far from where Ellen Tower (Nell an Túir) lived. She was a healer and a 'wise woman', listed in the 1821 Census as *bean feasa*, a woman of occult knowledge. There's Ciarán's Well at Mainistir; dry now. But if you want healing you can stretch a silk scarf for healing through the circle of a stone sundial there.

Illus. 12.5. Many wells are no longer the object of pilgrimage, like this well at Teampall Chiaráin. Yet a sense of grandeur and tranquillity lingers.

Illus. 12.6. Stone sundial by Ciarán's church on the big island where, tradition has it, you may be healed by drawing a silk scarf through the circular 'eye'.

Illus. 12.7. Blessed Well by the church of an Ceathrar Álainn – the Four Beautiful Ones. My sister and I visited the well and nearby bullauns with Fr Dara Molloy and my sister's eyes felt the benefit of making the rounds there.

Illus. 12.8. The Well of St Colman Mac Duach by Kilmurvey House. You may spy it among little woods as you commence the climb towards Dún Aonghasa. Legend recounts that Colman's mother, when pregnant with him, was thrown into a well to be drowned by a jealous relative. They survived to cause further wonders.

Nearby, St Sourney's bowl is hidden in thickets by her little hermitage. Later on she had an alm's house for pilgrims and a well at Drumacoo on the old road to the Burren. The wells of the Four Beautiful Ones — an Ceathrar Álainn — to restore sight are set above Corrúch and there's the Seven Churches with their well near Eoghanacht. At Cill Mhuirbhigh, Colman Mac Duach's Well is almost lost among small trees. He, too, set sail for the Burren and at Eagle's Rock encountered Guaire, his kinsman on the road of the dishes (another famous legend!). And I've set eyes on Colmcille's stone boat beyond the airstrip; the notion of men flying through the air would have seemed as fabulous and far-fetched long ago as the notion of a seaworthy stone craft does to us now. That's legends for you ...

Illus. 12.9. Colmcille's fabulous stone boat, drawn up on the rocky shore close by the airstrip at Cill Éinne.

Illus. 12.10. Tobar na mBróg, Well of the Shoes, a wayside well on the path above and east of Tobar Éinne on Inis Oírr – so called, one islander suggested, because the shape of the well resembles a shoe or shoes – 'it's as good an explanation as any!' she said.

At Inis Oírr, there's Enda's Well, Tobar Éinne, where sight of the eel confirms a cure. Then, beyond it, Tobar na mBróg, well of the shoes; St Gobnait's Well (far from her native Cork), for eye complaints above Baile an Lurgáin; the well of the Gleann and Tobar na Líne near the President's tree. And there's the vigil in the catacomb of Teampall Chaomháin before the island's pattern day. It is said that young women make the vigil to find a husband, but a wag declared that it's the fellows at night who'd come in search of sport! One man told me that the fishermen take a little bag of sand from near the chapel to save their lines from being swept away.

Illus. 12.11. Tobar Éinne, Inis Oírr. The well is still visited especially around the Saint's pattern day in June.

Cinndearg, the red-haired one, is believed to be a daughter of the King of Leinster and her well lies by the sepulchre of the King's Seven Sons on Inis Meáin. The custom is to do the round seven times, circling in a clockwise direction. The little well of Seven Streams in Creaga Dubha is said to have a cure for eyes but at Ceannanach's Well down by the graveyard the cure is no longer remembered. Making the turas now is a pilgrimage to remote gods.

Illus. 12.13. St Cinndearg's Well – Tobar Chinndeirge, Inis Meáin, set in a field behind the chapel. Nowadays, it is surrounded by stone and grassy earth but in olden times it seems that small trees grew around the site.

Illus. 12.12. The modest beauty of a smoothed, circular stone fits snugly into the little bullaun (bowl) above Tobar Éinne, as if to decorate it.

'Is this the place?' asks Nora as we near the well that thirsty animals have visited. We peer into Isleamán's Well, searching for print of hand and knee, then say our prayers and sup.

Resuming our perigrination by the seashore, Nora points out the boulders ranged against the massive tides. She halts to admire the prospect across Galway Bay and then enquires: 'where are the dead?' – 'It is said they are near-by to help us'. She still mourns her husband and the loss of his company and goodness. A Connemara woman whom I once met said to a friend: 'Is poll dubh dóite é an t-uaigneas; ach

Illus. 12.14. Nora at Tobar Isleamáin. Of the many words for water – aqua, eau, Wasser, the Irish word uisce is the most perfect, containing it its two syllables the stillness and the whisper.

má dhúnainn tú suas é, dúnfaidh tú amach go leor eile atá go hálainn' – 'Loneliness is a black burnt hole; but if you shut it in, you will shut out a lot that is beautiful as well'.

The uncertainty of life and the sureness of death are all one fabric here. The Irish language seems to make communication with all of nature and her gods more homely. It draws them into the family circle – as in this prayer of an old person hoping for God:

O Lord, give me strength for another while yet
Until I see your face of pity.
I am going down the hill, maybe I would not
   see much to please me.
But, O Lord, until death do not let my spirit
   faint
Everything is slowing down, astore, the night
   is not far from me
But aid me at the end, bright love of my heart.

A Thiarna, tabhair láidreacht domhsa go ceann
   tamaill eile
go dtí go bhfeicfidh mé d'aghaidh thruacánta.
Tá mé dul síos an cnoc, b'fhéidir nach bhfeicfinn
   mórán féilteach,
ach, a Thiarna, go dtí an bás ná lig m'anam bheith
   marbhánta.
Tá sé ag éirí mall, a stór, ní fada uaim an oíche,
ach fóir orm sa deireadh, a ghrá geal mo chroí.

'We like people to be born in the hospital but to die in their own beds at home', one Aran medicine woman said. She believes that there are many resemblances between Native Americans and Aran islanders in their attitudes to nature and spirituality, mentioning a prayer (based on the ley-lines of the body) called The Three Narrowings. She also described an Aran prayer, petitioning for a death that would be acceptable and against one not to be wished for. Here is the nearest I could find:

Death with anointing,
Death with bliss,
Death with illumination,
Death with consolation,
Death with repentance.

Death without torment,
Death without shadow,
Death without death,
Death without dread,
Death without sorrow.

Seven angels of the Blessed Spirit,
And the twin guardian angels,
Be around my roof tonight,
Until daybreak and the light.

Bás ola,
bás sona,
bás solais,
bás sóláis,
bás aithreachais

Bás gan chrá,
bás gan scáth,
bás gan bhás,
bás gan scanradh,
bás gan dólás.

Seacht n-aingeal an Spioraid Naoimh,
agus an dís aingeal coimhdeachta
do m' dhíonsa anocht agus gach oíche,
go dtig soils' is camhaoir.

My English does not do justice to the austere and beautiful cadence of the verse nor the respectful but pressing requirement in the language.

Yet, as with Nora, impishness keeps breaking through. Reporting on a wake, one islander said: 'It was a pity. The rain came and put a damper on things'.

Resilient, full of feeling, independent; rich and poor lead the same life upon the island rockery. They run the hazard of earthly and primordial forces that rage and allure, buffet and roast, bury and drown. Wind, fire, earth, air and water, neighbour and stranger demand an endurance, which responds with cleverness, conviviality, tolerance. 'Tá an nadúr ag imeacht as na daoine', the old people say. If the good nature has gone from the people of Aran, then there is nature nowhere. Generation after generation have sewn it into the perpetual spiral of island life in the likes of Nora – frail, intrepid sky-walkers. The sound of a footfall brings the promise of a story – and a story, like a journey, has permission to go anywhere.

Acknowledgements and thanks to the following for their generosity with advice, knowledge, help and hospitality. All errors are, however, mine:

Bríd Bean Mhic Dhonnchadha; Mary Bean Uí Conghaile, Margaret Sharry, Róisín Folan, Eileen Lund McCarthy, Seosamh Flatharta, Bríd and Tomás Ó Conghaile, Bríd Ní hEithir, Micheál Ó hAmhlain, Brigín Seoige, Pádraig Standún, Máire Bean Uí Mhaolchiarán, Nora Phaidín Saidhbhín — Bean Uí Conghaile, Padraig Pheait Sheáin Ó Conghaile, Dara Molloy, Connla Ó Dushláine, Marion Broderick, Clara Gill, Colie and Michael Hernon, Joel d'Anjou, Mairtín Neachtáin, John O'Donohue, Rionach Uí hÓgáin, Padraig Ó hEalaí.

Acknowledgements for Illustrations

Illus. 12.1, 12.5, 12.7, 12.8, 12.11, 12.12, Photos, Anne Korff.
Illus. 12.2, Photo, Ciarán Ó Coigligh.
Illus. 12.3, 12.9, 12.10, 12.13, 12.14, Photos, Lelia Doolan.
Illus. 12.4, Photo, Ulster Museum, Belfast.
Illus. 12.6, Photo, John Waddell.

CHAPTER 13

Máire an Túirne – Spinning Maura

A short story by Dara Ó Conaola

Bhí Máire an Túirne ann fadó.

Bhí sí ina cónaí tí Mháire an Túirne, an bhean bhocht. Agus bhí sí bocht. Bhí a fear básaithe agus bhí muirín lag le tógáil aice. Ní raibh acu ach an ganntan.

Mar bharr ar an donas bhí an tiarna talún a bhí ann ag bagairt go dtóigfeadh sé an túirne uaithi muna mbeadh an cíos aici dó an chéad uair eile a thiocfadh sé.

Bhí údar imní aici.

Bheadh sí féin agus a clann óg i ngéarchall ceart gan an túirne, mar sin é an t-aon chaoi amháin a bhí aici leis an oiread a shaothrú agus a choinneódh beo iad. Bhí sé deacair ag baintreach bhocht airgead a fháil.

Ach dhá bhfágfadh Dia an tsláinte aici agus dhá bhfágfadh an tiarna talún an túirne aici bheadh sí ceart go leor. Sin é an rud a dúirt sí léi féin agus lena clann go minic.

'Sé an túirne a sheasfas an báire dúinn,' a deireadh sí.

'Sé a sheasfas an báire dúinn anois freisin,' dúirt sí, agus í ag tagairt don chruachás ina raibh siad. 'Oibreoidh mé an túirne, go háithrid.'

Bhí éileacht uirthi. Baineadh ceol as an túirne. Agus níor spáráil Máire í féin ach an oiread. Í ag casadh léi; ag sníomh is ag cárdáil. Daoine ag teacht chuici le olann agus ag imeacht uaithi le snáth. Í ag sníomh léi ó dhubh go dubh – sea, agus uaireanta go mbíodh sé ina lá gheal...

Nuair a chuaigh a cáil amach mar bhean sníomhacháin bhíodh daoine ag teacht chuici as gach uile cheáird ag iarraidh uirthi olainn a shníomh dóibh. Ar ndóigh ní in aisce a

Spinning Maura lived a long while ago.

She was poor. Her man had died and she had a young family to raise. They had nothing but want.

On top of it all the landlord was threatening to take the spinning wheel if she hadn't the rent next time he called. She had cause to be worried.

Herself and her family would be at their wit's end without the wheel, because that was all she had to earn enough to keep them alive. It wasn't easy for a poor widow to earn money.

But if God left her health to her, and the landlord the wheel, she'd be alright. That's what she said to herself, and to her family, many is the time.

'The wheel will see us through,' she would say.

'The wheel will see us through now,' she said referring to the present hardship. 'I'll spin the wheel anyway.'

She was in demand. The wheel sang. Maura didn't spare herself. She spun away; spinning and carding. People coming with wool and leaving with yarn. She spun from blackest night to blackest morning – yes, and sometimes too into the brightening day.

When her fame went out as a weaver people came from near and far asking her to weave some wool. Of course she wasn't working for nothing and before long she was piling

bhí sí ag obair dóibh agus do réir a chéile bhí sí ag cur na bpingeacha os cionn a chéile.

Dhá leanfadh sí uirthi ar an gcuma sin bheadh an cíos aici don tiarna talún nuair a thiocfadh sé, 'Agus nár dhéanfa sé maith ná geir dhó, an bithiúnach.'
D'imigh sin ann féin.
Ní dhearna an tiarna breá aon dearmad ar an lá a bhí ceaptha aige leis an gcíos a bhailiú. Bhí sé féin agus a chuid fear agus a chuid capall taobh amuigh den doras le bánú an lae. Agus ní haon deá-rún a bhí ina chroí ach an oiread, mar ba ghnách leis. Sé féin nach mbeadh i bhfad ag caitheadh duine bocht amach as teach is as árus. Go bhfóire Dia ar an gcréatúr nach mbeadh an cíos aige dó. Sin é an dlí a bhí ann.

Ach is maith an buachaill é an t-airgead. Nach raibh sé sin ráite ariamh? An té a mbeadh sé sin ina phóca bhí sé in ann labhairt go teann le duine ar bith.

Bhí a dóthain den earra cúmhachtach sin ag Máire an Túirne le tabhairt don tiarna ar an ócáid phráinneach seo.
Thug sí dó an t-airgead agus d'imigh leis – é féin agus a chuid capall, is go n-imí an ghaoth aduaidh leo...
Bhí Máire as imní anois. Bhoil, bhí an anachain sin curtha thairte aici, ar aon chaoi. Ach ní h-in le rá go raibh gach uile shórt ar sheol na braich fós acu.
Bhí bia uathu. Bhí éadach uathu. Agus sin rudaí nach raibh le fáil in aisce an t-am sin, ach an oiread. Is maith a bhí fhios ag Máire é sin.
Bhí cleachtadh mhaith aici ar an nganntan, agus, ar ndóigh, níorbh é ab fhearr leí.
Shocruigh sí ina hintinn go mbeadh a dóthain aici an geimhreadh aithrid seo ní he fearacht blianta eile é. Ó bhí sí bainte amach ar obair anois cén dóchar a dhéanfadh sé cúpla pingin a chur i leataoibh i gcóir lá na coise tine ...
Choinnigh sí uirthi ag sníomh léi, ó dhubh go dubh agus go mbíodh sé doimhin san oíche.
Ar ndóigh, ní raibh sí ag déanamh tada as an mbealach. Céard a bhí sí ag déanamh ach ag obair go cneasta. Ní coir ar bith a bheith ag obair go crua, ná ró-chrua féin mar a bhí Máire. Ní raibh aonduine ag cuir iachall uirthi é a dhéanamh. Má bhí sí tuirseach tnáite féin nach hí féin a bhí

the pennies on top of the other.

If she continued like that she would have the rent next time the landlord came. 'Let him not thrive nor fatten on it, the scoundrel!'

The fine landlord didn't forget the appointed day for collection. Himself and his men and his horses were outside the house by first light. As usual, the milk of human kindness wasn't flowing from him. He wouldn't be long throwing some wretch out of house and home. God pity the creature without the rent. Such was the law.

Ah, money's the fine lad. Many a time it's been said. If you have it in your pocket you can talk proudly to any man.

Spinning Maura had enough of the aforementioned to hand over to the lord on this pressing occasion.

She gave him the money and off he went – himself and his horses, and may the north wind go with them ...

Maura had no worries now. Well, she had put one calamity aside anyway. But it wasn't plain sailing yet. They needed food. They needed clothes. Things that had to be paid for, even in those days. As Maura knew well.

She knew the meaning of want and she knew she didn't want it. She decided that this winter anyway they would have enough. Now that she had work to do, what harm to put a few pennies aside, for a rainy day.
She kept on weaving, all through the day and through the night.
She wasn't doing anything wrong, of course. Just working away nicely. It's no sin to work hard, or even too hard, as was the case with Maura. Nobody was forcing her. If she was worn out there was no one to blame but herself. It was nobody else's concern. She was harming no one. That's what she believed, the dear woman.

But there's another side to everything. She never thought her own story would have another side to it – but it did, and

síos leis? Níor bhain sé le duine ar bith eile. Agus taréis an tsaoil ní raibh sí ag cuir isteach ná amach ar aonduine. Sin é an rud a cheap sí, an bhean chroí.

Ach bíonn dhá thaobh ar gach uile scéal agus is gearr go mbeadh fhios aici faoi, freisin.

Bhí dream eile ann nár thaithnigh an obair seo leo ar chor ar bith, agus bhí a mí-shástacht ag dul i méid do réir a chéile ... Ní fad mór eile a d'fhanóidís síochánta!

Oíche chiúin sheaca. Dorchadas an gheimhridh. Diamhaireacht na Samhna dhá chur féin in iúl. Gach nídh ciúin. Gíoscán an túirne ag tabhairt dubhshláin an chiúnais. Máire an Túirne ar a ham is ar a buille ag sníomh léi. Gan áird aici ar an saol ciúin dorcha mórthimpeall.

Máire an Túirne. Ar uair an mheán-oíche.

Stop sí den sníomhachán ar feadh nóiméid go gcaithfeadh sí cúpla caorán ar an tine.

Sin é an t-am a d'airigh sí an sioscadh ag an doras. Nó cheap sí gur airigh. D'éist sí go haireach.

An raibh rud éigin ag an doras? Bhí gach nidh ciúin arís. Ara, ní raibh sí ach dhá cheapadh. Cheap sí nach raibh ann ach siota gaoth a shéid go tobann an oíche chiúin seo.

Ach mo léan!

Thosaigh sé arís. Agus ní gnáth ghaoth a bhí ann, ach an oiread, ach sop aisteach gaoth nár chuala sí a leithéid cheana le fada an lá.

Gaoth neamh-shaolta.

Baineadh geit aisti. Bhí tuairim aici nach le maith a bhí sé ann.

Thosaigh an sioscadh arís. Bhí sí cinnte anois gur sioscadh a bhí ann, ach ní raibh sí in ann meabhair a fháil ar an gcaint a bhí ar siúl.

Thosaigh an chaint ag éirí níos árdghlóraí. Thosaigh an bhagairt is an rí-rá. Anois bhí sí in ann cuid den chaint a thuiscint.

'Húrla hárla,
Túirne is cárda
Húrla hárla
Annseo.
Húrla hárla
Túirne Mháire,

soon enough she'd know about it.

There was another crowd that didn't like these goings on at all: they were getting more and more annoyed as time went on.

Soon they'd lose their patience.

A quiet frosty night. Winter darkness. The mystery of Samhain letting itself be known. All was still. Spinning Maura was at it. Not noticing the dark quiet world around her.

Spinning Maura. The very dead of night.

She paused for a moment and threw a few sods on the fire. It was then she heard the rustling at the door. Or thought she heard. She listened carefully. Was there something at the door? Everything was quiet again. Ah, she was only dreaming. A sudden gust of wind teasing the torpor of the night.

It started again. It wasn't an ordinary wind either but a strange wispy fluttering the likes she hadn't heard in a long long time. From another domain. She took fright. She had an idea it meant no good.

It began again, a murmuring. Now she knew it was murmuring but for the life of her couldn't make out the talk that was going on.

The talk got more noisy. Ominous hubbub. Now she could understand some of it:

'Hoorla haarla
Spinning Maura:
Spin and weave
Morn to eve!
Hoorla haarla
Spinning Maura:
Morn to eve
Spin and weave ...'

Over and over they keened and keened. Fading away, coming back again. Up and down and around.

Húrla hárla
Annseo ...'

a bhí siad ag canadh arís and arís eile. Ag imeacht uaithi
agus ag teacht níos gaire. Ag dul soir is anoir an tsráid.
Ansin tharla an rud is iontaí agus is aistí dá bhfaca Máire an
Túirne go dtí sin.
D'oscail an doras. Sí an ghaoth aisteach sin a bhrú isteach é.
Agus ansin tháinig siad isteach. Iad féin.
Na daoine maithe!
Ach ní thabharfá daoine maithe anois orthu. Sé cuma an
uafáis a bhí orthu.
Nuair a fuair Máire a hanáil thosaigh sí ag déanamh iontais
díobh. Ba údar iontais iad, freisin. Bhí rud éigin ag baint leo
a chuirfeadh scáth ort. Bhí súile dorcha agus fiacla fada acu.
Ó, bhí cuma dhrochmhúinte orthu.

An chéad cheann a tháinig isteach shuigh sé ar an stól mór a
bhí leis an mballa ó thuaidh. Chuir sé cos os cionn na coise
eile. Chuir a chloigeann faoi. Ní raibh le feiceáil de ansin ach
a hata mór agus a dhá bhróg.

Tháinig ceann eile ansin agus shuigh lena thaobh. Feairín
beag tanaí a bhí ansin agus carabhat mór bán timpeall a
mhuineál. Níor dhúirt sé sin tada ach an oiread.

Tháinig an oiread acu isteach ansin is nach raibh sí in ann
iad uilig a thabhairt faoi deara. Bhí an chistineach lán leo.
Fir and mná.

Bhí camáin agus maidí agus sceana géara acu. Bhí fonn
díoltais orthu. Ní raibh aonduine díobh ró-mhór ach ní
raibh siad ró-bheag ach an oiread. Bhí cuid acu tanaí agus
cuid acu beathaithe. Ach bhí an ghnúis dhorcha céanna
orthu uilig.

Cótaí glasa agus treabhsair gairide a bhí ar na fir. Seáilíní
ioldaite agus gúnaí dubha a bhí ar na mná. Thug sí faoi
deara gur raibh péire stocaí de cheannabháin bhána ar gach
uile dhuine acu. Ach níl ansin ach cuid den scéal – ní fhéad-
fadh sí níos mó a thabhairt faoi deara mar bhí an oiread
rudaí ag tárlú in éindí. Ina theannta sin bhí na glórtha ais-

Then something happened that Spinning Maura would
never like to see the likes again. The door opened. It was the
strange wind that opened it. And then they came in. It was
them.

The good people.

But you wouldn't call them good now. They were horren-
dous. When Maura got her breath she stood there in amaze-
ment. No wonder. There was something about them that
would put the fear of God in you. They had dark eyes and
protruding teeth. A brazen looking lot.

The first one to come in sat himself on a stool by the north
wall. He crossed his legs. Letting his head drop, all you
could see of him was the big hat. And the two shoes.
Another one came in and sat beside him. A small rake of a
man with a grand white cravat around his neck. He said
nothing either.

So many of them had come in by now she couldn't make
them all out. The kitchen teemed with them. Both sexes.

They had hurleys, sticks and sharp knives. They were on
the warpath. None of them was very big, but none too small
either. Some were thin and some were bloated. But they all
had the same dark face on them.

The men wore grey coats and knee-breeches. The women
coloured shawls and black dresses. She noticed they all had
socks of bog cotton. But that's only part of it – she couldn't
take in everything, so much was happening together.
Coupled with that their strange voices had begun to weaken
her brain.

They didn't speak directly to Maura at all. She thought,
maybe, there was a taboo against that. That's not to say they
weren't saying what they wanted to say, they were – in their
own queer fashion.

As soon as they were in they started chanting in their own
odd lingo. Implying all the time how outraged they were.

teacha a bhí acu ag baint an mheabhair di.

Níor labhair siad go díreach le Máire ar chor ar bith. Bhí sí ag ceapadh gur raibh sé sin toirmeasca orthu. Ach ní hin le rá nár chuir siad iad féin in iúl, mar chuir – ar a mbealach sainiúil féin.

Chomh luath is a tháinig siad isteach thosaigh siad ag cantaireacht san teanga aisteach a bhí acu. Iad ag inseacht di go hindíreach cé chomh míshásta is a bhí siad leí.
'Bhfeiceann tú thall ansin?' arsa ceann acu.
'Bhfeiceann tú thall arís,' arsa ceann eile, dhá fhreagairt.

> 'Is nár chuala muid ariamh
> Is bhí muid ann ariamh
> Gur ceart a cuid féin
> A thabhairt don oíche,'

arsa ceann eile ag bualadh a chamán faoin teallach is ag cur luath in aer.

> 'Fágfadh siad muide
> Lenár n-imní féin
> Is an té nach bhfágfaidh
> Caith sí íoc as,'

arsa beainín bheag thanaí, agus í ag damhsa timpeall agus í ag caitheamh sceana mara in áirde agus ag breith orthu arís chomh héasca céanna.

> 'Tabhair di an Lá,
> Tabhair dúinne an oíche
> Tabhair beagán scíth
> Don túirne, arsa glór eile.'

Ansin le chéile:

> 'Húrla hárla
> Túirne is cárda
> Húrla hárla
> Annseo ...'

agus níos díoscasaí fós:

> 'Gabhaillí, gabhaillí,

'D'ya see over there?' says one
'D'ya see over there?' says another, in answer.
'An didn't we always hear –
Since we've been always there –
No matter how cheap or dear,
The night must get its share ...'

says one, giving the hearth a belt with his hurley and scattering ashes in the air.

> 'They'll leave us alone
> With worries of our own,
> And those that won't, I say.
> Will pay, will pay, will pay...'

said a wisp of a little woman, dancing around, throwing razor shells in the air and catching them again with the greatest of ease. And another said:

> 'Give her the day,
> The night is ours,
> Put the wheel away,
> For a couple of hours ...'

And altogether :

> 'Hoorla haarla
> Spinning Maura ...'

over and over. And then, with more force than ever before:

> 'Come here, come here,
> Come here, come here:
> The Pooka draws near
> The Pooka draws near ...'

Maura's heart froze. She believed she and her children, sleeping through all this, were in terrible danger. She didn't know what was best to do, but she knew something had to be done. She never saw the likes of these before, but she knew their ways were inclined to no good. Hopping around the house in ghoulish fashion. But the mention of the Pooka,

Gabhaillí annseo
Is gearr anois
Go dtiocfadh
An Púca
Is gearr anois
Go dtiocfaidh
An P-Ú-C-A.'

Bhí faitíos a croí ar Mháire anois. Cheap sí gur raibh sí féin agus na páistí, a bhí ina gcodladh i gcaitheamh an achair, i mbaol mór.

Ní raibh fhios aici cén rud ab fhearr di a dhéanamh, ach bhí fhios aici go gcaithfeadh sí rud éigin a dhéanamh. Ní fhaca sí a leithéidí seo cheanna riamh, ach muna bhfaca féin bhí sí cinnte gur dream dhíobhálach iad. Iad ag pocléimnigh thart ar fud an tí agus cuma an uafáis orthu. Ach sé an tagairt don Phúca, nár tháinig fós, a scanradh ar fad í.
'O, muise, muise, cén chaoi ar tharraing mé orm iad ar chor ar bith?' ar sise, go cráite.
Rinne sí iarracht labhairt leo ag iarraidh síochán a dhéanamh leo ach níor thugadar áird dá laghad uirthi.
B'fhéidir dhá dtabharfadh sí rud éigin le n-ithe nó le n-ól dóibh go ndéanfadh sé maith éigin. Chuirfeadh sí síos pota breá tae dóibh. Cá bhfios nuair a bheadh sé sin ólta acu nach maolódh ar a gcuid feirge? Nach minic a bhain muigín deas tae an cantal di féin? B'fhiú di é a thriall, ar aon chaoi.
Ach barr ar an mí-ádh ní raibh aon deoir uisce sa mbuicéad. Nach deabhaltaí tráthúil. Ansin chuimhnigh sí nach raibh an tobar i bhfad as láthair.
D'éirigh sí agus fuair an buicéad. Níor chuir aonduine acu bac léi. Is dócha gur cheap siad gur raibh an oíche fada acu. B'eol dóibh nach ngabhfadh Máire i bfhad as láthair. Ba leo féin an oíche. Bhíodar i gceannas go hiomlán. Shuigheadar fúthu go ciúin. Ag fanacht.
D'ardaigh Máire léi an buicéad agus d'imigh léi go dtí an tobar. Bhí a hintinn tré-na-chéile.

Oíche bhreá ghealaí a bhí ann. Is gearr a bhí Máire ag dul síos go dtí an tobar agus ag líonadh an bhuicéid. Bhí an tobairín a bhí thíos faoi'n aill ag cur thar maoil.
Aníos léi go deifreach – agus gan fhios aici ó Dhia anuas

that hadn't come yet, was what frightened her most.

'Musha musha', she cried pitifully, 'how did I draw them down on me at all?'

She tried to talk to them and placate them but they took no notice of her. Maybe if she gave them something to eat, or drink, it might do some good. She'd put down a fine pot of tea for them. Maybe when they had that inside them their anger might subside? But as ill-luck would have it, not a drop of water was left in the bucket. Of all the unfortunate times for it to happen. But the well wasn't too far away.

She rose up and grabbed the bucket. No one stopped her. I suppose they thought the night was long. They knew Maura wouldn't travel very far. The night was theirs. They were completely in control. They settled down nice and quietly . Waiting.
She went with the bucket to the well. Her mind was upside down.
A fine moonlit night. She wasn't long going to the well and filling the bucket. The little well under the cliff was bubbling over.

Back she came in a hurry – not knowing under God's heaven what was best to do. In her haste she stumbled over a stone.
'Misfortune on you stone,' she said angrily, 'is it no where else you could have been?'
'Will you not be talkin' to me like that', said the stone.
Did the stone speak? Impossible. No one ever heard of stones talking before. But she heard more.
'Do you not recognise me?' said the stone.
Now she knew it was definitely the stone that was talking. God above ! What a night !
'I'm afraid', says Maura, 'I'm afraid I don't ...'
'I'm your mother, dear. Listen carefully to what I have to say ...'
'My mother, that's dead for years...'
'It's me surely – and don't be wasting time because every minute counts. Take heed of me now and you'll be better off. Listen now, carefully. That's a bad shower that's visiting you. There's two types of good people, those that are friend-

céard ab fhearr di a dhéanamh.

Leis an deifir bhuail sí a cos faoi chloch agus baineadh tuisle aisti.

'Mo chuid tubaiste ort, a chloch,' ar sise, go gangaideach, 'mura gann a chuaigh áit ort.'

'Ó bhó, bhó, ná habair é sin liom,' deir an chloch.

Labhair an chloch?

Níor bhféidir. Ar ndóigh, níor airigh aon duine riamh gur raibh caint ag na clocha. Ach chuala sí tuilleadh.

'Ní aithníonn tú mé?' d'fhiafraigh an chloch.

Anois bhí Máire cinnte gur raibh an chloch ag caint. Dar fia! A leithéid de oíche!

'Ó ,' deir Máire, 'ní aithním ... thú ...'

'Mise do mháthair, a mhainín. Éist go haireach liomsa anois ...'

'Mo mháthair, atá básaithe le blianta...'

'Is mé atá ann go cinnte – agus ná bí ag cuir am amú mar ní tráth faillí é. Má thugann tú áird ormsa beidh tú níos fearr as. Éist anois, go haireach. Tá droch dhream ar cuairt a'd. Tá dhá chineál daoine maithe ann, an chuid atá cáirdiúil agus an chuid nach bhfuil. An chuid nach bhfuil atá in do theach-sa agus ní bheidh siad sásta go mbainfidh siad díoltas amach ...'

'Ach' adeir Máire, 'ar ndóigh ní rinne mise tada orthu ...'

'Ní dhearna?' deir an chloch. 'M'anam, muise, nach hin é an rud a chuala mise. Céard a bhíonn tú a dhéanamh gach uile oíche leis an bhfad seo ... sea – ag obair san oíche. Ní maith leo é sin ar chor ar bith. Is leo féin an oíche. Coinníonn siad sin súil ghéar ar a gcuid, agus go bhfóire Dia ar an té a ghabhfadh i mbradaíl orthu, mar a rinne tusa.'

'Ach céard a dhéanfas mé anois?'

'Aon rud amháin atá le déanamh a'd,' deir an chloch. 'Seo é an rud a dhéanfas tú: Nuair a ghabhfas tú abhaile anois fan taobh amuigh den doras agus tosaigh ag béiciúch. Abair in árd do chinn is do ghutha go bhfuil Cnoc Meá trí lasadh. Feicfidh tú féin ansin céard a thárlóidh.'

'Agus an bhfuil Cnoc Meá lasta?'

'Níl ná a leithéid de rud – ach is cuma dhuit, ach é a rá.'

Bhí Máire ag dul ag rith léi go beo – ach ansin bhuail an fhiosracht í. Ar ndóigh, ní i gcónaí a gheobhfadh sí an deis a fháil amach céard a bhíonn ag tárlú ar an saol eile.

ly and those that are not. Those that are not are in your house now and they won't be happy till they've had their revenge'.

'But sure I did nothing on them', protested Maura.

'You didn't ? ' said the stone. 'Upon my soul, that's not what I heard. What are you up to every night this long while now...yes, working at night, every single night. They don't like that one bit. The night is theirs. They keep a sharp eye on what's theirs and God look down on anyone that poaches on them, as you did ...'

'But what'll I do now?'

'One thing you must do', the stone said. 'This is what you must do: when you go home now, stay outside the door and let you start howling. At the very top of your voice say Cnoc Meá is on fire. You'll see yourself then what will happen'.

'And is Cnoc Meá in flames?'

'It is no such thing – but don't mind that, you just say it.'

She was going to race off – and then she got curious. It's not often she'd get the chance to find out what goes on in the other world. She'd put a few questions now.

'Tell me', says she to the stone.

'Tell me nothing', says the stone, 'and off you go in a hurry and if you fall don't pause to get up ...'

That was the end of the talking and the stone was as quiet and as mute as any other stone on the side of the road.

Maura took off in a hurry.

She became afraid as she approached the house. They were still there. Sitting quietly around the kitchen. Waiting.

When Maura came near the flagstone by the front door she threw the bucket aside and started to howl:

'Cnoc Meá is on fire'.

'Cnoc Meá is on fire'.

When the crowd inside heard this they got up in a hurry and absconded one on top of the other. They took off like the wind.

Maura was as quick as them going in. When she found herself inside, she bolted the door. Wasn't it she that was grateful the trick worked.

Chuirfeadh sí cúpla ceist anois.

'Cogar?' deir sí leis an gcloch.

'Ná bac le do chogar,' deir an chloch, 'ach gread leat go beo ... agus má thuiteann tú ná fan le n-éirí ...'

Stop sí den chaint ansin agus d'fhan chomh ciúin chomh balbh le aon chloch eile a bhí caite ar thaobh an bhóthair. Ghread Máire léi go beo.

Tháinig faitíos uirthi nuair a tháinig sí gar don teach. Bhíodar ann i gcónaí. Iad ina suí go ciúin ar fud na cisteanaí. Iad ag fanacht.

Nuair a tháinig Máire gar don leic a bhí ag béal an dorais chaith sí uaithi an buicéad agus thosaigh ag béiciúch:

'Tá Cnoc Meá thrí lasadh'.

'Tá Cnoc Meá thrí lasadh'.

Nuair a chuala an dream istigh an cur-i-gcéill sin d'éirigh siad go beo agus amach leo i mullach a chéile. D'imigh siad ar nós na gaoithe.

Bhí an siúl céanna ag Máire ag dul isteach.

Nuair a fuair sí í féin istigh, chuir sí an bolta ar an doras. Sí a bhí buíoch gur éirigh leis an gcleas.

Chuir sí a beannacht ar an gcloch, más cloch a bhí ann, a chuir an chomhairle uirthi.

Ní leaghfadh sí a lámh ar an túirne sin arís anocht, ná aon oíche eile ach an oiread. Bhí beagán faitís uirthi fós féin. Níor bh'fhéidir léi dearmad a dhéanamh ar eachtraí na hoíche.

D'fhan sí. Agus d'éist sí. Níor chuala sí tada. Ní raibh tada anois ag cur isteach ar an gciúnas. Bhí gach uile nídh go deas síochánta. Bhlais sí den suaimhneas a théann leis an oíche.

She sent her blessing to the stone, if stone it was, that had given her the advice.

She wouldn't touch the wheel again that night, or any other night either. She was still frightened a bit. She couldn't forget the night's adventures. She waited. She listened. She heard nothing. Nothing was disturbing the stillness now. Everything was nice and peaceful. She tasted the calm that comes with the night.

Illus. 13.2. Ruairí Ó Cualáin, story teller of Inis Meáin with his wife Nora pictured outside their home in 1937. Ruairí was Dara Ó Conaola's grand uncle. (Photograph courtesy of Ceard Siopa Inis Oírr Teo.).

Acknowledgements

'Máire an Túirne' was first published in *Amuigh Liom Féin* by An Ceard Siopa in 1988.

'Spinning Maura' was first published in *Night Ructions* by Cló Iar-Chonnachta in 1990, and translated from Irish by Gabriel Rosenstock.

CHAPTER 14

The Irish Language in Aran

James J. Duran

Introduction

Aran Irish has been the object of linguistic description for nearly one hundred years. Around 1895, the Aran Islands were visited for several months by two prominent continental European scholars: Franz Nikolaus Finck from Germany and Holger Pedersen from Denmark. Each scholar worked independently of the other, and tended to be critical of the other. Finck's research was published in a two-volume work in 1899 under the title *Die Araner Mundart*, but Pedersen's linguistic notes have never been published. In the middle of this century, the Swiss linguist Heinrich Wagner and the Irish scholar Myles Dillon visited Inis Oírr and Inis Meáin, respectively, administering comprehensive dialect questionnaires whose phonetically transcribed data were later published as part of the massive *Linguistic Atlas and Survey of Irish Dialects* (henceforth LASID), published by the Dublin Institute of Advanced Studies. In the mid-1950s, the American scholar Michael Krauss did linguistic fieldwork on Inis Meáin Irish for his doctoral dissertation at Harvard University (*Studies in Irish Grammar, Phonology and Orthography*. Dept. of Linguistics, Harvard University, 1958). In more recent years, Mícheál Ó Siadhail has published a study of specialised vocabularies relating to house construction, clothing, house furnishings, and foods on Inis Meáin, *Téarmaí Tógála agus Tís as Inis Meáin*. More recently still, Jacqueline Wardlaw completed an unpublished M.A.

thesis, *Liosta Focal as na hOileáin Árann*, University College, Galway, 1988, containing a comprehensive list of distinctive vocabulary items from the islands. Brian Ó Catháin has also recently completed an M.A. thesis on the verbal system in Inis Oírr Irish, *Cuntas Sioncrónach ar Mhoirfeolaíocht an Bhriathair i nGaeilge Inis Oírr, Oileáin Árann, Co. na Gaillimhe;* University College, Dublin, 1990, which has not yet been published. Finally, I myself have just completed three summers of linguistic fieldwork in the Aran Islands under the auspices of the School of Celtic Studies, Dublin Institute of Advanced Studies. The object of the investigation was to round off and update the material already collected in Inis Meáin and Inis Oírr, but also to document massively the speech of Inis Mór, which, incredible as it may seem, had never had its distinctive speech forms recorded in a comprehensive way.

With the help of eight linguistic informants, mainly relatives and friends representing different areas of Inis Mór, I believe that the main outlines of linguistic variation in Inis Mór can now be clearly seen, and that the last big gap in the linguistic data for the Aran Islands has now been filled. With the help of some nine other linguistic informants scattered over Inis Meáin and Inis Oírr, plus the extensive data gathered by the researchers mentioned above, a comprehensive picture is emerging of the relationships of the forms of Irish spoken in the three islands to one another, as well as to the forms of Irish spoken in Connemara and northern Clare. Hopefully, the results of the dialect survey will be published as a monograph by the School of Celtic Studies, Dublin Institute of Advanced Studies, in a couple of years.

A brief mention should be made here of the importance of folklore materials and of ethnographic texts, particularly folk tales and descriptions of everyday life by local people given verbatim in their dialect. Such materials will frequently contain large chunks of relatively natural speech reflecting the casual speech of the local population, in addition to unusual words and turns of speech which are distinctive of the dialect. Fortunately, the Danish scholar Holger Pedersen, mentioned earlier, recorded a large number of folktales in phonetic script, which are finally being prepared for publication by the scholar's grandson Ole Munch-Pedersen. The original transcriptions should yield valuable information on the speech of Inis Mór at the end of the nineteenth century. Since my own collection of speech samples is heavily based on tape recorded material from the neighbouring townland in Inis Mór, comparisons of the two bodies of material may yield valuable information on linguistic continuity and change over a one hundred year period.

A collection of materials gathered from schoolchildren in Inis Meáin in 1938 was published recently, *Seanchas Inis Meáin as Bailiúchán na Scol*, (Ciarán Ó Coigligh, ed.) and a folklore researcher from University College, Dublin, Pádraigín Clancy, has been gathering an extensive collection of tape recorded materials from Inis Mór. The importance of such materials is that they provide large samples of relatively natural, connected speech, invaluable to the dialectologist as he or she examines the folklore texts for specific linguistic features in their natural social and linguistic contexts.

Aran Irish : Myth and Reality

What is Aran Irish? How does it differ from the Irish of neighbouring Connemara and Clare? Do the islands differ from one another? Are there speech differences between geographical areas on a single island, particularly on Inis Mór?

Looking at the dark shapes of the Aran Islands from Connemara or from Clare, one tends to emphasize the mystery and isolation of the islands. One visiting linguist described the dialect spoken in the town of Cill Rónáin on Inis Mór as 'one of the most archaic forms of Irish still spoken'. In fact, however, nothing could be further from the truth. The subdialect of the eastern half of Inis Mór, in whose area the town of Cill Rónáin lies, ranks with Cois Fhairrge Irish on the adjacent Connemara mainland as one of the most innovating dialects in Ireland. As for the town of Cill Rónáin itself, a point from which strong Anglicising forces have radiated outward over the rest of the island since the British administration tightened its hold on Inis Mór centuries ago, the suggestion that Cill Rónáin has been a sanctuary for the preservation of archaic forms of Irish Gaelic would bring smiles, if not peals of laughter, from local people, especially those from the western part of the island. The fact that good, fluent Irish can today be heard from one end of the town to the other is the result of a Gaelicization of the town over the last twenty years, so that, contrary to Reg Hindley's assertions in *The Death of the Irish Language: A Qualified Obituary*, that there has been a 'collapse' of the Irish language in Cill Rónáin, there has been a striking resurgence of Irish in the shops and government agencies of Cill Rónáin (of which, more later).

Having disabused ourselves of the romantic notions of Aran Irish as a mysterious entity, archaic and exotic, we are then prepared to see its close connections with its neighbouring dialect areas. In fact, we could look upon the Irish of Inis Mór and Inis Meáin as simple extensions of the dialects of eastern Connemara, particularly that of Cois Fhairrge. The descriptive works of Tomás de Bhaldraithe and of Mícheál Ó Siadhail on the Cois Fhairrge dialect could in fact be used as handbooks for learning Aran Irish, and the details of Inis Mór Irish or Inis Meáin Irish could be then mastered in the course of a summer or two spent on the islands.

This is in fact the very course I myself followed in conducting my research. The LASID materials mentioned earlier for Inis Meáin and Inis Oírr are also very useful, but the learners would have to become familiar with Wagner's somewhat idiosyncratic phonetic script. As for Finck's massive work, *Die Araner Mundart*, even those fortunate enough to read German would be faced with a conflation of linguistic material from all three islands, so that the learner who managed to master this rather hybrid material might wind up sounding odd wherever he or she went in the islands! (We will see a little later why Finck's well documented work must be used with caution).

In sum, then, the Irish of Inis Mór and Inis Meáin differs from that of eastern Connemara only in very small details; these differences, though numerous, hardly impede communication, and the visitor who speaks Connemara Irish will hardly realise that the small differences are numerous until he or she really begins to listen carefully. Sometimes, of course, a number of differences all strike the listener at once, in a single rapidly spoken utterance, leaving the listener at a loss. For example, when I called over to a young man at a bicycle rental shop in Cill Rónáin to ask if he could provide my friends with a bicycle for the afternoon, his reply was *'Tiúir anseo a'inn éad'*, (=Tabhair anseo chugainn iad) 'Bring them over to us'. Luckily, this was my second summer in Inis Mór, and I was able to do some fast speech processing!

As mentioned earlier, the subdialect of eastern Inis Mór and the dialect of Cois Fhairrge represent two of the most innovative dialect areas in Ireland. The same can be said of the relatively conservative subdialect areas of western Inis Mór and Inis Meáin. All share the linguistic innovations of the eastern Connemara dialect area, of which 'h-dropping' is one of the most striking, so that '**m'fhear**' ('my husband') and '**m'athair**' ('my father') sound almost alike, as do the last two words in *'ag caint faoi mháthair Mháire'* ('talking about Mary's mother').

One of the features that distinguishes Connemara Irish from the Irish of Inis Mór and Inis Meáin is the form of the contrastive pronoun **seisean**, e.g. *'D'imigh mise abhaile, ach d'fhan seisean'* ('I went home, but he remained'). One will hear **seisean** in Connemara and generally throughout the Aran Islands, but local forms occur with great frequency: **sosan** in eastern Inis Mór and in the other two islands, but **siosan** in western Inis Mór, an apparent blend of **seisean** and **sosan.** A great divider of eastern and western Inis Mór Irish (with the boundary running through the middle of the island between Corrúch to the east and Fearann an Choirce to the west) is the treatment of the diphthongs **ia** and **ua** in a large number of words; e.g. **siar** ('westward') and **suas** ('upward'). The Irish speaker from western Inis Mór will pronounce these words as they are pronounced in Standard Irish, but the speaker from the eastern Inis Mór will intersperse the standard forms with the forms **séar** and **sós**. Notice that we do not say that speakers will always use the forms characteristic of his or her area – only that such characteristic forms will tend to crop up in his or her speech, but not in the speech of people from other areas.

Another form which is peculiar to eastern Inis Mór is the pronoun form **muinn**, 'we/us', used for the Connemara form **muid** (cf. Standard Irish **sinn**); e.g. *'Tá muinn anseo'* (=Tá muid anseo, 'We are here').

Four linguistic forms that set off Inis Meáin from Inis Mór is the use of the prepositional pronouns **tharab** and **rúb** (cf. Inis Mór **thartab** 'past them' and **rumpab** 'before them') and the demonstrative forms **inteo** and **intin** (cf. Inis Mór **anseo** 'here' and **ansin** 'there').

Sometimes the differences between geographical areas can be very subtle. For example, speakers from Inis Mór and Inis Meáin will both say *'tiúra mé Máire abhaile'* ('I will take Mary home') whereas speakers from Inis Oírr will say *'túra mé Máire abhaile'*. On the other hand, with negative forms of the same verb in the same tense, the speakers from Inis Mór will say *'ní thiúra mé Máire abhaile'*, the speakers from Inis

Meáin and Inis Oírr will cluster together, both saying *'ní thúra mé Máire abhaile'* ('I won't take Mary home'). In other words, here the pronunciation of the initial consonant of Standard Irish **tabharfaidh** is the only difference between the islands, but the three islands cluster together differently, depending on whether the positive or the negative form of the verb is used.

We have stressed how similar Connemara Irish, Inis Mór Irish, and Inis Meáin Irish are to one another. We have said very little of Inis Oírr Irish. The reason, of course, is that Inis Oírr Irish reveals some sharp differences from the Irish of the other two islands (and from Connemara) owing to strong influences from Clare Irish. Nevertheless, Inis Oírr Irish is clearly Aran Irish (and by implication, part of eastern Connemara Irish), and not Clare (ultimately Munster) Irish.

How can we best explain this hybridized form of Aran Irish? My immediate solution is to invoke the concept of 'linguistic substratum'. We know that the islands were settled historically by people from Clare, and that the colourfully named Murchadh of the Axes (Murcha na dTua) invaded the islands from Connemara with boatloads of fellow Flaherties and a writ from Queen Elizabeth of England in the latter part of the sixteenth century. Presumably the islands were flooded with people from Connemara at that time – if not earlier. Certainly the earliest census records (those of 1821) show 'Flaherty' to be by far the dominant surname in the Aran Islands, with a strong presence in Inis Oírr (80 individuals) and an especially strong presence on Inis Mór (374 individuals) – with a distribution suggesting an earlier military occupation of the two strategically most important islands, and some kind of accommodation made with the pre-existing population in Inis Oírr. Certainly one's impression of the sociolinguistic history of Inis Oírr on sifting all the linguistic evidence is that of a flood tide from Connemara washing over Inis Oírr and of great tidal erosion, but with the harder rock of the linguistic substratum on Inis Oírr resisting the tidal erosion. Striking linguistic features characteristic of Clare Irish (and ultimately Munster Irish) appear in Inis Oírr Irish, particularly in the forms of the verbs. In a sentence such as *'Dhion sé obair gos na cailíní nuair a tháinig sé thar n-ais'* (= Standard Irish *'Rinne sé obair do na cailíní nuair a tháinig sé ar ais'*, 'He did work for the girls when he came back') one can see the Munster influence clearly. Another clearly southern trait is the lack of strong palatalization in the doubled 'slender' consonants **ll** and **nn**, e.g. **bainne** ('milk') pronounced as though it were **baine** or **Gaille** (=**Gaillimh**) pronounced as though it were **Gaile**. Other interesting Inis Oírr forms are the verb form **gau**, e.g. **gau mé** (for Inis Mór/Inis Meáin **gheabh mé**, 'I will get'), the future form in **-fe** (e.g. **rife mé**, for Standard Irish **rithfidh mé**, 'I will run'), and the preterite passive form in **-av** (e.g. **rugav mé,**) for Standard Irish **rugadh mé**, 'I was born'. Yet other sounds that strike the ear immediately are the strongly palatalized articulation of slender 'd' and 't', so that **d'iarr** in **d'iarr sí** ('she asked') sounds like the English word 'jeer', and of course the shibboleth **pionta** ('pint') pronounced **piúnta**, which is the first thing some one in Inis Meáin or Inis Mór will think of in trying to characterise Inis Oírr Irish. Finally we might mention again **inteo** and **intin** (= Standard Irish **anseo** and **ansin**, 'here' and 'there' respectively), which are strongly characteristic of both Inis Meáin and Inis Oírr Irish.

Clearly, these are not kinds of linguistic differences that speakers or neighbouring dialects 'pick up' from one another. Speakers of 'Anglo' ancestry in Texas, for example, borrowed hundreds of words from their Spanish speaking fellow Texans (many of them the original inhabitants of Texas), to describe the landscape features and activities new to them in Texas, but they have yet to borrow features of Spanish pronunciation, even when using vocabulary items of Spanish origin. This separateness of Inis Oírr Irish is the principal problem in using the work of Finck, who conflated all Aran forms together, without distinguishing between the subdialects of the three islands.

The reader may have noticed by now that the crucial differences that seem to separate the different regional varieties of Irish spoken in the Aran Islands are centred in pronunciation of certain verbs and of certain pronouns, though the features that distinguish dialects – or sub-dialects – from one another can be found anywhere in their linguistic systems. In fact, it is precisely the nuances of the pronunciation of key items from the grammatical core of a language or dialect that allow the historical linguist or dialectologist to construct a family tree for languages or dialects. Most people might associate dialect differences with differences of vocabulary as well as of differences in pronunciation, but here again the dialectologists and historical linguists will concentrate on the pronunciation of key vocabulary items considered basic to the dialect or language – words handed down in the family and not borrowed from strangers. Thus core words like 'arm' or ' leg' will be of far greater interest in sorting out the genealogy of languages and dialects, whereas non-core words like 'rodeo', 'safari', and 'sauerkraut' – or even 'pail' vs. 'bucket', will be more useful to the sociolinguist or social historian in establishing the linguistic contacts of language or dialect speakers with their neighbours. This is why the pronunciation of core grammatical items occurring with high frequency in the everyday, relaxed speech of speakers of a language or a dialect receive such attention from dialectologists. What for most people are the most prosaic and uninteresting elements of everyday conversation actually hold the keys to the mystery of a language or dialect's evolution.

The Present State of Aran Irish

How strong is Aran Irish among the resident population in the Aran Islands? Is it in danger of being largely or entirely replaced by the English language? In estimating the prospects for the survival of Irish anywhere in Ireland, it is easy to err in two directions. One error is to conclude that the Irish of a given area is doomed – and that any public money spent on its survival would be wasted. The opposite error is to see the local population as so stalwart and loyal to the language that it is in no danger of extinction, hence,

any public money spent on aiding its survival would be superfluous and therefore wasted. Both outlooks achieve the same (perhaps unconscious) objective – the avoidance of expenditures of public money on the survival of Irish. The linguist Wagner and the geographer Hindley both erred in the first direction. Wagner concluded that Inis Mór was not worth including in his dialect survey since he viewed it as an area where 'Irish (was) spoken in some houses and by part of the older generation, (but) English (was) the vernacular of the place'. In fact, Irish was spoken by some 900 people from one end of Inis Mór to the other, with the possible exception of some households in and around Cill Rónáin. Hindley similarly describes the present state of Irish in Cill Rónáin itself as a 'collapse' of the language, when it is in fact a remarkable example of language resurgence in the Irish speaking areas. Cill Rónáin has always been an English-speaking town, but Irish independence and the small government grants of money awarded to Irish speaking families (now the '£10 grants') stimulated the interest of families in Cill Rónáin in the language. Nevertheless, only thirty years ago, it was common for people from western Inis Mór to be shamed into speaking English by the shopkeepers when they went into Cill Rónáin to do their shopping. Something happened in the mid 1970s, however, which totally reversed the situation, as the following incident illustrates. A young woman from western Inis Mór went overseas in 1972 and returned in 1977. When she went into a Cill Rónáin shop to make a purchase, and spoke English to the shopkeeper, as she was used to doing, she was greeted with 'Well, aren't we posh now that we've been overseas and have learned a bit of English!' The enraged customer then responded with 'Well isn't it nice that we've learned enough Irish to do business with the customers! When a similar incident happened to the woman in another shop, she concluded that something had happened in Cill Rónáin since she had gone. And indeed it has, as I can well attest !

Why, then, is Hindley so alarmed? He is alarmed because of the precipitous fall in the number of £10 grants given to Irish-speaking families, and concludes that the children do not have the linguistic competence in Irish to qualify for a grant. In fact the mothers of families in Cill Rónáin often do not even apply for a grant since a condition of the grant is that the families awarded the grant remain monolingual Irish-speaking households, and no mother wants to place her children at a disadvantage when her sons may be fishing off the coast of Alaska or California and her daughters may be earning university degrees. The mothers feel no antipathy to Irish nor do they feel that the quality of the Irish is suffering due to exposure of the children to English within the household. In cases that I am familiar with, one parent usually speaks Irish, and the other parent speaks English, which is the 'one-parent, one-language' situation normally recommended by proponents of bilingual education so that the children do not become 'linguistically confused'.

It is certainly reasonable to be concerned for the future of Irish among children. My own experience is that teenagers are clearly Irish - dominant, speaking the language at lightning speed. If I, a stranger, go in to have my bicycle fixed at the Cill Rónáin pier, and drift into English while discussing the virtues of bicycle parts, it will be the teenagers that insist on continuing in Irish while we handle the technological problems of the modern world. Teenagers are proud of being bilingual. They are catching up educationally rapidly with the rest of Ireland, and in fact the large floods of foreign visitors to the Aran Islands every summer can help foster a sense of being 'European', that is, multilingual and multicultural in a world where knowing the English language is an advantage, but not the sole measure of a person's intellectual capacity or of his/her cultural refinement.

Certainly Irish is undergoing change among the young in the Irish speaking areas; and these broad, sweeping changes can be noted in the speech of the teenagers in the Aran Islands. Nevertheless, the young on each island are holding on strongly to the Irish of their particular islands; and this can be seen in the speech of teenagers on Inis Oírr, where local speech forms are not yielding quickly to speech forms from other areas – even from the neighbouring islands. The schools, especially the vocational school in Inis Mór, can do much to support the use of the language among the young people and to help provide the new terminology in Irish needed for the rapidly changing modern world. Outdated and inadequate textbooks in Irish and the persistent use of English by educational authorities in their communication to island schools, however, can seriously undermine the confidence of young people in the viability of Irish. Comprehensibility of 'civil-service Irish' is another problem. One woman complained to me that she would never ask for census forms in Irish again, since she found them incomprehensible.

Raidió na Gaeltachta, the Irish language radio broadcasting service, is a great help in modernising the local Irish. I have never encountered anyone – no matter how old – who had difficulties in understanding the floods of new words coming into the local language via Raidió na Gaeltachta, since such words tend to be introduced one word at a time over a period of years of listening to the radio. To the person returning to the islands after ten or twenty years of absence, however, the language of the radio, with its flood of neologisms, can sound incomprehensible. The only difficulties reported by local people in regard to Raidió na Gaeltachta have to do with the dialects heard on broadcasts; Aran people consistently report difficulty in understanding the Irish of Donegal.

Increasing use of English is reported from the schoolyards, and this can be a cause for concern. Relatives and their families will return from overseas in the summer, and it is understandable that the children may play together in English, but during the normal school year, when children from outside the islands are not usually present, the use of English is not necessary and may weaken the position of Irish over time. It is important to emphasise here, however, that such trends are subject to correction, and that the concerted action of parents, teachers, and students can quickly 'save the situation'.

Speaking of families, one cause for concern is the increasingly small size of families, locally as elsewhere in the modern world, so that even if the number of young people marrying and establishing families locally remains the same, the number of young children in the local population will continue to shrink. Another potential problem is the lack of opportunities for young couples to find work and settle down in the islands; if they are 'priced out' economically by people buying retirement or summer homes, or 'squeezed out' through lack of 'meaningful' employment opportunities, the Aran Islands may suffer from the 'California coastal syndrome'. Yet another potentially serious problem is the demographic split in the local population on Inis Mór, with young men staying home to participate in the fishing industry while young women leave the island for a university education and/or work outside the island. A continuing situation of that sort bodes ill for those who would like to see compatible, stable marriages among the island's young Irish speakers.

What of the floods of summer visitors now coming to Aran from all over western Europe? The number of visitors has been estimated to be as high as 70,000 or 80,000 per summer. Certainly the strain on public services in Inis Mór – especially in the areas of water supply and sanitation – is great, but here the psychological effects on the local population can be quite varied. As mentioned earlier, the large numbers of non-English speaking visitors can demonstrate that English is not the only language of wider communication, and that 'everyone has his own language' – which is not necessarily English. Secondly, the English language skills of the local people are often far superior to the well-dressed visitors they meet, no matter how much the local people may have been ridiculed before by English speakers. Thirdly, the attitudes of almost all Irish visitors and of many German or Scandinavian visitors tend to be very positive toward both the language and the culture, and this helps shore up the pride of the local people in their heritage. Indeed, to be the teachers rather than the pupils of visitors can be a very rewarding experience. Certainly the young Japanese students who have learned Irish are invariably spoken of with great respect, and are never the subject of jokes. The only problem might lie with more recent visitors from France, Italy and Spain, who seem to come for the physical landscape, and often seem to regard the local people as part of a vast *tableau vivant*. The islanders, who love television, video recorders and decent housing as much as the rest of us, will of course no longer consent to be treated as exhibits in a 'living museum', though the genuine 'cultural tourism' now being promoted by the Irish government will certainly find favour in the Aran Islands.

What's in store for Aran Irish? God knows, but the islanders are intelligent, energetic, and resilient. They have survived a lot of hardship, and they have been exposed to the most intense pressures of the outside world, despite the physical isolation of the islands. As the late Brendán Ó hEithir pointed out, Inis Mór has been effectively bilingual in English for at least a hundred years, and people remember the time – before the grants to Irish speaking families – when Inis Oírr seemed on the point of shifting to English. It seems like half the population of Inis Mór either has spent ten or twenty years living overseas – often in Boston, New York, or Chicago – or else has immediate family members living there now – yet no cultural or linguistic damage seems to have been done! The Irish language in Aran can survive – and even quietly thrive – in the twenty-first century, provided that the government and people of Ireland honour their obligations to the Irish speaking areas, and offer intelligent, timely assistance in the preservation and development of the national heritage.

CHAPTER 15

'And here's John Synge himself, that rooted man'
W.B.Yeats [1]

J.W. O'Connell

The name of John Millington Synge is inextricably linked to the Aran Islands, and it is to him that we owe that enduring image of Aran as a place where a hardy, redoubtable people maintained a precarious hold on a culture and way of life that was, he came to believe, doomed to disappear as the 20th century invaded the islands.

The Synge family were well-off Protestants, who had estates in County Wicklow not far from the village of Roundwood, between Bray and Glendalough. One of Synge's uncles, the Rev. Alexander Synge, who had studied Irish at Trinity College, arrived in Inis Mór in 1851, fired with the zeal of his mission to convert the islanders to the Church of Ireland form of evangelical Protestantism. A school was established, and the Rev. Synge wrote enthusiastically to his brother, that numbers were 'daily increasing'. However, a truer picture of his difficult task is given in the same letter: 'The sermon writing is the most difficult of all and takes up a great deal of time — then preaching it to a very small number makes it some thing harder I think'.[2]

The Rev. Synge left Aran in 1855. The memory of the islanders, however, was long, and a few days after John Synge arrived on Inis Mór in May 1898, he met an old man who reminded him of the earlier 'family connection'—'I was standing under the pier-wall mending nets', he said, 'when you came off the steamer, and I said to myself in that moment, if there is a man of the name of Synge left walking the world, it is that man yonder he will be'.[3]

John Synge was born in Rathfarnham near Dublin in 1871. Always shy and never in very good health, the young boy had early demonstrated an independence of mind by turn-ing his back on the strict evangelicalism of his family for the greater attractions of nature and the many colourful people he met on his solitary rambles outside Dublin in the Wicklow Mountains.

Another sharp difference from the strongly English tradition of his family that began to emerge in his late 'teens was a consuming interest in the country of his birth. He noted ironically, 'Soon after I had relinquished the Kingdom of God I began to take a real interest in the kingdom of Ireland. My politics, went round from a vigorous and unreasoning loyalty to a temperate Nationalism. Everything Irish became sacred ...'.[4]

'Go to the Aran Islands'

It was W.B. Yeats who shrewdly recognised that it was Synge's imaginative encounter with the Aran Islands that made him 'the greatest playwright the Abbey had discovered, one of the greatest Ireland has ever produced, and the first who might be called truly Irish'.[5] Furthermore, it was after reading *The Aran Islands* that Yeats 'came to understand how much knowledge of the real life of Ireland went to the creation of a world which is yet as fantastic as the Spain of Cervantes'.[6]

Synge graduated from Trinity College in 1892 with a degree in music, and in 1893 left Ireland for Germany. In April of 1895 he quit Germany and settled in Paris. It was here in 1896 that he was to meet Yeats, who was not only to be closely connected with his subsequent career, but probably decisive in Synge's crucial decision to visit the Aran Islands. Yeats had returned to Ireland in the late Summer of 1896 with Arthur Symons, a friend and one of the most influential literary critics of the *fin-de-siècle*. After spending several days with Edward Martyn at his home at Tulira, a few miles from Gort, where they met Martyn's cousin, the writer George Moore, the party made a visit to the Aran Islands for a couple of days. Symons, who was writing a book on islands, published an account of his visit,[7] and Yeats too was deeply impressed.

In December of 1896 Yeats travelled to Paris, where he stayed at the Hotel Corneille near the Luxembourg Gardens, and learned from a chance conversation with another resident that there was 'an Irishman living on the top floor'. Yeats found Synge 'reading French literature,

Illus. 15.2. The Pier.

Racine mostly', and hoping to make a living 'by writing articles upon it in English papers'. Many years later, in the first draft of his auto-biography, Yeats recalled, 'I liked him, his sincerity and his knowledge'.[8]

As they talked, Yeats urged him to go back to Ireland, and when he learned that Synge knew Irish, the visit he had recently made to the Aran Islands came back to him. 'Give up Paris', he told Synge, 'You will never create anything by reading Racine...Go the Aran Islands. Live there as if you were one of the people themselves; express a life that has never found expression'.[9]

Ulick O'Connor clearly indicates the attraction and importance of the culture of Aran for the Irish writers of the time: 'These islands were the last outpost of the culture that was at the root of the literary renaissance. It was almost as if they were acting as a magnet to those who were unconsciously seeking to express the Irish imagination. Here it was concentrated in its purest form...'.[10]

Synge had met Yeats in late December 1896, but another year and a half passed before he made his first visit to the Aran Islands. On the morning of May 10th 1898, the steamer from Galway landed him on the pier at Cill Rónáin. 'A little later I was wandering out along the one good roadway of the island, looking over low walls on either side into small flat fields of naked rock. I have seen nothing so desolate'.[11]

Synge spent the first fortnight on Inis Mór, but he learned from two of his new acquaintances that 'several men stayed on Inishmann to learn Irish', so he decided to move to the middle island, 'where Gaelic is more generally used, and the life is perhaps the most primitive that is left in Europe'.

Once on Inis Meáin he took up lodgings in the home of the McDonagh family, and Martin, the youngest son called 'Michael' in *The Aran Islands*, became his teacher. Synge stayed on

Illus. 15.3. The McDonagh cottage on Inis Meáin where Synge lodged. On one occasion Synge made the crossing with the curate. While waiting in the priest's kitchen with a group of men, he was told by one of them, 'A man who is not afraid of the sea will soon be drowned, for he will be going out on a day he shouldn't. But we do be afraid of the sea, and we do only be drowned now and again'.

developed a style of writing that he was to use in his plays to great effect. Unlike Lady Gregory's artificial 'Kiltartanese', Synge took pains to find a way to render Irish idioms and Irish syntax in such a way that they preserved the flavour and tone of the originals. Yeats records a remark made some years later by Synge that sums up the literary significance of his exposure to Aran – 'Style comes from the shock of new material'.[12]

The Aran Islands

Part of the pleasure of the book lies in the way Synge's inquisitive eye notes such details as the dress of the islanders: Of the women he writes: 'The simplicity and unity of the dress increases in another way the local air of beauty. The

Inis Meáin, with short visits to Inis Mór and Inis Oírr, a total of eighteen weeks stretched over five years – 1898, 1899, 1900, 1901 and 1902. The material that forms the basis of *The Aran Islands* is drawn from the first four of the visits he made.

Synge came to Aran as a curious outsider; the four sections of *The Aran Islands* show him gradually winning the confidence of the islanders by his eagerness to learn and speak Irish, his sharing in the intimate events of life and death that characterised the daily round, and even his ability to play new and traditional tunes on the 'fiddle' that he once imagined he might play in a concert orchestra. The Synge we meet at the end of the book is a changed man, ready to make his mark as the first genuinely Irish dramatist.

Perhaps most importantly, Synge on Aran

Illus. 15.4. Carrying seaweed for kelp.

women wear red petticoats and jackets of the island wool, stained with madder, to which they usually add a plaid shawl twisted round their chests and tied at the back. When it rains they throw another petticoat over their heads with the waistband around their faces, or, if they are young, they use a heavy shawl like those worn in Galway... Their skirts do not come much below the knee and show their powerful legs in the heavy indigo stockings with which they are all provided'.

The men, he observed, 'wear three colours: the natural wool, indigo, and a grey flannel that is woven of alternate threads of indigo and the natural wool. In Aranmore [i.e. Inis Mór] many of the younger men have adopted the usual fisherman's jersey, but I have only seen one on this island [i.e. Inis Meáin]...the men seem to wear an indefinite number of waistcoats and woolen drawers one over the other'.[13]

After he had been with the McDonagh family for a while, Synge tells us, 'The family held a consultation and in the end it was decided to make me a pair of pampooties, which I have been wearing to-day among the rocks. They consist simply of a piece of raw cowskin, with the hair outside, laced over the toe and round the heel with two ends of fishing-line that work

Illus. 15.5. An eviction scene on Inis Meáin. Synge described an eviction on the island which may be the one shown in this photograph: 'At a sign from the sheriff the work of carrying out the beds and utensils was begun in the middle of a crowd of natives who looked on in absolute silence, broken only by the wild imprecations of the woman of the house. She belonged to one of the most primitive families on the island, and she shook with uncontrollable fury as she saw strange armed men who spoke a language she could not understand driving her from the hearth she had brooded on for thirty years'.

round and are tied above the instep'.[14]

Sitting in the kitchen of the McDonagh home, or watching the men threshing in the fields, or observing the skill with which a roof was thatched aroused in Synge a genuine feeling of respect for the instinctive artistry and crafts-manship of the islanders: 'Every article on these islands has an almost personal character, which gives this simple life, where all art is unknown, something of the artistic beauty of medieval life. The curaghs and spinning-wheels, the tiny wooden barrels that are still much used in the place of earthenware, the home-made cradles, churns, and baskets, are full of individuality and being made from materials that are com-mon here, yet to some extent peculiar to the

Illus. 15.6. The Eviction.

island, they seem to exist as a natural link between the people and the world that is about them'.[15]

Running through the narrative are a great many stories (all too long, unfortunately, to reproduce here), most of those in the earlier part of the book told to Synge by Pat Dirrane, an island storyteller. Synge's retelling of these stories, which he heard in Irish, is masterly, employing a simple diction, and reproducing typical expressions of the storyteller's art, such as the formal openings – 'There was once a man...', or 'One day I was travelling...', as well as the equally standard conclusion – 'That is my story'. Synge also comments on the fact that 'in stories of this kind he always speaks in the first person, with minute details to show that he was actually present at the scenes that are described'.[16]

Synge appears to have had mixed feelings about the traditional sean-nós singing he heard: 'The mode of reciting ballads in this island is singularly harsh. I fell in with a curious man to-day beyond the east village, and we wandered out on the rocks towards the sea. A wintry shower came on while we were there together, and we crouched down in the bracken, under a loose wall. When we had gone through the usual topics he asked me if I was fond of songs, and began singing to show me what he could do'...'The music was much like what I have heard before on the islands – a monotonous chant with pauses on the high and low notes to mark the rhythm; but the harsh nasal tone in which he sang was almost intolerable'.[17]

Synge attended several island funerals during his yearly visits although he felt initially awk-ward intruding on such occasions of island inti-macy. He was struck, as so many other folk-lorists have been, with the phenomenon of 'keening', the lament over the dead raised by the women of the islands: 'While the grave was

Illus. 15.7. Thatching.

feel their isolation in the face of a universe that wars on them with winds and seas'.[18]

As islanders, the sea formed an important part of their lives. Synge listened to tales of disasters and near-disasters, rode in currachs manned by his island friends back and forth between the three islands, and observed the funeral of a young man who had been drowned and whose badly decayed body had been washed up on the shoreline (providing him with the kernel of his great one-act play *Riders to the Sea*). Because death by drowning was an ever-present danger, Synge came to understand the potential for tragedy the island way of life placed on the wives, sisters and mothers of these men: 'The maternal feeling is so powerful on these islands that it gives a life of torment to the women. Their sons grow up to be banished as soon as they are of age, or to live here in continual danger on the sea'.[19]

The book contains many passages of exception-

being opened the women sat down among the flat tombstones, bordered with a pale fringe of early bracken, and began the wild keen, or crying for the dead. Each old woman, as she took her turn in the leading recitative, seemed possessed for the moment with a profound ecstasy of grief, swaying to and fro, and bending her forehead to the stone before her, while she called out to the dead with a perpetually recurring chant of sobs...'

'This grief of the keen is no personal complaint for the death of one woman over eighty years, but seems to contain the whole passionate rage that lurks somewhere in every native of the island. In this cry of pain the inner consciousness of the people seems to lay itself bare for an instant, and to reveal the mood of beings who

Illus. 15.8. Two Inis Meáin islanders, possibly Martin McDonagh, J. M. Synge's guide on Inis Meáin and teacher of Irish, and a youth.

al beauty, in which Synge responds to nature in all its benign and malign aspects – the sea, the raging wind, the heavy and sometimes terrifying fogs that seemed to cut the islands off from the rest of the world, the penetrating sound of birds singing among their nests along the high cliffs. For example: 'It is a Holy Day, and I have come to sit on the Dun while the people are at Mass. A strange tranquillity has come over the island this morning, as happens sometimes on Sunday, filling the two circles of sea and sky with the quiet of a church. The one landscape that is here lends itself with singular power to this suggestion of grey luminous cloud. There is no wind, and no definite light. Aranmor seems to sleep upon a mirror, and the hills of Connemara look so near that I am troubled by the width of the bay that lies before them, touched this morning with individual expression one sees sometimes in a lake.

On these rocks, where there is no growth of vegetable or animal life, all the seasons are the same, and this June day is so full of autumn that I listen unconsciously for the rustle of dead leaves.

The first group of men are coming out of the chapel, followed by a crowd of women, who divide at the gate and troop off in different directions, while the men linger on the road to gossip.

The silence broken; I can hear far off, as if over water, a faint murmur of Gaelic'.[20]

Synge died of Hodgkin's Disease in 1909, just thirty-nine years old, and seven years after he made his last visit to the Aran Islands. If evidence is required to show the impact Aran made on his imagination, all one has to do is examine the dates of the plays, in which the fruits of his island education are so evident, on which his reputation rests: *In the Shadow of the Glen* in 1903; *Riders to the Sea* in 1904; *The Well of the Saints* in 1905; *The Tinker's Wedding* in 1907;

and his masterpiece, *The Playboy of the Western World* also in 1907.

Declan Kiberd, sums up the significance of Synge's achievement in the context of the Irish literary renaissance: 'It was a period of brief cultural idealism, in which many writers and revolutionaries attempted Irish but never even achieved an elementary mastery of the language, and lived to regret it. Yeats' famous advice to Synge to live on the Aran Islands and express life that had never found expression may be seen in terms of his own inability to master the language which held the key to that life'.[21]

Writing about his friend the year after his death, Yeats remarked of *The Aran Islands* that 'nothing that he has written recalls so completely to my senses the man as he was in daily life, and as I read, there are moments when every line of his face, every inflection of his voice, grows so clear in memory that I cannot realise that he is dead'.[22]

As we said at the beginning, the name of John Millington Synge is inextricably linked to the Aran Islands. He came to love the people, and, it is fair to say, they certainly came to honour, respect and even perhaps love him. He came not as a 'colonist' to plunder, but as a student, to learn.

Illus. 15.9. John Millington Synge (1871-1909), drawn by Harold Oakley 1905. Synge's plays, such as 'The Playboy of the Western World', 'Riders to the Sea', *and* 'The Tinker's Wedding', *were important contributions to the Irish Literary Revival and the fame of the Abbey Theatre. He published his account of the islands,* 'The Aran Islands', *in 1907.*

Acknowledgements for Illustrations

Illus. 15.1, 15.3, 15.5, 15.8, photos, J.M. Synge, Trinity College Library, Dublin. Illus. 15.2, 15.4, 15.6, 15.7, drawings by Jack B. Yeats by kind permission of Michael and Anne Yeats. Illus. 15.9, drawing, Hugh Lane Municipal Gallery of Modern Art.

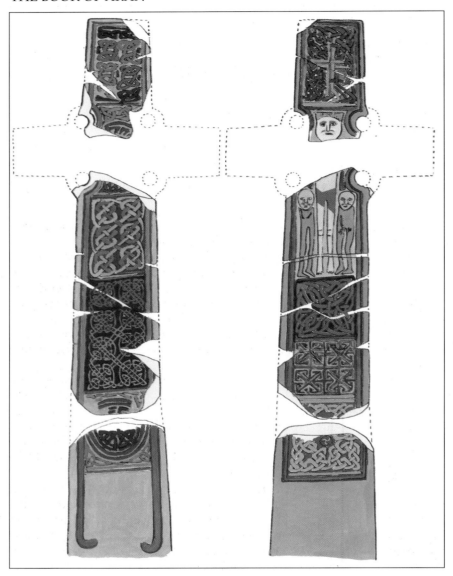

Illus. 16.1. North Cross at Teampall Bhreacáin, Inis Mór.
Reconstruction by Anne Korff and John Waddell.

The artistic creativity of the people of Aran finds its earliest expression on some of the simple cross-inscribed stones of the early Christian period. For all its simplicity the engraved cross was a new and potent symbol. The high crosses at Cill Éinne and Teampall Bhreacáin were more ambitious undertakings, with a different but no less significant repertoire of designs. It is generally assumed that the figured scenes and the intricate panels of knot-work and fret patterns were originally painted and picked out in contrasting colours.

Of course we have no clear idea what sort of paints may have been used or indeed whether the available pigments could withstand the western weather for any length of time. If crosses *were* painted, perhaps they were protected by a wooden canopy.

The North Cross at Teampall Bhreacáin — whether carved and painted or not — must have been a prominent and eye-catching feature of the pilgrims' circuit there, perhaps until the 1600s.

Although showing considerable skills in design and execution, high crosses like this one served specifically religious functions and may be seen, in the words of Kathleen Hughes, as 'prayers in stone, invocations for help, reminders of important events and festivals, and perhaps they conveyed other messages which have become lost over the long span of time separating the crosses from our own day'.

CHAPTER 16

The Artist's Eye

Anne Korff

In the beginning all art was craft and the artist was a 'maker'. For the Greeks the word we now translate as art was *techne*, while for the Romans it was *ars*. Both words have the meaning of a craft or specialised form of skill, like carpentry or sculpture, painting or even poetry. It was not until the Renaissance that a new understanding of the process of 'making', in which the activity of the craftworker is differentiated from that of the 'artist', whose activity was understood on the Biblical analogy of divine creation, led to a radically new emphasis on the 'creative' impulse involved in a 'work of art'. In time this separation of craft and art led to further distinctions, such as that between the applied arts and the fine arts. But it is important to remember that in the beginning no such distinction was made, nor was the need of it felt.

So when we consider such examples of creative activity as the inscribed crosses found on Aran dating from the early Christian centuries, the building of a currach, the construction of a wooden plough, the weaving of a woolen garment or even the playing of a musical instrument, we should recognise that what we see in each case is the exercise of a particular skill out of which the distinction between craft and art originally emerged. We should remember that it is we, viewing the particular work through the spectacles of a distinction that the original 'makers' themselves would not have recognised, who choose to describe, for example, a piece of sculpture or a piece of fine pottery as a 'work of art'.

Another distinction brings us on from that between craft and art and this concerns purpose or function. A wicker basket, however aesthetically pleasing, is, first and foremost, a container for holding something. A pattern in a woven shawl may be strikingly beautiful, but essentially the garment is meant to be worn as an article of clothing. But what happens when we come to a beautifully sculpted stone cross? Here we have something which is certainly beautiful, and as such can be appreciated by anyone with an eye for superb design, but its purpose was initially a religious one.

A final distinction, which is related specifically though not exclusively to what this chapter is concerned with, is that between anonymous works and those attributed to particular individuals. Much, indeed most, of the creative work of antiquity in the Middle Ages, is anonymous. It is from the Renaissance onwards that the sigificance of the individual artist starts to become important.

The Aran Islands are one of the most visually recorded places in Ireland, especially when it comes to photography, as is demonstrated by the many examples given throughout this book. While the primary importance of many of these photographs relates largely to their function as records of people and places as they once existed, others can be legitimately described as works of art.

What this chapter aims to do is to present a selection of paintings and drawings from particular artists who, attracted to the Aran Islands for many different reasons, took their inspiration from the people, the landscape and the rich collection of ancient monuments they contain.

George Petrie (1789-1866)
Illus. 16.2. 'Dun Aengus Fort, Inishmore, Aran Islands',
1850s
Watercolour on paper, 29.8 x 46.4 cms
National Gallery of Ireland

George Petrie was an antiquarian, writer, musician and artist. He illustrated many Irish guidebooks in the early part of the nineteenth century. Between 1835 and 1842 he was head of the topographical and historical department of the Ordnance Survey of Ireland and was the first since Roderic O'Flaherty in the 17th century to describe the monuments of Aran. His watercolour *'Dun Aengus Fort'* was painted in the 1850s and is a typically romantic presentation of a monument that was soon to become famous all over Ireland and Europe as one of the most striking antiquities of the pre-Christian world. The artist's imagination is primarily concerned with the dramatic aspects of the cliff-edge fort, and he takes considerable liberties with the actual topography in order to achieve his effects.

William Frederick Wakeman (1822-1900)
Illus. 16.3. 'The church of Kilcannanagh, middle Isle of Aran', 1839
Pen and ink and wash, approx. original size
Royal Irish Academy

William Frederick Wakeman held a position in the Ordnance Survey and was a pupil of Petrie. His drawing of *'The Church of Kilcannangh, middle Isle of Aran'*, 'sketched the spot', as he notes in the right hand corner, was drawn for the O.S. in 1839 and shows that he was an excellent traditional draughtsman.

Frederick William Burton (1816-1900)
Illus. 16.4. ' The Aran Fisherman's Drowned Child', 1841
Watercolour on paper, 88.4 x 78.5 cms
National Gallery of Ireland.

Frederick William Burton was born in Corofin, Co. Clare. He started his artistic career as a miniature painter and was introduced by George Petrie to the antiquities of the Irish countryside. He went with Petrie on sketching trips around the west of Ireland and was exposed to the emerging sense of national identity through people like Sir William Stokes, his daughter Margaret Stokes, Sir Samuel Ferguson, Sir William Wilde, Thomas Osborne Davis and Lady Gregory.

'The Aran Fisherman's Drowned Child' was painted in 1841 after excursions with Petrie to Connemara, which provided stimulus for a number of pictures, completed between 1838-41, representing ordinary scenes in daily life. Despite the title,'The Aran Fisherman's Drowned Child' actually shows the interior of a Galway or possibly a Connemara fisherman's cottage, and the clothing of the different figures is also more characteristic of Galway and Connemara, the only exceptions being the 'pampooties' worn by the fisherman and possibly the clothing and hat of the sailor. The position of the masts seen through the open door indicates the nearness of a pier, such as would be the case in the Claddagh, while the absence of fishing lines hanging from the ceiling and the presence instead of nets such as were used by mainland fishermen is another indication that this scene is not located in Aran. The artist is said to have made up to 50 preliminary sketches before he arrived at this final composition. Burton did not visit the Aran Islands until 1857, but Petrie, who had been there in 1821, would have offered him some detailed observations. This, together with his studies in folklore and costume on his travels in Connemara, would have given him enough material to paint this picture in his Studio in Dublin. The painting, which is typical of 19th century European Romantic style, reflects Burton's feelings about the people in the west of Ireland and their lifestyle, while presenting them in a knowledgeable and sympathetic manner.

Illus. 16.5. ' The Altar of the Church of the Four Beautiful Saints, Inishmore, Aran Islands.' 1857.
Black chalk and watercolour, 26 x 37 cms
National Gallery of Ireland.

This second picture by Burton was produced when he served on the Council of the Royal Irish Academy and was drawn on an excursion to Aran with George Petrie and Margaret Stokes. In contrast with the highly romanticized painting discussed above, it has an almost photographic realism about it, demonstrating not only his superb draughtmanship but also his deep appreciation and interest in Irish antiquities. The inscription on a label attached to it reveals that it was drawn for Margaret Stokes in September 1857.

Jack B. Yeats (1871-1957)
Illus. 16.6 'A Four-oared Currach', 1906
Ink and Watercolour on Card, 29.9 x 23.8 cms
National Gallery of Ireland

'*A Four-oared Currach*' contains authentic details of Aran wear, like the typical collarless shirt, pampooties and the tweed waistcoat. In this drawing Yeats provides a vivid impression of the dangers of the swelling waves, which are nearly as high as the prow of the tossing boat in which four oarsmen seem to row tense but nearly expressionless. This drawing is one of twelve Yeats provided for J.M. Synge's book *The Aran Islands* published 1907, in which he describes the islanders' activities. The emergence of a new *vision* of Ireland in visual and literary culture arose in large part through the attachment of Jack B. and W.B.Yeats to the life of the west.

Illus. 16.7. ' The Man from Aranmore', 1905
Black chalk and Watercolour on board, 38 x
27.3 cms
National Gallery of Ireland

Jack B.Yeats painted *'The Man from Aranmore'*
in 1905 after a visit, together with J.M. Synge,
to districts in South Galway. Yeats uses the
name 'Aranmore' for the largest of the Aran
Islands. The confident, proudly upright stance
of the figure standing on a pier which could be
Cill Rónáin indicates as much a 'type' as an
individual. The mast from the boat, probably a
hooker, indicates he is a seaman, but apart
from his hat, which is similar to those worn by
Aran Islanders, his other clothes seem not particular to an Aran islander. Jack B.Yeats was
hailed by *The Art Journal* in 1904 as 'the most
distinctively Irish painter', and it was in pictures like *'The Man from Aranmore'* that a powerful archetype began to emerge.

William Orpen (1878-1931)
Illus. 16.8. 'The Holy Well', 1916
Tempera on canvas, 234 x 186 cms
National Gallery of Ireland

William Orpen visited the west of Ireland probably in 1908 when he painted *'Old John's Cottage, Connemara'*. From 1913 to 1916 Orpen painted several pictures which relate to the Celtic Revival. The *'Holy Well'* painted in 1916, was produced as one of a series of large canvasses executed in the new 'marble medium' (a tempera, soluble in water, today's acrylic). Asked to explain the nudes in this clearly symbolic painting, Orpen referred to cultural regeneration and the impulse lying behind the new Sinn Féin movement, the partially clothed and unclothed men and women representing the spirit of a renewed Ireland. Seán Keating, who acted as a model (the figure standing on the beehive hut in the left hand side of the picture), strongly criticised the painting on the grounds that its portrayal of nudity was implausible in Catholic Ireland. Other critics have held that Orpen intended to be provocative and was dealing with myth and religion in a satirical manner.

'The Holy Well' was painted in Orpen's Studio in London, with Seán Keating supplying Orpen with costumes as well as his own paintings and drawings from his visit to Inis Oírr. The actual setting of the *'Holy Well'* is a product of the artist's imagination and represents a rearrangement of features, such as the beehive huts and the high cross, that certainly exist but not in this combination. Interestingly, an element of actuality suddenly asserts itself on the right hand corner where the small church of Cill Cheannannach on Inis Meáin, on the strip of land seen from Inis Oírr looking across the Foul Sound, is faithfully depicted. William Orpen was called to work as official War Artist in 1917 and left Seán Keating, his student, Charles Lamb, Maurice MacGonigal and others to continue the revival of the Irish visual arts.

Seán Keating (1889-1977)
Illus. 16.9. 'Steamer to the Aran Islands'
Watercolour, 29.2 x 46.5 cms
Private Collection

Seán Keating visited the Aran Islands from 1914 onwards and he is the painter who gives us the most informative and realistic image of the islands at that time. In pictures like *'Steamer to the Aran Islands'* we can feel the danger of living with the sea, and the everyday risks for the men rowing the currachs to the steamer is depicted in the most dramatic and realistic

Illus. 16.11 below. 'Men of Aran'
Oil on Board, 93.5 x 115.6 cms
Private Collection.

Illus. 16.10 below. 'Self Portrait in Aran Clothes'
Oil on Canvas, 71.5 x 69.2 cms
Private Collection

fashion.

'Everything comes to an End', also called *'Vanities of Vanities'* (an allusion to the Biblical book of Ecclesiastes with its constant refrain, 'Vanity of vanities, all is vanity') is an attempt to convey a complex symbolism and was painted in 1916, a time when he was producing illustrations for *The Playboy of the Western World*, a work which greatly influenced him. By contrast, *'Men of Aran'* gives us the atmosphere of a fine day at the pier and is painted in a more conventional way. In his numerous paintings and drawings of life on Aran, Keating depicted Irish characters as upright and self-confident people in a manner which supported the search for a new

Illus. 16.13 'Everything Comes to an End'
Oil on Board, 62.3 x 75 cms
Private Collection

national identity. Also shown here are two self portraits; one, *'Self Portrait in Aran Clothes'*, is a romantic study of the young artist dressed like an islander, while the other, a sketch done in later life, is equally dramatic but much more realistic.

Illus. 16.12. 'Self Portrait'
Charcoal
Private Collection

Charles Lamb (1893-1964)
Illus. 16.14. 'A Quaint Couple'
Oil on Canvas, 61 x 73 cms
Crawford Municipal Art Gallery, Cork.

Charles Lamb worked in similar ways, distilling the 'national essence' of Irishness in both his landscapes and figurative paintings. *'The Quaint Couple'*, painted in 1930, is a portrait of a tired but noble, elderly Irish country couple. Although most of his visits to the west were to Connemara, it seems that he was in Aran in 1928 living in a caravan, but none of his work is attributed to Aran. His painting *'Taking in the Lobster Pots'* could have been painted in Connemara or Aran, and it gives a genuine view of the daily life in the west at that time.

Illus. 16.15. ' Taking in the Lobster Pots'
Oil on Canvas
Armagh County Museum

Maurice MacGonigal (1900-1979)
Illus. 16.16. 'Gort na gCapall', 1932
Oil on Board
Private Collection.

Maurice MacGonigal first travelled to the Aran Islands in 1924; then a student at the Metropolitan School of Art (today's National College of Art and Design), he came under the influence of William Orpen, Sean Keating, Patrick Tuohy and James Sleator. Being an active member of the Irish Republican Army, arrested and interned in 1920, released in 1922, after which he resigned from the old I.R.A., he had the appropriate nationalist background to join in the project of creating a visual identity for the new independent Ireland. A visit to

Holland in 1927 broadened his outlook, and he was very impressed by Vincent van Gogh's paintings.

'*Gort na gCapall*', painted 1932, is pulsating with the elements of nature, as well as a rebellion against constrictions and mannerism. MacGonigal was Assistant Professor in 1937 and was appointed Professor of painting at the N.C.A.D. in 1950, a position he held until his retirement in 1969. He was a regular yearly visitor to Connemara (and Aran in the '50s) a demonstration of his deep attachment to the west of Ireland. His landscapes could, he believed, assist the establishment of national identity. He also painted many other subjects of social and political importance.

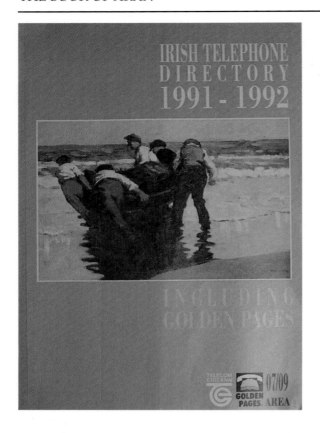

Paul Henry (1876-1958)

Paul Henry lived with his wife Grace, also a painter, from 1912 to 1919 on Achill Island. His new interpretation of the western landscape was enormously successful and his images of western scenes were used in tourist literature and in Government publications in the 1920s. His enduring popularity is shown by the reproduction of his painting *'Lobster Pots'* (c. 1934) as a postage stamp by An Post in 1976, and his painting *'Launching the Currach'* was the cover of the 1991-92 telephone book for the 07/09 area. Both paintings have become standard images which could have been modelled on the Aran Islands. *'Launching the Currach'* can be viewed in the National Gallery of Ireland.

Mainie Jellett (1897-1944)
Illus. 16.19. 'Rain clouds approaching Chevaux-de-Frise'
Pencil on paper, 20.2 x 33 cms
National Gallery of Ireland.

Mainie Jellett was influenced by Cubism while studying in France, and her work was abstract in the 20s. She moved towards semi-abstraction in the 30s, and during this period she travelled the west of Ireland, mostly to Achill Island, Co. Mayo. Her *'Chevaux -de -Frise'* drawing might have been done on Inis Mór. With its spare lines and clarity of image, it shows her tendency for construction towards a composition in this, one of many of her well observed nature studies.

Jacob Epstein (1880-1959)
Illus. 16.20. 'Man of Aran'
Bronze
Hugh Lane Municipal Gallery of Modern Art.

Jacob Epstein was born in the United States and settled in London in 1905 where he rapidly gained a reputation as a portrait and monumental sculptor. His best known commissioned work is the semi-relief of 18 figures, carved for the British Medical Association building in London's Strand. The circumstances in which Epstein executed the bronze head entitled 'Man of Aran' or ' Tiger King' are not known, but it seems likely it was done sometime during the mid-30s, when the film was enjoying success. It powerfully expresses a sense of character and resilience that shows the sculptor read his subject well.

Illus. 16.21.
St Gregory.

Illus. 16.22. Detail

Illus. 16.23. St Caomhán

Harry Clarke's (1889-1931) stained glass studio supplied the Parish church in Inis Meáin in 1939 with several beautiful windows, which make reference to some of the saints associated with the islands, as well as charming details, reminiscent of medieval stained glass windows, reflecting contemporary activities. One window shows St Caomhán patron of Inis Oírr, with an interesting detail behind the Saint's feet of two men rowing a currach.

A later addition to the church's windows was made in 1991, supplied by the **Abbey Stained Glass Studios**. This window depicts St Gregory, who is associated with Inis Meáin, seated in a boat heading towards an island on the horizon. The saint is associated with Gregory's Sound, the expanse of water between Inis Meáin and Inis Mór. A further reference to the saint is the depiction in the lower panel of the window of the early Christian church of Cill Cheannannach, which may take its name from Gríoir Ceannfhionnadh, or Gregory the Fairheaded.

Illus. 16.24.
Detail

George Campbell (1917-1979)
Illus. 16.25. ' Dun Aengus'
Oil on Canvas
Private Collection

George Campbell was a painter of great range and ability, with a wide diversity of subject matter. In particular his love of music influenced his paintings throughout his life. Campbell spent the 50s to the 70s moving between Ireland and Spain. His visits to the west were mainly to Connemara. In '*Dun Aengus*', painted probably in the 1960s, he displays a mastery of colour and light, great skill in using the abstract qualities of paint, and an appreciation of the contrasting textures of the rugged Aran landscape – its curved and edged coastline and the semi-circular form of the fort in the immediate foreground all unite to convey a powerful sense of atmosphere.

Heinrich Becker (1907 -)
Illus. 16.26. 'Fisherman's Wife on Aran (Cill Éinne)'
Oil on Canvas
Private Collection.

Heinrich Becker was born in Germany, and came to Ireland in 1938 to study Irish folklore and the Irish language at University College, Galway, undertaken on behalf of the German Research Council (Deutsche Forschungs-gemeinschaft). Becker is well remembered on the Aran Islands from the mid 1940s, when he lived and studied there. He achieved an excellent knowledge of the Irish language and became a fluent speaker. Becker recorded in writing, drawing and photographs many aspects of daily work and activity on Aran, including a detailed account of fishing methods which was written in Irish. He worked not only as a scholar but as an artist as is shown in the *'Fisherman's Wife on Aran (Cill Éinne)'*. He has published articles on the folklore of Aran and the west coast in German, English and Irish.

Gertrude Degenhardt (1940 -)
Illus. 16.27. 'On to Inis Meáin', 1993.
Drypoint Etching
Private Collection

Gertrude Degenhardt was born in New York and was brought up in West Berlin. Since 1966 she has worked as an independent painter and graphic artist. In 1968 she received the award of the Graphic Art Biennial in Cracow, Poland, and in 1976 the award of the Graphic Art Biennial in Fredrikstad, Norway. Ms. Degenhardt, who has had numerous exhibitions at home and abroad, lives and works in Mainz, Germany. For the past 20 years she has been a regular visitor to Ireland, especially Connacht, and has had several exhibitions in Kenny's Gallery, Galway. Her drypoint etchings are of international standard and unique, as her coloured etching '*On to Inis Meáin*' shows.

Noreen Walshe (1953 -)
Illus. 16.28. 'Seálta II', 1993
Oil on Canvas, 152.5 x 91.5 cms
Private Collection

Noreen Walshe was born in Limerick and studied Irish at U.C.G., graduating in 1975. After teaching for a while, she returned to her earlier love of art and graduated in 1992 from the National College of Art and Design, Dublin, with a degree in Fine Art. She now lives and works in Navan, Co. Meath, Deeply influenced by Irish culture, she gives us a fresh interpretation of the people and the seascapes of the Aran Islands. Shown here is *'Seálta II'*, one of a series of oils that explore the patterns and colours of the traditional shawls worn by the island women.

Gwen O'Dowd (1957 -)
Illus. 16.29. 'Poll na bPéist', 1992
Oil on Paper, 31 x 41 cms
Private Collection.

Gwen O'Dowd was born in Dublin where she studied Fine Art at the N.C.A.D. from 1976 to 1980. During the 1980s she travelled on a grant in the West Indies, Trinidad and Venezuela, Barcelona and the south of Spain, and was Artist in Residence in Wales. She has also worked as part-time lecturer at the Limerick and Cork schools of Art and Design and the N.C.A.D. She has had a number of exhibitions at home and abroad. Her current work is inspired by the west coast and the Aran Islands. The painting *'Poll na bPéist'* is her response to an environmental experience, relating more to self-exploration than to direct representation.

Seán Ó Flaitheartha (1964 -)
Illus. 16.30 'Eangach', 1993.
Mixed Medium on Canvas, 122 x 244 cms
Private Collection.

Seán Ó Flaitheartha was born on Inis Mór and studied at the N.C.A.D., the Pennsylvania School of Arts, U.S.A. and the École Nationale Supérieure des Arts de la Cambre, Brussels. He received a scholarship to study abroad from the Belgium Government and Údaras na Gaeltachta. At the moment he travels between Inis Mór and Connemara where he has a studio. His paintings relate to social and political realities dealing with issues that address the human situation, be it in a rural or an urban landscape.

My special thanks to: Ciarán MacGonigal and Patricia Móriarty of the RHA Gallagher Gallery, Robin Eyre Maunsell, Martha Hanbury, John Reihill, Justin and Michael Keating, Máire MacConghail and Tom Kenny, in helping me to obtain transparencies and permissions.
The National Gallery, The Hugh Lane Municipal Gallery of Modern Art, The Ulster Museum, Belfast and the Armagh County Museum, The Crawford Municipal Art Gallery, Cork, The Royal Irish Academy, An Post and Telecom, for their kind assistance.

CHAPTER 17

The Making of the Man of Aran

Joe McMahon

Illus. 17.1. 'We select a group of the most attractive and appealing characters we can find, to represent a family and through them tell our story'. The basis of O'Flaherty's approach to film and narrative: Maggie Dirrane, Coley King (Tiger King) and Mikleen Dillane, were chosen to represent the family.

On the 25th April 1934, the Aran Islands enjoyed, if that is the word, a degree of attention from the centres of the artistic world that is seldom bestowed on communities preoccupied with economic survival and unchanging modes of expression. On that day Robert Flaherty's film 'Man of Aran' had its premiere in the New Gallery, London, before a fashionable audience in evening dress. Music was provided by the Irish Guards and the cast of Aran islanders was also in attendance dressed in their own native home-spun fashions. A basking shark, though not at the premiere, had also been brought from the wild seas of the west Atlantic to be stuffed by a London taxidermist and displayed in the window of the film's production company. Flaherty was annoyed that a piece had to be cut from the middle of the fish to accommodate the window display. This, he felt, diminished the intended dramatic impact. Drama, as the people of Aran discovered during his almost two year stay on Inis Mór, was a quality much admired and sought after by Flaherty.

The man and his background

Robert Joseph Flaherty was born in Iron Mountain, Michigan, in 1884.[1] His father, an Irish Protestant, emigrated to Canada in the middle of the nineteenth century and married Susan Klockner a Catholic woman of German ancestry. He received little formal education but inherited from his father a love for the wilderness and by early manhood had developed a reputation as an explorer of the sub-arctic regions of Canada. In his own words 'first I was an explorer and then I was an artist'.[2] During the course of his adventurous career however the artist gained ascendancy over the explorer although the two aspects of the man never entirely separated.

His first and arguably most successful film, 'Nanook of the North' came about almost by accident when his patron suggested that he take with him into the arctic wilderness 'one of those new fangled things called a motion picture camera'. Released in 1922 after many years of development, Nanook was enthusiastically received by American and European critics and established Flaherty as one of the great founding fathers of film 'documentary' ('documentary may be said to have had its real beginnings with Flaherty's Nanook', Paul Rotha[3]). Nanook's critical, and even more important, commercial success led to an open invitation from Hollywood to repeat the formula and resulted in several futile attempts to adapt his idiosyncratic approach to that of the Hollywood studio system. A number of South Sea Island films (including 'Moana', released by the studio with the subtitle 'The Love Life of a South Sea Siren') were completed, one in collaboration with the German Expressionist director, F.W. Murnau (perhaps best remembered for 'Nosferatu'). In 1930 Flaherty moved to Europe and after spending a short period in Germany, where he was much impressed but not over influenced by the work of such European directors as Ivens, Eisenstein and Pudovkin, he moved to England where he made a short film called 'Industrial Britain'. Flaherty's critical reputation if not his 'bankability' was highly regarded world-wide and when he approached Michael Balcon, head of

British Gaumont Pictures, with a proposal to make a film in the Aran Islands, Balcon agreed hoping that the work would enhance the reputation of his company. 'Man of Aran', conceived as a silent film, was allocated a generous budget and allowed to proceed in the way Flaherty liked best without the preconceptions imposed by a script.

Arrival and attitude

Flaherty made slow progress towards the Aran Islands, staying some time in Dublin in the Autumn of 1931 where it was difficult to tell, according to his biographer Arthur Calder-Marshall, whether he was 'drinking-in' the atmosphere or simply 'drinking'.[4] He proceeded from there to Achill Island where he talked for a while of not proceeding to the Aran Islands but of shooting the film on Achill. This was apparently a process of preparation, a desire to get to know the western islands and their inhabitants, before arriving at his ultimate destination. Leaving at last for Aran, his first sight of Galway banished all thoughts of using Achill. When he disembarked from the *Dun Aengus* on to Inis Mór pier with his wife Frances and three daughters, one of the first people he encountered was Pat Mullen who was to become his assistant director and 'contact man' with the islanders and whose book *Man of Aran* provides an invaluable insight into the making of the film and into Flaherty's relationship with the islanders. Mullen's first reaction to Flaherty, whom he describes as 'a great giant-bodied man, white-haired and blue-eyed', was that Flaherty 'was bound to be a leader in any game where he played a hand'. After a short sight-seeing tour, the Flahertys departed but returned shortly afterwards in early January 1931 for what was to be an almost two year stay. They took the best house on the island which was situated near the sea in Cill Mhuirbhigh and proceeded immediately to convert a nearby fishing shed into a studio with developing and drying rooms. The islanders, as is their way, did not immediately take to the Flahertys and for a long time in Mullen's words continued to 'look sideways' at them.

Despite Flaherty's commitment to primitivism, he and his family, as well as various assistants, lived rather well on the island. Kevin Rockett, referring to the contrast between Flaherty's lifestyle and the 'island primitivism' depicted in the film, quotes Harry Watt, an assistant on the film, 'the extraordinary thing was that Flaherty lived like a king in these primitive places ... I never lived so well in my life'. They had brought a cordon bleu cook to Aran and

Illus. 17.2. Pat Mullen, the main contact between O'Flaherty and the islanders, whose book Man of Aran *provides an individualistic view of O'Flaherty's stay on Inis Mór.*

Illus. 17.3. Maggie Dirrane's cottage.

'we had two grown men just to put peat on the fire'.[5] An islander describes the Flaherty household: 'there is more thrown away out of this house, they say, than would give food to half the villages in the Island. Where there are quarters of beef and quarters of mutton and millions of tins of everything that come from every land on which the sun shines'.[6]

In his approach to 'Man of Aran', Flaherty followed a method that was essentially common to all his films. In pursuing his central theme of the confrontation between man and nature the first rule, he claimed, was that the material must be approached without preconceptions and that the film must grow 'naturally' out of the film-maker's exposure to and involvement in the community whose struggle for survival he has chosen to represent. This meant spending long periods on location and shooting vast amounts of film as he sought again and again to find in the developed images a conception that matched his 'vision'. The difficulty with this, of course, was that his 'vision' may have involved a more fundamental preconception than the one he was trying to avoid in the first place and that Flaherty in fact may have brought to all of his material a romantic notion of what he thought should be there in the first place.

He prepared for Aran by reading Synge's *The Aran Islands* (1907) and *Riders to the Sea* (1904) and arrived on the islands determined to find life there as it was in Synge's time and before. In fact most of Flaherty's films depict life not as he experienced it but rather as an idealised reconstruction of its past. Eskimo life as portrayed in 'Nanook' had disappeared by the time he encountered it and the life depicted in 'Man of Aran', in so far as it ever existed, belongs to the nineteenth century. Similarly he imposes a preconceived narrative pattern on most of his films. The male protagonist, adept at survival in a hostile environment because of skills he has inherited from the traditions of his people, provides for his family and passes these same skills on to his son. The hero is an integrated member of a community and is supported and comforted by the subsidiary skills of his wife and usually one male child.

Assembling a cast

One of the first things Flaherty did after arriving on Aran was to observe the islanders carefully with a view to assembling his cast. 'We select a group of the most attractive and appealing characters we can find, to represent a family, and through them tell our story. It is always a long and difficult process, this type finding, for it is surprising how few faces stand the test of the camera'.[7] His first concern was to find the archetypal family group which would form the basis of whatever narrative would evolve in the course of filming. He first saw Mikleen Dillane, the young boy featured in the film, at a dance in Cill Éinne village and after testing him decided he was right for the part.

Illus. 17.4. Woman of Aran. Despite Flaherty's tendency to insist on the subordinate role of women, Maggie Dirrane established the most vivid human presence in the film.

Illus. 17.5. Maggie Dirrane in the midst of friends at her cottage on Inis Mór.

Mikleen's mother however had different ideas being deeply suspicious that Flaherty's intentions were to tempt the boy into Socialism or even worse Protestantism. It took protracted negotiations between Pat Mullen, Mrs Dillane

(Mr Dillane deciding such matters were his wife's responsibility), the Garda sergeant and apparently the Parish Priest to bring matters to a satisfactory conclusion.

Maggie Dirrane, a young woman living in extreme poverty with four children and a husband who had 'run himself out' with years of back-breaking work, was chosen, after first being turned down, for the part of the mother. Maggie, who was described as being 'absolutely without fear',[8] established a memorable presence in her part. Tiger King (the Man of Aran), 'a fine looking man, six feet in height, supple as a deer and as light on his feet as a cat',[9] was discovered sitting on Cill Mhuirbhigh pier and, after some reluctance, was persuaded to sign on. The two older members of the cast were recruited because Flaherty recognised inherent dramatic quality in their appearance. Patch Ruadh, a man with a fine red beard, who was discovered while working as a builder on the set became convinced that this mysterious but valuable quality called drama was contained in his whiskers and right through the filming could be seen disappearing each day behind a large boulder with a piece of cracked glass and broken comb to groom his newly found asset. Bridgid, the old woman in the film, found that her face was 'full up entirely of drama'[10] which caused her concern at first until Pat Mullen assured her that 'a dropeen of whiskey' was the best cure for it.

Shooting

With his cast in place and the basic shape of his story beginning to take shape Flaherty plunged himself into work. His established method of filming was to shoot great quantities of film with little thought for the editing process that was to follow. All in all, he was to shoot over 200,000 feet of film for 'Man of Aran'. In one day alone, using two cameras he shot 5,600 feet.[11]

He had, as John Goldman, his editor, suggests, 'sensitivity only for the shot itself and not for its place within the overall rhythm and structure of the film'.[12] His tendency was to resist the rapidly developing technology of film making as if he wanted or needed the independence of approach that is available to a writer or painter but is close to impossible in the inescapably collaborative medium of film. Such an 'open', unpremeditated approach involved a considerable degree of uncertainty and tension and as shooting progressed Flaherty's temperament, equable indeed sociable when not under the pressure of a shoot, became increasingly irritable. John Goldman describes the atmosphere:

Illus. 17.6. Man of Aran. Sean Keating's striking drawing of Tiger King described by Pat Mullen as 'a fine looking man, six feet in height, supple as a deer and as light on his feet as a cat'.

'Bob on the job was not only bereft of all humour and wit, but was utterly concentrated on the film. His being was, as it were, both wrapped around the subject and at the same time engulfed in the subject. The result was an atmosphere difficult to describe if not experienced, heavy, thick and charged. There was tension everywhere, an unbearable tension, thunderous black tension, a tension you could feel with your hand, smell and sweat in. It would swell and grow thicker and darker. Your very blood thickened into and life slowed down into profound depression, compressed, dangerous and explosive. The final explosion was like a volcano blowing its top. It had to be. The atmosphere then lightened, work started anew and grew into a furious pace until the tide ebbed again and the fog gathered round and the tension grew again and stretched and brooded. And there was no relief'.[12]

While Flaherty's earlier conception was more elaborate, involving eviction and shipwreck scenes, the completed narrative structure of 'Man of Aran' is simple in the extreme, involving the struggle of the islanders, represented largely by one small family, with the barren land they live on and the raging sea that surrounds them. It opens with a number of short peaceful scenes of the boy catching crabs, the mother with baby in cradle surrounded by lambs and chickens and moves to the sea when the waves, at first calm, are seen building to a raging storm. A currach is seen beaching dangerously in the surf and Maggie rushes to help her husband and rescue the family fishing nets from the waves. The family is seen walking home together, beautifully framed against the shore. Next we see Tiger and Maggie making a potato bed by breaking rock and filling the small space cleared with seaweed (laboriously carried by Maggie on her back from the beach) and handfuls of earth recovered (again by Maggie) from crevices between the rocks. The currach damaged in the landing is repaired. Mikleen is seen carelessly fishing from the edge of a terrifyingly high cliff. He sees a gigantic basking shark in the waters below him. There follows a series of shark hunts by the island men (rapidly, sometimes confusingly, edited) in which the fragility of the small boats used is dramatically contrasted to the size and power of the sharks. Maggie and Mikleen attend the fire under a large cauldron which will be used for turning the shark's liver into oil. The final sequence shows a night scene with suggestions of a gathering storm. Maggie is seen next morning gathering seaweed against a huge sea. In 'some of the most extraordinary sea footage ever recorded on motion picture film'[13] we see the currach making repeated efforts to land before being broken in pieces by the violence of the sea. The men struggle to safety. Maggie rails against the sea.

Land, sea and sharks

The three main set-pieces of the film, the 'making' of land, the shark hunts and the landings of currachs in very heavy seas are to differing degrees anachronistic to life on the Aran Islands in the time the film was made. The practice of carrying large baskets of seaweed on their own backs had long been abandoned by the islanders who invariably used donkeys for the task. It also seems to be a matter of debate as to whether this task was commonly undertaken by women.[14] The islanders had not hunted basking sharks for a hundred years as their usefulness as a source of oil for light had been replaced first by paraffin and later by electricity. The landing of currachs in the kind of seas depicted in the film would be a most unusual event indeed as the islanders, except when tempted by film makers like Flaherty, had too much sense and respect for the sea to get caught in such situations.

To shoot the shark hunting sequences the islanders had to learn a craft long forgotten on the islands. Shark hunting was at that time part of the folklore of the islands with stories told and retold of boats being towed by harpooned sharks out into the Atlantic never to be seen again (hookers, much larger boats than those depicted in the film, were originally used). Rusty harpoons were found in sheds and hanging ornamentally over fireplaces and copied by the local blacksmith. A trip was undertaken to the Claddagh area of Galway to learn from an old dying shark hunter, Martin Quinn, as to where the harpoon should be aimed at the sharks (a grey streak under the big fin). A Connemara boat called a púcán, somewhat bigger than the island currachs, was bought for the shark hunters and the first sequences were shot from a camera based on a platform attached to two currachs which worked reasonably well in very calm seas but became impossible in even moderate swells. Later a number of increasingly bigger motor vessels were hired from Galway which were used for camerawork and often for the actual harpooning of the sharks. An old friend of Flaherty's, Captain Murray, who had worked for the Hudson Bay Co., and had experience of whaling was eventually hired to instruct the men in harpooning technique. He brought with him a harpoon gun, which while not of course seen in the film, was frequently used. The basking shark is not a maneater and when left alone is perfectly harmless, however as Pat Mullen put it:

'I have read accounts here and there lately about these basking sharks, some of which say they are harmless and inoffensive. This may be true, but I don't think it mattered a great deal to us whether a shark meant it or not, when a sweep of his tail was able to smash our boat or

knock us into Kingdom Come at a moments notice! Boats ten times bigger than ours had been lost with their crews that way in the old shark hunting days.'[15]

The storm scenes were the ones most hazardous to the islanders. These involved real risk and acts of heroism on the part of a small group of currach men which were undertaken for little material gain but apparently because of a sense of pride in their heritage and a determination that their island was going to be represented to the world in the way they saw fit even if it did involve a certain exaggeration. The first successful storm scenes were shot on Mainistir shore and the first response from the local currach men to the request to put to sea was, 'no man living in Mainistir has even seen a canoe put out in such a sea'.[16] Flaherty's face on hearing this 'looked as stormy as rounding Cape Horn'.[17] When the currach eventually did brave the stormy seas the perilous landing had

Illus. 17.7. 'The land upon which Man of Aran depends for his subsistence – potatoes – has not even soil' says the intertitle to the second sequence of the film. Maggie's heroic contribution to the 'Making of Land' is memorably depicted but the practice of carrying large baskets of seaweed on their backs had long been abandoned by the islanders who invariably used donkeys for the task.

Illus. 17.8. The three-man currach (top right hand corner) in the final storm scene, shot in mountainous seas in the channel between Bun Gabhla shore and Brannock Island.

The sea and nature has always been the main pre-occupation of Flaherty's films and in 'Man of Aran' the sea in all of its moods is the principal 'character' and the main focus of his dramatic attention.

Whatever reservations have been expressed on other aspects of 'Man of Aran', there is wide acceptance of the greatness of the climactic storm scene. 'Some of the most extraordinary sea footage ever recorded on motion picture film'.

Looking back later Flaherty said 'I should have been shot for what I asked these superb people to do'.

to be repeated four times before Flaherty declared himself satisfied. Various other sequences were shot or attempted at Cill Mhuirbhigh strand, Gort na gCapall and particularly in a channel between Bun Gabhla shore and Brannock Island where the final storm scene was shot. This sequence, shot in mountainous seas, in which a three man currach navigates a narrow channel described as 'a hell of tossing, tumbling seas coming from all directions at once' marks the high point of the film and involved very real risk to the currach men. When eventually the three men scrambled ashore, the currach having been smashed to pieces in the process, Pat Mullen says with some justification 'a great thrill of wild pride shot through me as I looked at them, for here had

been a trial of some of the old, old stock, and the blood still ran true'.[18] Looking back later Flaherty said 'I should have been shot for what I asked these superb people to do'.[19]

Release and reception

After nearly two years on Inis Mór everybody knew that the film was completed. That is everybody but Flaherty himself who went on obsessively shooting material he had already shot and covered from every angle. When Michael Balcon eventually recalled him to London he was relieved to have the decision to terminate the shoot made for him. Conceived as a silent film, it was decided in London that sound should be added and Tiger King, Maggie and Mikleen were brought over to London to add snatches of dialogue to the soundtrack. Their presence in London was exploited to the full, with Flaherty's consent, by Gaumont-British, the film's producers. As mentioned before, the film opened in April 1934 in London with members of the cast present and was later given gala presentations in a number of large English cities.

Critical reception was mixed with the beauty of the photography, particularly its seascapes, being generally admired but the film received heavy censure for its historical inaccuracy and avoidance of the social and economic reality of life on the islands. Graham Greene remarked 'how meaningless that magnificent photography of storm after storm. "Man of Aran" did not even attempt to describe truthfully a way of life'.[20] John Grierson in an article which is generally defensive of his friend Flaherty says: 'I like my braveries to emerge otherwise than from the sea, and stand otherwise than against the sky. I imagine they shine as bravely in the pursuit of Irish landlords as in the pursuit of Irish sharks'.[21] The film had its New York premiere on 18th October, again with members of the cast present, and here the critical response was more positive but by no means unanimously so.

'Man of Aran' was premiered in Dublin on 6th May with Mr de Valera, members of the Executive Council, the Diplomatic Corps and many distinguished persons, including W.B.Yeats in attendance. The reception was overwhelmingly positive and the film was enthusiastically grasped upon as delivering Irish representation at last from the grip of stage Irish caricature. Dorothy Macardle writing in the Irish Press enthuses: 'these are our countrymen and their actual, constant achievements are no less than these ... We have become almost resigned to being traduced ... Not three generations of protesting could do as much to rehabilitate the Irish people in the imagination of the peoples of other countries as this faithful and beautiful motion picture will do'.[22]

From our contemporary perspective however, such an easy solution to our problems of representation (as Luke Gibbons argues well in his essay 'Romanticism, Realism and Irish Cinema') is less sustainable. But to end on a more favourable note it is necessary to quote the defence of Flaherty's methods in Dudley Andrew's biographical study of Andre Bazin:

'All these fabrications were calculated attempts to make the images on the screen breathe the truth of a way of life that goes beyond immediate experiences. Flaherty believed that appearances must often be transformed from life to the screen (indeed events must be altered) if the equation of a man's life in his environment is to retain its essential significance'.[23]

Acknowledgements for Illustrations

Illus. 17.1, 17.7, 17.8, photo-stills from the film 'Man of Aran' by courtesy of the Rank Organisation Plc. Illus. 17.2, photo, U.C.G. Illus. 17.3, 17.4, 17.5, photo, The Mac Quitty Collection. Illus. 17.6, drawing, Sean Keating, private collection. Illus. 17.9, photo, G.A. Duncan. Illus. 17.10, photo, Fr Browne S.J. Collection.

Illus. 17.9. Maggie Dirrane, twenty years after the shooting of 'Man of Aran'.

Illus. 17.10. Another Man of Aran, photographed in 1938 by Fr Browne.

CHAPTER 18

Aran, Paris and the Fin-de-Siècle

Patrick Sheeran

In the course of a meditation on the sea and its thresholds, the novelist James Hamilton-Patterson remarks succinctly: [1]

'Four small things about small islands:

1. They look like objects, and hence like property.

2. The concept of the 'private island' satisfies most people's major fantasies.

3. The effect of islands is almost wholly regressive.

4. An island's boundaries can never be fixed.'

Every close observer of islands will want to add to the list. This essay suggests a fifth thing about islands:

5. An island lucky enough to be 'discovered' by urban intellectuals during the 1890s acquires a special cachet.

The story of the *fin-de-siècle* creation of Aran begins on 5th August 1896 aboard Tom Joyce's hooker sailing out of Cashla for Inis Mór. Had the 'half-decked, cutter-rigged fishing boat of seventeen tons' foundered, it would have brought with it to the bottom of Galway Bay a large part of the future of Irish literature. Aboard were W.B.Yeats, George Moore, Edward Martyn and the only non Irishman present, Arthur Symons. Symons, then co-editor of the *Savoy* with Aubrey Beardsley, wrote an account of the expedition for the London journal that would be of seminal importance.

The hooker, Symons recorded, was becalmed for nearly an hour under a very hot sun.[2] The future author of the classic study of French Symbolism observed that 'we were passed by a white butterfly that was making straight for the open sea'. A soul, perhaps, on its way to A.E.'s – and later Yeats's – 'holy city'? (See below). The article reveals, in a disarming way, that a sense of place is derived not so much from geographical experience as from reading competence. It points too to the intertextual, selective nature of perception, to the way in which all experience is mediated. In Symons' case the immediately relevant texts were Emily Lawless's *Grania* ('supposed to be the classic of the islands'), the 'quaint, minute seventeenth-century prose' of Roderic O'Flaherty's *Chorographical Description of West or H-Iar Connaught*, maps, and the sailor's chorus from Tristan and Isolde – all of which receive due mention before the hooker as much as puts into Cill Mhuirbhigh. Aran was already a much traversed erogenous zone. 'Nothing is more mysterious, more disquieting, than one's first glimpse of an island', wrote Symons, 'and all I had heard of these islands, of their peace in the heart of the storm, was not a little mysterious and disquieting. And later: 'We seemed also to be venturing among an unknown people, who, even if they spoke our own language, were further from us, more foreign than people who spoke an unknown tongue and lived beyond other seas'. Given the *fin-de-siècle* equation between the spatially distant and the temporally remote it could hardly be otherwise.

Declan Kiberd argues, convincingly, that Symons' essay *The Isles of Aran* rather than Pierre Loti's *Pêcheur d'Islands* was to become the primary model, both in content and method, for Synge's *The Aran Islands*.[3] The similarities Kiberd notes are very remarkable: a common focus on primitivism, on the combination of wildness and reserve in the people, on 'pre-historic heroism' and a special sympathy between man and nature. Symons was even the first to publish in his article the story of the man who killed his father that would later form the plot of Synge's *The Playboy of the Western World*.

There is another aspect of Symons' account (properly disregarded by Kiberd in his strictly comparativist paper) that, in a larger context, would have even greater resonance. It is the notion, most unashamedly stated in a number of A.E.'s essays, that there are privileged places where 'the veils between the worlds are thin'. Here is Symons' rendition of the theme:
'We loitered on the cliffs for some time, leaning over them and looking into the magic mirror that glittered there like a crystal, and with all the soft depth of a crystal in it, hesitating on the veiled threshold of vision. Since I have seen Aran and Sligo, I have never wondered that the Irish peasant still sees fairies about his path, and the boundaries of what we call the real, and what is for us the unseen, are vague to him. The sea on those coasts is not like the sea as I know it on any other coast; it has in it more of the twilight. And the sky seems to come down more softly, with more stealthy step, more illusive wings, and the land to come forward with a more hesitating approach; the land and sky to mingle more absolutely than on any other coast. I have never believed less in the reality of the visible world, in the importance of all we are most serious about. One seems to wash off the dust of cities, the dust of beliefs, the dust of incredulities'.

An Ending
By Arthur Symons

I will go my ways from the city and then, maybe,
My heart shall forget one woman's voice, and her lips;
I will arise, and set my face to the sea,
Among stranger-folk and in the wandering ships.

The world is great, and the bounds of it who shall set?
It may be I shall find, somewhere in the world I shall find,
A land that my feet may abide in; then I shall forget
The woman I loved, and the years that are left behind.

But, if the ends of the world are not wide enough
To out-weary my heart, and to find for my heart some fold,
I will go back to the city, and her I love,
And look on her face, and remember the days of old.

Illus. 18.1. Arthur Symons (1906).

On Inishmaan
(Isles of Aran)

In the twilight of the year,
Here, about these twilight ways,
When the grey moth night drew near,
Fluttering on a faint flying,
I would linger out the day's
Delicate and moth-grey dying.

Grey, and faint with sleep, the sea
Should enfold me, and release,
Some old peace to dwell with me.
I would quiet the long crying
Of my heart with mournful peace,
The grey sea's, in its low sighing.

From *Images of Good and Evil.*

It is a superb example of the Theosophical Sublime. Indeed, the extent to which such tremulous, transcendental expectations were 'in the air' with regard to Aran is shown in a letter written to Symons by an Indian lady, Sarojini Naidu, prior to his departure for the islands. Sarojini was accomplished in what post-colonial theorists would today, approvingly, call mimicry. To her contemporaries she seemed merely lacking in originality. Thus she fully expected Symons to have 'visions' on Aran and asked her friend: 'Do the gods speak unto the children of men in that sacred spot, and do beautiful demons lure mad poets to their destruction in that magical haunt?'[4] Clearly the '90s creation of Aran had infinitely more to do with the needs of urban, cosmopolitan intellectuals and less with the actual inhabitants of the place. The gaze of these tourists of transcendence yielded a liminal landscape, an island terminus that was to be the threshold of another world.

There is nothing quite so directly claimed in Synge's more empirical account of Aran, though he relates story after story of fairy and ghost lore in illustration of the statement that 'These people make no distinction between the natural and supernatural'.[5] Plainly, Synge does make such a distinc-

tion. It only breaks down once in the distanced account he gives of a dream which 'seems to give strength to the opinion that there is a psychic memory attached to certain neighbourhoods'. He had been 'walking in a dream among buildings with a strangely intense light on them' (cf. A.E. below) when he was swept into a maelstrom of music and dancing:

'Then with a shock the ecstasy turned to an agony and rage. I struggled to free myself, but seemed only to increase the passion of the steps I moved to. When I shrieked I could only echo the notes of the rhythm. At last with a moment of uncontrolled frenzy I broke back to consciousness and awoke. I dragged myself trembling to the window of the cottage and looked out. The moon was glittering across the bay, and there was no sound anywhere on the island'.

Synge too had been away with the fairies on Inis Meáin – but in the ambiguous ontology of a dream. The dramatic, even sinister, contrast between outer peaceful prospect and inner psychic turmoil is the quintessential *fin-de-siècle* moment on Aran. Perhaps the islands were not holy ground after all but a pathogenic zone?

Tim Robinson, in his edition of Synge's *The Aran Islands* will have no truck with such interpretations: Synge's psychic memory theory he reads as 'a nod to Yeats' (who better to nod to under the circumstances?). More generally, Synge's mind was 'too positivistic' to entertain such transcendental flights. We can approach the question of the textualizing of such attitudes via some recent work on the discourse of primitivism.

It is usual, when thinking of Synge's writing on Aran, to place them within the context of the primitivist strain in modernism which he shared with, for example, Paul Gauguin. We have recently learned to see primitivism as historically specific, as related in the first instance to Parisian modernisation ('Baudelaire's capital of the nineteenth century') rather than belonging to a realm of eternal ideas.[6] It is a discourse which each artist could appropriate to his own ends in the specific historical circumstances in which he found himself. Synge's deployment of it in *The*

Aran Islands is not a matter of juxtaposing peasant vitality with modern debility but more an attempt to open up a space where both could be seen as historically contingent. James Knapp, in his study of these matters, points to a revealing episode in *The Aran Islands* where Synge is climbing the crags of the most remote coastline in Europe. He sees a gull trying to break a white shellfish by dropping it from a great height. What could be more 'natural', more emblematic of the struggle for survival ? Except that the shellfish turns out to be a golf ball. Knapp comments: 'Through gestures such as this one, the primitive is constituted as contrary to modernity, but not as an alternative to it. Rather than inviting the reader into a dream space where modernity may be forgotten, this kind of textuality holds both terms before us in a dissonance that tends to undermine the absolute dominance of either'.

Primitivism and modernity, however, were not the only terms of the *fin-de-siècle* debate. A related set of oppositions were the natural and supernatural, positivism and transcendence. Here again Synge can be seen as opening a textual space where one term questions and undermines the other – as in the dream sequence quoted above. The extraordinary number of supernatural stories he places in the mouths of local informants without editorial dismissal have a similar function. If you were a spiritualist you could read them as evidence that Aran was indeed a privileged locale and look to Swedenborg for an explanation – as Yeats was to do with related material collected by Lady Gregory. If not, you could put it all down to too much poteen and no street lighting. Or you could, as the text seems to invite us to do, hold both natural and supernatural together in suspenseful excitement.

Aran as the locus of the primitive, as the last redoubt of the true Celt, as a Gaeilgeoir's Nirvana, as a saintly refuge – all these images have been scrutinized, deconstructed, ridiculed even, in what has become an academic cottage industry. Even more offensive to our contemporary sensibility is the notion of Aran as a place of enchantment. Yet within the context of *fin-de-siècle* Europe it is readily comprehensible. It had to do with the recurrent human need for romance, for magic and providential mystery and the necessity to ground such desires in a specific locale. One of the great themes of late nineteenth century European literature is the quest for adventure and Otherness in far away places – Africa, Asia, the Middle East. How alluring, then, to consider that Otherness might exist one hundred and fifty miles from Paris or Dublin, in Brittany or Aran! Hence the need to insist, as Arthur Symons does, that in the three days he spent on the islands he had been 'so far from civilisation, so much further out of the world than I had even been before'. Further, the religious impulse that could no longer satisfy itself with orthodox creeds and that had begun to turn to the occult and heterodox systems of all kinds hoped to find a new pantheon, a liberating polytheism among the peasantry. People at different times locate yearnings of this kind in different sorts of places. Islands were one such 'elective site' (the phrase is André Breton's) for the artists of the 1890s. Poets and painters discovered in them the symbolic equivalent of their own subjective impulses. Yeats's alter-ego Oisin, 'led by the nose / Through three enchanted islands' in 'The Wanderings of Oisin' is only the most flamboyant of these liminars.[7] Indeed, when the poet came to write the 'island' version of his unfinished novel *The Speckled Bird*, he set it on Aran for predictable reasons: 'Everything about the island, even the gulls rising and falling as they fed, had that unreal look, that look of being beyond the ramparts of the world, which had perhaps made John de Burgh choose if for his home'.[8] There is a postmodern novel to be written which would, with permissible manipulation of times, dates and ontological levels, bring John de Burgh, assorted Norwegian and German linguists, W.B.Yeats, Lady Gregory, Edward Martyn, George Russell, Padraic Pearse, Arthur Symons, Thomas Bán Ó Conncheanainn (home from Mexico) and the members of the Royal Irish Academy together in Dún Aonghasa for a *conversazione*. There have been, as Marc Bloch once remarked, mythomanic times as well as individuals.

It would be erroneous to underestimate the fascination felt for the Celt and the supposed possibilities of transcendence offered by places on the margins of Europe until quite late in our century. Three brief examples will establish the point.

A surrealist map of the world published in Brussels in 1929 shows Paris (minus France) alone of European cities. Europe itself consists of a huge Ireland, Germany and an immense Russia– no Great Britain, Italy etc. The islands of the Pacific occupy two thirds of the world.[9] (More locally, of course, the Revivalist mental map of Ireland suffered from similar distortions – it had a huge Connacht but no north-east Ulster).

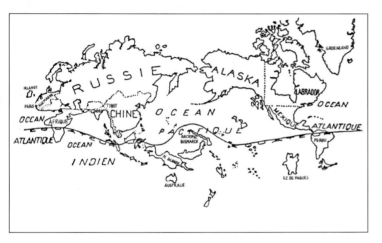

Illus. 18.2. Surrealist map of the world.

Equally telling, though tragic, was the impulse that drove Antonin Artaud, the great proponent of the Theatre of Cruelty, from Paris to seek revelation at the world's end. Artaud followed his mystical quest to Aran (he claimed to have been sent to Ireland by divine decree) carrying with him what he took to be the staff used by Christ to banish demons in the desert. Christ, in Artaud's understanding, was a magician who had come to earth to restore the truth of pagan religion: 'I am in search of the last authentic descendants of the Druids, those who possess the secret of druidic philosophy, who know that men descend from the God of Death "Dispater" and that humanity must disappear by water and fire'.[10]

The date of Artaud's visit to the west of Ireland is significant. He had come to the conclusion that the world would be destroyed on November 3rd, 1937, and had set out in his pamphlet *The New Revelation of Being* the terms of that destruction by fire. August 23rd, 1937, found him in Cill Rónáin. The details of his sojourn on Inis Mór are sketchy but he seems to have had some sort of apocalyptic vision. (Others would later explain it as a premonition of the horrors to come in Europe.) Something of the venom and fury stirred up in Artaud by his visit to Aran may perhaps be captured in remarks he made on Irish Catholicism: 'The Irish are stubborn Catholics, and the basis of Catholicism is to taste God the ego with all of its obscene tendencies, with the obscene phallic weight of a praying tongue, as though from the breath of its chest it lasciviously ejaculated its milk during an organism'.[11]

One element, at least, in Artaud's phantasmagoria we can hope to locate more clearly than heretofore. His biographer states that he brought to Aran a mysterious 'cane of St Patrick' given to him by a French magus. The reference is evidently to a relic of St Patrick first referred to in 789 in the *Annals of Ulster* as the Bachall Ísu, the Staff of Jesus. In the

Illus. 18.3. Antonin Artaud.

Tripartite Life it is described as the crozier bestowed by God on the Saint. Thereafter, it became part of the insignia of the abbacy of Armagh.[12] The Bachall eventually fell into the possession of Christ Church Cathedral where it was destroyed by an iconoclast in 1538. Artaud's version came to a more farcical end. He got into trouble with the Gardaí in Dublin and was thrown out of the country, leaving the pseudo-Bachall Ísu under the mattress of his bed in a doss house.

Irresistibly, the French genius's vision on Aran calls up another, earlier moment of negative transcendence and another visionary. Artaud on the crags of Inis Mór crazed by frenzies: Yeats on the battlement of Thoor Ballylee seeing 'Phantoms of Hatred and of the Heart's Fullness and of the Coming Emptiness' ('and I, my wits astray / Because of all that senseless tumult, all but cried / For vengeance on the murderers of Jacques Molay'. Jacques Molay (burned at the stake, 1314) was Grand Master of the Knights Templars, an order that Yeats curiously associated with the Parisian mob and the French Revolution.

It was not meant to be like this. A.E. in 'Ireland Behind the Veil' had told it like it ought to be: 'Perhaps these visions, to which the Celt is so liable, refer as much to the future as to the bygone, and mysteries even more beautiful than the past are yet to unfold. I think it is so. There are some to whom a sudden sun-lustre from Tir-no-nogue revealed a hill on the western shore overlooking the Atlantic. There was a temple with many stately figures: below at the sea's edge jetted twin fountains of the golden fire of life, and far off over a glassy calm water rose the holy city, the Hy-Brazil, in the white sunlight of an inner day'.[13]

In the grey light of an outer day it was probably raining. Yet A.E.'s is the true *fin-de-siècle* vision of Aran, a version of the Theosophical Sublime. Put differently, this particular narrative construction of Iar Connacht and the western islands tells a story of imminent revelation. Only Artaud had the foolhardiness to force the tale to its horrifying denouement. But then, as Yeats remarked in *Mythologies,* 'Paris was as legendary as Connacht'.[14]

Not surprisingly, the *fin-de-siècle* images and excitements degenerated into trite stereotypes and reflex responses. A few generations on and we find the following in *L'Opera d'Aran*: 'Aran, sentinelle avancée de l'Irelande en plein Atlantique. Trois îlots de granit ou s'accrochent quelques familles de pêcheurs. Rudes gens de mer pour qui vivre, c'est se battre contre la tempête et la faim. Coeurs nobles et simples, âmes mystiques tourmentées de rêves et de superstitions'.

Only granite (hard, acidic, igneous) can provide an appropriate *mise en scène* for the contest of such fiery souls as are presented in the opening paragraph of the libretto to *L'Opéra d'Aran* composed by Gilbert Bécaud and first performed in Paris in 1962. Bécaud, with his mixture of jazz and traditional *chanson* style singing, once provoked audiences in France to the same kind of frenzy as Elvis Prestley in the U.S.A. His *Opéra d'Aran* is similarly hybrid and reveals an archetypal island romance, a mixture of Bizet's Carmen, spaghetti western, and John Synge's *Playboy of the Western World.*

Angelo from the warm Mediterranean is cast up on Aran where Maureen ('the purest daughter of the isle') falls in love with him though she is bethroed to Sean who is away seeking his fortune in the Big World. The action of the opera is premised on the fervid notion, 'in ancient Ireland even the dead demanded of their women or fiancees an eternal, absolute fidelity and they returned to earth to take their revenge on those who forgot them'. Angelo and Sean come to blows. Maureen is accidentally blinded by Sean in the course of a fight between the two rivals after Mass. She goes off with the stranger who reveals himself to be a Christy Mahon - like impostor.

It all seems a little unfair until one recognizes that, of necessity, a male, mainland writer must weigh the scales against an island stripling – for how otherwise could the fantasy of possession fulfil itself? And exogamously inclined colleens must suffer mutilation in order to expiate their guilt at breaking with island fidelities. Maureen is a cipher for Aran and answers to all four 'things about islands' listed above (especially 'The effect of islands is almost wholly regressive').

Clearly it is a mistake to look to opera for an accurate representation of the world in which it is set. In opera, if anywhere, extravagant demands are made on the willing suspension of disbelief and formal elaboration is allowed a fine excess. Nontheless, *L'Opéra d'Aran* is primitivism gone to seed in the language and the city of its first conception.

The *fin-de-siècle* appropriation of Aran and the west of Ireland generally as a site of transcendental homelessness and our current end-of-century obsession with deconstructing that appropriation, leads one to consider, one last, sixth thing about islands:

6. Islands are ripe for re-mythologising.

Illus. 18.4. An Island Horseman.

Acknowledgements for Illustrations

Illus. 18.1. Photo, Clarendon Press, Oxford.
Illus. 18.4. Drawing by Jack B. Yeats, by kind permission of Michael and Anne Yeats.

Illus. 19.1. 'Goodbye Father' by Seán Keating. (Ulster Museum, Belfast.)

CHAPTER 19

The Aran Islands Today: A Personal View.

Pádraig Standún

I set foot on Aran for the first time on an August Sunday in 1970. To be more precise I set both feet on Inis Meáin that day. Within the islands, Aran (Árainn) tends to mean Inis Mór, Inis Meáin and Inis Oírr being referred to as *'na hoileáin'* the islands. I was on my way to the well of the Irish language, following in the steps of John Millington Synge, Padraig Pearse, Douglas Hyde, Eoghan O'Growney and many more. As a student priest I knew that I was likely to be posted at some stage to a Gaeltacht parish, and was preparing myself rather belatedly at the beginning of my final year for such an eventuality.

I had spent the previous couple of weeks on a building site in Mervue, then on the outskirts of Galway city. Tired from the work and a beery farewell to my mates in the Trapper's Inn the night before, I slept most of the way out through Galway Bay on that quiet foggy Sunday morning. It was the noise of the *Naomh Éanna's* anchor that woke me as the big ferry lay to about a hundred metres from an Inis Oírr still cloaked in fog. I had reached a new world.

Currachs suddenly appeared out of the mist, frail looking basins of lathes and canvas bouncing on the sea as men that spoke in a strange language collected people and cargo from the 'Steamer', which then steamed on to my destina-tion, Inis Meáin. Here I too was disgorged from the bowels of the ferry into a currach to be rowed ashore to the narrow slip beside a stubby pier.

Although born and reared in the middle of Mayo, about sixty miles to the north, I wasn't ready for the culture shock of traditional homespun trousers and waistcoat type bheist worn by the men, not to speak of the footwear of rawhide pampooties. The women were altogether more spectacular in brilliant red petticoats with multicoloured dreamcoats of shawls thrown over their shoulders.

And then there was Irish, Gaelic, the language that I, the stranger did not know, even though I had spent the best part of twenty years at school and college. It came as an even bigger surprise later that day to hear children speak this tongue that I was unpsychologically prepared to think of as a natural language.

Thus began my romance with Aran. The sun soon burned off the fog and dried the rocky grey expanse of creig before shining out to reveal a blue sea, with the faraway Twelve Pins of Connemara and the skies overhead painted by Paul Henry, on secondment from that great studio in the sky. This romance hasn't died although I'm a more realistic romantic now that I have wintered ten years in the smaller islands with a twelve year stint in Carraroe across the Bay in between.

The local curate, Paddy Gilligan, had thrown me in at the deep end. I was to visit every house in the island doing a kind of census. This forced me to meet the people, speak the language, realise my inadequacy. But it sent me back to Maynooth for that final year in the knowledge that Irish was learnable and that priesting the islands would be anything but the punishment station it was considered by many of my fellow students.

I had one intimation of the harsh reality of island life during that fortnight as a deacon on the island. A storm broke on the Feast of the Assumption, August 15th, an important feast day on an island with a great devotion to Mary, mother of Jesus. The *Naomh Éanna* was unable to sail but a trawler from Inis Mór managed to bring the people stranded in Galway home late in the evening. I realise my age now when I see the baby that came home wrapped in his mother's shawl that day is now a big strong man building his own house.

It was under a different kind of fog that I returned as curate to Inis Oírr and Inis Meáin something more than a year later, the 10th November 1971. Four days after the publication of an article in *The Western People* under the title 'The Dog Collar – From the inside', I found myself on the *Naomh Éanna* again, this time with full bags and baggage for my new posting. The article had described my previous job as Prefect of Studies in St. Jarlath's College, Tuam, as 'babysitting for the children of the rich'. On publication of the article it was suddenly remembered that I had earlier volunteered for service on the islands. What some may have construed as a punishment was in fact a blessing, a release.

The most exciting and dangerous aspect of priesting the islands at that stage was the Sunday morning crossing by currach between first and second Mass. Each house on the island took it in turn to transport the priest from island to island, a pleasant experience on a summer Sunday, a hair raising drama on a wintry morning.

With all due respect to the Gospel story of Jesus calming the waters, there was no way I or anyone else was going to sleep on the transom of a currach as he did on Galilee. Waves like rows of two-storey houses thundered through the aptly named Foul Sound between the islands. Currents, tidal changes, and the sudden rush of wind that accompanies a shower caused further complications. But the skill and coordination of the men on the oars was a beauty to watch and I always felt safe unless they began to show signs of panic.

It takes a landlubber like me a long time to begin to understand the sea. On a day I'd look out on a seemingly calm surface men would talk of a farraige mhór, a big sea, and sure enough there would be a swell causing treacherous breakers on the shore. Another day the wind would have the sea alive with white horses, but the verdict would be 'Níl farraige ar bith inniu ann'. (There's no sea at all today). The swell is infinitely more dangerous than the harmless splashes the wind would cause.

I always had a sense of exhultation afterwards. Maybe it was the excitement, the danger, or just the freshness caused by seawater splashing the face. By the time second Mass would begin in Inis Meáin with the vivid colours of the Harry Clarke studio windows kaleidoscoping on the altar before me, I used be ready to levitate. But I was never one for showing off. By the time Mass was over the morning adventure on the sea had changed from the frightening to the romantic. The shape of the currach conjured up images for me of the shoe of Christ walking on the water.

A Saturday morning in December 1972 brought currach, crew and priest within a hairsbreath of a disaster that might have left three widows and twelve fatherless children in Inis Oírr. It was one of those relatively calm days with a farraige mhór breaking. As we approached the slip it seemed out of character for the men of Inis Meáin not to be at the head of the pier to read the waves and shout instructions to their neighbours. Instead they stood away back, waving frantically to the Inis Oírr men to go home.

The currach was already too close. A great wall of water arose outside us, curling white on top. With a flick of the oars the currach faced it and somehow went through or across it. Seconds later we would have been meat and matchsticks on the rocks. Island councils conveyed the danger to Archbishop Joseph Cunnane, and as soon as he had a priest available he was sent to Inis Meáin, with me remaining a further two years in Inis Oírr. Twelve years later I was to return to Inis Meáin.

I'm telling you all this to establish my credentials. After ten years on the islands which include spells in the seventies, eighties and nineties I'm around longer than any tourist, journalist or anthropologist. But I'm still a blow-in, a stranger, an interloper. I wouldn't dare say 'I know the islands' or 'I know the people'. I don't think anyone is entitled to say that, and it irks me to read of anthropological studies on islands by people from distant cultures quoted as scientific gospel. There is no surer way for a well meaning American to have the wool pulled over his or her eyes than to go around asking questions in an Irish village or island. That said, I offer some personal opinions on the recent past, present and possible future of the Aran Islands.

I returned as curate to Inis Meáin in 1987 to find that electricity and its attendant timesavers and living-support machines had arrived, fridges, washing machines, television and, possibly most important of all, freezers. In the old days, I like many another, fried spam to put taste on it when ferries were delayed and fresh food was scarce. It is possible to live for months now on a freezer full of milk, bread, meat, local fish and vegetables. With a thin but productive layer of limestone soil that grows excellent potatoes, cabbage, parsnips, turnips, onions, spinach as well as wild garlic and blackberries by the ton, lack of variety on plate or palate certainly isn't a problem.

A strong co-operative, Comharchumann Inis Meáin, in which each family has shares has been the driving force behind community development. It has been involved in organising the electricity scheme, running water to every house, the building of an airstrip, first grass now tarmac, pier improvements and extensions, tarring of the roads. A knitting factory started by the co-op and later bought out by its first manager, Tarlach de Blácam , employs over twenty people and sells high fashion knitwear from Tokyo to Toronto.

A similar co-op Comhar Caomhán has been very successful on Inis Oírr. An Inis Mór venture of the same kind did not work out originally but a replacement seems to be working well. As an outsider living on the islands I am aware that many islanders don't realise they have far more control of their lives at a local political level than most small communities in the country. Co-op meetings can often be heated affairs with strong views being expressed on a range of issues not unlike Dáil Éireann. But here are both men and women factory workers, farmers, shopkeepers, fishermen, housewives successfully running what is as near as you will get to a socialist commune, though nobody will call it that.

On an island you learn patience, resignation. There is a fog or a storm. Planes can't fly, boats can't sail. You wait. Most of all you learn to use the resources you have, not depend on anyone in so far as possible. No state agency is going to do anything for you unless pushed, pulled, cajoled, maybe even blackmailed. Co-operatives have learned how to use the system. They know journalists will crawl out of the seaweed when a politician turns up to use the islands for a photo opportunity. The same journalists seem hard to find when questions need to be asked about what was promised and when will it be delivered? People learn to stand on their own feet, fight their own battles.

Many island children have travelled by plane more often than by car. Aer Arann's sturdy Islander planes run scheduled services to the islands morning and evening, adding flights when the need arises and the numbers warrant it. The building of a new airstrip at Minna on the South Connemara coast has reduced airtime from twenty to about six minutes. The availability of the plane for daytime emergency services and of a Shannon based helicopter service at night as well as the Cill Rónáin lifeboat greatly reduce fears of isolation and insularity.

I have been known to claim that more prayers are said over Galway Bay between mainland and island than are ever said in the churches. If you were being buffeted by a force nine gale you would know why. Hardened atheists have been known to sprout angels' wings on that short crossing, but people have a deep appreciation of the skill and dedication of the Aer Arann pilots and their groundstaff who keep the planes (air) shipshape.

Many visitors expect to find the islands and their people backward, but are amazed to find people who have walked the world, who know Boston better than Ballinasloe, whose interest in foreign affairs is phenomenal. Not just interest but care. This is something I often see reflected in collections for Third World agencies that are much higher than the national average.

I like the way in which the old and new can exist comfortably side by side on the islands. I see a man winnowing corn in the oldest method known, beating a sheaf on a bare limestone rock. A neighbour up the road works at a state of the art computer knitting machine. There is no sense of competition or contradiction between old and new. They will have a pint side by side, equals.

That is not to suggest that island life is some kind of heaven on earth. Having done some three month stints without setting foot on the mainland, I'm well aware of the build up of tension and isolation that can make small problems big,

molehills mountains, that can make one forget that there is a world out there beyond the sea. That is one of the downsides of island life and it can affect the born islander as much or more than someone from outside. People need to get away from time to time.

The compensations are spring and summer especially. One day a tourist wanders up the road. A rare Burren/Aran flower blooms. A lark sings. A feed of new spuds, fresh salmon, spinach. There is swimming and sunbathing on big unpolluted beaches. I reappoint myself chaplain to the island pub for another long lazy summer.

Tourism is welcome more for the buzz it brings to the islands for a couple of months, than from the commercial point of view. The commercial side of the business is welcome too, of course, but it is of benefit to a small enough number of people. Many people would make a sweeping claim that daytrippers with packed lunches leave nothing behind on the islands but litter. That's not to say that anyone would want to discourage them. Many a daytripper has fallen in love with the islands, returning again and again for longer holidays.

So far Inis Meáin is the least touristed of the islands, but it too has a tradition of family holidays, going back as far as the founding of Conradh na Gaeilge, the Gaelic League, in 1893. Parents intent on raising their children through Irish, holidayed year after year on the island. Many of those who came as children return again and again, often with their own families. The availability of chalets and houses to rent makes this kind of holiday particularly attractive.

Inis Oírr, more than any other island, has seen the value of the Irish language as an amenity. For more than thirty years now about five hundred teenagers each year have come to learn Irish there each year. This too has sparked off many long term love affairs with the island or with someone met there, and draws people back again and again. Inis Mór now has an Irish college and there are plans to revive one on Inis Meáin. The language is at least as important a part of the Aran environment as the beauty of the flowers, the surge of the sea or the great sweep of the cliffs.

If I speak of Inis Meáin more than the other islands it's because I've spent more of my time there. Inis Mór I know least as I'm only there twice yearly for a week of 'Station' Masses. But even these visits give the lie to claims that Inis Mór is 'destroyed' by tourism. Despite having anything from 1,000 to 3,000 visitors a day during Summer the island is back to what I would consider itself at the times of the year I'm there in March and October. As far as I can see tourism has no major impact on the character of the people of the islands themselves.

Huge influxes of people undoubtedly cause problems, litter, water shortages, lack of a proper dumping system for rubbish etc. Such problems are solvable by Galway County Council, with money and political will. As such they are minor problems. I think it important that organs of State recognise that the islands bring far more to the country in terms of culture, environment, and the tourism generated by such riches than whatever the expense of clearing up after tourists adds to Department or Council costs.

Some people regret the loss of most of the thatched houses. John Millington Synge, looking across from Inis Mór saw the houses as a straw rope across the back of Inis Meáin. Most island people would associate the thatch with the hard life, remembering the yearly repairs and the fear that the roof would come in on top of them in winter storms. Other people see the telephone and electricity poles and wires as a blot on the landscape. In an ideal world and with plenty of money they could have been put underground. I have to say that I only notice them in photographs and am delighted to see a phone in virtually every house, a vital link with family members far across the sea.

Like all rural communities in the west of Ireland the Aran Islands, like so many islands before them face the danger of

being denuded by emigration, migration and death. A population of well over a thousand people looks healthy, but school numbers are low, families are small and work is scarce. The very success of Inis Mór fishermen has meant that a number of them have had to move with their families to the mainland to be near the deeper and larger port of Rossaveal.

Inis Meáin National School, which once had 107 children now has 26, and at one stage in 1992 dropped to 19. The Department of Education tried to remove one teacher but the combination of a strong political campaign, the return of some families with children and the arrival on the island of a family with three young children as part of the Rural Resettlement Scheme turned the tide, temporarily at least.

Removal of one teacher from a two-teacher school on an island with no other educational establishment could have a disastrous domino effect on the community. Whole families might move out or decide not to come back if they saw one teacher burdened with having to teach all classes ranging in age from four to fourteen. Comharchumann Inis Meáin is addressing the population decline by building houses in the hope of attracting back island families or people interested in rural resettlement.

Despite the unbalanced population structure, 40 of an Inis Meáin community of about 200 are over 70 years old, I am more hopeful now than I was twenty years ago. Families were bigger then but everyone seemed set on emigration or jobs on the mainland. Quite a few of those came back and reared families here since. Many of the younger generation seem less interested in emigration as an option, if there was work available at home. So here I am hoping and praying for a dramatic increase in births and marriages, and I'm glad to see quite a few of the younger generation working along those lines.

Some people look at the Inis Oírr waterfront and see a mini Manhattan, a sprawl of unplanned looking oversized buildings. I see vibrant young families where children were scarce in the seventies. Without people, without children the islands are hunks of Burren rock, beautiful but barren like the Kerry Blaskets. I often wonder why the Aran Islands survived as living communities while the Blaskets were denuded, despite seeming to be better equipped as regards closeness to the mainland, as well as having better land, and bogs for turf or peat.

I think it was because the Aran Islands were far enough away from the mainland to warrant their own church and state infrastructures. Aran is a selfcontained parish of the Archdiosese of Tuam, while the Blaskets were an adjunct to a mainland parish with no church or clergyman. The people went to Mass, baptisms, weddings, funerals on the mainland. Inis Mór and Inis Oírr had lighthouses and lifeguards which connected them with state officialdom. Incidentally it is a proud boast in Inis Meáin that no foreign flag ever flew over the island. Inis Oírr people counter by saying the British Empire conquered every place worth taking over.

If the necessary infrastructure is there to provide people with what is accepted as a normal modern lifestyle, I feel that people will stay on the islands. At least it will provide them with the choice to do so. Without such an infrastructure there is little choice except for people who find a nineteenth century lifestlye attractive. Over the years co-operatives and Government agencies have been painfully and painstakingly putting together the necessary infrastructure, piers, a major new ferryboat, the *Oileáin Árann*, airstrips, Aer Arann, electricity, telephones, roads, water schemes.

Environmental consciousness is growing and will continue to grow with people's confidence as a new generation which never knew thatch begins to look at what has been lost. Already a number of buildings faced in local limestone have made an appearance among the white plastered houses. Semi-state agencies such as Telecom Éireann and the Electricity Supply Board have shown imagination in their

most recent buildings as have the Office of Public Works with the new interpretative centre Ionad Árann in Cill Rónáin.

Water is still, as I write, a major problem. The major priority for all three islands just now is a clean and plentiful supply of water capable of outlasting the longest summer drought. With that and a proper disposal system for rubbish and sewage I don't think it matters how many tourists visit the islands. But water and waste disposal, like ferries and everything else should be for the people of the islands first. With the infrastructure in place I'm sure you will have people, though I wouldn't for a moment attempt to predict the future of the Aran Islands. History has a habit of overturning all predictions.

As the Minister for Arts, Culture and the Gaeltacht, Mr Michael D. Higgins, TD, officially opened the 1993 Synge Week in Inis Meáin an Aer Arann plane rose like a crucifix above us in the sky. I thought that even such an imaginative man as Synge could hardly have stretched his imagination to foresee the changes a hundred years have wrought on the islands, all the mod cons I have already mentioned, but especially the flying machine to carry people across the sea, and the box in the corner on which we watch things as they happen in Beijing, or Bangladesh, Belfast or Bohola.

I'm sure Synge wouldn't have been too bothered as long as the islanders retained the distinctive imagination he found among the people of the islands. I would contend that they do, despite tourism, television and emigration. These things embellish people's lives without doing away with the past, with stories that shaped and stretched imagination, with folk memory that has known hardship and drowning, loss and return. Eavesdropping on my Mass servers I find imaginations that include the exploits of the Irish soccer team as well as ancient giants tossing a hammer back and forth a mile between them as they built the great Dúns or stone forts.

From my own professional point of view I find for the most part a rugged faith, a faith shaped as much by Catholic theology as by tragedy and drownings, from the daily danger of living close to the elements, on land, on sea and in the air. Synge's *Riders to the Sea* is relived all too often, most mothers far younger than Maurya, the mother pieta-like accepting the body of her dead son is usually portrayed on stage. As a fairly unorthodox clergyman I find a great tolerance among people deep rooted in oldfashioned piety and spirituality. People might not agree with you but accept your right to be different.

My own favourite place in the world is the clifftop south of Synge's chair on the west coast of Inis Meáin. This is my spiritual home to which I retreat regularly to have the cobwebs of life blown away. I love to sit and listen as great waves thunder at the base of the sheer cliff, green water exploding white on slimy brown birdshitted rock. I was a seagull here once ... But that's another story.

NOTES AND REFERENCES

CHAPTER 2
The Aran Flora - Cilian Roden
Notes

There are many scattered references to the flora of the Aran Islands in the botanical literature. I refer the interested reader to Prof. D.A. Webb's comprehensive survey of the Aran flora for pre-1980 references. Much of the content of this work is summarized in the more recent *Flora of Connemara and the Burren* (Webb and Scannell 1983). For post 1983 articles I have provided individual references. However, if the intending botanical explorer wishes to limit herself or himself to a single work, I would suggest that she or he obtain a copy of Webb (1980).

References
1. Robinson (1980).
2. Webb (1980).
3. Praeger (1934).
4. McArthur and Wilson (1967).
5. Curtis and McGough (1988).
6. Curtis and Robinson (1985).
7. Curtis *et. al.* (1988).
8. Clapham (1987).
9. Tierney, M (1980).
10. Scannell and Synnott (1987).

CHAPTER 3
The Natural History of the Sea - Michael O'Connell and Cilian Roden
Further reading
De Valera, M. (1958).
Mac an Iomaire, S (1938).
O'Connell *et.al.* (1992).

CHAPTER 4
The Wildlife of the Aran Islands - Gordon D'Arcy
References
1. Lansbury (1965) and Reynolds (1985).
2. F.L.Clark (1971).
3. Haverty (1859).
4. List of Aran birds published in *Iris Leabhair na Gaelige : the Gaelic Journal* 9 (1899), 305 : Swallow : fáinleog (also fathach and

athach) ; Jackdaw: caitheog; Sparrow : gealbhan; Linnet: gealbhan croige; Yellowhammer: buídheog; Robin: spideog; Starling: druid; Raven: fiach dubh; Stonechat: caislín cloch; Wagtail: glasóg; Sandpiper: ladhrán tragha; Snipe: faosg; Meadow pipit : caológ riabhach; Corncrake: traineach; Lapwing: filip-a-chleite; Owl (barn?) : olcadan; Eagle (sea ?) : iolrach; Seagull: faoiléan; Curlew: cruiteach. Additions by Editor: Sea swallow :(tern) : geabhróg; Sand-snipe (sanderling ?) : ladhrán; Grey crow: préachán; Shag: cailleach dhubh; Cormorant: braigheall; Guillemot: Éun aille; Redshank (Oystercatcher?) : roilleach ; Puffin: crosán.
5. Ruttledge (1989). Whilde (1977).
6. Fairley (1981).

CHAPTER 5
The Archaeology of the Aran Islands - John Waddell
Notes
1. Early Irish legend attributes some of the Aran forts to the westward migration of a defeated community of Fir Bolg led by Aonghus whose name is supposedly perpetuated in the great fort of Dún Aonghasa (O'Rahilly 1946). The Atlantis myth is more recent: e.g. Westropp (1912), Day (1903), Ó Síocháin (1962).
2. Ó Máille (1957). See also J.T. O'Flaherty (1825), O'Donovan (1839), Fraser (1922), Ó Móghráin (1945).
3. Burke (1887): 'nation might rise against nation ... but the islanders in happy repose ... would in their isles of peace have happily lived on in blissful ignorance of the painful turmoils that reigned around'.
4. Banim (1891).
5. Kinahan (1871).
6. Hardiman (1846) edited O'Flaherty's *A Chorographical Description of West or H-Iar Connaught*, a work written in

1684 for the Dublin Philosophical Society but not then published.
7. Ogygia is a name given by Plutarch to an island west of Britain. O'Flaherty's great work was in Latin and an English translation was published by Hely in 1793.
8. Lhuyd (1712). Campbell (1960).
9. Petrie (1845), (1972).
10. Twenty-three years later, the year after O'Donovan's death, Wakeman(1862) published an engaging account of their Aran adventure. They stayed in Galway with the historian James Hardiman, later librarian of the Queen's College, who generally entertained them at dinner with his personal piper. On Aran they were conscious that they were following in the footsteps of George Petrie, the 'only one true antiquary' to have examined the islands. They visited all the major monuments and on reaching famous Dún Aonghasa, O'Donovan threw his umbrella in the air with an exultant shout and then 'threw himself on the ground and shouted again and again'.
11. Wilde (1858). According to his *Lough Corrib*, he also visited Aran in 1847 when Dún Aonghasa was sketched (1872, 265, and fig.). This sketch of the exterior also appeared in Babington (1858) and Haverty (1859).
12. Haverty (1859). A short preliminary account of the excursion in *The Freeman's Journal*, September 7th, 1857, contains no details of the ancient monuments.
13. Wilde (1858). The name 'Western' or 'Southern' Aran Islands was sometimes applied to the Galway islands by nineteenth-century writers to distinguish them from similarly named islands in Donegal and Scotland.
14. Dunraven (1875).
15. Westropp (1895, 1899, 1902,

1905, 1910, 1910a, 1914).
16. Kinahan (1867), Kilbride (1869).
17. Barry (1886, 490). The Royal Historical and Archaeological Association of Ireland, as the Royal Society of Antiquaries of Ireland was then known, made representations to the Board of Works in 1883 about the condition of the Aran monuments: Graves (1883), 175.
18. Murphy (1888).
19. See the *Journal of the Royal Society of Antiquaries of Ireland* 25 (1895), 239-249.
20. Macalister (1895, 1922, 1949).
21. Crawford (1907, 1913).
22. Scantlebury (1926).
23. Goulden (1953, 1953a, 1955). Waddell (1988).
24. Ó Síocháin (1962), Mould (1972), Daly (1975), Powell (1984). Also to be noted is Messenger (1969), an anthropological study of a thinly disguised Inis Oírr, and O'Sullivan (1976) with brief notes on monuments. More important are *The Shell Guide to Ireland* by Killanin and Duignan (same information in the 1962 and 1967 editions) and Harbison's *The National Monuments of Ireland* (1964), *Guide to the National Monuments in the Republic of Ireland* (1970) and *Guide to the National and Historic Monuments of Ireland* (1992).
25. Waddell (1973, 1976, 1981).
26. Maps: Robinson (1975, Revised editions with greater detail 1980). Book: *Stones of Aran. Pilgrimage* (1986). The first edition of the six-inch (1:10560) Ordnance Survey maps of Aran (Sheets 110, 111, 119, 120) was published in 1841. The last revised editions appeared in 1910 but a very useful 1:25000 (approximately 2 inches to the mile) map was published by the Ordnance Survey in 1993.
27. Gosling (1994).
28. *Discovery Programme Reports* 1, Dublin, 1993.
29. Details of the Eochaill and

Ceathrú an Lisín tombs are to be found in DeValera and Ó Nualláin, *Survey of the Megalithic Tombs of Ireland*, Vol.III (1972), where the three destroyed sites at Ceathrú an Lisín, Corrúch and Fearann an Choirce, are also noted. The Ceathrú an Teampaill tomb was identified in 1978 and two possible examples are recorded by the Galway Archaeological Survey, one on Inis Oírr, the other at Fearann an Choirce (which may conceivably be the site thought destroyed). The former is marked 'grave' on Robinson's 1980 map in Ceathrú an Phoillín, the latter is located near the western-most stone shelter (no. 30 on Inis Mór) on the same map.

30. Three axeheads were found and two are preserved in the National Museum of Ireland (1962:104-5): Messenger (1969), Lucas (1964). One from a shell midden on Inis Meáin is also preserved in the National Museum (R2598) as is the bronze socketed axe and the battle-axes mentioned. A stone hand-axe (a primitive hand-held chopper or pounder of chipped stone) was discovered in a crevice among the *chevaux-de-frise* at Dún Aonghasa in 1974 (Murphy 1977); though a genuine artefact probably made over 70,000 years ago, this is a suspect find probably introduced in recent times. There is no evidence of human activity in Ireland at this early date.

31. Murphy (1888) and National Museum of Ireland register 1885:350, Wk. 48.

32. Westropp may have been referring to this strange monument in 1895: 'a curious square enclosure with twenty-seven early graves, each with an edging of flags, while to the west are two pillar stones and an entrance, the whole surrounded by a circular wall, has been uncovered by the wind'. It is difficult to see how

twenty-seven graves would fit in the present site and perhaps the figure is a mistake. According to Messenger (1969, 100, and fig. 12) the single 'pookah' of the island resides in this Bronze Age tumulus which became a medieval cemetery. Another illustration is to be found in Ó Síocháin (1962). Other graves of unknown date have been found on Inis Oírr: Barry (1886, 493) records several rock cut graves, one measuring 1.06m by 61cm and containing unburnt human bones, about '80 perches' (400m) north of the lighthouse in Ceathrú an Chaisleáin.

33. Lucas (1958, 120).

34. Dunraven's (1875) plates II and III are reproduced in Powell (1984).

35. Petrie (1972, 248). This, his essay on military architecture, was written in 1833 and 1834. O'Donovan (1839, 118): his description and measurements with his reference to a lower 'internal division' led several later writers to imagine a peculiar sunken way in the middle of the Dún Aonghasa rampart. Wakeman drew a reconstruction of Dún Chonchúir on Inis Meáin with such a lowered central section around the top of its rampart (in Wood-Martin 1902, Vol. 1, 317). Westropp, too, accepted this interpretation but corrected it in his 1910 study when he realised O'Donovan was referring to a lower terrace.

36. Petrie and O'Donovan (note 35) refer to a lower terrace four to seven feet above ground level. An anonymous writer in *The Irish Builder*, 15th August, 1886, 237, writing in part from notes of a visit made in 1877, notes 'the course of the *banquette*, which forms a portion of the eastern side, may be quite plainly discerned'. Westropp (1910, 31) is confident that there were two terraces. Hartshorne (1853) noted one terrace and steps.

37. Neither Petrie's nor O'Donovan's plans show any steps.

38. Westropp (1902, 655) but precise locations not recorded. Petrie (1972, 248) does mention that in 1821 'the steps that led to the parapet are destroyed'. That 1877 visitor's account in *The Irish Builder* (note 36) records simply that 'the traces of stairs are still to be distinguished'. According to Wakeman (1862, 470) in 1839 there were 'several flights of steps leading to the top of wall'.

39. Westropp (1910, 39) has published John Windele's brief notes which refer to 'at the west side, a succession of stairs, just as we find in the inside of Staigue Fort'. Westropp (1910, 31) also declares the pair of sidelong flights visible today to be reset but marked on Petrie's plan. This plan, however (as published in Petrie 1972, 244) shows only a wall chamber at this point). In 1878 Westropp did note 'slopes' with some trace of a terrace here.

40. As far as Dún Aonghasa is concerned, Westropp's initial assessment was harsh (1902, 692) 'the whole fort underwent extensive and in parts injurious repair during its conservation as a National Monument in 1881, and many of the flights of steps date from that time'. His judgement in 1910, after detailed study, was that very little falsification took place and most if not all of the reconstructed features probably had some basis in fact.

41. Petrie (1972, 244). Ferguson (1853, 494). Also Dunraven (1875, 6).

42. All three seem to be original features. Petrie and O'Donovan record only the then ruined north-eastern entrance. Westropp (1910, 26) recorded the lintelled north gateway and the north-west entrance (then a shapeless gap) in 1878; the latter is visible, he argues, in

Dunraven's plate III on the left (reproduced in Powell 1984, 15).

43. Also shown on his plan along with terrace and entrance.

44. Literally means 'horses of Friesland'; because they had few horses the Friesians employed pointed timbers sometimes shod with iron to check enemy cavalry charges. Some writers on Dún Aonghasa have used the name *abattis* derived from the military term for a defensive line of felled trees with their branches pointing upwards and outwards.

45. Ferguson (1853, 494).

46. O'Donovan records 'two distinct divisions'

47. Westropp's (1910, 13) suggestion was that the fragment of rampart originally ran all the way behind the *chevaux-de-frise* from west to east and joined what is now the middle rampart in the area of the north-east gateway. The original middle rampart continued to form an oval concentric with the inner fort. Thus the original plan consisted of at least two concentric ramparts and a third enclosing a larger sub-rectangular space also protected by the *chevaux-de-frise*. At some stage two rampart sections were demolished and the materials used to build what is now the central section of the middle rampart.

48. Westropp (1910a, 182) 'thought' there was 'a terrace' in 1878. Dunraven's sketch plan (1875, facing p. 4) seems to show one terrace and (possibly) two flights of steps but it is far from clear. According to Dunraven the rampart is in two sections with a medial wall facing. The lower plinth is probably of 19th century date.

49. Westropp states that when Petrie visited the monument in 1821 there was a perfect gateway at the end of the rampart to the west but Petrie (1972, 249) merely notes that the passage through the *chevaux-de-frise*

'winds in a serpentine and intricate way, narrow, difficult, and tedious to be traced'. O'Donovan (1839, 140) records that an entrance 'in the east side near the margin of the cliff had been destroyed some time before'. He may also be referring to a western entrance when he writes 'to the north-west of this fortress are the evident traces of a similar one, but the cliff has fallen in ...' and then proceeds to describe a stone hut and a wall chamber obviously within the fort.

50. Named after the western part of the island, Eoghanacht, from the Eoganachta of Munster who once ruled Clare and Aran. O'Donovan noted that the rampart had 'three distinct divisions regular faced with stones of considerable size, and which would stand firm independently of each other'. So did Windele (RIA. Ms. 12 K 27, f. 522). Petrie (1972, 246) recorded the two terraces and provides the earliest known sketch plan.

51. Petrie's plan merely indicates what seems to be one set of straight steps to a second terrace immediately to west of the lower steps on the northern part of the rampart. Dunraven refers to just one terrace.

52. Dunraven (1875, 11) recorded 'three recesses in the wall [of the fort] about 4 or 5 ft. deep and about the same width, one opposite the door and the other at right angles to it'.

53. Westropp (1910a, 187).

53. Westropp's account of O'Donovan's description is confused. Dunraven follows O'Donovan.

54. British Library Stowe Ms. 21024, f.155. The plan, possibly by Edward Lhuyd (1660-1709), is in a collection compiled by John Anstis (1669-1744).

56. The sketch plan is merely titled 'The Great Fort in the Island of Aran, Hib.' but the two-rampart plan and most of the measure-

ments given correspond to Dún Eochla. The area of the inner fort is described as '60 paces in circuit' implying a diameter of just over 19 paces. Since the pace in question was certainly the geometric pace (the distance between successive stationary positions of the same foot) which like the ancient Roman pace was about 5 feet, the actual diameter indicated is about 96 feet (29m). The outer rampart is described as being 'in circumference about a hundred paces distant from the inward walk, in some places about 12 yards'. The distance between the two ramparts at Dún Eochla does vary from about 30 feet (9m) to just over 100 feet (30m); presumably the figure of 100 paces is an error.

57. According to O'Donovan in 1839 the wall was 16 feet (4.80m) high on the east, the lower terrace was 7 feet 9 inches (2.30m) below the top of the rest of the wall, the two divisions of which were of equal height. This terrace was 7 feet (2.13m) above the floor of the fort and 2 feet 6 inches (0.76m) wide. On the west the wall was 13 feet (3.96m) high. Most of the 1700 measurements are broadly similar: the lower wall was 'not above 2 yards high and 2 foot broad at the top'; the second terrace (the top of the wall in O'Donovan's time) was 'about 4 yards high'. However 'the wall was higher than this walk but at present it is demolished, and is at present about 8 yards high save at the entrance'. Such a height (24 feet or 7.30m) may perhaps be an overestimation bearing in mind the maximum height of 5.5m recorded for the inner rampart at Dún Aonghasa.

58. Noted by Windele in 1854 who described it as 'a great circular pile of stones, the debris of its cloghan now made up regularly by the adjacent light-house peo-

ple' (RIA. Ms. 12 K 27, f. 524).

59. Named after Conchúir the legendary brother of the no less legendary Aonghas. Brief published accounts in Dunraven (1875), Westropp (1895) and (1902). The earliest useful description is by O'Donovan in the Ordnance Survey letters (1839). Wakeman drew a fanciful reconstruction (Wood-Martin 1902, Vol. 1, 317; note 35 above).

60. Ferguson (1853, 93) recorded that 'the outer envelope, as rising higher than either of the others, and having only its own thickness to oppose to the elements, has fallen all round Dun Conor to the level of the second, and in some places below it; so that what formerly constituted the upper banquette behind the parapet, now forms the top of the rampart'. He also notes several tiers of steps to both banquettes or terraces but does not record their location. According to O'Donovan steps on the north led to the lower terrace with a lateral flight from there to the upper terrace; there was a similar flight on the north-west and a vertical flight to the lower terrace on the west. Dunraven (1875, 7 and plan) also records lateral flights on the west, north and north-east.

61. Ferguson (1853, 93) also noted the remains of stone huts and thought he saw traces of chambers in the wall of the fort but admitted 'the discoloration of the loose materials renders this a very uncertain speculation'.

62. Dunraven (1875, 7) claims to have found a narrow doorway in it on the south-east and compared it to that in the outer rampart of Dún Eochla and the middle rampart of Dún Aonghasa.

63. O'Donovan records the remains of an ancient house or clochan (about 8m by 4m) some 50 paces to the north of the sub-rectangular outwork. Today only an irregular mass of stones can be

traced.

64. Dún Fearbhaí 'is named from the area, An Fhearbhach, and is also called An Mothar (which is still the usual Co. Clare word for an old fort or cattle enclosure) whence the name of the village below' (Robinson 1980).

65. Macalister (1949a, 281; also 1935, 58); it is interesting to note that in the 1920s, before the Second World war, he thought tales of Fir Bolg refugees to be highly improbable (1921, 268; 1928, 170).

66. 'In the scheme of Leabhar Gabhála [The Book of Invasions] all that has preceded is merely by way of leading up to the advent of the Sons of Míl, whose descendants, the Gaels, were henceforth to be the dominant people of Ireland. The scholastic provenance of the account of this invasion is obvious: the Sons of Míl came to Ireland from Spain because it was believed that Hibernia, the Latin name for Ireland, was derived from Iberia, while their father's name Mil Espaine is simply the Latin miles Hispaniae, "soldier of Spain" in Irish dress' (MacCana 1970, 64). See also McCone (1990, 69ff) who argues that the story of the Fir Bolg is broadly based on the tale of the partly subjugated Canaanites of the Old Testament.

67. Harbison (1968).

68. Harbison (1971).

69. Etienne Rynne (1991 and 1992) has argued that Aran forts like Dún Aonghasa were primarily ceremonial centres. See Long (1992).

70. MacNeill (1923, 305). Kelly (1988, 30).

71. This enclosure was recorded by Kinahan (1866, 28, no. 28) who noted that it was then called 'The Doon'. He also recorded the lintelled doorway but did not realise it was part of an annex; this door is of dry masonry construction with one lintel slab. It is 96cm wide and 1.25m deep.

72. The name Baile na mBocht was given to an indefinite parcel of land hereabouts in 1590 (Goulden 1953).

73. Kinahan 1856, who recorded the name 'Baile na Sean': village of the ancient ones.

74. Mason (1938).

75. Waddell (1988).

76. First described and illustrated by Petrie (1845) who visited it in 1821 but overlooked by O'Donovan and not marked on the O.S. first edition.

77. From *Iter Hibernicum*, a picaresque, poetic account of Ireland written in 1675, as quoted by Aalen (1966).

78. Leask (1943).

79. Piggott (1954). The Achill huts are believed to be 'booley houses' associated with the practice of transferring cattle to summer pastures. See also McDonald (1992, 145).

80. It has been claimed (in Gosling 1994) that Clochán na Carraige is 'probably of 17-18th century date'. It should be noted, however, that in 1684 Roderic O'Flaherty recorded that 'They have Cloghans, a kind of building of stones layd one upon another, which are brought to a roof without any manner of mortar to cement them; some of which cabins will hold forty men on their floor; so antient that no body knows how long agoe any of them were made' (Hardiman 1846, 68). If stone roofed huts were still used as dwellings in the 17th century O'Flaherty would probably have said so.

81. First briefly described by O'Donovan in the Ordnance Survey letters who just gives general dimensions and notes opposing doorways; the roof of the northern one was 'half collapsed' in 1839.

82. Kinahan (1867) plate VI, figs. k and l. Two short stone walls now forming a sort of forecourt to the northern door are not figured in Kinahan's sketch and are

presumably recent.

83. Kinahan's 1867 sketch shows the north door and window; the roof is partly collapsed. In 1972 much of the exterior of the southern wall had also collapsed and it was not possible to ascertain whether two stone-built openings on either side of the site of the door were windows or wall niches. The clochan had been rebuilt by 1984, a southern door constructed and these openings presented as small windows. Two of Kinahan's drawings of the Eoghanacht clochans were reproduced by Brash (1875, 150).

84. Goulden (1955).

85. Ryan (1931); Hughes (1966).

86. Conroy (1870); Scantlebury (1926).

87. Miraculous stone boats are not as rare as one might suspect: legend and topography are scrutinised by Tim Robinson (1986) in his superb account of his circuit of the island.

88. The use of large stones in ancient structures in Greece and southern Italy was attributed to the legendary race of Cyclopes – hence the architectural term. An 1839 sketch in the Ordnance Survey letters and a photograph taken in the 1860s in Dunraven (1875, pl. xli), republished in Powell (1984, 36) and Manning (1985) show that the church is unchanged.

89. Manning (1985, 117): 'the remainder of the church is a late or post-medieval reconstruction which was probably carried out as late as 1666 when Sir Morogh O'Flaherty of Bunowen was buried within it ... For a similar use of an early church as a monastery chapel compare Temple Dowling at Clonmacnoise, which according to a plaque over the door was rebuilt for this purpose by Edmund Dowling in 1689 ...'.

90. Petrie (1878, 18) noted 'in the list of saints given by Colgan,

March 22, as belonging to the family of St. Enda of Aran, there is mention made of the father of Flann Febhla, Archbishop of Armagh, who was named Scandlan', and guessed that 'it is not unlikely that this Scandlan, of the same race as Enda, was buried in the church dedicated to this saint in Aran. He died, it may be presumed, in the seventh, or the beginning of the eighth century. The death of his son Flann, is entered by the Four Masters in the year 704, and in the Chronicon Scotorum at A.D. 702'. Also published by Macalister (1949, 5) and Higgins (1987, 153, 383).

91. A number of instances of the name Sanctán are recorded as in Cell Sanctáin or Kilsantel, Co. Antrim (MacNeill 1938) but none are likely to be connected with the Cill Éinne inscription. Also published by Henry (1940, 53), Macalister (1949, 5) and Higgins (1987, 288).

92. Manning (1985).

93. See Henry (1970, fig. 13, 137) who illustrates most, but not all, of the cross.

94. The cementing of the sides of the three fragments to the wall in Teaghlach Éinne has served to obscure some decoration.

95. See Manning (1985) and references therein. The church at Kilbannon, Co. Galway, may be dedicated to the same individual who is commemorated in the first station on the pilgrims' climb of Croagh Patrick in Co. Mayo (Harbison 1991) which is traditionally known as Leacht Mhionnáin, St. Benignus' Monument, where several *deiseal* prayerful circuits are made.

96. Charcoal in the mortar of the church has been radiocarbon dated to about the 11th century AD: Berger (1992, 883). For the CARI inscription see Higgins (1987, 151).

97. Manning (1985).

98. O'Donovan may have mistak-

en these remains for those of two buildings in 1839. He is the first person to record the existence of a six foot high cross slab some 40 paces to the south-west of this church.

99. Haddon and Brown (1893, 818).

100. For the name atharla see Goulden (1953). O'Donovan records an elder tree growing in the centre of the enclosure and notes that there was a well here called Tobar Rónáin.

101. The east window is illustrated in Barry (1886, 491, fig. 2).

102. Wood-Martin (1902), Vol. II, 240.

103. Macalister (1922).

104. The cross-inscribed slabs and fragments have been published by Higgins (1987): nos. 1-7 here are respectively his nos. 91, 98, 56, 57, 54, 110 and 32.

105. Ordnance Survey letters, p. 159.

106. The cross-inscribed stones here numbered 1-6 have been published by Higgins (1987), nos. 22, 27, 13, 15, 48 and 23 respectively.

107. Dunraven (1875, 82) notes that Petrie recorded this tradition. The church has been slightly restored: it was a little more ruined in the early 19th century: Dunraven, pl. XLII.

108. It has been 'partially restored' according to Barry (1886, 491). The convexity of the north wall was noted by Dunraven. For the cross-inscribed slabs see Higgins (1987), nos. 36, 40, 41, 77 and 84.

109. Haddon and Browne (1893, 822); they also record a plain 'holed-stone' near this 'well'.

110. Killanin and Duignan (1967, 60). For sacred trees: see Lucas (1963).

111. O'Donovan (1839).

112. Haddon and Browne (1893, 818).

113. The story is recorded in Synge's *The Aran Islands*.

114. A radiocarbon determination from charcoal in the mortar: Berger (1992, 884).

115. Leask (1955, Vol. 1, 66) has

published a small plan and a sketch by Westropp.

116. Crawford (1923, 99). A horse is likely: there is a carving of a somewhat similar sway-backed horse (with rider) in Inishmaine Abbey, Co. Mayo (see *Journal of the Royal Society of Antiquaries of Ireland* 35, 1905, 7, fig.).

117. Higgins (1987, 119, no. 94).

118. Petrie (1845, 449) and (1972, 250).

119. Higgins (1987, no. 14).

120. Waddell (1976).

121. Waddell (1973). It is thought that the use of the name 'The Seven Churches' may reflect a belief that the Seven Churches of the Apocalypse were represented.

122. An early church now named Carntemple at Noughaval is probably Brecan's foundation: Westropp (*Proceedings of the Royal Irish Academy* 22, 1900, 103, 147).

123. O'Sullivan (1983). The meaning of some words in the poem (like Cláiringneach) is not clear.

124. Higgins (1987, 145, no. 80). When Petrie first saw this slab in 1821 it was broken but complete. He recorded that it had been found in the early years of the 19th century 'within a circular enclosure known as St. Brecan's tomb, at a depth of about six feet, on the occasion of its being opened to receive the body of a distinguished and popular Roman Catholic ecclesiastic of the county of Galway, who made a dying request to be buried in this grave' (1845, 140). There is no circular enclosure visible today and there is some confusion as to which leaba or grave plot is actually Brecan's grave. To compound the confusion, the 1898 six-inch Ordnance Survey map distinguishes between St Brecan's Bed and his grave but does not clealy indicate their locations: according to O'Donovan in 1839 the grave was located near the remains of a house to the south-east of the church, according to Dunraven (1875) and Westropp (1895) Brecan's Bed lay west of the church with the shaft of a high cross standing at one end (this is the West Cross and Leaba an Spioraid Naoimh), and according to Robinson (1980) Brecan's grave is to be tentatively identified with a rectangular grave plot south-east of the church marked by several slabs including one inscribed VII ROMANII (yet Petrie appears to differentiate between this grave of the 'Seven Romans' and that of the elusive St Brecan). Robinson locates Leaba Bhreacáin some distance to the south (where the South Cross now lies). The identification of both grave and leaba in Waddell (1973) rests mainly on the fact that the inscribed Brecan grave slab was located at this spot in 1972 (where it was quite obscured by vegetation) and was sufficiently heavy not to be easily transported from one location to another. It was there in the last century too (Macalister 1895).

125. Macalister (1949, 7, no. 538) read the inscription as ORAIT AR ANMAIN SCANDLAIN. Petrie (1845, 22) thought the name was SEMBLAIN. Higgins (1987, 143, 324, no. 50) suggests both SCANDLAIN and SCANDLAN.

126. Haddon and Browne (1893, 819).

127. Macalister (1913). One commentator (Ganly 1886) takes six pages of print to say that nothing is known of the 'Seven Romans'. Higgins (1987, 143).

128. In the *Passio* of Aelfric and in the *Leabhar Breac*. It must be noted that almost all versions of the tale of the Seven Sleepers refer to *Septem dormientes*, calling them sleepers rather than Romans. However, one north European version recounted by the 8th century Paul the Deacon does refer to them as 'Romani'. See M. Huber, *Die Wanderlegende von den Siebenschläfern*, Leipzig, 1910, and E. Honigmann, *Patristic Studies,* Vatican City, 1953.

129. Higgins (1987, 147, no. 85).

130. Higgins (1987, 149, no. 92).

131. In 1821 on the occasion of Petrie's first visit, this slab was located in the church Teampall Bhreacáin and was recorded there by Crawford (1913, 154). A photograph in Ó Domhnaill (1930, facing p. 168) shows only three slabs at the grave plot, two erect and one recumbent (presumably the CRONMAOIL slab). See also Scantlebury (1926, plates on p. 20 and 23).

132. Various possible locations; Waddell (1973) for older references; Robinson (1980).

133. Waddell (1973) and (1981); Harbison (1992a, 169) and references.

134. Harbison (1991, 52).

135. Anon (1886, 196). For the story of Ultan and his shrine see A. Campbell (1967), *Aethelwulf — De Abbatibus* : an early 9th century poem by a Northumbrian monk.

136. Robinson (1986, 22).

137. An 1839 sketch in the Ordnance Survey letters shows that this simple church had a pointed doorway in its north wall and a narrow window in the east wall.

138. Ó Domhnaill (1930, 202).

139. A date suggested by radiocarbon dating a sample of mortar: Berger (1992).

140. Mason (1938, 199).

141. Westropp (1895).

142. Leask (1955, 73). Mortar from the earlier part of the church suggests a date in the 11th century: Berger (1992).

143. Hedderman (1917).

144. From a drawing kindly supplied by W. Walsh. For references to the *flabellum* see Higgins (1987, 109).

145. Mason (1938, 198, pl. xx, fig.

1) shows it intact. Higgins (1987, no. 82, pl. 26B) shows it broken.

146. Robinson (1990, 28).

147. There is a fine aerial photograph in Daly (1975, 75), reproduced in Powell (1984, 20). Dunraven (1875, 15) implies that two enclosing walls were visible in the 1880s.

148. Anon (1887). *The Irish Builder*, 1st February, 45 (these are notes of a visit made in 1877).

CHAPTER 7
Arkin Fort - Paul Walsh
Abbreviations used in notes

BL British Library, London. NAI National Archives, Ireland. PRO Public Record Office, London. RIA Royal Irish Academy. SP State Papers. TCD Trinity College, Dublin.

Notes

1. The most comprehensive published account of the castle and Cromwellian fort is that by T. Robinson, *Stones of Aran. Pilgrimage* (1986), 239-58. It is intended that this paper should complement his narrative.

2. T. Robinson, *Mapping South Connemara* (1985), 27.

3. Arkin castle is listed, in 1574, as been in the possession of one James Lynch; J.P. Nolan, 'Galway castles and their owners in 1574', *Journal of the Galway Archaeological and Historical Society* 1(1900-01), 116. In 1595, one Captain Fildew was murdered there; *AFM, s.a.* 1595; *Cal. S.P. Ire. 1592-6*, 418. Various inquisitions are recorded as being held at Arkin, and these, undoubtedly were taken in the castle. The earliest of these dates to 6 Oct. 1590; RIA MS 14.D.4, 83. Arkin may well have been the site that Queen Elizabeth I had in mind when she authorised the construction of a fort on Aran. Nothing, however, came of this proposal; *Cal. Carew MSS 1603-24*, 296.

4. J. Goulden, writing in the early 1950s records that the name Arkin was then seldom ever heard on the islands. The remains of the fort were known as ballaí Chromwell; *Irish Sword* 1 (1949-53), 263. In more recent times this has been superseded by the name Caisleán Arcín, Arkin Castle.

5. The articles are printed in J. Hardiman, *History of Galway* (Dublin, 1820), App., xxxi. Sir Robert Lynch, who owned the Aran islands, commanded the detachment sent there; J. Smyth de Burgh, ed., *The memoirs of the Earl of Clanricarde* (London, 1757), Lorraine Proceedings, 21.

6. Roderic O'Flaherty, writing in 1684, records the destruction of both these buildings; J. Hardiman, ed., *A chorographical description of West or H-Iar Connaught* by Roderic O' Flaherty, 1684. (Dublin, 1846), 82. St Enda's church was a completely separate building to Teaghlach Einne which still survives. John O' Donovan, who visited the islands, in 1839, recorded the local tradition that the round tower, of which only the stump now remains, was also pulled down to obtain materials for building the fort; RIA. Ordnance Survey Letters, Co. Galway iii, 337.

7. They took advantage of the fact that the Parliament ships had departed from Galway bay. This, undoubtedly, was the main reason why the fort was so easily captured; J. T. Gilbert, *Contemporary history of affairs in Ireland* (Dublin, 1885), iii, 361; R. Dunlop, *Ireland under the Commonwealth* (Manchester, 1913), 303, 305.

8. This was scheduled to be observed on the 30th December; C. H. Firth, ed., *Ludlow's Memoirs* (London, 1894), i, 533, n.1.

9. The articles of surrender are printed in Dunlop, op. cit., 311,

n. 2. The account of the monies expended in constructing the new works formerly survived in the Public Record Office, Ireland (now, the National Archives): 'Arran Islands, 1652-3. Account of Captain Thomas Graham for building the fort of Arkin'; *P.R.I., Rep. Dep. Keeper, 33, Appendix*, 55. One full company is recorded as been stationed on Inis Mór, in February 1657, and Captain Nicholas Bayly, in his report on the forts in Inis Mór and Inishbofin (1663-4), noted that up until 1662, there had been one full company on each island; W. Petty, *The history of the survey of Ireland commonly called the Down Survey. AD 1655-1656*, ed. T. Larcom (Dublin, 1851), 162; *Ormonde MSS*, i, 296.

10. Extracts from Commonwealth Council Book; RIA MS 24.I.12, 38. Roderic O Flaherty, writing in 1684, records that the islands contained 'noe fuell but cowdung dryed with the sun, unless they bring turf in from the western continent.' Hardiman, ed., op. cit., 67-8. Captain William Webb, an engineer, writing in August 1662, records that Lettermullan castle was specifically garrisoned for the purpose of bringing firing over to the islands; *Ormonde MSS*, n.s., iii, 26. It is very likely that this was a continuation of an existing practice which had probably started during the Commonwealth period. Lettermullan is listed as being garrisoned in 1655 and 1656; Dunlop, op. cit., 524, 616.

11. Hardiman, ed., op. cit., 294. In January 1658, a John Shaw is recorded as minister on Inis Mór; St. John D. Seymour, *The Puritans in Ireland, 1647 - 1661* (Oxford, 1921), 149. For the history of the fort on Inishbofin and description of the surviving remains see P. Walsh, 'Cromwell's Barrack: a Commonwealth garrison fort on

Inishbofin, Co. Galway.' *Journal of the Galway Archaeological and Historical Society* 42 (1989-90), 30-71.

12. J. P. Prendergast, *The Cromwellian settlement of Ireland* (Dublin, 1875), 324.

13. [J. MacCaffrey], 'Commonwealth records'. *Archivium Hibernicum* 6 (1917), 179-81; Dunlop, op. cit., 675. Unfortunately, the surviving records do not enable us to determine precisely the number held there during this period; Walsh, art. cit., 38-9 and notes.

14. P. F. Moran, *Historical sketch of the persecutions suffered by the Catholics of Ireland* (Dublin, 1907), 306.

15. This much is recorded by the authors of the *Commentarius Rinuccianus* (Dublin, 1944), v, 406. Nevertheless, it appears that not all the clergy were liberated at the one time for Fr Brian Conny OFM, died on Inishbofin after the others had been released; see Walsh, art. cit., 39, 64, n. 66.

16. For Alderman Deey's appointment as mayor, commissioning and quarters see *Cal. S. P. Ire. 1660-1662*, 39, 48, 447; *Ormonde MSS*, i, 351; ii, 181. Deey had been a shoemaker and was sheriff of Dublin in 1646-7; J. T. Gilbert, *Cal. Ancient Records of Dublin* (Dublin, 1892), iii, 442. In September 1662, Deey was appointed to take charge of the forts and garrisons on Inis Mór and Inishbofin with all the arms, ammunition etc.; *Ormonde MSS*, i, 251. He was transferred form Arkin during the summer of 1663. Having served at various stations in Leinster and Connacht his company was eventually disbanded in 1672; C. Dalton, *Irish Army lists, 1661-1685* (London, 1907), *passim*. Deey returned to Dublin and was elected mayor for 1672-3; Gilbert, op. cit., v, 18. The gunners are listed in the Military

Establishment for 1662; PRO SP 63/310, fol. 77v.

17. The guns comprised one culvern, two demi-culvern, and four sakers (all of iron); NLI MS 2274, fol. 10; a list of ordnance, August 1662. The condition of the ordnance at Arkin was typical of that in the other forts around the country. Most of the guns on Inishbofin and all but one in Galway were unmounted; ibid. The troopers were from Sir Oliver St. George's troop of horse; *Ormonde MSS*, i, 245, 274; M. Ó Duigeannáin, 'Three seventeenth century Connacht documents', *Journal of the Galway Archaeological and Historical Society* 17 (1936-7), 153.

18. *Ormonde MSS*, i, 251, 265-6.

19. In his petition to the King he records that it was he who 'brought to Brussels the happy news of the change in England'. It was there he had been introduced to the King by the duke of Ormond; *Cal. S. P. Dom. Ser. 1661-62*, 619; *Ormonde MSS*, n.s., vii, 494. The King recommended him for a troop of horse but all the vacancies were filled and he had to settle for a foot company; *Cal. S. P. Ire. 1660-62*, 350.

20. He requested £150 that 'both these islands may be so provided with boats, and the forts so repaired, that your grace need not be at any further charge for some years with them.' *Ormonde MSS*, i, 295-303, 320-3. He is addressed as Major Bayly in a letter dated 16 Jan. 1665; ibid., 321.

21. The duke of Ormond's son, Richard Butler, was created a peer, in 1662, and took the title 'Earl of Arran'. He immediately set about establishing a claim to the Aran Islands. He was appointed governor of them, in March 1666, and Bayly was authorised to act as such in the earl's absence; *Ormonde MSS*, i, 342. Some interesting insights into Bayly's character and the

land-hungry politics of the period can be gleaned from the accounts of the hearings and petitions relating to the ownership of the islands at this time; see T. Robinson, op. cit., 254-5; *Hist. MSS Com.*, Rep. IX, Part ii, 175-6, 178-9. Arran had the title to the islands confirmed to him, in 1669, under the Acts of Settlement and Explanation; *Rec. comm. Ire. rep.*, 11-15 (1821-5), 219.

22. NLI MS 802, fol. 32v; an estimate of the charge for repairing fortifications, Oct. 1677. In June 1677, William Robinson, surveyor general of the fortifications, was ordered to compile a report on the state of forts around the country; TCD MS 1179, fol. 89; PRO SP 63/361, fol. 167. The account in NLI MS 802, a contemporary copy of extracts from various Ormonde documents and letters, is probably taken from his report.

23. In 1672 and 1676, he was in Galway (*Ormonde MSS*, ii, 200; NAI Wyche 2/1), in 1677-8, he was in Inishbofin (*Ormonde MSS*, ii, 208; NLI MS 802), in January 1680, he was in Inis Mór (NLI MS 802), and in July on that year he was in Galway (*Ormonde MSS*, ii, 224). It is at this time also that the name 'Arkin' disappears from the records and the fort is simply referred to as Aran fort.

24. Arran was also eager for Bayly to sell his company for he owed the earl £200 in rent from the islands. Bayly stayed on in London and, in 1683, petitioned the earl to find a position for his son. The earl obliged and he was made an ensign. In the following year he again petitioned the earl for an administrative post for himself but does not appear to have been successful on this occasion. By 1687, he had fallen on hard times and wrote to Ormond in June of that year for a loan of £10 to help him feed his

family and stay at Winsdor in the hope of receiving some position or other from the King. And so he fades out of recorded history; *Ormonde MSS*, n. s., vi, 26, 150, 176, 181, 186, 226; vii, 15, 37, 208, 494.

25. Walsh, art. cit., 43. The transfer of the gunner from Inis Mór is noted in the military establishment for 1682; NAI 999/308/1; NAI Wyche 2/48. It is likely that the ordnance were transferred to Charles Fort at the same time as they are listed in the fort's inventory contained in Lord Mountjoy's account, dated 25 March 1685; *Ormonde MSS*, i, 377-8. Some of the ordnance from Inishbofin are also listed as being in Charles Fort and others at Galway; ibid., 387. Bushe is returned as quartered on Inis Mór in 1682, 1683, and 1684; NAI Wyche 2/3 & 4; NLI MS 2559, fols. 622r, 655r and 670v.

26. In March 1685, Bushe is listed as being quartered in Inis Mór and in September of that year at Edenderry, Co. Offaly; *Ormonde MSS*, i, 404; NLI MS 2559, fol. 698v. In March of the following year Nicholas Plunckett is recorded as 'captain of that company whereof Captain Amyas Bush was late captain' and so Bushe too fades from the record; *Ormonde MSS*, i, 413.

27. Letter from Colonel Henry Belasyse to George Clarke, Secretary of War; TCD MS 749.12, no.1159. Hardiman states that at this time a 'garrison was sent to Arran, and a barrack was built, in which soldiers were stationed for many years'; *History of Galway* (Dublin, 1820), 320. I have found no mention of this barrack in the various returns for the late 17th and early 18th centuries; see Walsh, art. cit., 45, 67, n. 111. Neither the fort on Inis Mór or that on Inishbofin in represented on the two maps of Ireland, drawn by William Robinson (Surveyor General of

fortifications) in 1700, showing the location of the barracks in the country; BL King's Top. LI. 15-16.

28. *Ormonde MSS*, n. s., viii, 319; Hardiman, ed., op. cit., 430, n. u. In 1708. on a rumour of an invasion by the Scottish Pretender James, Galway was put into a state of defence and a detachment of soldiers sent to the Aran islands; Hardiman, *Hist. of Galway*, 168.

29. All that survives is the rough draft of these proposals which he submitted to Major General Hutchinson, the officer commanding the western district; Oireachtas Library MS 8.H.21. Colonel Robertson records little detail about the islands save to note that Inis Mór could be easily defended by having a few heavy guns placed in one or two prominent positions, one of which to be located at the point in front of the old fort and town of Cill Éinne to protect the main harbour there. The only other landing place was at Cill Mhuirbhigh, but this was seldom used. He estimated that there were 1,500 inhabitants on Inis Mór with as many cattle, 400 inhabitants on Inis Meáin and 150 inhabitants on Inis Oírr; both with 300 cattle a piece. Nothing, however, ever came of his proposals.

30. Paul Kerrigan has published an extensive series of articles on the defences of Ireland (1793 - 1815) in *An Cosantóir*, the Irish Defence Forces magazine. The west coast defences are described in Part 12 of the series; *An Cosantóir* XLII, No. 2, April 1982, 39 - 44.

31. RIA Ordnance Survey Letters, Co. Galway, iii, 403. Though the curtain wall by the seaside was recorded by the Ordnance Survey the position of this tower was not. J. Goulden, in his article on Arkin in the *Irish Sword* cites a source in the then Public

Record Office (PROI Ia/45/4, p.76) which indicated that parts of the fort were standing in the year 1821; art. cit., 262, n. 5. I am grateful to Aideen Ireland and Frances McGee of the National Archives who successfully tracked down this elusive reference. It refers to the 1821 census of Galway. One of the houses listed in the townland of Cill Éinne is described as 'a round tower built by Cromwell's men'. It had three stories and was inhabited by Pat and Kate Donoughoe with their son Michael; NAI CEN 1821/18, 100.

32. The roadway is represented on the 1841 Ordnance Survey 6-inch map as finishing just north-east of Cill Éinne, which is depicted as a dense cluster of cabins. Routeways tend not to change over time and it is likely that the present road through the village follows the line of the original thoroughfare. A superimposition of the roadway and houses recorded on the revised Ordnance Survey 6-inch map (1899) on the earlier one also supports this suggestion. This area of Cill Éinne is still known as An Bábhún; ie the bawn or courtyard of the fort. See Robinson, op. cit., pp. 256-7.

33. Some twenty-two examples are known to this writer from Galway city and there is a further example at Menlough village some 3km north of the city. The essential feature of these carvings is a cross which is sometimes represented as standing on a base or on the horizontal bar of the letter H in the monogram IHS. Nearly three quarters of the carvings are dated: the dates range from 1815 - 1818, (1816 being the commonest), and many have the name J or I Healy carved alongside. It has been suggested that these stones commemorate the laying of the foundation stone, in 1816, of the former Pro-Cathedral in

Middle St., Galway. Other than the fact that they share a similar date there is no evidence to support this and their origin and purpose are still a mystery. For these carvings see E. Rynne, *Tourist Trail of Old Galway* (Galway, rev. ed., 1978), *passim* and P. O'Dowd, *Old and new Galway* (Galway, 1985), 108-9.

34. This pillar was first recorded by Tim Robinson, op. cit., 257. To Paul Gosling goes the credit for its identification as part of a late medieval cross-shaft.

CHAPTER 15
'And here's John Synge himself, that rooted man' - Jeff O'Connell.
Notes

1. Yeats, W.B. (1978), 'The Municipal Gallery Revisited,' *Collected Poems*, 368-369.
2. Ó hEithir, B. and R. (1991), *An Aran Reader*, Dublin, 29-33.
3. Synge, J. M. (1966, 1982), *Collected Works II Prose* (ed. Alan Price) London , 53.
4. Synge, Ibid., 13.
5. Brady, A. M. and Cleeve, B. (1985), *A Biographical Dictionary of Irish Writers*, Dublin, 232-233.
6. Yeats, W. B. (1961), *Essays and Introductions*, London, 326.
7. Symons original account appeared in the *Savoy Magazine*, Nos. 6,7,8, (Oct. Nov. Dec. 1896). It later appeared as a chapter in *Cities and Sea-Coasts and Islands*.
8. Yeats, W. B. (1972) *Memoirs* (ed. Denis Donoghue) London, 104.
9. Yeats, W. B. (1961), *Essays and Introductions*, 299.
10. O'Connor, U. (1984), *All the Olympians*, New York, 123.
11. Synge, J. M., *Collected Works II Prose* , 49.
12. Yeats, W. B. *Memoirs*, 105.
13. Synge, J.M. *Collected Works II Prose*, 59.
14. Ibid., 65
15. Ibid., 58-59.
16. Ibid., 72.
17. Ibid., 140-141

18. Ibid., 74-75.
19. Ibid., 108.
20. Ibid., 82.
21. Kiberd, D. *Synge and the Irish Language,* Dublin, 2nd edition, 1993, 93.
22. Yeats, W. B. *Essays and Introductions*, 327-328.

CHAPTER 17
The Making of the Man of Aran - Joe McMahon
Notes

1. Biographical detail taken largely from Arthur Calder Marshall, *The Innocent Eye : The Life of Robert J. Flaherty*, London, 1963.
2. Calder Marshall, op. cit, p.72
3. Paul Rotha (in collaboration with Sinclair Road and Ricard Griffith), *Documentary Film*, London, 1936, p.79.
4. Calder Marshall, op. cit, p.143.
5. Quoted by Kevin Rockett in *Cinema in Ireland*, London, 1988, p.91, from Helen Seller's *The Rise and Fall of the British Documentary: The Story of the Film Movement Founded by John Grierson*. Berkeley, University of California Press, 1975, p.29.
6. Pat Mullen, *Man of Aran*, Cambridge Mass., 1970, (original edition 1935) p.170.
7. Quoted by Richard Barsam in *The Vision of Robert Flaherty*, Bloomington and Indianapolis, 1988, p.67. from William T. Murphy's *Robert Flaherty : A Guide to References and Resources*, Boston, 1978, p. 24.
8. Mullen, op. cit, p. 93.
9. Mullen, op. cit, p. 115.
10. Mullen, op. cit, p. 74.
11. Calder Marshall, op. cit, p. 151.
12. Calder Marshall, op. cit, p. 152
13. Barsam, op. cit, p. 67,
14. See *How the Myth was Made*, a film by George Stoney released in 1978 dealing with the making of *Man of Aran*.
15. Mullen, op. cit, p. 225.
16. Mullen, op. cit, p. 81.
17. Mullen, op. cit, p. 82.
18. Mullen, op. cit, p. 275.
19. Calder Marshall, op. cit, p. 153.

20. Quoted in Calder Marshall, op. cit, p.166.
21. Quoted in Calder Marshall, op. cit, p. 170
22. Quoted by Luke Gibbons in *Cinema in Ireland*, London, 1988 from *Irish Press*, May 7th 1934.
23. Dudley, Andrew, *Andre Bazin*, New York, Columba University Press, 1990 (originally published 1978), p.108.

CHAPTER 18
Aran, Paris and the Fin-de-siècle. - Patrick Sheeran
Notes

1. Hamilton-Patterson, James (1992), *Seven Tenths: The Sea and its Thresholds*, London, 63.
2. Symons, Arthur (1897), *Cities and Sea-Coasts and Islands*, London. (This volume includes Symons's essay from the *Savoy*.)
3. Kiberd, Declan (1989), 'Synge, Symons and the Isles of Aran', *Notes on Modern Irish Literature* 1, 32-40.
4. Beckson, Karl (1987), *Arthur Symons – A Life*, Oxford.
5. Synge, John (1992) *The Aran Islands* (ed. Tim Robinson), London.
6. Knapp, James (1989), 'Primitivism and Empire: John Synge and Paul Gauguin', *Comparative Literature* 41, 1, 53 - 68.
7. Yeats, W.B. (1990), *The Poems* (ed. Daniel Albright), London.
8. Yeats, W.B. (1977), *The Speckled Bird* (ed. William H. O'Donnell), Toronto.
9. Wood, David (1992), *The Power of Maps*, London.
10. Knapp, Bettina (1980), *Antonin Artaud : Man of Vision*, London, 157.
11. Knapp, ibid., 158.
12. Bourke, Cormac (1993), *Patrick: The Archaeology of a Saint*, Belfast.
13. A.E. [George Russel], (1988), *The Descent of the Gods*, part 3 of *The Collected Works* (ed. Raghavan Iyer and Nandini Iyer), London.
14. Yeats, W.B. (1959), *Mythologies*, London.

BIBLIOGRAPHY

Aalen, F.H.A. 1966. 'The Evolution of the Traditional House in western Ireland', *Journal of the Royal Society of Antiquaries of Ireland* 96, 47-58.

Admiralty Hydrographic Department., 1954. *The Irish Coast Pilot* (1954 ed.). London.

Anderson, R.J. 1904. 'Irish Cetaceans', *Proceedings of the International Congress of Zoology*, Berne, 703 -711.

Anon. 1884. 'Irish local legends No. V—Naomh Greoihir or St Gregory of Inishmaan...', *The Irish Builder* 26, 329.

Anon. 1886-87. 'Antiquities of the Aran Islands, County Galway', *The Irish Builder*, Vol. 28 (1886): 15th April, 119-120; 1st May, 126-7; 15th May, 151; 1st June, 165; 15th June, 175-6; 1st July, 196-7; 15th July, 201; 1st August, 223; 15th August, 237-8; 1st September, 249; 15th September, 255. Vol. 29 (1887): 15th January, 22; 1st February, 45; 15th February, 49-50; 1st March, 73; 15th March, 88; 1st April, 103-4.

Anon. 1905. 'Ára', *St Stephens* 2,175.

Armstrong, E.A. 1957. 'Birds of the Aran Islands', *Irish Naturalists Journal* 12, 207-8

Babington, C.C. 1858. 'On the Firbolgic Forts in the South Isles of Aran, Ireland', *Archaeologia Cambrensis* 4, 96-103.

Banim, M. 1891. *Here and there through Ireland*. Dublin.

Barrett, J. H. 1958. 'Birds seen on Inishmore, Aran Islands, 6th-9th November, 1957', *Irish Naturalists Journal* 12 (12), 314-316.

Barrington, J. S. 1928. 'Barred warbler on north Aran', *Irish Naturalists Journal* 2 (1), 6.

Barrington, R. M. 1912. 'Wryneck on Aran Islands', *Irish Naturalists Journal* 21 (10), 207.

Barry, J.G. 1886. 'Aran of the Saints', *Journal of the Royal Society of Antiquaries of Ireland* 17, 488-494.

Baynes, E.S.A. 1961. 'Report on migrant insects in Ireland for 1960', *Irish Naturalists Journal* 13 (9), 200-204.

Baynes, E.S.A. 1964. 'Report on migrant insects in Ireland for 1963', *Irish Naturalists Journal* 14 (11), 253-254.

Bécaud, G. 1962. *L'Opera d'Aran*. Paris.

Becker, H. 1960. 'Seetangwirtschaft und Tangfluren an der Atlantischen Küsten', *Festgabe Kurt Wagner*, 299-314.

Bell, J. 1860. 'Note on the meaning of the name of the Aran Islands, County Galway', *Ulster Journal of Archaeology* 8, 74-75.

Berger, R. 1992. [14]C Dating Mortar in Ireland', *Radiocarbon* 34, 880-889.

Bouvier, N. 1990. *Journal d'Aran et d'autre lieux. Feuilles de route*. Paris

Boyne, P. 1987. *John O'Donovan (1806-1861), a biography*. Kilkenny.

Brash, R.R. 1875.*The Ecclesiastical Architecture of Ireland*. Dublin.

Brunicardi, M. 1914-15. 'The shore-dwellers of ancient Ireland', *Journal of the Royal Society of Antiquaries of Ireland* 44, 185-213; 45, 176.

Burke, O. J. 1887. *The South Isles of Aran (County Galway)*. London.

Butler, Dame Columba. 1952. 'Agnes O'Farrell and Aran...', *The Capuchin Annual* 1952, 473-8.

Butler, Hubert. 1990. *'Influenza on Aran'* in *The Sub-Prefect should have held his tongue*. (edited and with an introduction by R. F. Foster). London.

Byrne, F. J. 1958. 'The Eóganacht Ninussa', *Eigse* 9, 18-29.

Campbell, J. L. 1960. 'The Tour of Edward Lhuyd in Ireland in 1699 and 1700', *Celtica* 5, 218-228.

Chinery, M. 1986. *Guide to the Insects of Britain and Western Europe*. London.

Clancy, P. 1993. 'Seachain a Taibhse: a study of the custom of Hallowe'en Guisers in the island of Aran (Árainn), Co. Galway', *Sinsear . The Folklore Journal* 7, 29-38.

Clapham, A.R., et. al. 1987. *Flora of the British Isles* (3rd edition). Cambridge.

Clark, F.L. 1971 'The Common Lizard (*Lacerta vivipara*) and Pigmy Shrew (*Sorex minutus*) on Inishmore, Aran Islands, Co. Galway', *Irish Naturalists Journal* 17 (1), 24.

Colgan, N. 1893. 'Notes on the flora of the Aran Islands', *The Irish Naturalist* 2, 3-4.

Colgan, N. 1895. 'Witchcraft on the Aran Isles', *Journal of the Royal Society of Antiquaries of Ireland* 25, 84-85.

Conroy, G. 1870. 'A Visit to the Aran-More of Saint Enda', *Irish Ecclesiastical Record* 7, 19-31, 105-123.

Cotter, C. 1993. 'The Western Stone Fort Project', *Discovery Programme Report* 1, 1-19.

Crawford, H.S. 1907. 'A descriptive list of early Irish crosses', *Journal of the Royal Society of Antiquaries of Ireland* 37, 187-239.

Crawford, H.S. 1913. 'A descriptive list of early cross-slabs and pillars', *Journal of the Royal Society of Antiquaries of Ireland* 43, 151-169.

Crawford, H.S. 1923. 'Carvings from Aran churches', *Journal of the Royal Society of Antiquaries of Ireland* 53, 99-100.

Curtis, E. 1935. 'Original documents relating to Aughrim, Burrishoole and Aran...', *Journal of the Galway Archaeological and Historical Society* 16, 134-43.

Curtis, T.G.F. and H.N. McGough. 1988. *The Irish Red Data Book 1 Vascular plants*. Dublin.

Curtis, T.G.F. and T.D. Robinson. 1985. 'Salvia verbenaca L. in the Aran Islands: an extension of range in western Ireland', *Irish Naturalists Journal* 21, 408-409.

Curtis, T.G.F., et.al. 1988. 'The discovery and ecology of rare and threatened arable weeds, previously considered extinct in Ireland, on the Aran Islands, Co. Galway', *Irish Naturalists Journal* 22, 505-512.

Dall, I. 1931. *Here are stories : an account of a journey to the Aran Islands*. London.

Dalton, J. P. 1929. 'Who built Dun Aengus?', *Journal of the Galway Archaeological and Historical Society* 14, 52-76, 109-32.

Daly, E.P. 1977. *A Hydrological investigation on Inismaan, Aran Islands*, Geological Survey of Ireland internal paper No. 3, Groundwater Division.

Daly, L. 1975. *Oileáin Árann. The Aran Islands*. Dublin.

Danaher, K. 1972. *The Year in Ireland —A Calendar*. Cork.

D'Arcy, Mary Ryan. 1985. *The Saints of Ireland*. (3rd ed) Cork and Dublin.

Day, R. 1903. 'The lost island of Atlantis off the Aran islands, Galway', *Journal of the Cork Historical and Archaeological Society* 9, 202.

De Courcy Ireland, J. 1981. *Ireland's Sea Fisheries: a history*. Dublin.

De Courcy Ireland, J. 1986. *Ireland and the Irish in Maritime History*. Dublin.

De Hórsaigh, A. 1933. 'Seán an Mhoinfhéir Ghlais agus na bromaigh. (Told by P. Ó Conghaile of Aran)...', *Béaloideas* 4, 182-190.

De Paor, L. 1956. 'The Limestone Crosses of Clare and Aran', *Journal of the Galway Archaeological and Historical Society* 26, 53-71.

De Paor, L. 1993. *Saint Patrick's World*. Dublin.

Destombes, M. 1987. *Contributions Sélectionées à l'Histoire de la Cartographie*. Utrecht.

De Valera, M. 1958. *A topographical guide to the seaweeds of Galway Bay*. Dublin Institute of Industrial Research and Standards.

De Valera, R. and S. Ó Nualláin. 1972. *Survey of the Megalithic Tombs of Ireland, Vol. III, Co. Galway etc.* Dublin.

Dockrell, R. B. *et al.* 1954. 'The Faces, Jaws and Teeth of Aran Children', *Transactions of the European Orthodontic Society 1954.*

Dublin Naturalists Field Club. 1931. 'News of Societies' *Irish Naturalists Journal* 3 (8), 178 - 179.

Dunn ,T.C. 1969. 'Collecting in the Aran Islands', *Entomologists Gazette,* July 28th - August 10th, 20, 271-278.

Dunraven, E. 1875. *Notes on Irish Architecture* (edited by Margaret Stokes). London.

Elcock, C. 1884. 'Abstract of lecture on Antiquities in Mayo, Galway, and the Arran Islands', *Proceedings of the Belfast Naturalists Field Club* 3, 248-51.

Fairley J. 1981. *Irish Whales and Whaling.* Belfast.

Farmer, D.H. 1987. *The Oxford Dictionary of Saints.* New York.

Feehan, J. 1991. 'The Rocks and Landforms of the Burren', in *The Book of the Burren,* (eds.) J.W. O'Connell and A. Korff, Kinvara, 14-30.

Ferguson, S. 1853. 'Clonmacnoise, Clare and Arran', *Dublin University Magazine,* 79-95, 492-505.

Ferguson, S. 1872. 'On paper-casts of ancient inscriptions in the Counties of Galway and Mayo...', *Proceedings of the Royal Irish Academy* 15, 257-260.

Finck, F.N. 1899. *Die Araner Mundart.* Marburg.

Fitzgerald, W. 1905. 'An ancient Irish cooraun or brogue found in Ballyhagen bog With an illustration of the pampooties worn in the Isles of Aran', *Journal of the Kildare Archaeological Society* 4, 376.

Fitzpatrick, T. 1922. *Connemara and the Burren,* Dublin.

Foras Forbartha 1978. *Distribution Atlas of Ireland's Dragonflies.*

Foras Forbartha 1979. *Distribution Atlas of Ireland's Amphibians.*

Foras Forbartha 1980. *Distribution Atlas of Ireland's Butterflies.*

Fraser, J. 1922. 'Irish *Aru "Aran" ', Révue Celtique* 39, 353-354.

Gailey, R. A. 1959. 'Settlement and Population in the Aran Islands', *Irish Geography* 4, 65-78.

Gailey, R.A. 1959. 'Aspects of change in a rural community (Aran Island)', *Ulster Folklife* 5, 27-34.

Ganly, W. 1886. 'The Seven Romans of Arran', *Irish Ecclesiastical Record,* August 1886, 727-732.

Gannon, J.B. 1945. 'The unveiled Aran', *Irish Monthly* 73, 519-22.

Godinho, V.M. 1990. *Mito e Mercadoria, Utopia e Praticá de Navegar.* Lisbon.

Gosling, P. 1994. *Archaeological Inventory of Co. Galway,* Vol.1. Dublin .

Goulden, J.R.W. 1953. 'Aharla', *Eigse* 7, 52-54.

Goulden, J.R.W. 1953a. 'Arkin: an outpost in Aran', *The Irish Sword* 1, 262-267.

Goulden, J.R.W. 1955. 'Killnamanagh: the lost church of Aran', *Journal of the Galway Archaeological and Historical Society* 26, 35-40.

Graves, Rev. J. 1883. '...Representation made to the Board of Works about the forts on the Aran Islands', *Journal of the Royal Society of Antiquaries of Ireland* 16, 175.

Greene, D.H. 1956. 'The Aran Islands. Last Fortress of the Celt', *The Commonweal* (New York), 64, no. 25, 609-610.

Gwynn, A. and R. N. Hadcock 1988. *Medieval Religious Houses —Ireland.* Dublin.

Gyles, L. 1898. 'The wryneck in Ireland', *Irish Naturalists Journal* 7 (1), 16-18.

Hackett, E. and M. E. Folan. 1958. 'The ABO and RH Blood Groups of the Aran Islanders', *Irish Journal of Medical Science, June 1958,* 247-261.

Haddon, A.C. 1893. 'The Aran Islands, County Galway. A study in Irish ethnography', *The Irish Naturalist* 2, 303-8.

Haddon, A.C. 1893. 'Abstract of lecture on the Aran Islands, a study in Irish ethnography', *Proceedings of the Belfast Naturalists Field Club* 3, 538-44.

Haddon, A.C. 1893. 'Studies in Irish craniology the Aran Islands, Co.Galway', *Proceedings of the Royal Irish Academy* 18, 759-67.

Haddon, A.C. and C.R. Browne. 1893. 'The Ethnography of the Aran Islands, County Galway', *Proceedings of the Royal Irish Academy* 18, 768-829.

Harbison, P. 1964. *The National Monuments of Ireland.* Dublin.

Harbison, P. 1968. 'Castros with *chevaux-de-frise* in Spain and Portugal', *Madrider Mitteilungen* 9, 116-147.

Harbison, P. 1970. *Guide to the National Monuments in the Republic of Ireland.* Dublin.

Harbison, P. 1971. 'Wooden and Stone *Chevaux-de-Frise* in Central and Western Europe', *Proceedings of the Prehistoric Society* 37, 195-225.

Harbison, P. 1991. *Pilgrimage in Ireland. The Monuments and the People.* London.

Harbison, P. 1992. *Guide to the National and Historic Monuments of Ireland.* Dublin.

Harbison, P. 1992a. *The High Crosses of Ireland.* Bonn.

Hardiman, J. 1846. *A Chorographical Description of West or H-Iar Connaught written A.D. 1684, by Roderic O'Flaherty, Esq.* Dublin.

Harper, T. and Molloy, D. (eds) . *The Aisling Magazine.* Aisling Árann Teo., Eochaill, Árainn.

Hartnett, P.J. and B. Ó Ríordáin. 1969. *The Aran Islands and Galway City including Westropp's Account of the Aran Islands.* Dublin.

Hartshorne, C.H. 1853. 'Early Remains in the Great Isle of Aran', *Archaeologia Cambrensis* 4, 291-306.

Haverty, M. 1859. *The Aran Isles: or a report of the excursion of the ethnological section of the British Association from Dublin to the western islands of Aran in September, 1857.* Dublin.

Hedderman, B.N. 1917. *Glimpses of My Life in Aran.* Bristol.

Hely, J. 1793. *Ogygia or a chronological account of Irish events ... by Roderic O'Flaherty translated by Rev. James Hely.* Dublin.

Henry, F. 1940. *Irish Art in the Early Christian Period.* London.

Henry, F. 1970. *Irish Art in the Romanesque Period (1020 - 1170 AD).* London.

Higgins, J. 1987. *The Early Christian Cross Slabs, Pillar Stones and Related Monuments of County Galway, Ireland. British Archaeological Reports, International Series* 375. Oxford.

Hillis J.P. and R.F. Haynes. 1980. 'Report on migrant Insects in Ireland for 1979', *Irish Naturalists Journal* 20 (3), 122-124.

Huggins, H.C. 1928. 'Collecting in the Aran Islands', *The Entomologist* 61, 43-44.

Hughes, K. 1966. *The Church in Early Irish Society.* London.

Hughes, K. and Hamlin, A. 1977. *The Modern Traveller to the Early Irish Church.* London.

Humphreys, G.R. 1930. 'Observations on the migrations of birds at Irish lightstations during the year 1928', *Irish Naturalists Journal* 3 (4) , 83-89.

Humphreys, G.R. 1931. 'Observations on the migration of birds at Irish lightstations during the year 1929', *Irish Naturalists Journal* 3 (9), 185-191.

Humphreys, G.R. 1932. 'Iceland Redwings in Ireland', *Irish Naturalists Journal* 4 (1), 14.

Humphreys, G.R. 1933. 'Observations on the migrations of birds at Irish lightstations during the year 1930', *Irish Naturalists Journal* 4 (8), 151.

Johnston, T.H. and A.J. Stattersfield. 1990. 'A global review of Island endemic birds',

Ibis 132 , 167 - 180.

Kane, Rev. P. 1898. 'Aran of the fishermen', *New Ireland Review* 9, 235-46.

Kearns, K.C. 1976. 'The Aran Islands: an imperilled Irish outpost', *Proceedings of the American Philosophical Society* 120, 421-438.

Kelly, F. 1988. *A Guide to Early Irish Law*. Dublin.

Kenny, J.F. 1929. *The Sources for the Early History of Ireland*. Dublin.

Kershaw, P. 1957. 'The Aran Islands', *Trident*, May 1957, 309-310.

Kiberd, D. 1989. 'Synge, Symons and the Isles of Aran, *Notes on Modern Irish Literature*, 1, 32-40.

Kiberd, D. 1993. *Synge and the Irish Language*, 2nd edition. Dublin.

Kilbride, W. 1869. 'Some notes on antiquities on Aranmore in the bay of Galway ...', *Journal of the Royal Society of Antiquaries of Ireland* 10, 102-118.

Killanin, M. and M.V. Duignan. 1962. *The Shell Guide to Ireland*. London.

Killanin, M. and M.V. Duignan. 1967. *The Shell Guide to Ireland*. Second revised edition. London.

Kinahan, G.H. 1867. 'Notes on some of the ancient villages in the Aran Isles, County of Galway', *Proceedings of the Royal Irish Academy* 10, 25-30.

Kinahan, G.H. *et. al.* 1871. *Explanatory Memoir ... of the Geological Survey of Ireland illustrating a portion of the County of Galway*. London.

Klimm, L. E. 1927. 'Inishmore: an outpost island', *Geographical Review* 17, 387-396

Klimm, L. E. 1935. 'The relation between field patterns and jointing in the Aran islands', *Geographical Review* 25, 618-624.

Klimm, L. E. 1936. 'The rain tanks of Aran. A recent solution to an old problem', *Bulletin of the Geographical Society of Philadelphia 1936*, 73-84.

Lansbury, I. 1965. 'Notes on the Hemiptera, Coleoptera and

Diptera and other invertebrates of the Burren, Co.Clare and Inishmore, Aran Islands', *Proceedings of the Royal Irish Academy* 64 (B), 7.

Lawson, T.D. 1906. 'Aran with a (geological) note by Richard John Anderson', *Journal of the Galway Archaeological and Historical Society* 4, 24-35.

Leask, H.G. 1943. 'Finding of a Whale's Vertebra in Clochan-na-Carraige, Inishmore, Aran, Co. Galway', *Journal of the Royal Society of Antiquaries of Ireland* 73, 24.

Leask, H.G. 1955. *Irish Churches and Monastic Buildings*, Vol. 1. Dundalk.

Lewis, S. 1837. *A Topographical Dictionary of Ireland*. London.

Lhuyd, E. 1712. 'Some further observations relating to the antiquities and natural history of Ireland', *Philosophical Transactions of the Royal Society of London* 27, 524-6.

Long, H. 1992. 'Dún Aonghasa', *Journal of the Galway Archaeological and Historical Society* 44, 11-27.

Lucas, A.T. 1958. 'National Museum of Ireland: Archaeological Acquisitions in the year 1957', *Journal of the Royal Society of Antiquaries of Ireland* 88, 115-152.

Lucas, A.T. 1963. 'The Sacred Trees of Ireland', *Journal of the Cork Historical and Archaeological Society* 68, 16-54.

Lucas, A.T. 1964. 'National Museum of Ireland: Archaeological Acquisitions in the year 1962', *Journal of the Royal Society of Antiquaries of Ireland* 94, 85-109.

Macalister, R.A.S. 1895. 'Crosses at Kilbreccan, Aran', *Journal of the Royal Society of Antiquaries of Ireland* 25, 379-80.

Macalister, R.A.S. 1913. 'The stone of the "Seven Romans" on Aran Mor', *Journal of the Royal Society of Antiquaries of Ireland* 43, 344.

Macalister, R.A.S. 1921. *Ireland in Pre-Celtic Times*. Dublin.

Macalister, R.A.S. 1922. 'Note on the cross-inscribed "holed-stone" at Mainistir Chiaráin, Aran Island, County Galway', *Journal of the Royal Society of Antiquaries of Ireland* 52, 177.

Macalister, R.A.S. 1928. *The Archaeology of Ireland*. London.

Macalister, R.A.S. 1935. *Ancient Ireland*. London.

Macalister, R.A.S. 1949. *Corpus Inscriptionum Insularum Celticarum*, Vol. II. Dublin.

Macalister, R.A.S. 1949a. *The Archaeology of Ireland*. Second edition. London.

Mac an Iomaire, S. 1938. *Cladaí Chonamara*. An Gúm. 1985.

McArthur, R.H. and E.O.Wilson, 1967. *The theory of island biogeography*. Princeton.

MacCana, P. 1970. *Celtic Mythology*. London.

McCarthy, P.M. and M.E. Mitchell, 1988. *Lichens of the Burren Hills and the Aran Islands*. Galway

McCone, K. 1990. *Pagan Past and Christian Present in Early Irish Literature*. Maynooth.

MacCullagh, R. 1992. *The Currach Folk*. Dublin.

McDonald, T. 1992. *Achill: 5000 BC to 1900 AD. Archaeology, History, Folklore*. Achill.

McGrail, S. 1987. *Ancient boats in Northwestern Europe. The archaeology of water transport to AD 1500*. London.

MacNeill, E. 1923. 'Ancient Irish Law. The Law of Status or Franchise', *Proceedings of the Royal Irish Academy* 36C, 265-316.

MacNeill, E. 1938. 'An Inscription at Killeany, Aran Islands', *Journal of the Royal Society of Antiquaries of Ireland* 68, 143.

MacNeill, M. 1982. *The Festival of Lughnasadh*. London.

'Máire'. 1916. 'The school of St Enda of Aran', *Catholic Bulletin* 6, 624-5.

Manning, C. 1985. 'Archaeological excavations at two church sites on Inishmore, Aran Islands', *Journal of the Royal Society of Antiquaries of Ireland* 115, 96-120.

March, H.C. 1894. 'Remarks on the date of Dún Aengus', *Proceedings of the Society of Antiquaries of London* 15, 224-228.

Mason, T.H. 1936.*The Islands of Ireland*. Dublin.

Mason, T.H. 1938.'The Antiquarian Remains of Inisheer, Aran, County Galway', *Journal of the Royal Society of Antiquaries of Ireland* 68, 196-200.

Messenger, J.C. 1966. 'Man of Aran revisited, an anthropological critique', *University Review* 3, 15-47.

Messenger, J.C. 1969. *Inis Beag. Isle of Ireland*. New York.

Milligan, S.F. 1896. 'Antiquities, social customs, and folklore of Tory, Inishmurray, and the South islands of Aran', *Proceedings of the Belfast Natural History and Philosophical Society* 1896, 27-36.

Mills, S. 1987. *Nature in its Place*, London.

More, A. G. 1877. ' Report on the flora of Inishbofin, Co. Galway, including a comparison with the flora of Aran', *Proceedings of the Royal Irish Academy* 2, 553-78.

Mould, D.P. 1972. *The Aran Islands*. Newton Abbot.

Mulholland, R. 1900. 'The islands of Ireland', *Irish Monthly* 28, 609-10.

Mullen, P. 1970. *Man of Aran* Cambridge (Mass.)

Murphy, B. 1977. 'A Handaxe from Dun Aenghus, Inishmore, Aran Islands, Co. Galway', *Proceedings of the Royal Irish Academy* 77C, 257-259.

Murphy, D. 1888. 'On two sepulchral urns found, in June, 1885, in the south island of Arran', *Proceedings of the Royal Irish Academy* 12, 476-479.

Murphy, J.R. 1896. 'South Aran Irish', *Gaelic Journal* 6-7, 125, etc.

Murphy, R.C. 1931. 'The Timeless Arans', *National Geographic Magazine* 59, 747-775.

Nairn, R.G.W. and J.R. Sheppard, 1985. 'Breeding waders of sand dune machair in north-west

Ireland, *Irish Birds* 3 (1), 53-70.

Ó Briain, L. 1934. 'Sgéal ó Inis Meadhoin (Told by Bartlí Ó Flaharta)', *Béaloideas* 4, 391-2.

Ó Coigligh, Ciarán. 1990. *Seanchas Inis Meáin : as bailiucháin na scol*. Dublin.

Ó Conaola, D. 1988. *Thatched Homes of the Aran Islands*. Inis Oírr.

Ó Conghaile, M. 1988. *Conamara agus Arainn 1880-1980: gneithe den stair shoisialta*. Béal an Daingin.

O'Connell, M., J. Fives and P. Ó Céidigh, 1992. 'Littoral fishes on Inishmore, Aran Islands, Co. Galway', *Proceedings of the Royal Irish Academy* 92B, 109-31.

O'Connell, M., J. Fives and P. O'Céidigh, 1992. 'Ecological studies of littoral fauna and flora on Inishmore, Aran Islands, Co. Galway', *Proceedings of the Royal Irish Academy* 92 B, 91-107.

O'Connor, U. 1984. *All the Olympians*. New York.

Ó Direáin, M. 1955. 'Aran 1947 : a poem (translated by Valentin Iremonger) beginning 'Whistling in the night...', *Poetry Ireland* 28, 57-8.

Ó Direáin, M. 1980. *Dánta 1939-1979*. Dublin.

Ó Direáin, M. 1984. *Selected Poems — Tacar Dánta*. Newbridge.

Ó Domhnaill, M. 1930. *Oileáin Árann*. Dublin.

O'Donovan, J. 1839. *Ordnance Survey Letters: Co. Galway*. Royal Irish Academy (Typescript copy).

Ó Duilearga, S. 1940. 'An triúr naomh a'dul go hÁrainn. (Told by Máirtín Beag Ó Cualáin...)', *Béaloideas* 10, 203.

O'Flaherty, J.T. 1825. 'A Sketch of the History and Antiquities of the Southern Islands of Aran ...', *Transactions of the Royal Irish Academy* 14, 79-140.

O'Flaherty, R. 1684. *A Chorographical Description of West or H-Iar Connaught*. Edited by J. Hardiman 1846. Dublin.

O'Flaherty, R. 1685. *Ogygia seu*

rerum Hibernicarum chronologia. London.

O'Flaherty, T. 1991. *Aranmen All*. Dingle.

Ó Flannagain, D. 1985. *Ó Thrá Anoir*. Cathair na Mart.

Ó Flannagáin, S. 1931. 'Beart sgéalta ó Árainn...', *Béaloideas* 4, 228-53.

Ó Flannagáin, S. 1933. 'Tiachóg sgéalta ó Árainn...', *Béaloideas* 3, 47-52.

Ó Flannagáin, S. 1937. 'Sean-Phaidreacha ó Árainn', *Béaloideas* 9, 66-85.

Ó Flannagáin, S. 1939. 'Sean-sgéalta ó Árainn', *Béaloideas* 9, 66-85.

O'Growney, E. 1897, 'Ón domhan Thiar', *Gaelic Journal* 8, 84-6.

O'Growney, E. 1900. 'Words from the spoken Gaelic of Aran and Meath', *Archiv für Celtische Lexikographie* 1, 151, 175, 550.

Ó hEithir, B. 1989. *An Nollaig Thiar*. Dublin

Ó hEithir, B. and R. (eds.). 1991. *An Aran Reader*. Dublin.

Ó Laoghaire, D. 1975. *Ár bPaidreacha D'chais*. FÁS.

Ó Máille, T.S. 1957. 'Ara mar áitainm', *Galvia* 4, 54-65.

O'Meara, E. 1866-69. 'On some new diatomaceae collected off the Arran Islands, by Dr.E. Perceval Wright', *Proceedings of the Natural History Society of Dublin* 5, 106, 155.

O'Meara J. 1982. *Topographia Hiberniae : Giraldus Cambrensis*. Portlaoise.

Ó Móghráin, P. 1945. 'Aran, Co. Galway', *Eigse* 4, 6-8.

Ó Murchú, S. 1992. 'An t-ainm áite Inis Oírr', *Eigse* 26, 119-123.

O'Rahilly, T.F. 1946. *Early Irish History and Mythology*. Dublin.

O'Rourke, F. 1970. *The Fauna of Ireland*, Cork.

Ó Siadhail, M. 1978. *Tearmaí Tógála agus Tís as Inis Meáin*. Dublin.

Ó Síocháin, P.A. 1962. *Aran: Islands of Legend*. Dublin.

O'Sullivan, A. 1983. 'Saint Brecán of Clare', *Celtica* 15, 128-138.

O'Sullivan, P. and N. Godwin 1976. *A World of Stone*. Dublin.

O'Sullivan, P. and N. Godwin. 1977. *Field and Stone*. Dublin.

Pearse, P.H. 1898. 'Names of birds and plants in Aran', *Gaelic Journal* 9, 305

Petrie, G. 1845. *Ecclesiastical Architecture of Ireland anterior to the Anglo-Norman Invasion*. Dublin.

Petrie, G. 1878. *Christian Inscriptions in the Irish Language* (ed. M. Stokes). Dublin.

Petrie, G. 1972. 'An Essay on Military Architecture in Ireland previous to the English Invasion', *Proceedings of the Royal Irish Academy* 72C, 219-269.

Philips, R.A. 1916. 'The non-marine mollusca of the Aran Islands', *Irish Naturalists Journal* 25 (5), 83.

Piggott, S. 1954. 'Some Primitive Structures in Achill Island', *Antiquity* 28, 19-24.

Powell, A. 1984. *Oileáin Árann. Stair na n-oileáin anuas go dtí 1922*. Dublin.

Power, P. 1926. *Aran of the Saints. A brief introduction to the islands' antiquities*. Dublin.

Praeger, R.L., 1934. *The botanist in Ireland*. Dublin.

Praeger, R.L. 1949. *Some Irish Naturalists*. Dundalk.

Raftery, B. 1991. 'Dun Aengus, Inismore, Aran, County Galway, Ireland', in *The Celts*, Milan, 613.

Rees, A. and Rees, B. 1961. *Celtic Heritage*. London.

Reynolds J. 1985. 'Karstic freshwater habitats of the Aran Islands, Co.Galway, with preliminary notes on their fauna', *Irish Naturalists Journal* 21 (10), 430-435.

Richards, O.W. 1961. 'The fauna of an area of limestone pavement in the Burren, Co.Clare', *Proceedings of the Royal Irish Academy* 62 (B), 1.

Robinson, T. 1975. *Oileáin Árann. A map of the Aran Islands, Co. Galway, Eire*. Kilronan.

Robinson, T. 1976. 'Aran surrounded by ocean', *The Geographical*

Magazine, December, 178-186.

Robinson, T. 1980. *Oileáin Árann. The Aran Islands, Co. Galway, Eire. A map and guide*. Cill Rónáin.

Robinson, T. 1986. *Stones of Aran. Pilgrimage*. Dublin.

Robinson, T. 1990. *Connemara. Part 1: Introduction and Gazetteer*. Roundstone.

Robinson, T. 1991. *Mementos of Mortality. The Cenotaphs and Funerary Cairns of Árainn*. Roundstone.

Robinson, T. 1992. 'Place/Person/ Book. Synge's *The Aran Islands*, vii-liii, 137-149, in J.M. Synge's *The Aran Islands*, London, 1992.

Romero, F.A. 1987. *Las Embarcaciones de los Celtas*. Lisbon.

Romero, F.A. 1991. *Santos e Barcos de Pedra*. Vigo.

Ross H.C.G. 1984. *Catalogue of the Land and Freshwater Mollusca of the British Isles*. Belfast.

Royle, S.A. 1983. 'The Economy and Society of the Aran Islands, County Galway, in the early nineteenth century', *Irish Geography* 16, 36-54.

Royle, S.A. 1984. 'Irish Famine Relief in the early nineteenth century: the 1822 famine on the Aran Islands', *Irish Economic and Social History* 11, 44-59.

Ruttledge, R.F. 1944. 'Siberian chiffchaff on migration: an addition to the Irish list', *Irish Naturalists Journal* 8 (6), 220

Ruttledge, R.F. 1945. 'Report on observation of birds at Irish lightstations, 1944', *Irish Naturalists Journal* 8 (7), 247-251.

Ruttledge, R.F. 1948. 'Report on observations of birds at Irish lightstations, 1947', *Irish Naturalists Journal* 9 (6), 142-147.

Ruttledge, R.F. 1954. 'Report on observations of birds at Irish lightstations, 1953', *Irish Naturalists Journal* 11 (7), 199-200.

Ruttledge, R.F. 1955. 'Unrecorded instances of continental Chaffinches in Ireland', *Irish Naturalists Journal* 11(9), 253-254.

Ruttledge, R.F. 1989. *Birds in*

Counties Galway and Mayo, Irish Wildbird Conservancy, Dublin.

Ryan, J. 1931. *Irish Monasticism. Origins and Early Development*. Dublin.

Rynne, E. 1980. 'Slate Medals and Amulets from the Aran Islands', *Journal of the Galway Archaeological and Historical Society* 37, 78-83.

Rynne, E. 1991. 'Dún Aengus - Fortress or Temple?', in B. and R. Ó hEithir (eds.), *An Aran Reader*, Dublin, 260-262.

Rynne, E. 1991. 'Dún Aengusa – Daingean nó Teampall', *Archaeology Ireland* 5, 19-21.

Rynne, E. 1992. 'Dún Aengus and some similar Celtic ceremonial sites', in A. Bernelle (ed.), *Decantations. A Tribute to Maurice Craig*, Dublin, 196-207.

Scannell, M. J. P. and D. M. Synnott, 1987. *Census catalogue of the flora of Ireland*, 2nd edition. Dublin.

Scantlebury, C. 1926. *Saints and Shrines of Aran More*. Dublin.

Scharff, R. F. 1899. *The History of the Irish Fauna*. London.

Scharff, R.F. 1920. 'A new Irish whale – a correction', *Irish Naturalists Journal* 29 (3), 27.

Scott, R. J. 1983. *The Galway Hookers*. Swords, Co. Dublin.

Sharrock, J.T.R. (ed.) 1973. *The Natural History of Cape Clear Island*. Berkhampstead.

Sheeran, P.F. 1976. *The Novels of Liam O'Flaherty: a study in romantic realism*. Dublin.

Sleeman, P. 1989. *Stoats and Weasels, Polecats and Martens*. London.

Stelfox, A.W. 1933. 'On the occurrence of a peculiar race of the humble bee, *Bombus Smithianus White*, on the Aran Islands, in western Ireland', *Irish Naturalists Journal* 4, 235-238.

Symons, A. 1897. *Cities and Seacoasts and Islands*. London.

Symons, A. 1899. *Images of Good and Evil*. London.

Synge, F. 1985. 'Coastal evolution' in *The Quaternary History of Ireland*, (eds. K. Edwards and W. Warren), London, 115-132.

Synge, J.M. 1907. *The Aran Islands*, London. [edited with an Introduction and Notes by T. Robinson, 1992].

Synge, J. M. 1966. *Collected Works II Prose*, (ed. Alan Price). London.

Tierney, M. 1980. *Eoin MacNeill: scholar and man of action 1867-1945*, (ed. F.X. Martin). Oxford.

Troadec, L. Dujardin. 1967. *Les Cartographes Bretons du Conquet*. Brest.

Ua Concheanainn, P. 1931. *Innismeadhoin. Seanchas agus Sgéalta*. Dublin.

Waddell, J. 1973. 'An Archaeological Survey of Temple Brecan, Aran', *Journal of the Galway Archaeological and Historical Society* 33, 5-27.

Waddell, J. 1976. 'Kilcholan: an early ecclesiastical site on Inishmore, Aran', *Journal of the Galway Archaeological and Historical Society* 35, 86-88.

Waddell, J. 1981. 'An Unpublished High Cross on Aran, County Galway', *Journal of the Royal Society of Antiquaries of Ireland* 111, 29-35.

Waddell, J. 1988. 'J.R.W. Goulden's Excavations on Inishmore, Aran, 1953-1955', *Journal of the Galway Archaeological and Historical Society* 41, 37-59.

Wakeman, W.F. 1862. 'Aran – Pagan and Christian', *Duffy's Hibernian Magazine* I, 460-471, 567-577.

Webb, D.A. 1980. 'The flora of the Aran Islands.' *Journal of Life Sciences*, Royal Dublin Society, 2, 51-83.

Webb, J.F. (Transl.) 1965. *Lives of The Saints. (The Voyage of St Brendan. Bede: Life of Cuthbert. Eddius Stephanus: Life of Wilfred)*.

Weir, A. 1980. *Early Ireland. A Field Guide*. Belfast.

Westropp, T.J. 1895. 'Aran Islands', *Journal of the Royal Society of Antiquaries of Ireland* 25, 250-274 [reprinted with different illustrations in Westropp 1905 and Hartnett and O Ríordáin 1969].

Westropp, T.J. 1899. 'Dun Aenghus, Aran', *Journal of the Royal Society of Antiquaries of Ireland* 29, 66-67.

Westropp, T.J. 1902. 'The Ancient Forts of Ireland: being a contribution towards our knowledge of their types, affinities, and structural features', *Transactions of the Royal Irish Academy* 31, 579-730.

Westropp, T.J. 1905. 'Aran Islands', in *Illustrated Guide to the Northern, Western, and Southern Islands, and Coast of Ireland*, Royal Society of Antiquaries of Ireland, Dublin, 60-96.

Westropp, T.J. 1910. 'A study of the fort of Dun Aengusa in Inishmore, Aran Isles, Galway Bay: its plan, growth and records', *Proceedings of the Royal Irish Academy* 28C, 1-46.

Westropp, T.J. 1910a. 'A study of the early forts and stone huts in Inishmore, Aran Isles, Galway Bay', *Proceedings of the Royal Irish Academy* 28C, 174-200.

Westropp, T.J. 1912. 'Brasil and the legendary islands of the north Atlantic: their history and fable. A contribution to the "Atlantis" problem', *Proceedings of the Royal Irish Academy* 30C, 223-260.

Westropp, T.J. 1914. 'The promontory forts and early remains of the islands of Connacht', *Journal of the Royal Society of Antiquaries of Ireland* 44, 297-337.

Westropp, W.H. 1870. 'Sketch of the physical geology of north Clare', *Proceedings of the Royal Geological Society of Ireland*, N.S. 3, 75-79.

Whilde, A. 1977. *The Birds of Galway and Mayo*. Irish Wildbird Conservancy, Dublin.

Whilde, A. 1985. 'The 1984 all Ireland Tern Survey', *Irish Birds* 3 (1), 1-32.

Whilde, A. 1994. *The Natural History of Connemara*. London

Whilde, A. and T. Fitzpatrick, 1992. *Connemara and the Burren*. Dublin.

Wilde, W. 1858. *A short description of the Western Islands of Aran, County of Galway, chiefly extracted from the programme of the ethnological excursion of the British Association to these interesting islands in the autumn of 1857, under the direction of W.R. Wilde, MRIA*. Dublin.

Williams, P.W. 1966. 'Limestone pavements with special reference to western Ireland', *Transactions of the Institute of British Geographers* 40, 155-172.

Wood-Martin, W.G. 1902. *Traces of the Elder Faiths of Ireland*. London.

Wright, E.P. 1866. 'Notes on the flora of the islands of Aran, West of Ireland', *Proceedings of the Natural History Society of Dublin* 5, 96-156.

NOTES ON AUTHORS

Jeffrey O'Connell is a freelance writer, journalist and historian. Born in the United States, he came to Ireland over twenty years ago. He took his Arts Degree at U. C. G. and taught at a Rudolf Steiner School outside London for six years. Since returning to Ireland he has lived in Kinvara. He is editor of *Tracht*, the Kinvara parish magazine, and has published two books devoted to aspects of Kinvara history. *St Colman's Church* is a study of a unique, pre-Emancipation church, making use of original manuscript material from the papers of Dr Nicholas Archdeacon, Bishop of Kilmacduagh and Kilfenora from 1800 to 1823. His other publication *Kinvara History : A Family Affair* is based on the research he conducted into parish family history. Since 1985 he has collaborated with Anne Korff on six Ramblers Guides and Maps to the Burren, South Galway and Medieval Galway. He also co-edited *The Book of the Burren* published in 1991. He is along with Anne Korff, one of the directors of Tír Eolas. Mr. O'Connell is married with four children and edits the Arts section of *The Galway Advertiser*.

Anne Korff was born in Germany and studied Fine Art, Visual Communications, Graphic Design, and Publishing in Berlin, taking a Masters Degree in Fine Art. Her professional career in Germany included design work for films and publishers. She came to Ireland in 1977 and worked freelance with various agencies. She also taught at the National School of Art and Design. Ms Korff moved to Kinvara, Co. Galway, in 1982 and continued to work freelance. In 1985 with Jeffrey O'Connell she produced *Kinvara, A Ramblers Guide and Map* which led to the production of six further Guides and Maps covering the Burren and South Galway regions. In 1988 she co-founded Tír Eolas with Jeffrey O'Connell.

Professor John Waddell lectures in Archaeology in University College, Galway. He received his Ph.D. from the National University of Ireland and also studied at the University of Glasgow. He was on the staff of the National Museum of Ireland for a number of years. His research interests lie in the prehistoric archaeology of western Europe and he has published several studies of Ireland's prehistoric relationships with Britain and the Continent. He has made a special study of the archaeology of the Aran Islands and of the royal site of Rathcroghan in Co. Roscommon. His publications include *The Bronze Age Burials of Ireland*. He was appointed by the then Taoiseach, Mr. C. J. Haughey, to the organising committee of the Discovery Programme which has initiated the major series of excavations at Dún Aonghasa.

John Feehan is a lecturer in environmental heritage and environmental resource management at University College, Dublin. He is a graduate of Trinity College, Dublin, where he also carried out his postgraduate studies in geology. Best-known for his television series on landscape and environmental heritage, his books include environmental histories of County Laois and the Slieve Bloom Mountains and (with Grace O'Donovan), a study of Coole. His special areas of interest currently include peatland heritage and the evolution of the postglacial landscape.

Cilian Roden took his degree in Botany at University College, Dublin, and subsequently studied marine and freshwater algae at University College, Galway, and at University College, Dublin, where he obtained his Ph.D. in 1979. Since 1980 he has worked on the west coast of Ireland, firstly at the Shellfish Research Laboratory in Carna, Co. Galway, and since 1987 at Redbank Shellfish, New Quay, Co. Clare. Throughout his working life he has been attracted to two very different types of plant: the marine plankton of the Atlantic coast and the flowering plants of the west coast of Ireland. This interest has led to participation in a project to restore Redbank Oyster Beds in Aughinish Bay on the north coast of the Burren. He has a particular interest in the arctic-alpine flora and has written an account of the mountain plants of Galway and Mayo, as well as contributing records to *The Flora of Connemara and the Burren* by D. A. Webb and M. J. P. Scannell. While much of his published work centres on the ecology and growth of marine algae, he has also written a number of papers dealing with the plants, both terrestrial and marine, of the west of Ireland, e.g. 'The Vascular Flora and Vegetation of Some Islands in Lough Corrib' in the *Proceedings of the Royal Irish Academy* and 'A Survey of the Flora of Some Mountain Ranges in the West of Ireland' in the *Irish Naturalists Journal* .

Michael O'Connell was attracted to Marine Biology while studying Zoology in University College, Galway. Since 1975 he has been teaching Biology and Mathematics at Gairmscoil Éinne in Cill Rónáin, Inis Mór. Living on the island has enabled him to develop his interest in the marine environment and he has taken part in a number of projects in this field. He has spent a number of years studying the ecology of the sea shores of Inis Mór and has recently been involved in publishing two scientific papers on this subject in the *Proceedings of the Royal Irish Academy*. At present he is studying the biology of sand eels in the waters of the Aran Islands as well as working on the ecology and biology of the shores of Inis Mór.

Gordon D'Arcy has an M.Sc. in Environmental Science from Trinity College, Dublin. He has published four books, including *Guide to the Birds of Ireland* (1981); *Pocket Guide to the Birds of Ireland* (1986); *Pocket Guide to the Animals of Ireland* (1987); *The Natural History of the Burren* (1992). In addition, he has contributed numerous articles to various journals, including *The Irish Naturalists Journal* and the *IWC News*, the newsletter of the Irish Wildbird Conservancy

Paul Walsh was born in Galway and educated at St. Joseph's College. He studied archaeology at University College, Galway, and presented a survey of the town walls and fortifications of Galway for his M.A. degree. He undertook further studies at the Angelicum University, Rome. In 1980-81, he was responsible for the survey of the architectural monuments as part of the archaeological survey of County Donegal. Since then he has worked as an archaeologist with the Ordnance Survey of Ireland, in Dublin. His academic interests include Irish prehistory, medieval architecture, and the history of his native city. He has published on all these topics in various books and journals. He is currently Joint Honorary General Secretary of the Royal Society of Antiquaries of Ireland, and vice-Chairman of the Irish Association of Professional

Archaeologists. His other interests include music, especially choral and barbershop music, and he is musical director of the People's College Choir, Dublin.

John de Courcy Ireland was born in 1911. His family came from Robertstown, Co.Kildare. After leaving school at the age of seventeen he embarked as a steward on a Dutch cargo ship. He spent some years aboard ships travelling to South America, the Baltic, North Italy, and Norway, during which time he learned French, Spanish, Italian, Portuguese and German, to enable him coverse with the remarkable number of beautiful girls to be met in each port. He worked for the Chinese government in Eurcpe during the Japanese occupation in the 1930s. From 1941-43 he was with the Local Defence Force in Inishowen, from 1943 to 1986 his career took the path of teaching. He was Secretary of the Dun Laoghaire Lifeboat from 1956-81, and is now President and Research Officer of the Maritime Institute of Ireland. In 1959 he founded the National Maritime Museum. He also holds the office of President of the Irish Campaign for Nuclear Disarmament. Dr de Courcy Ireland is author of *The Sea and the Easter Rising* (1966); *Ireland's Sea Fisheries: A Histcry* (1981); *Ireland and the Irish in Maritime History* (1986); *Ireland's Maritime Heritage* (1992). To date he has prepared approximately 60,000 words of a biography of Admiral Brown.

Anne O'Dowd is a Dubliner who works as a curator in the Irish Folklife Division of the National Museum. Her working life is taken up with caring for and developing the unique National Folklife Collection which has been in storage for many years. She has travelled around the country collecting artefacts for this collection which represents the lives of ordinary people during the 19th and 20th centuries. Her hope is that it will soon see the light of day and be exhibited for all to appreciate. Anne O'Dowd is the author of several articles on Irish folklife and she has published two books, *Meitheal: A Study of Co-Operative Labour in Rural Ireland*, 1981, and *Spalpeens and Tattie Hokers. History and Folklore of the Irish Migratory Agricultural Labourer in Ireland and Britain*, 1991. The latter was awarded the prestigious Michelis-Jena Radcliffe prize in folklore in 1992 and the Humbert Summer School book award in 1992. Her current academic interests are the uses of natural materials such as straw, hay and rushes in the manufacture of household furnishings and everyday objects and the beliefs and traditions surrounding amulets and reliquaries.

Dara Ó Conaola is a native of Inis Meáin, where he attended national school. After spending two years at the Technical School in Cíll Rónán he went to Galway to attend the Technical School there – Jack Mahon describes the scene in that establishment in his book *Only the Teachers Grow Old*. After five glorious years in Galway studying his favorite subjects – woodwork, drawing and city life he went to Wexford where he trained as a Woodwork Teacher. He moved to Dublin where he met his wife Pacella and, in 1973, they moved to Inis Oírr. He has published many books in Irish: *An Gaiscíoch Beag* (The Little Warrior), 1979 and *Mo Chathair Ghríobháin* (Labyrinth) (1981) were the first two and were published by An Gúm, the Department of Education's publications branch. *Night Ructions*, a selection of short stories (translated by Gabriel Rosenstock) was launched at the 1990 Sunday Times Festival of Literature in Hay-on-Wye, Wales. *Misiún ar Muir* (Sea Mission) was staged by Na Fánaithe as part of the Galway Arts Festival in 1992 and later at Expo '92 in Seville. He is currently working on a novel and a play .

Padraigín Clancy is a graduate in Irish folklore and history. She is currently pursuing her Masters Degree by thesis at the Department of Irish Folklore, University College, Dublin. Her research topic is 'The Yearly round in Ára na Naomh – Prayer, Pattern and Pilgrimage in an island community'. She has a keen interest in Irish/Celtic spirituality and folk tradition and she facilitates retreats and seminars countrywide on the subject. She has resided in Inis Mór for the greater part of the past seven years and is part of the 'Aisling Árann' network. She has published articles in *Sinsear-The Folklore Journal. Camcos - U.C.D. History Review* and the *Aisling Magazine*. She is a keen set dancer and tin whistler and is a member of Comhaltas Ceoltóirí Éireann, 'Brooks Dance Academy' and Cumann na Píobairí Uilleann.

Lelia Doolan has a primary degree in Modern Languages from University College, Dublin, and a Ph.D. in Social Anthropology from Queen's University, Belfast. She has worked in television, theatre, film and journalism, for RTE, the Abbey Theatre, the Irish Press, and many other leading national newspapers and magazines. She has lived and worked in Dublin, Belfast and Mayo and settled in south Galway some years ago, where she now freelances as a writer, teacher, film-maker, gardener and student homeopath. She is currently Chair of Bord Scannán na hÉireann – the Irish Film Board.

James J. Duran, Ph. D., is a native of Boston and a speaker of four languages including Irish. His father's parents were Irish speakers from Inis Mór in the Aran Islands. Dr Duran is an instructor in applied linguistics and second language acquisition at Loyola Marymount University and teaches Modern Irish with the UCLA Extension Program. He also spends his summers in the Aran Islands, carrying out linguistic research on the Irish language under the auspices of the Dublin Institute of Advanced Studies.

Joe McMahon took a B.A. degree in English and Philosophy as well as an M.A. in English Literature at University College, Galway. In the mid 1970s he became actively involved in the Galway Film Society and has remained involved in film organisations in Ireland ever since. An early organising member of the Federation of Irish Film Societies, he chaired the organisation for a number of years. As well as being a former Chairperson of the Galway-based Film Resource Centre, he was also, for many years, a member of the Governing Council of the Irish Film Institute. He was centrally involved in the setting up of the now very successful Galway Film Fleadh. Joe McMahon has lectured in the areas of English Literature and Film Studies and now works on the Administrative Staff of University College, Galway.

Patrick F. Sheeran is Director of the Centre for Landscape Studies at University College, Galway. The Centre promotes the interdisciplinary study of the natural and cultural landscapes in the region. Relevant publications by Dr Sheeran include: 'Genius Fabulae: the Irish Sense of Place' in *Irish University Review*, 'Sacred Geography' in *Eire-Ireland*, 'The Idiocy of Rural Life Reviewed' in *The Irish Review*, 'The Ideology of Earth-Mysteries' in *Journal of Popular Culture*, and 'Place and Power' in *ReVision*, California.

Pádraig Standún was born and reared on a small farm near Belcarra, Castlebar, Co. Mayo. After studying in Maynooth, he was ordained a priest in 1971. All of his priestly life has been spent in the Gaeltacht, between the smaller islands of Aran and Carraroe. His first novel, *Súil le Breith* (Cló Chonamara, 1983) was published in English by Poolbeg Press in 1991 as *Lovers*. Bob Quinn based his films 'Budawanny' (1986) and 'The Bishop's Story' (1994) on this book and on an idea from Standún's second, *AD 2016* (Cló Chonamara 1988). *Cíocras* (1991), from Cló Iar-Chonnachta, was quickly followed by *An tAinmhí* from the same publisher in 1992. 1993 was the year of the four novels, *Celibates* (Poolbeg), based on *Cíocras*, *The Anvy* (Cló Iar Chonnachta) a translation of *An tAinmhí*. Cló Iar-Chonnachta published *Cion Mná* (Winner of the 1991 Oireachtas literary prize) and *Na hAnthropologicals* later that year. *A Woman's Love* (Poolbeg 1994) is based on *Cion Mná*, and is soon to be followed by *Stigmat* (CIC) already translated for Poolbeg (1995). The author is at present working on a new Irish language novel, *Shaman*, to be followed by a translation of it and another of *Na hAnthropologicals*. He also has a couple of filmscripts, hopefully for Teilifís na Gaeilge, in the pipeline. Inis Meáin drama group have produced two of his plays in all three Aran Islands and Carraroe. The recipient of an Arts Council bursary in 1990, Pádraig Standún was given most of the following year free by Archbishop Cassidy of Tuam to write fulltime. He returned as curate to Inis Meáin in 1991.

Tír Eolas is a publishing firm based in Kinvara, Co. Galway. Since it was established in 1985, Tír Eolas has published six Guides and Maps, covering the Burren, South Galway, Kinvara and Medieval Galway. Its two Directors are Anne Korff and Jeff O'Connell.

Tír Eolas Books

The Book of the Burren, edited by Jeff O'Connell and Anne Korff, 1991.

The Shannon Floodlands, by Stephen Heery, 1993. A Natural History of the Shannon Callows.

Not a Word of a Lie by Bridie Quinn-Conroy, 1993. A portrait of 'growing up' in the West of Ireland.